ROBIN
SANDER

C000151678

THE FREE CHURCH OF ENGLAND

THE FREE
CHURCH
OF ENGLAND

Introduction to an Anglican Tradition

John Fenwick

T & T CLARK INTERNATIONAL
A Continuum imprint
LONDON • NEW YORK

T&T CLARK INTERNATIONAL LTD
A Continuum imprint

The Tower Building   15 East 26th Street
11 York Road   New York, NY 10010
London SE1 7NX, UK   USA

www.tandtclark.com

British Library Cataloguing-in-Publication Data
A catalogue record for this book is available from the British Library

ISBN 0 567 08433 7 (Hardback)
ISBN 0 567 08197 4 (Paperback)

Typeset by Servis Filmsetting Ltd, Manchester
Printed and bound in Great Britain
by Antony Rowe, Chippenham, Wiltshire

Firstly, we have promised to God . . . that the Church of England shall be free . . .

Clause 1, Magna Carta, 1215

Cultivate, then, brethren, a deeper and broader and more intimate acquaintance with your own ecclesiastical history.

Bishop Benjamin Price, 1867

Wake up! Strengthen what remains and is about to die.

Revelation 3.2

Contents

CONTENTS

Acknowledgments

I should first of all like to express my gratitude to the many clergy and laity of the Free Church of England who have shown me courtesy, kindness and friendship since I first came to know the denomination in 1988, and in particular to the congregation at Emmanuel Church, Morecambe.

Among the bishops I should like to pay tribute to the late Arthur Ward, who was my first contact with the denomination, and whose openness has made many things possible; and to the late Cyril Milner, who always made me most welcome. I have had conversations with all the recent bishops while preparing this book, and have gained insights from all of them. I owe a particular debt to Kenneth and Edna Powell, and to John and Betty McLean, without whose support this project might not have been possible. I am grateful to Bishop John, as the oldest serving bishop in the Free Church of England, for writing the Foreword.

Richard Fenwick's timely work has put all writers on the Free Church of England in his debt for many years to come. His enthusiastic encouragement has been most welcome. I hope that this book will give his work the wider recognition it deserves.

Thanks are due, too, to the following: The Bishop of Peterborough for his commendation; Mrs Margaret Staplehurst, Archivist of the Countess of Huntingdon's Connexion for providing me with copies of material from her invaluable archive; my former colleague Dr Richard Palmer and his staff at Lambeth Palace Library, for helping me track down some of the sources; and to the many people who have offered comments or insights into the history and current state of the denomination. My indebtedness to various authors will be evident from the footnotes.

I wish to thank National Archives (the Public Record Office) and St Edward's Orthodox Brotherhood for permission to use the reproduction of the 1863 Deed Poll and the icon of St Augustine of Canterbury on the cover.

I am grateful to Geoffrey Green of T & T Clark for accepting the book; to Fiona Murphy for seeing it through to publication; and to the graphics department for dealing with the illustrations.

Last, but by no means least, I should like to thank my wife Lis, who has shared my sympathy for the Free Church of England vision, and Craster, Louise and David who have on occasion occupied its pews.

A Note on Terminology

Words can produce strong responses. For many of the people involved in the story of the Free Church of England, basic words like 'Catholic' and 'Protestant' have carried an immense weight of association, history, emotion, prejudice and motivation.

In the present work words such as 'Anglican', 'Catholic', 'Ecumenical', 'Evangelical' and 'Protestant' are used with neutral intention to convey their 'plain and natural' meaning. None (as used by the present writer) is intended as a pejorative term.

The legal title of the Church whose story is told here is 'The Free Church of England, otherwise called the Reformed Episcopal Church', as it results from a union between two Churches bearing those names in 1927. Among its own members the present-day denomination is usually simply called 'The Free Church of England'. That usage has been followed here. It should be clear from the context whether the pre-union Free Church of England or the post-union united Church is being referred to.

Illustrations

Every effort has been made to obtain the permission of the copyright holders of the various illustrations. Any omissions or corrections will be included in subsequent editions.

1 King George III. Detail of portrait by Johann Zoffany. The Royal Collection © 2003, Her Majesty Queen Elizabeth II, used by permission.

2 George Whitefield. Detail of portrait by John Greenwood, gift of Mrs Frederick Lewis Grey. Photograph © Museum of Fine Arts, Boston. Used by permission.

3 Selina, Countess of Huntingdon. From a portrait by P. Solidi, reproduced by permission of the Cheshunt Foundation, Westminster College, Cambridge.

4 Thomas Haweis. Lithograph in the *Evangelical Register*, April 1825. Used by kind permission of the Archivist of the Countess of Huntingdon's Connexion

5 Archbishop Howley and Queen Victoria. Detail of painting in the Mansell Collection.

6 Edward Adolphus, 11th Duke of Somerset. Portrait photographed, and reproduced, by kind permission of the present Duke of Somerset.

7 The Revd James Shore. Portrait reproduced by kind permission of Richard Fenwick.

8 John Moore, Archbishop of Canterbury. Reproduced by kind permission of the Archbishop of Canterbury, Lambeth Palace.

Foreword

I am privileged and delighted to write this Foreword to Dr John Fenwick's book about the Free Church of England of which I have been a member for over 50 years and in which my wife was baptized and confirmed.

The Free Church of England has suffered from a great deal of mis-understanding over the years – both from outsiders and frequently from those who have joined it, believing it to be other than it really is. Here, however, Dr Fenwick has let the foundational documents speak for them-selves and shows the identity of the denomination to be 'essentially one with the Church of England', albeit in a form which we believe is closer to the Apostolic and Reformation heritage.

Having worked with every Bishop Primus since Frank Vaughan (who assisted at our wedding, and whose successor at Morecambe I have the honour to be), I can vouch for the fact that what is presented here is the authentic voice of the Free Church of England. In particular I welcome the way in which Dr Fenwick is able to substantiate the denom-ination's 'claims to great antiquity'. Readers may be surprised to learn just how deep our roots go.

The present volume – which must surely remain definitive for years to come – is uncomfortable reading in many places. It is clear that we in the Free Church of England have often failed to live up to the great hopes placed in us. Yet I hope that the honest acknowledgment of our failures will itself help us to overcome them by God's grace.

Foreword

It is my prayer that this book will serve as a wake-up call to the members of the denomination and inspire us to rediscover our authentic identity and to celebrate it with Christian joy. I pray, too, that others reading this will understand us better, forgive us our mistakes and be encouraged by the blessings we have received. For too long we have hidden our light under a bushel. I pray that this book will enable us to emerge from the shadows and join with others in restoring the unity of Christ's Church and winning our nation for Him.

John McLean
Bishop of the Northern Diocese

Introduction

This work is an introduction to what could be described as England's best-kept ecumenical secret.

Most English Christians, even those who consider themselves ecumenically informed, are totally unaware that for over 150 years there has existed in England (and at times in Wales, Scotland, Canada, Bermuda, Australia, New Zealand, Russia and the USA) an episcopal Church, similar in very many respects to the Church of England, worshipping with a Prayer Book virtually identical to the 1662 Book of Common Prayer, and served by bishops, presbyters and deacons whose Orders derive directly from Canterbury, ecumenically enriched by Old Catholic, Swedish, Moravian and other successions.

It is a Church which is a member of the Free Churches Group of Churches Together in Britain and Ireland and which sent bishops to Canterbury to attend the Enthronements of George Carey in 1991 and Rowan Williams in 2003. It is a Church whose official Conversations with the Church of England were described in the official Report of the 1998 Lambeth Conference as something that 'gives us hope'.[1]

The story of the Free Church of England as an independent jurisdiction within the Universal Church began in the reign of King George II. In 2002 the Church sent a Loyal Message to Queen Elizabeth II on the occasion of her Golden Jubilee. The years in between are the fascinating story of a body of Christians who have sought to serve Jesus Christ in the midst of great change and who still seek to proclaim Him at the dawn of the Third Millennium.

1

The nearest parallel in English history is probably the Non-Jurors – a body of bishops, clergy and laity who were deprived of their positions in the Church of England in 1691 for refusing to take the oath of allegiance to the new King and Queen, and who maintained an independent exist- ence as an episcopally ordered community until the dawn of the nine- teenth century. Like the Non-Jurors the original members of the Free Church of England, though forced by conscience into separation from the organizational structures of the Church of England, saw themselves as preserving and continuing a purity that the Established Church had lost. Curiously, though, while the Non-Jurors have been a source of continu- ing interest and study,[2] the Free Church of England, which presents many parallels and some points of contact with the earlier movement, has attracted hardly any interest at all, at least for the last 75 years.[3] Most Christians in England do not even know that it exists. Yet the Free Church of England, which is a much more highly organized community than the Non-Jurors ever were, has not only outlasted the Non-Jurors (whose history spans at most 114 years[4]), but is still with us.

This book, then, is intended as an introduction to this 'branch of the Holy Catholic Church of the Lord Jesus Christ'[5] which has maintained its worship, work and witness in England and beyond for so many years. It is intended for members of the Free Church of England itself (most of whom know surprisingly little of the breadth of their denomination's history) and for the wider Christian world which, I believe, ought to know more of this highly neglected Christian community.

It should also be of particular interest to those concerned with the current pressing issues of Anglican identity and to those interested in alter- native ways of being Anglican. This is, after all, the only sustained attempt to create an alternative Church of England as close as possible to the origi- nal. The present work therefore perhaps has a contemporary 'political' relevance beyond what its subject matter might initially suggest. Those who take opposing views on the question of Anglican unity will find both encouragement and warning in the story of the Free Church of England.

Should the Free Church of England suffer the same fate as the Non- Jurors (and one of its former bishops considers it will last no longer than 10 to 20 years unless substantial changes are made[6]) then my hope is that the present work will be a preliminary memorial to many godly men and women who have served in it over the years, and a starting point for the academic interest that will no doubt follow the denomination's demise.

Only two substantial books on the denomination have hitherto been published, both of them written by members of the Free Church of England. The earlier is that F. S. Merryweather in 1873, which is an invaluable 'snapshot' of the Church and what it stood for on the eve of the great changes that were to follow. The later work (which relies heavily on Merryweather in places) is by Bishop Frank Vaughan in 1936.[7] No work on the Free Church of England is now possible, however, without reference to the two-volume Ph.D. Thesis of the Dean of Monmouth, Richard Fenwick.[8] I am grateful to Dr Fenwick (to whom I am not knowingly related) for his advice and encouragement. Much of the detail of the Thesis has inevitably been omitted here, and the present work covers areas not treated by Richard Fenwick. (I also differ from Dr Fenwick somewhat in my interpretation of some of the data.) The present work is in fact broader in its scope than all three. Rather than simply give a historical account, I have attempted initial descriptions and analyses of various areas of the life of the Free Church of England – notably its constitution, liturgical tradition and doctrinal statements – which have never before received detailed attention. To assist the reader, a minimal amount of historical material is repeated in the more thematic chapters, thus saving repeated cross-referencing. It will be obvious that the preliminary findings presented here open up rich fields for further research. Many primary sources, within and without the denomination, remain to be explored.

Two significant areas are, however, omitted from this study. The first is any substantial treatment of the Reformed Episcopal Church in North America, whose British 'daughter' united with the old Free Church of England in 1927. The origins of the North American Church, together with an overview of subsequent developments, can be found in Allen C. Guelzo's *For the Union of Evangelical Christendom* published in 1994.[9] The Reformed Episcopal Church is itself currently exploring new possibilities in the North American context and deserves closer study. The second main area of omission is the overseas congregations and jurisdictions. At times individual congregations and even whole dioceses have come under the oversight of bishops in England. The present work, however, concentrates on the denomination in the United Kingdom and only the briefest glance has been possible at overseas work. This is true also of missionary work (especially in India) sponsored by the Churches in this tradition.

The task of writing about the Free Church of England is made all the harder by the fact that many of the archives have been lost. The denomination has never had a centralized headquarters and so the preservation of documents has been scattered around the churches and subject to the vagaries of neglect and damp. Even those held by the denominational solicitors were destroyed when their office was firebombed during the London blitz.[10] Bishop Vaughan created a major collection at Emmanuel, Morecambe, but this was inexplicably dispersed or destroyed after his death, by Bishop Burrell. During his period of research Dean Fenwick achieved what is probably the greatest assembly of denominational material since then. Much of it has subsequently been returned to the original keepers and is once again at risk.

Writing Church History or the story of a Christian community is a difficult task. The historian seeks to identify and analyse human causes, while the Christian looks for the hand of God. The two approaches are not, however, incompatible. The doughty Anglican Evangelical Daniel Bartlett, one of the founders of the Bible Churchmen's Missionary Society in 1922, pointed out how scriptural history 'never shrinks from recording realities – discords and doubts, mistakes and moods, separations and strifes – and so never attributes to poor human agents the glory which belongs to God alone . . .'.[11] All too many discords, doubts, mistakes, moods, separations and strifes can be found in the history of the Free Church of England. But so too can much that is good – vision, sacrifice, courage, toil, witness, loving pastoral care, faithful preaching of the Word and devout administration of the Sacraments. Perhaps inevitably, surviving records tell more of the former than of the latter. Disagreements are recorded in Minutes and may find their way into the press. No one, on the other hand, records the hours of work put in by clergy, Sunday School teachers, Readers, youth workers, magazine editors, committee members, churchwardens, cleaners, flower arrangers and countless others on whom the daily life of local congregations depends. No one records the stories of the thousands of men, women and children who have found a living faith in Jesus Christ through the witness of the Free Church of England and have lived lives of humble discipleship in her fold. Inevitably such an imbalance in sources makes this what the Church Historian Patrick Collinson would call a 'vertical' history – 'concerned with the descent and continuity of the Church as a visible organisation, through its professional personnel, the clergy; and, above all, the hierarchy',[12] rather than the 'horizontal' context and experience of the entire membership. For this, I apologize in advance to the faithful laity of the denomination.

It should perhaps also be recorded that researching and writing this book has produced results that I was not expecting. The essential nature of the Free Church of England – in terms of its history, constitution, worship, ministry, doctrinal definitions and the stated intentions of its representative spokesmen – is somewhat different to that which I expected to find. It has become clear that the Free Church of England has frequently been misunderstood, both by outsiders and by some of its own members. Some of the implications of this are discussed in the final chapter. In the meantime it is hoped that the present work will offer something of a corrective to such misinformation.

This, then, is an attempt at an honest, warts-and-all, account of the present-day denomination. There are events recorded here which are not honouring to the Lord of the Church and which will sadden the sympathetic reader. The same is no doubt true of every part of Christ's Church. The Free Church of England is not alone in having many things to be ashamed of and of which it needs to repent. But this study is written in the conviction that the Free Church of England deserves to be better known and that, in this time of renewed upheaval in the wider Christian community (and the Anglican Communion in particular), there are lessons that might be learned from the denomination's history. It may be that the Free Church of England still has a significant contribution to make to the purposes of God for His people. More important, perhaps, is the fact that, despite her imperfections, she *has* been a vehicle of salvation for many, and continues to be so until the present day.

Inevitably, there has to be a 'cut-off point' in a work of this nature. For most purposes it is the year 2002 – the 75th anniversary of the uniting of the original Free Church of England with the Reformed Episcopal Church. This anniversary (though it went strangely unnoticed in the denomination) seems a good point at which to take stock. Some matters referred to are slightly later than this.

Author's note

As the present book was being prepared for the press, Mr Alan Bartley of Middlesex, who has undertaken his own researches on the early development of the Free Church of England, kindly provided me with a copy of A. Theodore Wirgman's *Foreign Protestantism within the Church of*

England: The Story of an Alien Theology and its Present Outcome (London, The Catholic Literature Association, 1911). It has not been possible to make reference to it in the main body of the present work, but a number of points are sufficiently important to merit note.

Wirgman's main thesis is that Protestantism within the Church of England is essentially the result of foreign influence, and has no place there. He does, however, devote an entire chapter to 'The Story of the Cumminsite Schism' which in his view 'deserved the respect of all honest men at its formation' (p. 13; cf. Chapter 4 of this book). There are a number of historical inaccuracies in Wirgman's account, but his judgment of Cummins is significant. Wirgman considers Cummins to have had

> much more scholarship and learning than Bishop Ryle and the usual type of 'militant Protestant' clergy in England. He never descended to the depths of controversial vulgarity and profanity which characterised the extreme members of his school of thought in England. He was an honest, and in many respects, an able man . . . We may deplore the views of Bishop Cummins and his followers, but we cannot help contrasting with admiration the honesty and courtesy of these men with the polemical virulence of [those] who were responsible for the Victorian persecution [in England]. (pp. 231ff.)

Wirgman records the anticipation that 'at least a third of the Church of England' would join the Reformed Episcopal Church after the first English consecrations in the 1870s, and believes it was not fulfilled because English Anglican Evangelicals gave Cummins 'the cold shoulder' (pp. 236f.). He states that he had 'a slight acquaintance' with Huband Gregg, and judged him 'an honest man, with the courage of his convictions' (p. 237). In Wirgman's view

> the secessionist Bishops [Cummins and Gregg] certainly occupied a higher moral platform than their co-religionists of the 'Establishment', with their Palaces, large incomes, and seats in the House of Lords. The poor and humble 'Reformed Episcopal' Bishop who was trying his best to induce his Protestant co-religionists in the 'Establishment' to be honest men and follow his own example, was bitterly disappointed. (p. 236)

While Wirgman's style is deliberately provocative and polemical, it is difficult to avoid the impression that his professed admiration for

Cummins and the Reformed Episcopal Church was not entirely ironic. It is an interesting testimony, from an unexpected quarter.

Interestingly, too, there is no indication that Wirgman had any awareness of the existence of the original Free Church of England. This is in agreement with other evidence that the events of 1836, 1844 and 1863 had not impinged on the general Christian consciousness.

John Fenwick
Martyrdom of Thomas Cranmer, 2004
Ulverston

Notes

1. Mark Dyer *et al.* (eds), *The Official Report of the Lambeth Conference 1998* (Harrisburg, PA, Morehouse Publishing, 1999), p. 228.
2. A historical survey can be found in J. W. C. Wand, *The High Church Schism* (London, The Faith Press, 1951). The continuing interest is exemplified by J. D. Smith, *The Eucharist Doctrine of the Later Nonjurors*, (Alcuin/GROW Joint Liturgical Study 46; Cambridge, Grove Books Limited, 2000).
3. It receives no mention, for example, in most of the classic histories of the Victorian Church. The Church is also the subject of continued misinformation: the recently reprinted *New International Dictionary of the Christian Church* (Grand Rapids, Michigan Zondervan, 2001) states 'its ministry is presbyterian' – a fact which ceased to be true in 1876!
4. From 1691 when the bishops and other clergy were deprived, until 1805 when the last bishop died.
5. This is the Free Church of England's designation of itself in its Declaration of Principles.
6. J. B. Shucksmith, 'Agenda for Renewal 2002–2012' (paper prepared for the 2002 Convocation), pp. 1, 6.
7. F. S. Merryweather, *The Free Church of England: Its History, Doctrines and Ecclesiastical Polity* (London, Partridge & Co., 1873); hereafter cited as Merryweather. Frank Vaughan, *A History of the Free Church of England otherwise called the Reformed Episcopal Church,* first edn Bath 1936, second edn 1960, third edn 1994; hereafter cited as *History*. A number of pamphlets and booklets have also been produced over the years.
8. R. D. Fenwick, 'The Free Church of England otherwise called the Reformed Episcopal Church *c.*1845 to *c.*1927', Ph.D. Thesis, University of Wales, 1995. It is referred to in the present work as Fenwick, *Thesis*.
9. Published by Pennsylvania State University Press.

10. See Fenwick, *Thesis*, pp. xxviiff. for an account of the problem of locating primary sources.
11. W. S. Hooton and J. Stafford Wright, *The First Twenty-five Years of the Bible Churchmen's Missionary Society 1922–1947* (London, BCMS, 1947), p. x. The BCMS is now called Crosslinks.
12. Patrick Collinson, 'The vertical and the horizontal in religious history' in A. Ford, J. McGuire and K. Milne (eds), *As by Law Established: The Church of Ireland since the Reformation* (Dublin, Lilliput Press, 1995).

CHAPTER 1

The First Strand: Deep Roots and Evangelism

It has been the consistent claim of the Free Church of England and its constituent traditions that it is 'not a new Church, it [is] the old Church, *purified* and *free*'.[1] From the earliest beginnings of the movement that was to lead to the Free Church of England its apologists have declared that, 'We desire to be esteemed as members of Christ's Catholic and Apostolic Church, and essentially one with the Church of England'[2] and this claim to be in direct continuity with the historic Church in England has been repeated throughout the denomination's history.

The first official history of the Free Church of England was written by the Church's Registrar, F. S. Merryweather, as long ago as 1873.[3] In it Merryweather traced the continuity back through English history; indeed, back to before the arrival of the English – 'even before Augustine planted his mud-built church in Kent'[4] – and beyond the British Isles. The Free Church of England, stated Merryweather, 'has claims to great antiquity and is descended from the most ancient form of Christianity'. 'Its doctrines', he asserted, 'are the doctrines of the Bible and the elements of its constitution are apostolic'.[5] Far from repudiating a catholic heritage, Merryweather sketched a continuity from the apostolic era through the Fathers of the first centuries,[6] via Aelfric and the Anglo-Saxon Church to John Wycliffe and the Lollards, the martyrs of Mary Tudor's reign and the preachers of the eighteenth-century Evangelical Revival. In the light of this heritage 'the Free Church of England claims a connection with the evangelical thoughts and aspirations of antiquity: claims to be a lawful and

9

faithful descendant of that historical Church which English Protestants revere and love'.[7] The visible Church may at times have been sadly corrupt, but it has been the conduit for what Merryweather called the 'living streamlet' of Gospel faith.[8]

Here, then, is the twofold continuity: continuity in *apostolic faith*, expressed in terms of a simple unadorned gospel of salvation through personal faith in the atoning death of Jesus Christ; and continuity in a *structured Christian community*, expressed in terms of a liturgical, episcopal Church, rooted in the apostolic and patristic eras and shaped by English history.

Within this wider continuity, the origins of the Free Church of England 'as a distinct, visible, ecclesiastical organisation'[9] are complex. Put simply, the present-day Free Church of England is the result of the interweaving of three strands. Two of these have their origins in the nineteenth century: events that took place in England in the 1840s; and developments in North America in 1873 that reached Britain soon afterwards. These will be explored in the next three chapters. Pre-dating both of these is a continuity of people, intention and organization stretching back to the eighteenth century. This is explicitly acknowledged in the Preamble to the motion creating the first Free Church of England constitution in 1863:

> Whereas in the good providence of God, and by His Grace, there was a remarkable revival of Religion in the British Empire during the last century, wherein many persons were converted . . .[10]

Thus, from the very moment of its formal inception, the Free Church of England saw itself in direct continuity with (and to some extent a fruit of) the eighteenth-century Evangelical Revival. This fact has been surprisingly neglected by the Free Church of England itself which has tended to fix on 1844 as the year of its inception. Without an appreciation of this older strand, however, it is impossible adequately to understand the processes that led to the constituting of the Free Church of England as a distinct body, or the debates and tensions that characterized much of its existence up to the early decades of the twentieth century. Moreover, it is an important corrective to the oversimplistic view of the Free Church of England simply as an anti-Tractarian reaction.

The Evangelical Revival

Like most movements, the origins of the Revival are complex and it is impossible to explore them in detail. Only a bare outline is sketched here, with particular attention to those events and persons especially associated with the Free Church of England story. In recent years there has been a tendency to trace the origins of the Revival to events in Central Europe, and to see the events in the British Isles and North America a part of a much wider phenomenon.[11] Traditionally the English aspect of the Revival is traced to a group of Church of England presbyters and their associates at Oxford University. The 'Holy Club' had been started in November 1729 with the brothers John and Charles Wesley, sons of a High Church rector, as two of its original members. They had started by reading classical authors and the New Testament in Greek. Soon, later devotional writings came to dominate, including the medieval Thomas à Kempis's *Imitation of Christ*. Of particular influence were the Non-Juror William Law's *A Serious Call to a Devout and Holy Life* published in 1728, and *A Practical Treatise upon Christian Perfection* (1726).[12] Inspired by Law's call to single-minded discipleship, the Holy Club members began to attempt to live out their Christian profession by a structured 'method'.[13] A central element in this 'method' was strict adherence to the doctrines and practices of the Church of England. Despite being mocked for their seriousness, the Club grew and had about 14 regular members by 1735. Two of its most significant recruits in the present context were George Whitefield and Benjamin Ingham.

In 1735 the Holy Club dissolved and its members dispersed to various spheres of Christian ministry. It was precisely at this time that most of them underwent a spiritual experience that changed their lives and their approach to preaching and ministry. The central element for all of them was a sense 'of personal trust in Christ as expressed in repentance for sin and faith in the efficacy of his work on the cross'.[14] A sense of new birth by the Holy Spirit liberated them from seeking to win acceptance by demanding devotional practices. John Wesley's later description was of passing from the faith of a servant to the faith of a son.[15]

George Whitefield's life-changing experience pre-dated Wesley's by three years. A junior member of the Holy Club (although descended from a family of comfortable status which had produced a number of Church of England clergy, the reduced circumstances brought about by his father's early death required him to pay his way through Oxford by acting as a 'servitor' to other undergraduates) he had been left behind in the university when the Wesleys and others had left to sail to the colony of Georgia. Weakened by fasting, he became ill in the weeks following Easter 1735:

> One day, perceiving an uncommon drought and clamminess in my mouth and using things to allay my thirst, but in vain, it was suggested to me, that when Jesus Christ cried out, 'I thirst,' His sufferings were near at an end. Upon which I cast myself down on the bed, crying out, 'I thirst! I thirst!' Soon after this, I found and felt in myself that I was delivered from the burden that had so heavily oppressed me. The spirit of mourning was taken from me, and I knew what it was truly to rejoice in God my Saviour . . . After a long night of desertion and temptation . . . the Day Star arose in my heart. Now did the Spirit of God take possession of my soul, and, as I humbly hope, seal me unto the day of redemption.[16]

Returning to his native Gloucester for a few months, Whitefield was instrumental in awakening 'several young persons, who soon formed themselves into a little Society'.[17] As Dallimore recognizes: 'The founding of this little Society was an historic event. This was the first Methodist Society in the permanent sense of the word, and it remained a unit of Whitefield's work throughout his lifetime.'[18] It could also be described as the beginning of the Free Church of England.

Whitefield's zeal brought him to the attention of the Bishop, Martin Benson, who was so impressed that he ordained him deacon on 20 June 1736, despite the fact that he was only 21.[19]

Whitefield's ordination opened up for him a preaching ministry. He had a commanding voice and spoke with fervour of 'new birth' and justification by faith. His fame spread rapidly – long before John Wesley had even returned to England. It is a much overlooked fact that it was Whitefield, not the Wesleys, who began the Revival in England and who for many years was its acknowledged leader.[20] By 1753, for example, it was estimated that he had around 20,000 followers, compared with John Wesley's 12,000.[21]

For many of the Holy Club members a significant contributory factor in their 'conversion experience' and subsequent ministry was contact with the Moravians. In view of this Church's importance and subsequent contact with the Free Church of England, a brief introduction is necessary here.

The Moravians[22]

The Moravians were heirs to a fourteenth-century reforming movement in Bohemia (in the modern Czech Republic). This itself had been influenced by memories of the region's Orthodox past (it had been evangelized by Cyril and Methodius, though later came under Roman obedience) and by the writings of John Wycliffe (c.1330–1384).[23] Despite the burning at the stake of one of the movement's most prominent leaders, Jan Hus, in 1415, reforming groups proliferated. An episcopal ministry (though not in the historic succession) developed from 1467 and continued in the group that came to be known as the Unitas Fratrum (Unity of Brothers) or Bohemian Brethren. Nearly three centuries of intermittent persecution, interspersed with some periods of freedom and growth, resulted in the dispersal of several groups of Unitas members throughout Eastern Europe. In 1722 a small group were given refuge on the estate of Count Nikolaus von Zinzendorf in Saxon Upper Lusatia, where they founded a community called Herrnhut ('the Lord's protection'). After an experience of spiritual renewal in 1727 the Herrnhut community was characterized by intense Christ-centred piety, ordered communal living and evangelistic zeal. One of the community, David Nitschmann (1695–1772) was consecrated bishop in 1735 by one of the few remaining bishops of the old Unitas Fratrum.

Moravians (as the Herrnhut group came to be called, due to the presence among the first settlers of a number from German-speaking Moravia) began to visit England from 1728, not to evangelize, but en route to the American Colonies where other groups of Continental Protestants had also migrated in the search for religious freedom. They were enormously attractive. For many Church of England clergy there was the fascination of contact with another ancient Protestant episcopal Church. For ordinary Christians (especially those awakened by the Revival) there was the appeal of a living Christ-centred spirituality, liturgical worship (conducted by clergy in surplices), membership of what was rapidly becoming an international fellowship, disciplined pastoral care and well-ordered community life. So strong was the appeal of the Moravians that six of the original members of the Holy Club were eventually to join them.[24]

Whitefield's spiritual awakening seems to have taken place independently of contact with the Moravians. This was not true of the Wesleys and Ingham (and a number of other leaders of the Revival).

When John and Charles Wesley and Benjamin Ingham boarded the *Simmonds* in October 1735, they found a number of Moravians on board, including the newly consecrated David Nitschmann. Wesley was famously impressed by the calmness of the Moravians in a storm during the crossing, which suggested a depth of faith and assurance he lacked. He was further unsettled by conversations with the Moravians both on board and after landing in Georgia. In addition to the evident reality of their faith, the Moravians in their community organization seemed a closer reflection of the life of the apostolic Church than the complexities of the Church of England. Contact with the Moravians also brought Ingham's spiritual search to a climax. In 1737, 'having used all means, and finding them ineffectual, he looked in his deep darkness to Jesus, called upon Him for mercy and instantly obtained it'.[25] On his return to England later that year Ingham met up with Whitefield, each rejoicing to see the spiritual change that had taken place in the other.

Eventually John Wesley left Georgia in 1738, deeply oppressed by the failure of so many of his hopes there. He and Charles Wesley remained in frequent contact with the Moravians whose assurance in faith had already impressed them in Georgia, and who taught that justification by faith was not simply a doctrine to be assented to, but a reality to be experienced. That experience came first for Charles, at Whitsuntide 1738; John's followed a few days later. John Wesley was to say of his own experience when attending an exposition on the Letter to the Romans in a Moravian meeting at Aldersgate on 24 May 1738: 'I felt my heart strangely warmed. I felt I did trust in Christ, Christ alone for salvation; and an assurance was given me that He had taken away *my* sins, even *mine*, and saved *me* from the law of sin and death.'[26] It was an experience that others were sharing.[27] And it was the need for a life-changing experience of Jesus Christ, entered into by an act of personal repentance and commitment to Him that formed the central plank of their preaching, which increasingly took place out of doors as parish churches proved hostile.[28] The simple gospel message, accessible by people of all ages and sections of society, found a massive response in a context where not only the Church of England but older Dissenting groups had sunk into a lifeless orthodoxy.

The Revival was carried to parts of Yorkshire by Benjamin Ingham. It was through this ministry that there came about the conversion of perhaps the most significant person in the 'pre-history' of the Free Church of England – Selina, Countess of Huntingdon.

Born Lady Selina Shirley in 1707, the daughter of the second Earl Ferrers, she married in 1728 the ninth Earl of Huntingdon.[29] Largely through the witness and prayer of her sister-in-law, Lady Margaret Hastings, who had been influenced by Ingham's preaching (and who eventually married him, causing a scandal due to their different stations in society), Lady Huntingdon experienced a spiritual conversion in about 1738. It changed her life and from then on she took every opportunity to share her faith in Jesus Christ with others, particularly in the noble and Court circles in which she moved. Widowed at the early age of 39 she used her considerable resources and talents to promote the cause of the gospel. The Countess associated with many of the leaders of the revival, but as the years went by drew particularly close to George Whitefield, whom she appointed as one of her chaplains in 1748, so that she could invite her aristocratic friends to hear him preach, often in the drawing room of Lady Huntingdon's London house.

The Calvinist tradition within the Revival

The Revival looked unstoppable. It is, however, one of the tragedies of the movement that as early as 1741 a serious rift had occurred between its leaders, principally between John and Charles Wesley and George Whitefield. The basic disagreement was over the issue of Election and Predestination. To oversimplify, the question (which in the Western theological tradition was shaped by St Augustine of Hippo in the fourth century) is whether God has already chosen in advance certain people – 'the elect' – for salvation. If so, by an extension of the argument, it was then argued by some that He must have therefore chosen others for damnation. The question is clearly a critical one, especially in its bearing on Christian approaches to evangelism. The concept of Predestination is strongly associated with the sixteenth-century French Reformer John Calvin (though there is some debate as to precisely how central it was to his thinking) and therefore the term 'Calvinist' came to be used as a shorthand for those supporting a belief in Predestination. A contrary view is associated with the Dutch Reformer Jacobus Arminius (also of the sixteenth century) who insisted that Divine sovereignty *was* compatible with human free will and that Christ died for *all* and not only for the elect. Broadly, the Wesleys took an Arminian position as a justification for their evangelistic work – if God had already decided who was going to be saved or damned, why bother preaching? As the recent Anglican–Methodist *Common Statement* points out, 'Most leaders in the Evangelical Revival took a Calvinist position in the 18th century, albeit a "moderate" one, and this was true within the Church of England as well as without.'[30] It was Wesley who was taking a minority position. Whitefield followed the more Calvinistic line (though he claimed not to have read Calvin), and saw his preaching as God's means of awakening faith in those elect in whom the workings of grace were not yet manifest.[31] To this end Whitefield therefore wished to reach as many people as possible: 'If the Pope himself would lend me his pulpit I would gladly proclaim the righteousness of Jesus Christ therein!'[32] The clash (which was at times very public and acrimonious[33]) between the leaders of the Revival inevitably resulted in their followers dividing into two camps. Ultimately, in England, the societies outside the Established Church following the position of the Wesleys came to predominate numerically and, after their own divisions and reunions, formed the modern Methodist Church in Britain and overseas. It was the eventually smaller Calvinistic stream that was to be more closely associated with the origins of the Free Church of England.

The Calvinistic tradition was particularly strong in Wales where Daniel Rowland of Llangeitho and Howell Harris of Trevecca were the leaders of the first generation of preachers. Born in 1711, Rowland was a Welsh-speaking presbyter of the Church of England. The son of a clergyman, he was ordained deacon in London in March 1734 by the Bishop of St Davids, having walked there from Llangeitho in West Wales. He was ordained priest in August the following year at the Bishop's Chapel at Abergwili, near Carmarthen. Shortly after ordination his faith was 'awakened' by the preaching ministry of Griffith Jones of Llanddowror.[34] Harris was born in 1714 at Talgarth in Brecon. In 1735 he underwent a conversion experience.[35] He rapidly began to organize family prayers and to speak of his faith. This was to lead to a vigorous preaching ministry, despite his being a layman. It was this irregularity, and his 'enthusiasm' that prevented Harris from ever being ordained.

Under the ministry of Rowland, Harris and a few others, a Revival swept through Wales which was proportionately probably greater than that in England. Links with Whitefield were strong: 'Whitefield saw the Welsh work of Rowland and Harris, and his own English work, as one Calvinistic Methodism.'[36] Whitefield regularly visited Wales, unlike John

Wesley who went there only occasionally and whose 'Wesleyan Methodism' 'remained a small and stunted plant'.[37]

Organizing the Fruits of Revival

The Revival in both Wales and England resulted in many thousands of converts for whose spiritual and pastoral needs provision had to be made. Most of the first generation of leaders counselled their followers to remain in their parish churches. Many did, but the hostile reception often found there forced many others to seek Christian fellowship elsewhere.[38] Whitefield linked together his societies into a 'connexion' with its headquarters at the 'Tabernacle' – the large wooden preaching hall built at Moorfields in London in 1741. A surviving list from 1744 lists 36 societies and 25 preaching places 'in Connexion together under the care of the Reverend Mr Whitefield'.[39] At this time Whitefield's Connexion was divided into 4 Associations, each with its own Superintendent (who sent regular reports to Whitefield) staffed by approximately 50 'exhorters' – lay preachers.

Whitefield was also instrumental in organizing the Revival in Wales. With his active involvement Rowland and his colleagues began in 1743 to hold meetings known as 'Associations' to organize and provide for their converts. Despite great care being taken initially to do nothing that would constitute a breach with the Established Church, with the passage of time such structures inevitably evolved into distinct denominations. From the 1750s the Welsh Association began to sanction the building of 'Society Houses'. These were often humble creations – Rowland's first such structure at Llangeitho had mud walls and thatched roof.[40] Inevitably the erection of separate meeting places hastened the process of separation from the Established Church. In 1763 Rowland's bishop withdrew his licence. It made little practical difference to his powerful itinerant ministry, but helped to ensure that the Revival would be substantially lost to the Church of England in Wales. Over the next half-century the congregations which Rowland, Harris and their co-workers organized came to be known as the Calvinistic Methodists, a denomination which still exists, now called the Presbyterian Church of Wales.[41] After Rowland's death in 1790, the leadership of the movement passed to his fellow Welshman, Thomas Charles, who had been converted under Rowland's ministry in January 1773.

Following ordination at Oxford and curacies in Somerset and Merioneth, Charles (who had occasionally preached for Lady Huntingdon and was finding Church of England posts denied to him) moved to Bala in 1784 where he remained until his death in 1814, exercising a powerful preaching ministry and being much involved in the founding of many Day and Sunday Schools.[42] It was from the denomination reluctantly brought into separate existence by Charles, who oversaw the final break with the Church of England, that Benjamin Price, first bishop of the Free Church of England, came.

Initially Whitefield and the other English leaders of the Revival looked to the Moravians, with their longer experience of organizing small groups of believers, not simply as a model, but as a possible home for their converts. Ingham, for example, in 1742 placed the many societies that he had founded in West Yorkshire under the authority of the Moravians, though he did not join them himself until 1749.[43] Wesley, who had visited Herrnhut (with Ingham) shortly after his Aldersgate experience, soon separated from the Moravians after initial involvement in a congregation run on Moravian lines in Fetter Lane. As probably the most efficient organizer among the Revival leaders, he went on to create a disciplined 'class' system of local groups which laid the foundation of the modern Methodist Church.

From 1739 Whitefield had admired the Moravians and initially worked with them, especially in Georgia and Pennsylvania. Despite some misgivings about doctrinal differences, in December 1741 when attending a Moravian General Meeting, Whitefield 'declared publicly that he felt the grace among the Moravians in his heart and wished to unite with them'.[44] In February 1742 he wrote to the Moravian leader in London, August Spanenberg, formally requesting 'full union'. Twelve months later Whitefield attempted to bring the Wesleys, the Moravians and his own followers together in a reunion of the whole Evangelical Revival movement, but nothing came of it. After this, Whitefield's relationship with the Moravians cooled somewhat (he and Zinzendorf disagreed strongly on a number of matters) and Whitefield returned to America in 1744, leaving John Cennick, a lay evangelist, in charge of his English societies. In December 1745, with Whitefield still in America, Cennick announced that he intended to join the Moravians. In the event he took with him many members of the Moorfields Tabernacle and most of Whitefield's societies in the West Country. If the Moravians had not declined to receive all who applied to them, the transference 'could virtually have destroyed'

Whitefield's work.[45] In 1755 Whitefield published an *Expostulatory Letter* to Zinzendorf, criticizing many aspects of Moravian life and teaching at the time. Nevertheless, despite this distancing, Whitefield's Moorfields Tabernacle was modelled in a number of respects on Moravian practices.[46]

In addition to suffering the loss of much of his work to the Moravians, Whitefield seems to have been extremely unhappy at the growing rivalry between the young 'Connexions' – his own and John Wesley's in particular. Returning to England from the American Colonies in 1748 he found himself expected by his followers to build up 'Whitefieldian Methodism'. Had he chosen to do so it is likely that it would have overtaken Wesley's work. Instead, Whitefield attempted to quench the growing rivalry by making the sacrificial decision not to form any more societies, but to operate as an evangelist at large, without creating structures for his converts. In 1749 he made it known that he would no longer serve as 'Moderator of the [Calvinistic Methodist] Association'.[47] When urged to reconsider by disappointed followers, he replied, 'Let my name die everywhere . . . if by that means the name of the blessed Jesus may be promoted.'[48] A further important factor in Whitefield's decision was no doubt the fact that he frequently spent time away from England in America. He had paid his first visit to Georgia in 1738 and was to visit seven times in all, exercising a remarkable itinerant ministry in the British Colonies becoming 'the single best-known religious leader in America of [the eighteenth] century, and the most widely recognised figure of any sort in North America before George Washington'.[49] Scotland and Ireland also (as well as Wales) received Whitefield's ministry, increasing his international stature still further.

Although anxious not to promote his own glory, Whitefield nevertheless intended initially to make provision for his societies and hoped that Howell Harris would take on their leadership. Harris, however, suffered a breakdown in the early 1750s. Whitefield seems thereafter to have made no attempt to induce anyone else to lead them: 'he simply left the Societies to look after their own affairs and allowed the Association as an organisation to die away'.[50] Even so, a loose 'family' of societies continued in relationship with Whitefield, 'and after his death [in 1770] they were known as The Whitefield Connexion'.[51] Over the next few decades this Connexion began to dissolve, many of the surviving congregations feeding 'mainly into evangelical Independency'[52] and 'contributing considerably to the growth of evangelical Dissent'.[53] Whitefield's heritage was in danger of being lost to the Anglican tradition of which he counted himself a loyal son.[54] Something of it was saved by 'Whitefield's chief patron and supporter',[55] the Countess of Huntingdon.

The Contribution of the Countess of Huntingdon and Thomas Haweis

Lady Huntingdon had her own unique solution to the problem of providing places of worship and nurture to those awakened by the Revival. 'Anxious to keep the Methodist movement within the bounds of the Established Church',[56] she was nevertheless conscious of the need for her to do something to help those 'Methodists' who were being driven from their parish churches, and the Evangelical preachers who were finding more and more pulpits closed to them. She therefore 'embarked upon a scheme for building chapels in different locations which would serve as preaching stations for such men and where new converts might be built up in the faith'.[57] As a peeress the Countess had the right to appoint chaplains to minister to her and to have her own private chapels which could be open to the public.[58] In theory there was a limit to the number of chaplains each grade of the peerage could have, the maximum being six for an archbishop or duke, but the Countess 'regarded this as a dead letter and the law turned a blind eye'.[59] Lady Huntingdon opened her first chapel in 1761 and over the next 20 years established a network of them around the country, each served by one or more chaplains, clergy of the Church of England, and using the Book of Common Prayer.[60]

Lady Huntingdon's prominent social position made her for a time a natural focus for many of the leaders of the Revival. The majority of them were presbyters of the Church of England, often unpopular and hard-pressed as a result of their Evangelical preaching. It was natural that they should draw a degree of comfort and protection from an aristocratic patron.

In its early stages the Countess's circle almost constituted a religious community. Whitefield described the situation at the Countess's homes, where a number of clergy at a time resided under her roof: '. . . it looks like a college. We have the sacrament every morning, heavenly conversation all day, and preach at night. This is to live at Court indeed.'[61] Gradually there emerged a fluctuating group of clergy who, in addition to their duties as incumbents, were prepared to leave their parishes for a number of weeks or months and 'itinerate' – travel around the Countess's chapels and preach in them. Most of the great 'names' of the Revival, including Daniel Rowland, took part in this work at one stage or another. Among these presbyters was an 'inner core' who were formally appointed as her chaplains. As already noted, George Whitefield was one of this group. Another chaplain who was to play a unique role following the Countess's death, was Thomas Haweis.[62] It was Haweis's statement about the nature of the Countess's communities being 'essentially one with the Church of England' (quoted at the beginning of this chapter) that was to become authoritative in the Free Church of England. A brief examination of this significant figure is therefore necessary.

Originally from Truro, Haweis, who was born in 1734, had been converted as a boy by the ministry of Samuel Walker, curate of St Mary's Truro. After school he was apprenticed to an apothecary and physician as his family was too poor to send him to university. Eventually he came to the notice of Joseph Jane, Vicar of St Mary Magdalene, Oxford from 1748, who recognized Haweis's potential and arranged for him to study at Christ Church, himself providing the necessary financial assistance. As an undergraduate Haweis organized a group who met for prayer, fellowship and discussion, which has sometimes been described as 'a second Holy Club'. After encountering some initial opposition to ordination as a result of his Evangelical stance, Haweis was eventually ordained Deacon at Cuddesdon by Bishop Secker of Oxford on 9 October 1757 to serve as curate to Joseph Jane. He was ordained Priest in Christ Church Cathedral on 19 February 1758.

In 1762 Haweis left Oxford and for two years was appointed to the Lock Hospital in London. Being in the capital brought him into the company of the leading Evangelical laity of the time, most of whom were members of Lady Huntingdon's circle. He met the Countess, and by 1764 was preaching regularly at some of her chapels. Haweis was offered the parish of St Paul's, Philadelphia by Whitefield himself in 1763, but eventually in 1764 accepted the Rectory of All Saints, Aldwincle, in Northamptonshire, an ancient parish mentioned in the Domesday Book. He remained as Rector until his death in 1820.

After an initial period of establishing a Gospel ministry in his parish, Haweis was to find that there was insufficient work there to occupy all his talents. He therefore became involved in a number of projects, the story of most of which falls outside the present work.[63] He was appointed Chaplain to the Earl of Peterborough and in 1774 to Lady Huntingdon also. This latter appointment involved him spending several months of each year away from Aldwincle (where his curates looked after the parish) travelling around some of the Countess's chapels, principally, Brighton, London, Bath and Bristol. He was clearly deeply committed to Lady Huntingdon's cause: 'I am willing, while my taper burns, that it should be in that candlestick'.[64] However, 'Haweis does not appear to have regarded this allegiance to the Countess of Huntingdon as constituting any breach of loyalty to the Church of England.'[65] In fact he went so far as to insist that no one other than a clergyman of the Church of England should preach in any of the chapels where he ministered. Haweis's deeply Anglican commitment was to be significant as the network of chapels in time began to evolve to form the nucleus of the Free Church of England.

The establishing of this network of chapels caused much opposition, not least from many of the local incumbents in whose parishes they were situated. The story of one – Spa Fields Chapel in Clerkenwell, London – is worth recounting as it played an important role in both the Countess's work and in the story of the Free Church of England:

> In 1774 a large building which had formerly been used as a place of amusement [called the Pantheon] came on the market. It had a spacious circular auditorium and the Countess seriously considered its purchase as a preaching centre, but abandoned the idea on the grounds of expense. However, a group of Christian businessmen stepped in and acquired it. They called the building Northampton Chapel and appointed two men . . . as Ministers. Large congregations were drawn to the place and the attention of the Vicar of the Parish [William Sellon] was aroused. He strongly objected to what he regarded as an unwarranted intrusion into his Parish. A lawsuit followed and, as a result, the Chapel had to be closed. Quite undaunted the Countess thereupon acquired the premises which were re-opened in March 1779 as Spa Fields Chapel and she appointed Thomas Haweis and Cradock Glascott as her Chaplains.[66]

Sellon once again took legal action and the resulting Consistory Court ruling that the Countess could only have her lawful number of chaplains and chapels brought the Countess's work to a moment of crisis. If it was to continue within the Church of England many of her chapels would have to close and the work be severely curtailed. The Countess therefore took the decision to take her chapels *outside* the Church of England. In 1782 she registered Spa Fields Chapel as a Dissenting place of worship under the 1689 Toleration Act. Most of the rest of her chapels were eventually to be so registered. At this juncture all but one of Lady Huntingdon's chaplains (including Haweis) withdrew from her service and continued to minister in the Church of England.[67] The severity of this blow was eased somewhat by the fact that the Countess had already taken steps that would benefit both her own work and (unknown to her) that of the Free Church of England in years to come – she had established a training college for clergy.

The first Church of England Theological College for training men for ordination was not established until 1816 at St Bees on the Cumberland coast.[68] Until then the usual route for ordination was simply to read a degree at Oxford or Cambridge and then to present oneself to a bishop, who made such enquiries as he thought fit. There was no 'training for ministry' in the modern sense. Oxford and Cambridge were not only closed to non-Anglicans, but were also often unsympathetic to those who had been influenced by the Revival. The Countess therefore decided to found a college where men could be trained for Christian ministry and in 1764, together with Howell Harris, she leased a sixteenth-century farmhouse, Trefeca Isaf,[69] at Talgarth in Brecon, South Wales. The official opening took place on 24 August 1768 with George Whitefield as the preacher.[70] As well as studies in Greek, Latin, Church History and Philosophy, the students also – probably uniquely at the time – spent part of their time away from the college, often on short pastorates at one of the Countess's chapels. John Wesley preached at Trevecca and Daniel Rowland was a frequent speaker at the annual Anniversary Services.

In the early years of Trevecca's existence men trained from it were ordained by Church of England bishops to serve as the Countess's Chaplains.[71] Following the registering of the chapels as Dissenting Places of Worship, episcopal ordination was no longer available, so on 9 March 1783 ordination by presbyters commenced, with two Church of England presbyters, Thomas Wills and William Taylor, ordaining six young men in a five-hour service which culminated in Holy Communion. The candidates were required to subscribe to the *Fifteen Articles of Faith*, the new basic confessional statement of what was coming to be called the Countess's 'Connexion'. Thus was established a separate ministry from that of the Church of England.[72] The Countess now had a source of trained men for her network of chapels and a means of commissioning them for service.[73]

As Cook states, 'the Countess's chapels now embraced a halfway stance between Church and Dissent: they became "partial conformists"'. Lady Huntingdon 'still insisted that in all their services of worship the chapels in the Connexion should retain the Church Liturgy'.[74]

In 1789 Thomas Haweis actively rejoined the Countess's cause. This decision may have been influenced in part by his marriage the previous year to Jennett Payne Orton, a close companion of Lady Huntingdon. It was a rather anomalous position. As Haweis's biographer put it: 'He remained a clergyman of the Established Church whilst resuming an itineracy in what had become a Dissenting body.'[75] Despite the fact that its ministers were now mostly presbyterially ordained, Haweis seems still to have regarded the Connexion 'as in essence a society within the Church of England'.[76] A further factor in Haweis's decision to become involved with the Connexion again was almost certainly Lady Huntingdon's increasing age. By 1789 she was 82.

Even in her eighties the Countess still to a large degree ran the network of chapels herself, moving preachers frequently.[77] As her powers failed she began to look for some way of ensuring that her work survived her. In 1790 Lady Huntingdon commended to her chapels 'A Plan for Uniting and Perpetuating the Connexion of the Right Honourable the Countess Dowager of Huntingdon'.[78] The Plan divided the country into 23 geographical districts, each to be served by a committee consisting of the ministers and two laymen from each congregation. The district committees would report to a central body, the London Acting Association. There was to be a 1d a week levy on all members. In the event, some of those closest to the Countess, including Thomas Haweis, strongly opposed the Plan. Haweis disliked in particular the inclusion of the laity in the decision-making processes, and the weekly levy. Cook suggests that a deeper reason was that such a structure would tie his hands as 'heir apparent of the Connexion' after Lady Huntingdon's death.[79] In fact, Haweis's reaction to his new responsibilities when the Countess died suggests otherwise. It is more likely that he feared that adopting a formal structure and constitution would inevitably give the Connexion an existence independent of the Church of England. For Haweis the Plan would 'turn the Connection [sic] into a Dissenting denomination'.[80] Later generations were to regret the decision not to put the Connexion on a firm footing. As New put it, 'The auspicious moment, however, passed, and the golden opportunity has not yet returned.'[81] Too weak to fight, the Countess did not press the issue, but drew up a will naming Haweis and his wife, with two others, as Trustees of all her property, with power to appoint successors.

It was an unsatisfactory solution. Lady Huntingdon died on 17 June 1791.[82] She had not told Haweis of her intention to place her Connexion in his hands and the news, when broken to him by George Best, the Countess's secretary, 'burst on him like a thunderstroke'.[83] He was, after all, as a beneficed clergyman of the Church of England, being placed in effective charge of a Dissenting body numbering perhaps 120 chapels. After seeking advice, Haweis accepted the charge. Part of his motivation seems to have been that 'under his control the Connection [*sic*] might be kept as close to the Church of England as was possible'.[84] This is confirmed by his own statement: 'I strove very hard always to preserve the Chapels regular, to maintain a propriety and dignity in the service, and to admit none to preach where I was whom I did not think qualified to appear before a polite as well as intelligent auditory. . . . I struggled hard to prevent any departure from the Church'.[85] Lady Anne Erskine, one of the other original four Trustees, continued with a great deal of the 'secretarial' work, much as she had done in Lady Huntingdon's last years. Haweis oversaw the well-being of the chapels by regularly visiting at least the principal ones, and arranging the supply of preachers. He thus exercised a very real *episkope* over the chapels and their ministers, speaking – bishoplike – of 'those of my brethren that are more immediately under my care'.[86] It is from this period that Haweis's much-quoted statement about the identity of the movement derives:

> We have no secret; we wish the whole world to know the manner of our procedure . . . You ask of what Church we profess ourselves? We desire to be esteemed as the members of Christ's Catholic and Apostolic Church, and essentially one with the Church of England, of which we regard ourselves as living members . . . The doctrines we subscribe (for we require subscription, and, what is better, they are always truly preached by us), are those of the Church of England in the literal and grammatical sense. Nor is the liturgy of the Church of England performed more devoutly in any Church, nor the Scriptures better read for the edifying of the people, as those who attend our London congregations can witness.[87]

The reluctance of Haweis and the other Trustees to take any action that might increase the separation between the Connexion and the Established Church was to create its own problems. A Connexional Trust Deed was not drawn up until 1807, by which time most of the chapels had set up their own trusts. Despite the difficulties, Haweis was optimistic about the cause that had been entrusted to him and anticipated its continuation: 'I hope when I die I shall leave the Connection more flourishing than when I found it, and that my colleagues who have been such helpers in the truth will long continue in succession to see the pleasure of the Lord prosper in their hands.'[88] Haweis last preached at Spa Fields in 1815, when he was 81. He died at Bath in 1820 and is buried in Bath Abbey. His memorial there describes him as '57 years Rector of All Saints, Aldwincle, Northamptonshire; Chaplain and Principal Trustee to the late Countess of Huntingdon and founder of the [London] Missionary Society'. With Haweis's authority removed, it is significant that the following year the clergy met together for the first time in Conference and continued to do so annually thereafter.[89] In 1836 a Constitution was agreed,[90] but by then the Connexion was in trouble.

Like the chapels, the College also suffered from not being placed on a sufficiently firm foundation. It was refounded on its relocation to Cheshunt in 1792 in a form that weakened its Connexional character. In due course Principals were appointed who were not members of the Connexion. Even more extraordinary was the eventual appointment of Trustees of the Connexion's property who were not Connexion members.[91] In effect the Connexion was divided into three blocs – the clergy, organized into a Conference; the Trustees in charge of the buildings of the denomination; and the College with its own body of Trustees. The sad legacy of this situation was that for much of the nineteenth century the various elements of the Connexion were engaged in a succession of disputes (sometimes involving legal action) which sapped human and financial resources and left the Connexion in poor shape to deal constructively with new challenges and opportunities.[92]

Inevitably, decline set in. From a peak of over 100 affiliated congregations in the 1780s (including some of Whitefield's former societies), the number declined to just 34 chapels in Central Trust in 1842.[93] Most of the Countess's chapels and students 'dissolved into Independency'.[94]

There remained, however, a core of ministers and congregations who clung to the original vision of a community 'essentially one with the

Church of England'. They used the Book of Common Prayer – 'the devout, simple, humble, contrite, Catholic, and Christian utterances of her Liturgy'[95] – and adhered to 'the profound, massive and Scriptural theology of her doctrinal articles'.[96] In the Annual Conference they had a forum to voice their dissatisfaction and to plan for a better future.

By the 1840s many of those remaining in the Connexion were seeking what modern secular terminology would call a 'relaunch' – a new initiative to breathe life into the old vision.

The opportunity came in 1844.

Notes

1. Frank Vaughan, *Prospect and Retrospect: the Centenary Charge* (printed by the Wallasey and Wirral Newspaper Co., Wallasey, Cheshire, 1944), p. 6. The claim to be 'not an new, but an old Church (reformed)' occurs in *The Constitution and Canons of the Reformed Episcopal Church . . . also called the Reformed Church of England* (London, E. Marlborough & Co., 1883), Article XIII. See Chapter 6 for the place of the Reformed Church of England in the story.

2. The phrase derives from a letter of Thomas Haweis, Rector of Aldwincle, dated 21 December 1795, reproduced in Aaron Seymour, *The Life and Times of Selina, Countess of Huntingdon* (London, William Painter, 1840), vol. II, p. 521. It is reproduced in the first edition of Vaughan's *History*, and retained in each of the two subsequent editions. See below for the significance of Haweis.

3. Much of Merryweather's opening chapter is repeated (without acknowledgment) in Vaughan's, *History*.

4. Merryweather, p. 1. According to Bede, Augustine in fact began by restoring church buildings erected in Roman times (*A History of the English Church and People*, I.26.33, trans. Leo Sherley-Price; Harmondsworth, Penguin, 1968), pp. 70, 81). This in fact makes Merryweather's point even more strongly.

5. Merryweather, p. 1.

6. His list (p. 5) includes Justin Martyr, Clement of Alexandria, Tertullian, Origen, Eusebius, Cyril of Jerusalem, Gregory Nazianzen, Jerome, Augustine, Chrysostom, Theodoret and Gelasius. Merryweather sees in them 'a line of consecutive testimony' concerning the Eucharist, but finds them inconsistent.

7. Merryweather, p. 2. Merryweather is also aware of Continental reforming movements such as the Bohemian Brethren (see below) and the Waldensians.

8. Ibid.

9. The phrase is Merryweather's, p. 1.

10. Merryweather, p. 83.

11. See, e.g. Henry Rack, *Reasonable Enthusiast: John Wesley and the Rise of Methodism* (London, Epworth Press, 3rd edn, 2002), pp. 161ff. and the authorities quoted there.

12. 'There is scarcely one of [the pioneers of the awakening] who does not express his indebtedness to one or both of these treatises . . .' A. Skevington Wood, *Thomas Haweis 1734–1820* (London, SPCK, 1957), p. 6. 'God worked powerfully upon my soul, as He has since upon many others, by that . . . treatise', Whitefield (p. 45) was to write of *A Serious Call* (George Whitefield, *Journals*, Edinburgh, Banner of Truth Trust, 1960; hereafter cited as *Journals*). Law's influence at this stage provides an interesting point of contact between the Non-Jurors and the story of the Free Church of England. See also Eric W. Baker, *A Herald of the Evangelical Revival: A critical inquiry into the relationship of William Law to John Wesley and the beginnings of Methodism* (London, Epworth Press, 1948). For the text of *A Serious Call* see the edition by Paul G. Stanwood (London, SPCK, Classics of Western Spirituality series, 1978).

13. Greek for 'rule'; hence the adjective 'Methodist' which was applied loosely in the eighteenth century to anyone influenced by the Revival.

14. T. Grass (ed.), *Evangelicalism and the Orthodox Church*, London, ACUTE, 2001), p. 12.

15. See Rack, *Reasonable Enthusiast*, p. 156. See also R. Hattersley, *A Brand from the Burning: The Life of John Wesley* (London, Little, Brown, 2002) for a recent treatment of John Wesley's life and views.

16. *Journals*, p. 58. The most recent biography of Whitefield is Arnold Dallimore's two-volume *George Whitefield: The Life and Times of the Great Evangelist of the Eighteenth Century Revival* (Edinburgh, Banner of Truth Trust, 1970 (vol. 1), 1980 (vol. 2). See also John Pollock, *George Whitefield and the Great Awakening* (London, Hodder & Stoughton, 1972).

17. *Journals*, p. 61.

18. Dallimore, *George Whitefield*, vol. 1, p. 83.

19. The minimum canonical age for ordination as a Deacon is 23. Whitefield was ordained Priest on 14 January 1739: 'I find my not being in Priest's Orders is a great hindrance to my ministry . . . The good Lord prepare me for that second imposition of hands.' *Journals*, p. 146 (Sunday 2 April 1738).

20. 'In point of time, Whitefield was the pioneer of the Evangelical Revival in England . . . When John Wesley was returning from Georgia a sadder and wiser man . . . Whitefield was sounding the first clear trumpet of the Evangelical Revival,' Skevington Wood, *Thomas Haweis*, pp. 8f. This is acknowledged by Rack, *Reasonable Enthusiast*, p. 191, and by the recent Anglican–Methodist *Common Statement* (London, Methodist Publishing House/Church House Publishing, 2001), p. 4. Indeed, at the time of the

'unconverted' Wesley's return, Whitefield's first sermons were already appearing in print. See Dallimore, *George Whitefield*, vol. 1, pp. 165ff.

21. Colin Podmore, *The Moravian Church in England 1728–1760* (Oxford, Clarendon Press, 1998), p. 120.

22. A clear summary of Moravian history can be found in *Anglican–Moravian Conversations: The Fetter Lane Common Statement with Essays in Moravian and Anglican History* (London, Council for Christian Unity of the General Synod, (GS 1202) 1996).

23. Wycliffe was claimed as one of the 'ancestral spirits' of the Free Church of England. Merryweather called him, 'the instrument chosen to awaken the Church from the sleep of ages' (p. 14) and devoted seven pages to his work and that of his Lollard followers. See also Edward Langton, *History of the Moravian Church* (London, George Allen & Unwin, 1956), pp. 12f. Communion in both kinds is normal Orthodox practice; by Hus's time the cup had been denied to the laity, bringing the area into line with the rest of the Roman Church.

24. Podmore, *Moravian Church*, p. 107. Some, however, subsequently left the Moravians.

25. Quoted in William Batty, *Church History, Collected from the Memoirs and Journals of Mr Ingham and the Labourers in Connection with him* (John Rylands MS MAM P11B), p. 3.

26. See Rack, *Reasonable Enthusiast*, pp. 137ff. for a discussion of the context.

27. The list includes William Grimshaw, Henry Venn, William Romaine and, rather later, Charles Simeon.

28. Whitefield was the first to engage in open-air preaching to the miners at Kingswood in Bristol on 17 February 1739: 'Blessed be God that I have now broken the ice!' *Journals*, p. 216. John Wesley was at first very sceptical: 'I could scarce reconcile myself at first to this strange way of preaching in the fields . . .'; quoted in Rack, *Reasonable Enthusiast*, p. 191.

29. See Faith Cook, *Selina, Countess of Huntingdon* (Edinburgh, Banner of Truth Trust, 2001) and the works quoted there for an account of the life of this remarkable woman. A shorter version can be found in Gilbert W. Kirby, *The Elect Lady* (The Trustees of the Countess of Huntingdon's Connexion, 2nd edn 1990).

30. *Anglican–Methodist Common Statement*, p. 4.

31. For a relatively recent treatment of some of the issues see J. I. Packer, *Evangelism and the Sovereignty of God* (London, IVP, 1961 and reprints).

32. Quoted in Dallimore, *George Whitefield*, vol. 2 p. 90.

33. Whitefield's response to John Wesley's published sermon on *Free Grace* can be found in Whitefield's *Journals* pp. 569–88. The issue is much more complex than the brief sketch given here. Rack calls it 'a running sore in the bowels of the Revival', *Reasonable Enthusiast*, p. 202.

34. See Eifion Evans, *Daniel Rowland and the Great Evangelical Awakening in Wales* (Edinburgh, The Banner of Truth Trust, 1985) for an account of the life and ministry of Rowland. Griffith Jones had been preaching in the open air since 1714. See Rack, *Reasonable Enthusiast*, p. 224.

35. Evans, *Daniel Rowland*, pp. 52f. Interestingly, like a number of others, Harris's experience was brought to a head in the context of preparing to receive Holy Communion. His incumbent had told him, 'If you are not fit to come to the Lord's Table, you are not fit to live, nor fit to die.' Harris was also influenced by the Moravians, whom he first encountered in London (Evans, p. 136).

36. Evans, *Daniel Rowland*, p. 177.

37. Rack, *Reasonable Enthusiast*, p. 226.

38. For a discussion of that section of the Revival which remained in the Established Church see G. R. Balleine, *A History of the Evangelical Party in the Church of England* (London, Church Book Room Press, 1908 and subsequent editions); and Kenneth Hylson-Smith, *Evangelicals in the Church of England 1734–1984* (Edinburgh, T & T Clark, 1988).

39. Dallimore, *George Whitefield*, vol. 2, p. 153.

40. Evans, *Daniel Rowland*, p. 289.

41. Separation from the Established Church did not begin to become definitive until 1795, and the Church did not ordain its own ministers until as late as 1811. Throughout the nineteenth century the Calvinistic Methodists continued to have links with the Countess of Huntingdon's Connexion which, by 1851, they outnumbered by approximately 5:1. See Chapter 3 and Fenwick, *Thesis*, pp. 67f. Today (2002) it has 43,000 members served by 99 ministers and takes 'an active part in ecumenical activities' (statistics from official website: *www.ebcpcw.org.uk*). It is the Church in which the present Archbishop of Canterbury was baptized.

42. Cook, *Selina*, pp. 403f. For those familiar with the traditional story of the founding of the British and Foreign Bible Society, it was to Thomas Charles's house in Bala that Mary Jones walked from Llanfihangel-y-pennant, having over several years saved up enough money to purchase a Bible in Welsh.

43. Podmore, *Moravian Church*, p. 196. In 1751 Ingham left the Moravians and went on to build up a Connexion of his own, of which he became 'General Overseer', ordaining ministers himself from 1755. See H. M. Pickles, *Benjamin Ingham: Preacher amongst the Dales of Yorkshire, the Forests of Lancashire, and the Fells of Cumbria* (Coventry, published by author, 1995) for a recent account of Ingham and his legacy.

44. Podmore, *Moravian Church*, p. 82.

45. Ibid., p. 88.

46. Whitefield had two 'Tabernacles' in London. The first was intended as a temporary structure erected in 1741 at Moorfields (not far from John Wesley's

Foundery); the second was built on Tottenham Court Road in 1756 and registered as a Dissenting Meeting House. It is not always clear which is being referred to in post-1756 references.

47. Dallimore, *George Whitefield*, vol. 2, p. 256.
48. Quoted in ibid., vol. 2, p. 258.
49. Mark A. Noll, *A History of Christianity in the United States and Canada* (London, SPCK, 1992), p. 91.
50. Dallimore, *George Whitefield*, vol. 2, p. 302.
51. Ibid., vol. 2, p. 546.
52. Rack, *Reasonable Enthusiast*, p. 191.
53. Ibid., p. 284.
54. 'For my own part, I can see no reason for my leaving the Church, however I am treated by the corrupt members and ministers of it. I judge the state of a Church, not from the practice of its members, but its primitive and public constitutions. . . . I wish the Church of England was the joy of the whole earth . . .' Whitefield, *Journals*, pp. 256 (21 April 1739) and 312 (22 July 1739).
55. Rack, *Reasonable Enthusiast*, p. 164. Dallimore specifically states that some of the Whitefieldite societies joined the Countess's Connexion (vol. 2, p. 546). This continuity establishes the Free Church of England's continuity with the earliest years of the Evangelical Revival.
56. Cook, *Selina*, p. 154.
57. Kirby, *Elect Lady*, p. 30.
58. The arrangement can most easily be seen today in the continuation of chaplains to Her Majesty The Queen, and the collection of chapels among the 'Royal Peculiars'.
59. Pollock, *George Whitefield*, p. 240.
60. There were only about half a dozen such chapels by 1770, but the preaching of the Trevecca students (see below) resulted in there being an estimated 120 by the time of Lady Huntingdon's death. Cook, *Selina*, pp. 338 and 407.
61. Quoted in Cook, *Selina*, p. 135.
62. For his biography, see Skevington Wood, *Thomas Haweis*.
63. In addition to various writings, Haweis became passionately involved in promoting missionary work, especially in the 'South Seas'. He had links with the founders of the Church Missionary Society (CMS) and was highly instrumental in the founding of the London Missionary Society. See A. Skevington Wood for a full account, including Haweis's links with Captain Bligh of *Bounty* fame.
64. Letter of 1774, quoted in Skevington Wood, *Thomas Haweis*, p. 152.
65. Ibid.
66. Kirby, *Elect Lady*, p. 33.
67. The one who remained was Thomas Wills, whom Lady Huntingdon had appointed one of her personal chaplains in 1778. He was married to her niece.

68. See Trevor Park, *St Bees College 1816–1895* (Barrow-in-Furness, St Bega Publications, 1982).

69. Usually known as 'Trevecca'. Talgarth was of course Harris's home to which he had returned in 1752 having broken his health with itinerant preaching. He founded a small religious community there. See Evans, *Daniel Rowland*, pp. 284f. For details of the College's organization see Cook, *Selina*, pp. 233ff.

70. In 1792, the year after the Countess died, the College moved to Cheshunt in Hertfordshire, while in 1905 a further move was made to Cambridge. In 1968 the College linked up with Westminster College, Cambridge, serving the Presbyterian Church of England (now the United Reformed Church). The Cheshunt building was sold in 1967 and the Cheshunt Foundation set up to enable students to pursue theological training.

71. '. . . its students were trained in Church of England principles' (Merry-weather, p. 51).

72. An account of the service can be found in Seymour, *Life and Times*, vol. II, pp. 438–50. John Wesley found himself having to take the same step when he ordained Thomas Coke in 1784 to 'superintend' the work in the newly independent United States of America. From the 1784 Christmas Conference over which Coke presided, grew the Methodist Episcopal Church, one of whose bishops nearly a century later was to play a part in the story of the Free Church of England.

73. There is some evidence that Lady Huntingdon was ambivalent about this departure. She did not attend the 1783 ordinations. Haweis disapproved of them and (in his own words) 'studiously avoided being present on such occasions' (quoted in Skevington Wood, *Thomas Haweis*, p. 169).

74. Cook, *Selina*, p. 379.

75. Skevington Wood, *Thomas Haweis*, p. 169. Hylson-Smith describes Haweis as 'demonstrat[ing] something of the often ambivalent relationship between the Evangelicals [in the Church of England] and the Countess of Huntingdon' (Kenneth Hylson-Smith, *Evangelicals in the Church of England 1734–1984* (Edinburgh, T & T Clark, 1998), p. 49).

76. Skevington Wood, *Thomas Haweis*, p. 173. Whitefield had earlier seen his own Connexion, with its 'exhorters' in the same light.

77. 'Not until 1868 did regular pastorates become the official policy of the Connexion'; Cook, *Selina*, p. 439.

78. The full text is found in Cook, *Selina*, pp. 448–53. Its provisions will be discussed more fully in Chapter 9.

79. Ibid., p. 408.

80. Skevington Wood, *Thomas Haweis*, p. 173.

81. A. H. New, *The Coronet and the Cross* (London, Partridge & Co, 1858), p. 358.

82. John Wesley had died just over three months earlier, on 2 March.

83. Haweis, *Autobiography*, p. 196, quoted in Skevington Wood, *Thomas Haweis*, p. 182.

84. Skevington Wood, *Thomas Haweis*, p. 183.

85. Ibid., p. 158, quoting Haweis, *Autobiography*, p. 130.

86. Ibid., p. 255, quoting Haweis, *Diary*, p. 201.

87. Letter dated 21 December 1795 quoted in Seymour, *Life and Times*, p. 521. Interestingly, Haweis's statement echoes one by Zinzendorf in 1746: 'This is what we want, to be clearly and undoubtedly *acknowledged* as Members of the Established Church' (quoted in Podmore, *Moravian Church*, p. 191). It is not inconceivable that the Zinzendorf's concept of allowing what would now be called 'dual membership' influenced Revival leaders.

88. Letter, as above.

89. *Evangelical Register* (1854), p. 181.

90. See Chapter 9.

91. This anomaly was not removed until 1884. Fenwick, *Thesis*, p. 72.

92. Fenwick, *Thesis*, pp. 60–69, 83–84 describes the long-running disputes.

93. Cook, *Selina*, p. 439.

94. Rack, *Reasonable Enthusiast*, p. 286.

95. The phrases are those of Connexional minister Thomas Thoresby in 1863 (see next chapter). *The Free Church of England Magazine* (hereafter cited as *FCE Magazine*) 1870, p. 162.

96. Ibid.

CHAPTER 2

The Second Strand: Preserving True Anglicanism 1844–1863

Even Merryweather, who was at pains to stress the ancient continuities of the Free Church of England, acknowledged that the events of 1844 were determinative in the process that was to lead directly to the present denomination.[1]

Although not so long ago in historical perspective, 1844 is a year far removed from modern times. Just over two decades previously, on the other side of Europe, the Ottoman Turks had hanged the Patriarch of Constantinople from the gates of the Phanar in retaliation for the outbreak of the Greek War of Independence. France was a Monarchy; Germany still a patchwork of medieval states. In Britain the age was hardly even 'Victorian': the young Queen was still only 25 and it was less than a quarter of a century since King George III had died. The Duke of Wellington, hero of Waterloo a generation before, was still a respected figure in the land, and the Archbishop of Canterbury, the aged William Howley, still wore a clerical wig as his predecessors had done for over a century. The context, then, was almost Hanoverian – but only just. The world in which the Countess's Connexion had come into existence was about to vanish forever. Immense changes were taking place. Industrialization was accelerating at an immense rate, along with a transformation of the social and political life of the nation. There were contradictions in this time of ferment: great self-confidence and looking to the future co-existed with a sense of instability and a hankering after the past (exemplified by the Romantic Movement and Gothic Revival).[2] The changes in thinking which had contributed to and been strengthened by the American War of Independence of 1776 and the French Revolution of 1789 continued to work their way through society. Concepts such as human rights and representative government were winning acceptance and requiring political and social action.

The eighteenth-century Evangelical Revival had caused turmoil in the life of the Church of England, bringing new life in many places, and resulting, as seen in the previous chapter, in the loss of many parishioners to various 'societies' and 'connexions'. It had, however, left the constitutional position and structures of the Church of England relatively intact. Nor had there been a great deal of change in the style of worship encountered by people in their parish churches each Sunday. By contrast, it was precisely these things that the upheavals of the nineteenth century were to affect, which helps to explain the intense feelings they generated.

There is no space here to explore the immensely complex changes taking place in the first half of the nineteenth century. It is important, however, to understand the degree to which, at that time, political and religious issues were inextricably linked. The 'privatization of religion' with which we are now familiar simply did not exist. A person's religious affiliation determined how he or she stood before the law. Furthermore, for England, Wales and Ireland the government of the Church was carried out basically by Parliament, rather than by the independent or semi-independent synods that we are accustomed to today.[3] Consequently, Parliamentary legislation often directly affected a person's religious life. One of the results was that 'the great question of constitution in church and state affected every town and village in the country, embittered relations, bred enmity between church and chapel, governed the utterance and programme of political candidates, entered classroom and guildhall'.[4]

Out of a whole range of interrelated issues, it is necessary to isolate a few of particular relevance to the second phase of development of the Free Church of England.

The Roman Catholic Relief Act 1829

Since the late seventeenth century Roman Catholics in Great Britain and Ireland had not enjoyed what today would be called 'equal civil rights' with members of the Established Churches of England, Ireland and

Scotland or even with Protestant Dissenters. Slowly, however, this situation was changing. By the Papists Act of 1778 Roman Catholics were allowed to own landed property on taking an oath not involving denial of their religion. Life-long imprisonment for keeping a Roman Catholic school was abolished and legal protection extended to priests. Three years later the Roman Catholic Relief Act permitted Roman Catholic worship and schools and opened certain posts in the military and legal professions to Roman Catholics.

In 1800 Ireland was politically united to Great Britain, and the Irish Parliament (like the Scottish one in 1707) suppressed. From henceforth Irish MPs would have to be elected to Westminster. This meant that issues affecting the seven-eighths of the Irish population who were not Protestant and did not belong to the Established Church of Ireland now had to be addressed directly by Parliament in London. This hastened the emancipation process and resulted in the Relief Act of 1829 which removed most legal disabilities from Roman Catholics.

In today's climate of relative indifference to religious matters among the public at large, it is difficult to understand the fear and hatred felt towards the Roman Catholic Church by the majority of the English populace in the early nineteenth century. Views that would now be seen as extreme bigotry were widely held at all levels of society. From a post-Vatican II perspective it is important to realize that many non-Catholics would have found it hard to recognize Roman Catholicism as the same *religion* as their own, so alien did the dynamics, language (Latin) and ethos of its worship seem. As Bishop Colin Buchanan points out, as recently as the 1960s 'evangelicals looked with such horror on the Roman mass as hardly to view it as the Lord's Supper at all'.[5]

Important though it is to appreciate this assessment of Roman Catholic teaching and worship, it is necessary to understand that in the 1840s this was not the whole picture, nor even necessarily the most important issue. Benjamin Price, the first Bishop Primus of the Free Church of England, is surprisingly unworried about Roman Catholic theology: 'Romanism as a *religion*, I have nothing to say against, except to condemn its doctrines as unscriptural.'[6] What worried Price was what he believed to be something much larger and more sinister:

> as a system, I regard it as a monstrous conspiracy against truth and righteousness, a mystery of iniquity, a masterpiece of Satan, an enemy of God

and man, and therefore dangerous to the interests of the State, and subversive of the rights of men and the liberties of the world . . . it will never rest with equality; it must be supreme or nothing.[7]

Embarrassing though they may be to many ecumenically sensitive Christians today, Price's views were not for their time exceptional or extreme.[8] The service giving thanks for 'the happy Deliverance of King James I . . . from the most traitorous and bloody intended massacre by Gupowder' still appeared in the Book of Common Prayer.[9] Effigies of the Pope were burned every year on 5 November. Memories of the Spanish Armada and the Glorious Revolution of 1688 still informed people's minds. Historically, Roman Catholicism had been a threat to national self-determination and liberty. John Foxe's *Acts and Monuments of Matters happening in the Church*[10] had for over two centuries been one of the most widely read books in England. Generations had read in it the accounts of the terrible sufferings of the Protestant martyrs during the reign of Mary Tudor and gazed in fascinated horror at the woodcuts depicting the burnings. To many people Roman Catholicism was the religion that had done *this* to godly old men and was now seeking to reassert itself again.

The Suppression of the Irish Bishoprics 1833

At the accession of Queen Elizabeth I the vast majority of bishops in Ireland had (unlike their English counterparts) acquiesced in the Reformation Settlement and remained in their sees. They and their successors constituted the hierarchy of the Church of Ireland as established by law, eventually using a Prayer Book identical with that of England and sharing the same doctrinal basis. The Church of Ireland and the Church of England were united 'into one Protestant Episcopal Church'[11] in 1800. Irish Church matters thus became the responsibility of the Westminster Parliament. However, unlike England, where the majority of the population adhered to the Established Church, as already noted, the vast majority of the Irish remained Roman Catholic in allegiance. The historic church buildings remained in the possession of the Church of Ireland while the Roman Catholic population (much of which was desperately poor) worshipped in thatched barns, and (in addition to paying rent to

Protestant landlords) was required by law to pay tithes for the upkeep of the buildings and clergy of the minority Established Church. The situation was a great source of social and religious resentment and unrest, requiring the permanent presence of the British Army to keep the peace. Furthermore, as a legacy of its far-off Celtic past, the Church of Ireland was divided into 32 dioceses, with 4 archbishops and 18 bishops. Some of the dioceses contained as few as 20 parishes. Quite apart from the particularly Irish dimension, for a Parliament that had passed the Great Reform Act of 1832, tidying up the Church's 'rotten boroughs' seemed a logical next step.

Consequently in 1833 Parliament passed the Church Temporalities (Ireland) Bill, abolishing two of the four archbishoprics (Cashel and Tuam) and eight bishoprics by amalgamating them with neighbouring dioceses. While most people might, on calm reflection, agree that the Church of Ireland needed a degree of reform, what caused such a fierce reaction was that the reform had been undertaken, not by the Church, but by Parliament. The issue was thus one of authority. The King's brother (the Duke of Cumberland) and others insisted that the State had no right to abolish a single bishopric in Ireland without the consent of the Church.[12] Parliament had acted as though the Church of Ireland was simply a government department. What is more, the government's action had been to the disadvantage of Protestants and to the advantage of Roman Catholics. The perception was that, as Owen Chadwick put it: 'Without consulting church authorities a government which leaned on Catholic and dissenting votes abolished bishoprics and arranged endowments. What might such a government do to the Church of England?'[13]

For many members of the Church of England the actions of the government forced them to ask hard questions about the place of the Church in society and its relation to the State. 'From the tortures of imagination rose misty spectres, half-atheist ministers nominating heretical bishops, destroying as useless the beauty and grandeur of English cathedrals, cutting doctrines from the prayer book to make it more palatable.'[14] Alternatives began to be considered, including the model of Scotland and the United States where Protestant episcopal Churches lived without State control. And, significantly for the present story, 'clergymen debated the prospect of going out to a free Church of England, like the non-jurors after the revolution of 1688'.[15]

The Tractarian Movement

Among the plethora of pamphlets, speeches, sermons and petitions that sought to address the challenges and uncertainty in Church and State, one series was to be uniquely influential. This was a series of small publications – entitled *Tracts for the Times* – written in the main by a circle of Oxford-based clergy and their associates: John Henry Newman, John Keble, Edward Pusey, Hurrell Froude and William Palmer. In its earliest days the group presented some parallels with the Holy Club of almost exactly a century earlier. For both, a strict adherence to the rubrics and practices enjoined by the Book of Common Prayer provided an important starting point.[16] Keble had already made a public stand against State interference in the life of the Church in his sermon entitled 'National Apostasy' delivered before the Oxford Assize Judges on 14 July 1833, in which he condemned the manner in which the Irish bishoprics had been suppressed. All were agreed on the nature of the Church as a Divine society, not dependent on the State for its authority. In particular, the early Tracts emphasized the superior position of the Church of England 'against Popery and Dissent'. The first Tract was published in September 1833 and was by Newman. It was entitled 'Thoughts on the Ministerial Commission respectfully addressed to the Clergy'. In it Newman sought to locate the Church's independent authority in what he termed 'our Apostolical Descent' and 'the Apostolic Succession', which was to become a major theme in the Oxford Movement which grew out of the Tracts. Put briefly, the concept as expounded by the Tractarians was that bishops are 'the successors of the Apostles', deriving their orders and apostolic ministry from them via an uninterrupted sequence of laying on of hands, by which the gift of the Holy Spirit is given in a unique way to each candidate: 'The Lord JESUS CHRIST gave His Spirit to His Apostles; they in turn laid their hands on those who should succeed them; and these again on others; and so the sacred gift has been handed down to our present Bishops, who have appointed us as their assistants, and in some sense representatives.'[17] In its more developed form, the theory stated that the Church could only exist where there were bishops: 'we must necessarily consider none to be *really* ordained who have not been *thus* ordained'.[18] Non-episcopal bodies were therefore not the Church and could only be entrusted to the 'uncovenanted mercies of God'. Such a concept was, in its absolute form, new to the Church of England and deeply offensive to many, especially Evangelicals, who enjoyed fellowship and co-operation with Protestant Christians outside the fold of the Church of England.

As the series of Tracts progressed, they tended to become more extreme, until they culminated with Newman's famous Tract 90 in January 1841, which was understood to be arguing that the Thirty-Nine Articles were capable of a Roman Catholic interpretation.[19] Shortly after this Newman left the Church of England and was received into the Roman Catholic Church. Over the years he was followed by a number of those who had been prominent in the Tractarian Movement. The Movement itself, however, continued to grow in the Church of England. From the 1840s much of its energy was devoted to restoring to the Established Church the ornamentation and practices (particularly in relation to the Eucharist) that had been shorn away in the sixteenth and seventeenth centuries. There were different approaches to this – should the model be pre-Reformation English practice or that of contemporary Rome? – but the practical effect was that the ordinary parishioner found his parish church being transformed by a tide of ritual, ceremonial and architecture. Thus the *external* threat from an increasingly aggressive Roman Catholic Church was seen as being aided and abetted *within* the Church of England itself, by clergy who were seeking to undermine the very principles on which it had been reconstituted at the Reformation.

There is no space here to recount something of the associations, appeals, campaigns and court cases by which Churchmen sought to stem the Tractarian or 'Ritualist' tide. In the main, though, the impression was created that the authorities, and in particular the bishops, were either ineffectual or were secretly supportive of this movement that was seeking to change the character of the National Church. People began to despair of ever restoring the purity of the Church of England and to wonder whether they might not be better seeking a solution outside its fold.

The Free Church of Scotland, 1843

Like England, Wales and Ireland, Scotland was also to undergo great ecclesiastical change at this time.[20] The underlying issue was also that of the relative powers of Church and State, though in Scotland it focused on the rights of patrons to appoint ministers to parishes. As Chadwick points out, 'In both the established churches [i.e. of Scotland and England] a party stood decisively for the independent life of the church apart from the state. In England the party was Tractarian. In Scotland it was evangelical.'[21] Ecclesiastical patronage had been abolished in the 1707 Articles of Union, but was soon reinstated, depriving the local congregation of any significant say in the appointment of their minister. The details of the issue are not relevant here, but they culminated in a deep split within the Church of Scotland – the Great Disruption – precipitated at the General Assembly of 18 May 1843 when the Moderator of the preceding General Assembly, Dr David Welsh, instead of inaugurating the new Assembly, read a Protest, then led several hundred representatives out of the building to the cheers of the crowd. In the nearby Tanfield Hall Welsh inaugurated what he and those with him believed to be the true 'Church of Scotland – Free'. The first Moderator was Dr Thomas Chalmers, who, in 1838, had visited London to lecture on the principle of Established Churches. Some 454 out of 1,195 ministers left the Kirk, joined by between a third and a half of the lay membership.[22] The impetus was maintained and 'by 1851 the established Church represented less than a half of Scotland's Churchgoing population'.[23] Moreover, 'the Free Church of Scotland' attracted to itself many of the most energetic and committed ministers. Despite some persecution of Free Church tenants by largely Episcopalian landlords, 'the Free Church emerged as arguably the most dynamic denomination in Scotland, a great popular Church'.[24] Undoubtedly this was a great encouragement to the Evangelical dissentients from the Established Church in England. 'The success of this Church was marvellous,' wrote Merryweather.[25] If a 'free' form of one of the national Churches in the British Isles could eclipse its established counterpart in less than a decade, why should the same not occur in another part of the United Kingdom?

Continuing Disquiet

It has only been possible to take the briefest glimpse at the confused, complex and deeply unsettling social and religious context which formed the background to what was to be a highly formative phase of the Free Church of England's evolution. It was precisely these events that were to give the Christian community nurtured by Thomas Haweis and his successors the occasion for its 'relaunch'. Many of the developments touched on in this chapter were in their early stages by 1844 and were to continue throughout the century, reinforced by a succession of further issues and crises.[26] This sense that the Established Church was being irrevocably corrupted prompted a succession of individuals, clergy and lay, and congregations to look for an Anglican home outside the Church of England, and hence to join the Free Church of England movement. Given the climate of the times the secessions could have started in any number of places. In fact, what actually caused Free Church of England congregations to, as it were, begin to 'precipitate out' of the Church of England like crystals out of a saturated solution, was a complex sequence of events focusing on Bridgetown Chapel in the Diocese of Exeter and County of Devon.

The Events leading up to the 'first Free Church of England' Congregation, 1844

Bridgetown was a hamlet in the parish of Berry Pomeroy of which the patron with the right to appoint the incumbent was the Duke of Somerset. Around the year 1832 Edward Adolphus, the eleventh Duke, built a number of houses for some of his tenants and labourers on his estates.[27] At the same time he built a chapel, at the cost of £7,000, to provide them with a place of worship. The chapel was temporarily licensed for worship by the Bishop of Exeter, in order to see how viable a proposition it was going to be. On the Duke's nomination the Vicar of the parish, Mr Edwards, appointed the Revd James Shore as Curate in Charge. This innocuous arrangement was to be transformed by the clash between the Bishop and the Curate.

The Bishop of Exeter was Henry Phillpotts, who had been consecrated to that see in 1830 and continued as Bishop there until 1869. Phillpotts is one of the most extraordinary bishops of the nineteenth century. He has been described as 'an iron hand undisguised by any sort of glove'.[28] Chadwick describes him as 'a genuinely religious man with his religion concealed behind porcupine quills', one for whom 'aggression is the best defence'.[29] 'It was', says Chadwick, 'a weakness that he relished fighting, and lacked human sympathy for that majority of the human race with which he disagreed.'[30] Much of Phillpotts's belligerence took the form of legal action. At any one time he was involved in a number of lawsuits, not just involving clergy, but ranging from newspaper editors to a mine owner whose mine had flooded part of a neighbouring pit in which Phillpotts had a financial interest. Phillpotts believed passionately in the rights and privileges of the Church of England and was prepared to defend them against Rome and Dissent alike. His 'high' view of the Church meant, however, that he had some sympathy with the Tractarians and he seems to have done nothing to prevent their influence in his diocese. In 1844 and 1845 he provoked the so-called Surplice Riots, initially by insisting that the surplice should be worn in the pulpit by the minister preaching the sermon. The older practice had been for the surplice to be exchanged for an academic gown, at least at Morning and Evening Prayer, where the sermon did not strictly form part of the prescribed service.[31] Phillpotts' move was seen as an attack on the Protestant nature of the Church, and clergy who tried to obey their bishop found themselves mobbed by crowds of several hundred protesters. It all contributed to a raising of the ecclesiastical temperature in the Diocese of Exeter.[32]

Shore's ministry at Bridgetown seems to have gone peacefully until 1840, when he became involved in the appointment of a presbyter to the living of Chudleigh. Unusually for the Church of England, the candidates were, under the terms of a seventeenth-century trust deed, presented to the parishioners for election. Shore himself was a candidate at one stage but withdrew and circulated a handbill advising people to vote for one of the remaining candidates who happened *not* to be Bishop Phillpott's preference. The Bishop's candidate lost and Phillpotts was furious with Shore, who from then on was a marked man. The Bishop's opportunity for action came when a new incumbent, W. B. Cousens, 'a creature of the bishop'[33] was appointed to Berry Pomeroy in 1841.

Phillpotts informed Shore that he would need to be renominated for his post at Bridgetown Chapel, and at the same time the Bishop left Cousens in no doubt that he did not expect him to nominate James Shore. The affair soon degenerated into an acrimonious exchange of correspondence. The Duke of Somerset (who in the Table of Precedence far outranked a mere Diocesan Bishop[34]) backed Shore and refused to find an alternative minister for the chapel that he had built and which was still unconsecrated.

The impasse was broken by both the chapel and Shore leaving the Church of England and hence Bishop Phillpotts's jurisdiction. On 16 February 1844 the Duke's agent, Mr T. Michelmore, certified the building under the provisions of 52 Geo.III, c.155 as 'a place . . . for the religious worship of Protestants', in other words, as a Dissenting chapel. This the Duke was entitled to do as the chapel was still his property and had never been consecrated. On 11 November 1843 Shore had written to the Bishop stating that, 'I have no other alternative but the painful one of freeing myself . . . from the obligation of . . . legal jurisdiction'[35] and on 16 March 1844 he took the oaths as a Nonconformist minister.[36] The situation was almost exactly the same as that in which the Countess of Huntingdon had found herself back in 1782. A peer of the realm had created a chapel for Church of England worship, but outside the control of the Established Church.

James Shore continued to minister in the chapel, now with a different legal status and so, according to the accepted history of the denomination, 'This was the FIRST Free Church of England.'[37] This was not in fact true. As shown in the previous chapter, 'Free' Church-of-England-style congregations had been in existence for over half a century in the Countess's Connexion. It is also significant that the Bridgetown secession was not in itself a result of anti-Tractarianism; Phillpotts's antagonism towards Shore was motivated primarily by the latter's opposition to him concerning the election at Chudleigh. The belief (held by those within and without the denomination) that the Free Church of England 'began' in 1844 as an anti-Tractarian protest is an oversimplification. After exhaustive analysis Fenwick judges that the Shore case 'was actually less significant than the mythology in the denomination would make it'.[38] What significance it does have lies in the publicity it engendered. For this, Bishop Phillpotts was largely responsible.

Phillpotts did not of course accept the situation. He claimed that it was not possible for Shore simply to divest himself of his Orders as a priest and so he remained liable to the discipline of the Church of England. A series of legal actions resulted. The widespread publicity and the strong feeling then raging as a result of the Surplice Riots prompted other congregations to take action. At the end of September 1844 the Commercial Hall in Fore Street, Exeter, opened as a 'Free Church', with Shore as the preacher. The services used were 'those of the Book of Common Prayer, with some slight alterations . . .'.[39] A preaching visit to Ilfracombe by Pusey precipitated events there. The remarks of a writer to *The North Devon Journal*, printed in its 29 August 1844 edition show the reaction and where remedy was thought to lie:

... the doctrines of the reformation are not taught in the Reformed Church [i.e. of England]; and the cry is not for a new place of worship ... but for a man of God ... Were he an evangelical clergyman, or one of the Countess of Huntingdon's Connexion, there can be no doubt of his success. An immediate secession from the Established Church would take place ...

In fact a wealthy local gentleman did respond by building a chapel, which was officially opened on Sunday 1 September 1844 by Benjamin Woodyard, a minister of the Countess of Huntingdon's Connexion, 'who preached in both morning and evening to overflowing congregations'.[40]

The pattern was thus set. Local groups of Christians, unhappy with what was happening in their parish church (whether as a result of Tractarianism or of local circumstances) and not hopeful of any redress from their bishop, took matters into their own hands and organized themselves into 'free' congregations. Often a local person of means would provide a place for worship. If a sympathetic Church of England presbyter could not be found to minister, then the Countess of Huntingdon's Connexion was the natural place to turn to provide a clergyman. The idea was spreading rapidly. In its 20 March 1845 edition the *Exeter Flying Post* spoke of 'the necessity for a Free Episcopal Church ... to provide for those who have been driven from their parochial edifices by the semi-popish teaching of the clergy ...'.

Nationwide publicity was provided by the events of 1849. James Shore preached on 9 March of that year at the Countess's Spa Fields Chapel at the invitation of the Connexional minister there, Thomas Elisha Thoresby.[41] At the end of the sermon, as Shore came down from the pulpit, he was arrested by officers of the Ecclesiastical Court, almost certainly at the instigation of Bishop Phillpotts. Shore was taken to Exeter and imprisoned in St Thomas's gaol there. Before leaving for Exeter, Shore had been able to send a quick note to Thoresby (who seems not to have been in the chapel when the arrest took place): 'My Dear Sir, I am just apprehended in your chapel after preaching ... I am at last to be incarcerated for contempt of court – they say for the non payment of the Bishop's costs, but really and virtually for preaching the gospel out of the establishment ...'.[42] Thoresby leapt into action. He composed an appeal which he took to *The Times* at Printing House Square that very evening. It was nearly midnight when he got there and the presses were already rolling. The clerks refused to accept his text, but eventually inserted it as an advertisement, for which Thoresby was charged £8. His appeal 'To the Ministers and Friends of the Gospel in London of all Denominations' appeared the next morning. In it Thoresby recounted the circumstances of Shore's arrest and called for a meeting at Exeter Hall, Strand at 11.00 a.m. on Monday 12 March 1849 'to confer as to the best means of altering the law . . .'.[43] In the event about 5,000 people packed the hall. The Bishop's actions were denounced, sympathy was expressed with Shore, and pledges made to seek to alter the law in relation to ecclesiastical matters. Contributions were also made to a fund to fight Shore's case. The meeting was sympathetically reported in *The Times* and so brought the whole issue to the awareness of the nation. Despite offers to pay his costs for him, Shore chose to remain in prison on principle. He served three months in all and 'at no time during most of the three months was he away from the public eye'.[44] The attendant publicity left two impressions in people's minds: firstly, that those who made a stand for the gospel in the face of advancing Tractarianism were likely to be persecuted by the Establishment; and secondly, that a *free* liturgical church might be a realistic alternative (and, indeed, already existed in a number of places by the time of Shore's arrest). If such churches could be formed in Devon, why not in other parts of the country? North of the border the Free Church of Scotland was well on the way to eclipsing the Established Church. Surely the time was right for England to follow suit?

Careful thought was given to the name of the movement. Many years later, in 1871, Connexional minister Joseph Figgis recalled 'meeting in a drawing room to confer with two or three gentlemen respecting the name by which it should be called, when it was suggested that the most fitting name – most expressive of its peculiar character – was "The Free Church of England".'[45] Almost certainly a major deciding factor was the precedent set by the Free Church of Scotland, which, as Merryweather observed 'became, undeniably, the Church of the Scottish people' within a very short time.[46] 'This important event . . . helped, perhaps, to suggest a name for an idea that had for some years been working in the minds of a few earnest and devoted men.'[47] The first official use of the name seems to have been in 1846, when the church at Ilfracombe mentioned above was registered for the solemnization of marriages, the certificate bore the name 'Free Church of England'.[48]

The response of the Countess of Huntingdon's Connexion

The Connexion – itself a pre-existing network of 'free' Churches of Anglican heritage – naturally looked on this second wave of seceding congregations with great interest. Although Shore himself initially seems not to have been involved with the Connexion, from the very beginning the denomination was being seen as the natural focus for the new congregations, and a source of ministers for them, as the example of Ilfracombe illustrates. Merryweather states that the initiative was taken by 'several prominent ministers' of the Connexion.[49] Quite how this came about is not clear from the surviving sources, but it is likely that, for an older generation of Connexion members at least, Haweis's legacy of an abiding sense of Anglican identity noted at the end of the previous chapter made the link a natural one. This natural affinity was taken to a new level by Shore's arrest in 1849. This, after all, took place in what was the Connexion's principal chapel – Spa Fields – purchased by the Countess herself. The new cause thus instantly 'became, in a way, a *Connexional* cause . . . .'.[50]

As far back as October 1844 the editor of *The Circular for the Countess of Huntingdon's Connexion* had seen the challenge. He saw the provision of a Connexional minister for Ilfracombe 'as a probable indication of the line of usefulness open to the Connexion in these stirring times. Puseyism will draw many friends of the church to seek the truth out of its pale. We ought to be ready to assist all who desire our help in such circumstances.'[51] Five years later, looking at the growing number of 'free liturgical churches' coming into being beyond the Diocese of Exeter, the Revd Thomas Dodd, Connexional minister at Worcester, writing to the *Circular* commented on the similarity of their doctrine and government with those of the Connexion, and asked, 'Should we not as a body take the initiative in this matter . . . inviting them to unite with us, and thus extend our border . . . by the amalgamation of the . . . Connexion and the Free Church of England?'[52] Dodd's letter is significant because it appears to attribute a corporate identity to the scattering of congregations leaving the Established Church, despite the fact that no organizational bonds seem to have existed between them. Should the newly free congregations be left to develop their own structures, or should the Connexion take responsibility for them?

This ambivalence within the Connexion was to be a continuing theme for the next half-century. It is therefore helpful to explore it a little further. In his analysis, Richard Fenwick suggests two main differences between the Connexion and the new congregations that were becoming associated with it.[53] The first was that the origins and driving forces of the two movements were different. The Connexion came into being as a result of evangelistic attempts to inject life into what was seen as a moribund Church. The new Free Churches were making a stand against a Church of England that was becoming infused with a new life that was taking it in a doctrinal direction away from its foundational formularies and unacceptable to many in the country. The second main difference lay in the fact, as noted in the previous chapter, that the Connexion was losing its Anglican identity. In the words of Merryweather, 'It had, from various causes, gravitated down very far towards congregationalism, and lost some of its original characteristics.'[54] The Prayer Book was no longer the sole vehicle for worship, the surplice was less and less worn, and the general style, both of worship and of the denomination as a whole, made it in some respects unfamiliar to those accustomed to 'the ancient laws and customs of the Church of England'.[55] The desire of the growing number of 'Free Churches' was to continue as disciplined, liturgical, ecclesiastical communities very like the Established Church as it was before the incursions of the 'Puseyites'. This was no longer the nature of the Countess of Huntingdon's Connexion.

A third reason for the ambivalence lies in the complex structuring of the Connexion itself, already alluded to in the previous chapter. Complex debates, and conflicts surrounding these, dominated much of Connexional life in the 1850s. It seems very likely that many Connexional members who were supportive of the 'Free Church of England' concept, did not want it to be burdened by the unsatisfactory arrangements that fettered the older congregations affiliated to the Connexion. Certainly, the new congregations were *not* legally registered as part of the Connexion, even though the Connexion often supplied the minister.

Nevertheless, for the time being the natural focus for the new congregations was the Connexion and the 'Free Churches' appear in the minutes of its annual Conference. It is clear, however, that there were differences of opinion on how things should develop. For some it seemed obvious that the new congregations should simply become part of the Connexion; for others (including some influential Connexional leaders such as Thoresby and Dodd) the hope was that the 'Free Churches' would be, as it were, the flowering of the Connexion's bud. Yet others remained unsure whether any long-term partnership was in fact possible. Con-ference Minutes reflect the vexed question of identity; those of 1860 include the sentence: 'The position in which the several Free Churches stood in relation to the Connexion, formed a subject of considerable discussion.'[56]

While the debates continued throughout the 1850s, Thomas Thoresby worked on a solution, which was to make him a pivotal figure in the history of the movement. Born in Devonport in about 1818, Thoresby was the son of a Congregationalist minister. He entered the ministry himself and after eight years' pastorate in Bristol he came to Spa Fields in 1846 and remained there till his death in 1883. He is described in his obituary as 'a man of massive build physically and of strong mental calibre'.[57] Shore's arrest in his Spa Fields Chapel back in 1849 had won Thoresby over to the 'Free Church' cause and for 14 years he laboured at drawing up a constitution for 'The Free Church of England'.[58] In doing so, Thoresby believed himself to be following the vision of the Countess herself and to be following 'a draft plan, which she did not live to execute'.[59] This was clearly the 1790 Plan referred to in the previous chapter, the implementation of which had been prevented by Thomas Haweis. Very little primary documentation concerning Thoresby's years of work survives, and it is therefore unclear to what extent he was working alone. There is some evidence that several of the 'districts or dioceses' created by the Connexional Conference in 1862 considered some of the proposals.[60] Merryweather states that Thoresby submitted his draft to 'some evangelical churchmen' (i.e. members of the Church of England) and to 'the principal ministers in the Connexion' in order to achieve a constitution that was 'representative of the views entertained by the advanced evangelical party in the Church of England; was free and com-prehensive, truly catholic in spirit, and on points of ecclesiastical polity was evidently moulded closely upon New Testament authority'.[61] In addi-tion Thoresby consulted the Connexion's solicitor, Mr Lewis, on the pos-sibility of using the proposed Free Church of England scheme as a basis for the government of the Connexion itself. Lewis's advice was that it was not possible, though at a later date the Charity Commissioners might vest 'the old Trusts upon the new foundation, with the consent of the present Trustees of each particular chapel'.[62]

The fruits of Thoresby's consultation and labours were brought to the Connexional Conference in June 1863, held, appropriately enough, at Thoresby's Spa Fields Chapel. At the opening session he read a paper on

'The Connexion in Relation to the Free Church of England'. It is foundational in setting out the vision on the basis of which the legal inauguration of the Free Church took place. Thoresby began by asserting that the concept of a *free* Church of England already existed in the public mind; what was needed now was action to make the idea 'not only a fact, but a great one'.[63] He then went on to stress the continuity: 'That *the Connexion is already the Free Church of England*, virtually and substantially, both in principle and form, it is thought easy to prove.'[64] Thoresby's proofs included the intention and declaration of Lady Huntingdon and her associates, the doctrinal and liturgical continuity and the enshrining of those principles in the Constitution that he was now proposing for adoption. Only legal difficulties, Thoresby continued, preventing 'at once call[ing] the Connexion the Free Church of England'; indeed, the very name 'Free Church of England' 'would have been from the first [the] most appropriate appellation' for the Connexion.[65] The existing Connexion was to be absorbed – the intention was

> at the proper time by a vesting order of the Charity Commissioners, to get the chapels now included in the Trust under Lady Huntingdon's will, and the other Connexional chapels under local trusts, under the scheme and by the name of the Free Church of England. To do this is the best way of carrying into full effect the intention of the Countess of Huntingdon and her associates, as expressed in the plan sent out by her Ladyship just before her death, and in her will, in which she left her chapels for that purpose.[66]

To the question why should the Free Church of England succeed while the Connexion 'is now more feeble than ever'? Thoresby listed what he saw as the weaknesses of the Constitution: 'The name, The fact of its being a mere Connexion, The lamentable division between the trustees and its ministers, The want of government; and consequent want of enterprise.'[67] All of these the proposed Constitution would overcome. The proposed name 'has the great merit of a title of being not only accurate in itself, but clearly understood. Everyone knows what you mean by it, so far as the general idea is concerned; and it is distinctive; it would never be confounded with the Church itself, nor with any of the Dissenting bodies.'[68]

Thoresby's arguments clearly carried the day, for after debate the Conference on St John the Baptist's Day (24 June) formally inaugurated the Free Church of England by passing the following resolution. In view of its importance, it is quoted in full:

Whereas in the good providence of God, and by His Grace, there was a remarkable revival of Religion in the British Empire in the last century, wherein many persons were converted, and then, by the means and under the care of Selina, Countess Dowager of Huntingdon, her chaplains and their associates, were formed into Christian Societies, which societies, with their ministers, were known as the 'Countess of Huntingdon's Connexion':-

And whereas by a solemn statement made by one of the Countess's devisees,[69] the Connexion was declared to be essentially in the main, as to its doctrines and liturgy, one with the Church of England; and as to its government, whilst allowing the distinctness and separate government of the several Congregations, was held to be Presbyterian and Episcopal:-

And whereas the Congregations in the Connexion have, for the most part, borne a distinctive character, inasmuch as they have used with slight modifications the Liturgy of the Church of England, and in their general action have been subject to a general Conference of Presbyters, under the guidance of a President Bishop:-

And whereas in the present state of the public mind of Great Britain, there is a demand for the sound doctrine expressed in the general sense of the Thirty-nine Articles of the Church of England, to be held in Connexion with a revised Liturgy of the Book of Common Prayer – 'Not' (to quote the words of Archbishop Whately) 'by any departure from the principles of our Reformers, but by following more closely the track they marked out for us':-

And whereas the Connexion cannot change either its form or name; and the trusts contained in the several deeds upon which the existing Chapels are settled cannot be altered without a vesting order from the Court of Chancery or the Charity Commissioners, which would require the consent of the Trustees of the Chapels under Lady Huntingdon's Will, and also the consent of the Trustees of all the other Chapels in the Connexion:-

It is therefore Resolved by the Conference, for the perpetuation and development of the principles on which the Connexion is founded, that it is highly expedient from this time that any new Churches, and Congregations gathered in them, shall be known as 'The Free Church of England', holding the Doctrines, and governed by the Laws, Regulations and Declarations set forth in the printed scheme now submitted to this conference, and that the whole subject be referred to the special committee . . . with full power to carry the whole into legal and practical effect.[70]

The motion was carried. Having been duly authorized by Conference, the committee acted as required, and on 31 August 1863,

> the Laws, Regulations and Declaration forming the Free Church of England, were finally embodied in a Poll Deed, which was duly registered in Her Majesty's High Court of Chancery . . . giving to the body a legal basis, a legal status, and a legal security to all its vested properties and trusts, securing a recognised standard around which its scattered forces might be gathered.[71]

Interestingly, the Deed Poll[72] enrolled in Chancery contains a rather different interpretation of events to that contained in the preamble to the Resolution. Its own preamble refers to the 1790 Plan drawn up by the Countess which 'was not carried out and since her death has only been partially acted upon' with the result that the 'several persons whose names and seals are hereunto subscribed and affixed and other persons members of Congregations in the said Connexion, believe that the said Connexion is not governed in accordance with the original design of the said Countess and with sufficient regard to the plan proposed by her for the Propagation of the Gospel'.[73] The constituting of the Free Church of England is thus presented in the Deed as not simply a means of getting around legal complications involved in Connexional Trusts, but as a return to first principles – the formation of a self-sufficient and self-perpetuating 'Religious Community or Connexion' from which the gospel may be proclaimed.

The Free Church of England was now in legal existence. Was it a new body? With the passage of time, and the eventual failure of the existing elements of the Connexion to transfer (see below) the Free Church of England lost sight of its Connexional origins; so much so that in 1994 the denomination celebrated 150 years since its 'founding', categorically stated by Bishop Primus Milner to have taken place on '14th April 1844'.[74] The men who passed the Conference resolution in 1863 clearly did not see it like that. For them the Free Church of England was simply the next stage in the development of the Connexion, signalled by the adoption of a name that 'would have been approved by the Countess . . . in preference to the use of her own name at the head of a religious society'.[75] The intention was clearly to return to the 'Church principles' explicit in the early days of the Connexion, to create an *Anglican* body, rather than a *Dissenting* one: 'The body which we wish to see gathered and grow is the Church of England – that is to say, we will hold her doctrines, liturgy, and general outline of government, but all freed from what we consider unscriptural and objectionable.'[76]

This continuity is underlined by the fact that, as will be seen in the following chapters, the leadership of the Free Church of England did not initially come from the new congregations leaving the Established Church, but from those already in positions of leadership and influence in the Connexion. Further constitutional continuity will be demonstrated in Chapter 9. Later Free Church of England descriptions of the Countess's Connexion as 'scaffolding'[77] or 'the nursing mother'[78] are therefore misleading: the relationship is in fact much more intimate. Although something new did happen from the 1840s, its direction and development were determined solely by the Connexion. There is a very real sense in which the Free Church of England is a continuation of the Connexion, and hence a surviving expression of the heritage of Whitefield.[79]

At its legal inauguration the Free Church of England consisted of approximately 21 churches, including one in Canada and two in Australia.[80]

The community called into being by the ministry of Whitefield and his associates had now reorganized itself as an alternative to the Established Church.

Notes

1. Vaughan goes so far as to say, 'It began in Devonshire in 1844 . . .' *History* (1st edn), p. 22. Vaughan's origins, however, were in the Reformed Episcopal Church, which in the early twentieth century was antagonistic to the Countess of Huntingdon's Connexion (see Chapter 7). He acknowledges the role of the Connexion in the early years but chooses not to stress the continuity.

2. An example of this is provided by the decision that plans to be submitted for the new Houses of Parliament following the fire of 1837, must be in either Tudor or Gothic style. 'Both styles increasingly satisfied moves to define and assert a national identity, nurtured above all during the period of the Napoleonic Wars'; Christine and Jacqueline Riding (eds), *The Houses of Parliament: History, Art, Architecture* (London, Merrell, 2000), p. 105.

3. The Church of Scotland was also established and affected by Parliamentary action, but enjoyed a greater degree of autonomy via its General Assembly.

4. Owen Chadwick, *The Victorian Church*, (London, A & C Black, 2nd edn, 1970), p. 3.

5. C. O. Buchanan, *News of Liturgy* 281, May 1998 (Cambridge, Grove Books

Limited), p. 2. Buchanan goes on to say that the post-Vatican II changes 'have made it a hundred times easier for most people this side of Ian Paisley to recognise it as Christian. . . . I would urge now that their rite is simply Christian but with some passing hiccups for visitors', though he acknowledges that 'I would have great problems still in having to preside at such a rite. . . '

6. Quoted in Anne Elizabeth Price, *The Organisation of the Free Church of England, being Extracts from the Autobiography of the late Bishop Price . . .* (Ilfracombe, W. H. Smith & Son, 1908), p. 9.

7. Ibid.

8. There are of course still Christians who would see the Church of Rome in such terms. The writer has come across the view that the European Union and NATO are organs of the papacy. Nor is it only extreme Protestants who think in such terms. They are shared by some Orthodox.

9. The prayers spoke of the intended victims 'by Popish Treachery appointed as sheep to the slaughter' and asked for the deliverance of 'our Nation from Popish Tyranny and Arbitrary Power'.

10. The work was commonly called *The Book of Martyrs*. It was first published in England in 1563 and has been through many editions. It is still in print.

11. The Act of Union, Article V.

12. It was not, it was argued, for the Government to take away 'some of the candlesticks of the Irish Church'. Quoted in N. D. Emerson, 'The Last Phase of the Establishment' in W. A. Phillips (ed.), *History of the Church of Ireland* (London, OUP, 1933), vol. III, p. 302. The allusion is to Revelation 2.5.

13. Chadwick, *Victorian Church*, p. 60. Chadwick is incorrect in stating that there was no consultation. The list of sees to be amalgamated was actually suggested by Archbishop Beresford of Armagh, Primate of All Ireland; see Emerson, 'The Last Phase', p. 303.

14. Chadwick, *Victorian Church*, p. 64.

15. Ibid. Curiously, Chadwick seems unaware that some people *did* 'go out to a free Church of England'.

16. Some liturgical parallels can be found in Trevor Dearing, *Wesleyan and Tractarian Worship* (London, Epworth Press/SPCK, 1966).

17. *Tracts for the Times by Members of the University of Oxford* (London, J. G. & F. Rivington 1834), p. 2 (Tract 1).

18. Ibid., p. 3.

19. See Chadwick, *Victorian Church*, pp. 181–89 for a useful discussion of this. Chadwick's account makes clear that Newman's argument was more subtle than is usually supposed.

20. See Stewart J. Brown, *The National Churches of England, Ireland and Scotland 1801–1846* (Oxford, OUP, 2001) for a useful discussion of the issues.

21. Chadwick, *Victorian Church*, p. 224.

Notes for Chapter 2

22. Brown, *National Churches*, p. 358.
23. Ibid., p. 361.
24. Ibid., p. 360. In some places Free Church of Scotland congregations had to worship on the beach, below the high tide mark – where the jurisdiction of the landlord ended. See John MacLeod, *Highlanders* (London, Hodder & Stoughton/Sceptre, 1996), p. 213. The Free Church of Scotland itself suffered a secession in 1893, losing many Highland members to the Free Presbyterian Church of Scotland. In 1900 the majority of the remaining Free Church of Scotland congregations united with the United Presbyterian Church (heir to several bodies of eighteenth-century origin, usually of anti-patronage stance) to form the United Free Church of Scotland. The great majority of this body itself re-united with the Church of Scotland in 1929. Further divisions have taken place in that part of the Free Church which remained independent, the most recent on 20 January 2000, when the Free Church of Scotland (Continuing) came into existence (see *www.freechurchcontinuing.co.uk/history*). The Free Church of Scotland currently has 63 ministers, two thirds of them in the Highland region (statistics from official website: *www.freechurch.org/robbo.html*).
25. Merryweather, p. 72.
26. In September 1850 Pope Pius IX in the Bull *Ad Perpetuam rei Memoriam* created England an ecclesiastical province of the Roman Catholic Church, complete with Archbishop and Bishops. The advance of 'Romanism' *within* the Established Church seemed relentless: the Bennett Case (1872), the Ridsdale Case (1876), the trial of the Bishop of Lincoln (1890) and others all seemed to give sanction to various Tractarian practices and beliefs. Each 'victory' for the Anglo-Catholic cause tended to result in a modest wave of secessions to the Free Church of England. A further controversy of particular significance was the Gorham case of 1847–50, which will be discussed in Chapter 10.
27. By coincidence (which seems to have gone unnoticed in the Free Church of England) it was the Duke's ancestor, Edward Seymour, the first Duke, who, as Lord Protector during the first part of the reign of Edward VI had encouraged Archbishop Cranmer's production of the first English Prayer Book of 1549. The Duke was executed in January 1552, shortly before the 1552 Prayer Book was published.
28. Fenwick, *Thesis*, p. 8.
29. Chadwick, *Victorian Church*, p. 217.
30. Ibid.
31. The situation seems to be less clear in the case of the Holy Communion service, where the sermon is an integral part of the rite and occurs in the middle of the service. It seems unlikely that clergy removed their surplices,

put on a gown to preach, then resumed their surplices again. Communion was, however, relatively rare at this period and most people's reactions related to Morning and Evening Prayer.

32. Fenwick, *Thesis*, pp. 9–12 gives a detailed account of the Surplice Riots.
33. Ibid., p. 16.
34. See, for example, Charles Mosley (ed.), *Burke's Peerage and Baronetage* (Chicago, Fitzroy Dearborn, 106th edn, 1999), pp. xxxivff. Thirty-one categories of people separate a duke from a bishop.
35. H. Phillpotts, *The Case of the Rev. Mr. Shore A Letter to His Grace the Archbishop of Canterbury* (London, 1849), pp. 20f.
36. Fenwick, *Thesis*, p. 35.
37. Vaughan, *History* (1st edn) p. 23.
38. Fenwick, *Thesis*, p. 604. As Fenwick shows, the process was an extremely complex one. The facts presented here are merely a brief summary.
39. Ibid., p. 20.
40. Quoted in Fenwick, *Thesis*, p. 22.
41. For further details concerning Thoresby, see below.
42. Vaughan, *History* (1st edn) p. 24.
43. *The Times*, Saturday 10 March 1849, p. 6, col. 4.
44. Fenwick, *Thesis*, p. 39.
45. Quoted in *FCE Magazine*, July 1871, p. 178.
46. Merryweather, p. 73.
47. Ibid.
48. *FCE Magazine*, vol. iii, p. 31. According to an article in the magazine for February 1869, the choice was due to the churchwarden who was involved in the transaction with the registrar. It is unlikely, however, that such an important matter was left to the decision of a local individual. As Figgis's testimony shows, the leaders of the movement had given thought to the issue.
49. Merryweather, p. 73.
50. Fenwick, *Thesis*, p. 41.
51. *The Circular for the Countess of Huntingdon's Connexion*, October 1844, p. 24.
52. Ibid., September 1849, p. 237.
53. See Fenwick, *Thesis*, p. 33.
54. Merryweather, p. 66.
55. The phrase is from Article XIII of the present Constitution of the Free Church of England. The denomination is still committed by its Constitution and Canons to maintaining precisely those laws and customs.
56. *Harbinger*, August 1860, p. 193.
57. *FCE Magazine*, April 1883, p. 70. No likeness of Thoresby seems to have survived.
58. Curiously, Shore himself seems to have played no further significant part in

the denomination's development. He retired to Buxton in Derbyshire in 1861 where he lived until his death on 12 August 1874, following a fall from his horse.

59. Vaughan, *History*, (1st edn) p. 25.
60. Fenwick, *Thesis*, pp. 53ff.
61. Merryweather, p. 79. The Constitution will be considered in more detail in Chapter 9.
62. Ibid., p. 71. The hoped-for transfer of the older Connexional chapels to the Free Church of England did not happen.
63. The text of Thoresby's speech can be found in *FCE Magazine*, 1870, pp. 161–64.
64. Ibid., p. 162 (italics not in the original).
65. Ibid.
66. Ibid.
67. Ibid.
68. Ibid., p. 164.
69. This is clearly Haweis.
70. Merryweather, pp. 82–84. *Harbinger*, August 1863, p. 249.
71. Price, *Organisation of the Free Church*, p. 13. The names appended to the deed were those of Thoresby and eight others, including Thomas Dodd, William Woodhouse (President of Conference 1862–3) and George Jones (President of Conference 1863–5).
72. A Deed Indented is one between two or more parties, each of whom received a copy of the text, cut from the original parchment by an indented line (so that they could be matched up to check authenticity). A Deed Poll relates to only one subject or party and was therefore cut – 'polled' – with a straight line; see J. E. Penner, *Law Dictionary* (London, Butterworths, 2001). Members of the Free Church of England, from Price onwards, have tended to reverse the order of the words.
73. *A Deed Poll and Declaration* . . . PRO reference C54/16/16152. The details of the various plans and constitutions are discussed more fully in Chapter 9.
74. *FCE Year Book 1994–1995*, p. 8.
75. Merryweather, pp. 80f.
76. *FCE Magazine*, 1870, p. 164. The words are from Thoresby's 1863 address.
77. Bishop Cyril Milner in *FCE Year Book 1994–1995*, p. 10.
78. Vaughan, *History* (1st edn), p. 23.
79. Fenwick discusses the relationship with the Connexion in great detail, but as the title of his thesis ('The Free Church of England *c*.1845 – *c*.1927') suggests, he is less inclined to stress the continuity.
80. Fenwick, *Thesis*, p. 56 lists them. One, Christ Church Exeter, is still an active member of the Free Church of England. All subsequent numerical data are taken from Fenwick's *Thesis*.

CHAPTER 3

A Developing Identity 1863–1873

By its resolution of 24 June 1863, the Conference of the Countess of Huntingdon's Connexion had brought the Free Church of England into legal existence and provided it with a history.[1] What had hitherto been a scattered group of congregations in varying degrees of relationship with the Connexion was now a distinct denomination, heir to earlier aspirations.

Three challenges immediately faced the newly organized Church. The first was to provide a home for those who felt alienated from their parish church as a result of the 'romanization' of the Church of England. From the perspective of individual souls and the ministry of Word and Sacrament, this is of course, the most important aspect of the Free Church of England's work. It is, unfortunately, an area too great and too diverse to be explored in this present Introduction. Every single congregation had its own story and unique set of circumstances. Some of these have been published, others are now lost.[2] Behind the broad denominational events related here lie numerous stories of difficult decisions, fervent prayer and sacrificial initiatives (as well as, inevitably, a few less worthy motives). To all that was good in these, due honour should be paid.

The second challenge to the infant denomination was one of *identity*. What kind of Christian body was it going to be? How was it going to organize? What was its style to be?

The third challenge was to work out its *relationship* with the pre-existing structures of the Countess of Huntingdon's Connexion. What

58

form was that going to take? Were the two bodies going to merge, as envisaged in 1863? It is with these latter two challenges that the present chapter is concerned.

Benjamin Price

Before examining these challenges, it will be helpful at this stage to introduce briefly one whose importance to the life of the Free Church of England 'it would be hard to overestimate'.[3] It was Benjamin Price who was to lead the Free Church of England through this crucial formative period and beyond into the next stage of its development. To understand the remarkable way in which Price was able to hold the denomination together in what were to be very difficult years, it is necessary to understand him in context.

Price was born into a Mid-Wales Calvinistic Methodist family in 1805. The date is significant. Daniel Rowland, whose ministry was described in Chapter 1, had died only 15 years before. In England Thomas Haweis had 15 more years to live. Six years were to pass before Thomas Charles (himself an episcopally ordained presbyter) 'with the greatest reluctance . . . finally led the [Welsh] Methodist Societies to break with the Church of England by ordaining ministers of their own in 1811 and so forming the Calvinistic Methodist Church of Wales'.[4] Price's father (who was an elder in the Calvinistic Methodist Church) and his generation had grown up as technically members of the Church of England. Despite the growing apart of the two Churches that had begun in the late eighteenth century, the sense of Anglican identity must still have been quite strong. Price himself spoke of 'some secret but undefined attachment to the Church of England still lingering in our veins'.[5]

Price was ordained into the Calvinistic Methodist ministry in 1830 and spent his first seven years working in Wales (Welsh was his first language). After a spell as a master in a school, he moved to the new 'Free Church' congregation at Ilfracombe in 1845. Such a move, to a congregation under the auspices of the Countess of Huntingdon's Connexion, would have been natural for Price. As shown in Chapter 1, the Connexion was seen in many ways as the English equivalent of the Welsh denomination. Both shared a common heritage in the work of Whitefield, Harris, Rowland, Lady Huntingdon and their associates: 'Welsh and English

Calvinistic Methodism were seen as one movement, a readily identified piety which centred on the doctrines of grace propagated in the life and power of the Holy Spirit.'[6]

From this point on, Price's many gifts – oratory, pastoral experience, organizational ability and a shrewd judge of character – enabled him to play a leading role in the next formative stages in the movement's life. In 1866 he was elected President of the Connexional Conference (which meant that he was simultaneously President of the Free Church of England Convocation). From then on he was seen as the natural leader of the 'Anglican wing' of the movement. It would be wrong, however, to see him as coming to the tradition as an outsider. During his formative years the Calvinistic Methodists had not taken many steps away from their Anglican origins. For Price to become a bishop in the historic succession (see Chapter 5), though clearly a development for both him and the denomination, was nevertheless not *so* great a leap as might be imagined. Price shared Thoresby's sense of the continuity of the movement with the events of the eighteenth century and the historic Church in England. As early as 1867 (when the Constitution had only been in existence for four years) he told the Conference:

> We possess a history. We are not of yesterday. We are descendants of a noble ancestry. . . What is remarkable, or rather observable, in our history, though too much lost sight of, is, that we have been a Free Church from the beginning. The designation, it is true, was not used, unfortunately; but we had the thing, always had it, always were a Free Church, and a Free Church of England, too.[7]

Price's lasting legacy is that his credentials made it possible for the Free Church of England to follow him when the leap from Connexion to Establishment-style Church was eventually made. Something of this process must now be explored.

What Kind of Church?

Inevitably, there was much in the early years that was in a state of flux. As Richard Fenwick points out, 'Ideas and customs were neither standardized, nor were they even widely understood.'[8] The story of the first ten years was to be one of developing a sense of identity, both structural (constitutional and ministerial) and of ethos and style. The process would take longer than ten years, but some important foundations were laid in that period.

Thanks in the main to Thomas Thoresby, the Free Church of England had a Constitution.[9] He and others were determined that the new denomination should not suffer from the organizational chaos of the Connexion, and so from the very beginning ensured that a definite framework of regulations and prescriptions was in place. It was within this framework that the scattered congregations now brought together (and those others that would join later) developed their corporate identity.

The Constitution stressed, firstly, the *Anglican* nature of the new denomination. This often comes as a surprise to those encountering the Free Church of England for the first time,[10] but is an ineradicable element of the vision from the very beginning. The Deed Poll declares 'the movement to be essentially one with the Church of England'. This theme was elaborated by Merryweather in his 1873 history and apologia for the new body

> It is distinctly a Church movement, and opens up a middle way between the dangers of the State Church and an absolute form of dissent, is in all essential points 'one with the Church of England' . . . one in all essential Articles of Faith, and in the use of our national Liturgy. It is indeed, the Church of England, purged of Romanism and free in its constitution from priestly despotism.[11]

Here lies a fundamental claim that it is not the Free Church of England that is inaugurating change, but the Church of England. The Free Church of England is simply seeking to maintain and conserve principles and practices from which the Established Church is departing:

> The Deed Poll of the Free Church of England shows that her members are not necessarily Dissenters, even from the principles of an Established Church. Nor are they dissenters from the Episcopacy of the Established Church, considered as an ecclesiastical institution; they only desire to bring it into conformity with Scripture and the usages of Apostolic times. They are not dissenters from the Liturgy of the State Church, but love it, use it, and find therein nourishment for their spiritual life. . . . It is indeed the Church of England that has been faithless in her grievous *dissent* from the doctrinal standard of the Reformation . . . The Church of England in her

pure, reformed, and progressive character we love . . . To sum up in a few plain simple words a declaration of the noble title of the 'Free' Church of England, it means, that it is one in all essential points with the State Church, but that it is free to go into any parish where necessary, and preach the Gospel of our Lord and Saviour Jesus Christ.[12]

Not only was this the understanding of former Connexional ministers, but it was strongly shared by the growing number of Church of England clergy and laity who were joining the Free Church of England following its formal establishment. They were not seeking to become Nonconformists. On the contrary, it was their consistent claim that it was the 'Ritualists' who were not conforming to the historic doctrines and customs of the Church of England. It was inevitable, therefore, that the clergy and congregations joining the Free Church of England should wish to continue those very practices which they saw being replaced in the parishes of the Church of England.

This continuity was visible from the very moment of entering a Free Church of England place of worship. Though the buildings were to contain 'no crosses or candles, or Popish mummeries',[13] yet there was still a sense of 'the beauty of holiness': 'that kind of ornamentation which is simple and beautiful, and consistent with evangelical truth and purity, meets with sanction and encouragement'.[14] The rubric at the beginning of the Holy Communion service indicates that the Table is to be covered, though the colour of this covering is not to be changed to indicate the Church seasons.[15] The worshipper was to feel even more at home the minute the worship began: 'Nothing is discarded from its ceremonial that tends to solemnity, decency and order. Its Church character is fully maintained, and whilst free from the sensuous parade of the Ritualists on the one hand, it does not adopt the bald simplicity of the Puritan dissenters on the other.'[16] In practice this meant that the surplice was worn by the clergy (with a gown for preaching). Richard Fenwick gives several contemporary accounts of the use of the surplice (with black scarf, and occasionally academic cap) by Free Church of England clergy (including those not of Anglican background) at this period.[17] There was some debate on the propriety of robed choirs, but these too became part of Free Church of England worship in some places.

The liturgy was essentially that of the Book of Common Prayer. It was one of the results of the Oxford Movement that it sparked a fierce debate about the nature of the Prayer Book. Evangelicals defended it as a Protestant liturgy. The Tractarians found in it features such as fasting and the observance of saints' days which justified interpreting the book in a 'catholic' sense. The debate raged fiercely for much of the nineteenth century and well into the twentieth. Eventually a substantial body of Evangelicals adopted the position that if the Prayer Book did indeed contain features capable of a Tractarian interpretation, then it must be revised so as to remove them. In the Church of England this could only be done by parliamentary action. The *free* nature of the Free Church of England, on the other hand, meant that the modifications that many wished for could in fact be put into effect. A fuller account of the liturgical tradition of the Free Church of England will be given in Chapter 11. Here it is simply necessary to note that the changes made were generally modest and reflected the issues of the time. 'Formularies of a thousand years', wrote Merryweather, 'ought not to be touched except with reverence; if touched in any other spirit, they are likely to be desecrated.'[18] The word 'priest' was replaced by 'minister' or 'presbyter' and passages seen as teaching baptismal regeneration, a physical real presence in the Eucharist, and priestly absolution were modified or removed. Morning and Evening Prayer could be shortened.[19] Merryweather concludes his survey of the changes by saying, 'It will be thus seen how few are the alterations made in the ordinary service of the Church.'[20]

The Sunday experience of worshippers was of a Church hardly different from the Established Church. This similarity was carried over into its organizational structures as well, so far as circumstances permitted.

The Constitution of 1863 made provision for the common oversight of 'all the congregations in a given district or diocese'. Subdivision into geographical units was not new – it had been envisaged by the Countess herself, and by 1863 the Connexion was itself divided into four districts – Southern, Western, Northern and Eastern. What seems to have been new was the use of the word *diocese*. In his Thesis Richard Fenwick traces how, in Free Church of England usage, the term was originally used interchangeably with 'district'. Gradually, however, the term 'district' dropped out of use,[21] until by the mid 1890s 'diocese' is the sole term used.[22] Even as early as 1873 Merryweather could use a sentence like: 'The choice or nomination of diocesan bishops is one of the most important functions of the District Meetings.'[23]

From the districts/dioceses clergy and lay representatives were sent to a body that was initially referred to as 'Conference' (it was in the first few years in fact the same body as the Connexion's Conference), but which, after 1868, is called 'Convocation'. As will be discussed more fully below, from 1863 to 1866 the Free Church of England was simply administered by a committee of the Connexion, reporting to Conference. However, once the Free Church of England business began to be handled by a separate body, the name adopted for it was 'Convocation'. The word in fact occurs in the 1863 Constitution, but in a general sense; like the word 'diocese' it gradually took on a more specific and 'churchy' meaning. Thus the July 1868 edition of the denominational magazine contains a report on 'The Fifth Annual Convocation of the Free Church of England'. The choice of name was evidently deliberate, for Merryweather goes to some length to compare and contrast the Convocation of the Free Church of England with those of the Established Church. The roots of the Convocations of Canterbury and York go back to Saxon times and predate a unified English kingdom. Since the fifteenth century each has been divided into an Upper House (the bishops) and a Lower House (elected and ex officio clergy). Summoned by the Crown since the Reformation, between 1717 and 1852 they transacted no business[24] – hence Merryweather's comment that 'in the Established Church, Convocation is acknowledged by all parties to be a failure'.[25] Nor did the Convocations of the Church of England include laity; not until 1885 was a semi-formal 'House of Laymen' established, and not until 1920 did the laity have a statutory role in Church government at a national level. By contrast, the Convocation of the Free Church of England was not only more representative (it was not top-heavy with ex officio members), but it contained lay representatives, thus, says Merryweather, 'recogniz[ing] unreservedly the Apostolic idea that the Church is composed of laity as well as of the clergy . . .'.[26] Methodists and the Connexion might have *Conferences*, the Protestant Episcopal Church in the USA might have a General *Convention*, but the Free Church of England asserted its historicity and continuity by having a *Convocation* – and a superior one to those of the Church of England at that.

The 1863 Constitution also made detailed provision concerning the *ministry*. The stated intention was to combine in the new Church all that was best in the Congregational, Presbyterian and Episcopal systems. The Congregational element was demonstrated in the sense that each Congregation shall manage its own affairs; so far as those affairs begin and end with such Congregation, and are not so managed as to be contrary to the general rules and regulations for the government of the Church made from time to time by the Convocation.[27]

The Presbyterian element was located in the 'authority given to the District or Diocesan Meeting, and in the assembly of the whole presbytery and lay representatives of the laity in Convocation as the ultimate governing body in the Church'.[28] This structure was to be served by and overseen by a ministry that had an *episcopal* dimension.

Following its formal separation from the Church of England, the Countess of Huntingdon's Connexion had functioned with a single order of ministry. For the Free Church of England, however, this did justice neither to Anglican practice nor, more importantly, to the evidence of the New Testament itself. A modern perspective would see in the infant Church a wide range of ministries, given by charism of the Holy Spirit. The nineteenth-century debate focused on two 'generic' ministries – that of *service* ('waiting on tables' Acts 6.2) and that of *oversight* ('. . . the flock, of which the Holy Spirit has made you overseers' Acts 20.28). New Testament usage suggested that the term 'overseer' – *episkopos* – was used interchangeably with the term 'elder' – *presbuteros*.[29] The Deed Poll reflected this modified two ministry pattern:

> . . . there are two orders of Ministers, videlicet, Bishops and Deacons. The first order shall be designated Bishops, or Presbyters, or Elders, the words being applied in the New Testament to the same persons . . . After these follow the Deacons, under which name are also included Managers and Churchwardens.

The 'lay' administrative-type roles attributed to the deacons reflect both Nonconformist influence and a confusion over the diaconate which persists in the Western Church to the present day. The Presbyterate-Episcopate might, however, consist of one *order*, but it was understood to be divided into two *offices*. Thus the Constitution states that the Free Church of England is *episcopal*, 'in the sense that one of the Presbyters, chosen by his fellow Presbyters and the Deacons . . . shall have oversight for the common good of all the Congregations in a given District or Diocese'.[30]

Beyond this, there was yet one additional ministry: 'and further, that one of such Bishops shall be chosen by the said Convocation as President or Bishop Primus of the whole body'.[31]

The 1863 Constitution therefore created a hierarchical structure: Bishop Primus – Diocesan Bishop – Congregational Presbyter – Deacon – Laity. The theology undergirding this was vastly different from that of the Oxford Movement, but the *structure* was not so very different to that of the Established Church. This was reassuring to some and alarming to others.

It is important to realize that all the offices were *elected*. This was seen as having apostolic and patristic sanction, as Merryweather makes clear: 'the Free Church of England . . . recognizes in a bishop, elected by the suffrages of his fellow presbyters and their Christian congregations, an office having far more legitimate claim to Apostolic affinity than one appointed by the State, or who assumes prelatical power upon the base-less fabric of Apostolic succession'.[32] There was an ordination service, modelled on that of the Book of Common Prayer, but it seems only to have been used for the ordaining of presbyters.[33] It was the unsatisfactory nature of an annually elected episcopate that was to hasten further developments and a growing apart from the Connexion.

In summary, the Free Church of England sought to combine the best features of the Established Church and of Nonconformity. As Price put it:

> It sympathises with the Church of England, and does not frown on Dissent. It has diminished the distance between them by incorporating into its own system something from both. The Churchman finds much to gratify him, and the Dissenter meets with much to enlist his approval. Its basis is broad and catholic, its teaching sound and Scriptural, its constitution comprehensive and elastic.[34]

Such a synthesis, Price conceded, was not of universal appeal:

> The movement is too Churchy for some, and too Methodistical for others. The Nonconformist does not like its Churchism, and the Episcopalian is equally displeased with its Methodism. . . . Nevertheless, it is a position singularly adapted to the spirit of the times, and fitted to meet the wants of the age, and to do a great deal of good in the land.[35]

Arguably, however, the Free Church of England vision was ahead of its time. Certainly, many found it difficult to assent to, not least parts of the Connexion.

The Relationship with the Countess of Huntingdon's Connexion

As has been shown, over the first ten years of its life the Free Church of England, while still very definitely a Protestant organization, began to take on more of the vocabulary and style of the Established Church. Indeed, much of this was envisaged by the Constitution. It was only as the words on paper began to take form in the life of the new Church that a parting of the ways with the Connexion became inevitable.

Initially, as intended from the beginning, the door was left open for the Connexion to transform itself into the Free Church of England. The preamble to the Resolution of 24 June 1863 gives the impression that the only reason that the new body is being brought into existence is the inability of the Connexion to adapt itself quickly enough 'without a vesting order from the Court of Chancery or the Charity Commissioners' which itself would require the consent of diverse groups of Trustees. Ministers and office holders of the Connexion could become members of the Free Church of England as well by subscribing to its Articles and assenting to its forms of worship.[36] This holding of dual membership was to continue for many years. The very title of the denominational magazine reflected the high tide of expectation that the new body would subsume the old: *The Harbinger of the Countess of Huntingdon's Connexion* became in January 1863 *The Harbinger, a magazine of the Countess of Huntingdon's Connexion and the Free Church of England*. A more radical shift took place in 1867, the title becoming *The Free Church of England Magazine and Harbinger* [the following in small print] *of the Countess of Huntingdon's Connexion*.

This ascription of priority to the Free Church of England was seen in other ways. The 1867 *Magazine* lists 'The Free Church of England (including the Countess of Huntingdon's Connexion) arranged in Districts', naming the Presidents and Secretary of each of the 4 districts, together with the ministers, deacons, managers or churchwardens of each church.[37]

The same President, Treasurer and Executive Committee oversaw the whole enterprise; only the office of Secretary was divided, with one Secretary for the Connexion, and one for the Free Church of England. This rapid 'Anglicanization' of the Connexion created tensions. Price might argue that 'our present movement . . . and the direction which it is taking, are in strict accordance with the facts of our history',[38] but others were not happy.

Something of a crisis occurred in 1868 when the title 'Bishop' was used without qualification for Benjamin Price in the order of service and publicity notices for the consecration of a church in Tottington, near Bury in Lancashire. The details of the scenario need not concern us here. Price's own summary of the reaction was that the Connexion 'was not prepared for so bold and decided a step, and objected to the whole proceeding'.[39] In fact, at the meeting of Conference/Convocation[40] held later that year, two Connexional members moved a resolution that only the term 'President' be used, but were soundly defeated. The meeting then went on virtually unanimously to affirm the title 'Bishop'.[41] Fenwick sums up the result:

> The die was cast. Whilst the episcopate remained only a concept in the Poll Deed, the relationship could work easily enough between the two denominations. But the Bury decision had forced the pace. The fact was that if Convocation had accepted [the resolution in favour of President] it would have had to deny the basis of its Poll Deed, and the whole integrity of the denomination would have been accordingly questioned . . .[42]

At the same meeting of Convocation (June 1868) Benjamin Price was elected for a third year as President/Bishop Primus.[43] It is as though the denomination was coming, almost instinctively, to realize that an 'annual episcopacy', unlike an annual presidency, simply would not work. The episcopate had to be, if not permanent, then at least long term. The next year, while Price continued as Bishop Primus, the Revd George Jones was elected President of the Connexion. The denominations now had two separate 'heads' and worked less and less closely together. By 1870 Conference and Convocation were no longer meeting together simultaneously as they had done in the past.

Between 1871 and 1873 there were further attempts to heal the growing rift,[44] but they were ultimately unsuccessful. 'The fact remains,' concludes Fenwick, 'that the ministry, organisation and the theology of *both* denominations had grown too widely apart . . . the FCE was continuing to look towards the model of the Establishment . . . and the Connexion was not only looking back to its Calvinist roots, but was continuing to have internal troubles . . .'[45] Merryweather lamented the fact that with a few exceptions 'the congregations of the Connexion made no great effort towards amalgamation with the earlier Free Churches'[46] and took the view that 'the progress and legitimate work of the Free Church of England was hampered and hindered for years by the retention, by many of her ministers, of the name of the Countess of Huntingdon's Connexion'.[47] The Connexional tradition was becoming a millstone round the neck of the Free Church of England.

The ten years following the Conference Resolution of 1863 were thus crucial in the history of the Free Church of England. During those years an identity was forged which was determinedly Protestant, but at the same time determinedly episcopal and liturgical. Its style was virtually indistinguishable from the traditional practices of the Church of England as then maintained by the Evangelical wing of the Established Church.[48] It did not wish to be a network of Calvinist chapels; it sought to be a Protestant Episcopal Church and hence a spiritual home for all those English Christians who loved the Lord, loved their Bible and loved their nation's Christian heritage.

Merryweather's comprehensive description, published in 1873, is a most valuable 'snapshot' of what the Church had become by that date. It was, however, a picture of a state of affairs whose days were numbered. In 1873 no one in the Free Church of England could have foreseen the sequence of events about to unfold in far-off North America, which was to change the whole situation.

Notes

1. 'The Connexion has a history, and that history is a history of the Free Church of England'; Thoresby, *FCE Magazine*, 1870, p. 164.
2. Richard Fenwick has what is probably the most comprehensive collection of the histories of the individual congregations and the events by which they came into existence.
3. Fenwick, *Thesis*, p. 337.
4. R. Tudur Jones, 'Charles, Thomas' in J. D. Douglas (ed.), *The New International Dictionary of the Christian Church* (Exeter, Paternoster Press, 1974).
5. *FCE Magazine*, 1867, p. 198.
6. Evans, *Daniel Rowland*, p. 286.
7. *FCE Magazine*, 1867, p. 198.
8. *Thesis*, p. 104.

9. The development of the Constitution will be considered in detail in Chapter 9.

10. And, it has to be admitted, has discomfited some of the more radical members of the denomination over the years.

11. Merryweather, p. 85. The familiarity which many members of the Connexion/ Free Church of England felt towards Anglicanism is illustrated by the fact that F. W. Willcocks, one of the leading proponents of the Free Church of England, was for a period simultaneously a deacon of Spa Fields Chapel and church-warden of Clerkenwell (*FCE Magazine*, 1867, p. 193).

12. Merryweather, pp. 86ff.

13. Ibid., p. 96.

14. Ibid. The marginal heading reads 'Christian Art encouraged'.

15. At Communion time it was also to have 'a fair white linen cloth upon it'.

16. Merryweather, p. 96.

17. *Thesis*, pp. 93f. Fenwick implies that the use of the surplice was no longer common in the Connexion.

18. Merryweather, p. 155.

19. The Shortened Services Act of 1874 extended the same liberty to the Church of England.

20. Merryweather, p. 159.

21. It survives of course in Methodism.

22. Fenwick, *Thesis*, pp. 95ff. The Constitutional development and arrangements are discussed in greater detail in Chapter 9.

23. Merryweather, p. 106.

24. The Convocation of Canterbury began to discuss business this year; that of York did not do so until 1861.

25. Merryweather, p. 119.

26. Ibid., p. 120. Merryweather cites patristic precedent for the presence of laity at Councils of the Church, p. 122.

27. Deed Poll, para. 4.

28. Merryweather, p. 108.

29. This was very much the line taken by Thomas Wills, preacher at the first ordination service of the Connexion in 1783. Seymour, *Life and Times*, vol. II, p. 445.

30. Paragraph 4.

31. Ibid.

32. Merryweather, p. 104.

33. As will be discussed below, there was no attempt to consecrate a bishop until 1876, by which time the situation was very different. The central petition of the ordination rite was: 'Mayest thou receive the Holy Ghost for the office and work of a minister in the Church of God now committed unto thee by the

imposition of our hands; and be thou a faithful dispenser of the Word of God and of His holy sacraments; in the name of the Father, and of the Son, and of the Holy Ghost. Amen'; Merryweather, p. 153.

34. Opening Address at Convocation, 27 June 1871; *FCE Magazine*, October 1871, p. 171.

35. Ibid.

36. Merryweather, p. 124.

37. *FCE Magazine*, 1867, pp. 202–06.

38. *FCE Magazine*, 1867, p. 199.

39. Price, *Organisation of the Free Church*, p. 22.

40. The two bodies were still one at this stage.

41. Price, *Organisation of the Free Church*, p. 23.

42. Fenwick, *Thesis*, p. 102.

43. Price is usually referred to as 'the first bishop of the Free Church of England'. Strictly speaking, this is not true. Following the creation of the 1863 Constitution George Jones served for a year as President of Conference and hence technically as Bishop Primus of the Free Church of England. E. C. Lewis occupied the same position the following year. See Appendix 4.

44. See Fenwick, *Thesis*, pp. 105–08 for details.

45. Ibid., p. 108.

46. Merryweather, pp. 181f.

47. Ibid., p. 82.

48. F. W. Willcocks later complained about the movement's 'assumptions and imitations of ecclesiastical dress, orders and styles of address' in *An Old Attendant [F. W. Willcocks], Spa Fields Chapel and its Associations 1779–1884* (London, *c.* 1888), pp. 21f.

CHAPTER 4

The Third Strand: An Ecumenical Initiative 1873

From Church of England to Protestant Episcopal Church

The ease with which George Whitefield, Benjamin Ingham, the Wesleys and others ministered on both sides of the Atlantic is a salutary reminder that, prior to 1776, substantial areas of North America were part of the Church of England. Indeed, at the outbreak of the American Revolution, the Church of England was the Established Church in 6 of the 13 states, and in a few an organized geographical parish structure was in place.[1] In some places more than five generations had lived and died on American soil ministered to by clergy of the Church of England, using the services of the Book of Common Prayer of 1662.[2]

The links with England were strong. The 13 states were all part of the Diocese of London. In many of them the bishop was represented by a commissary, and Whitefield's *Journals* record his interactions with them.[3] Furthermore, every deacon and presbyter had received his ministerial commission in England. No bishop had visited the colonies.[4] Every minister was therefore either an Englishman who had gone to North America subsequent to ordination or, if a native-born American, had made the long and perilous crossing at least once to receive the laying on of episcopal hands, having taken the oath of allegiance to the sovereign. It is not surprising that the Church of England in North America has been described as, 'the most self-consciously British of the major Protestant Churches'.[5] This strength of identity was not matched by strength of numbers. On the eve of the Revolution there were only 318 active Church of England parishes in the colonies – an average of about 24 per state. In fact the distribution was uneven, with the Church of England presence weaker in the northern states where the Presbyterian and Congregational presence was strong.

The 1776 Declaration of Independence and the war that followed it 'almost destroyed American Anglicanism'.[6] Of the 286 resident clergy, 131 fled, either north to Canada or back to Britain. Those who remained were scattered and without a bishop.

There is no space here to recount the story of the recovery of what was to become the Protestant Episcopal Church in the United States of America.[7] All that can be done is to select a few developments which were to be of significance in the emergence of the Reformed Episcopal Church from the Protestant Episcopal Church approximately 80 years later.

Once it became clear that the 13 states were indeed going to achieve independence from Great Britain the Church of England clergy in each state began to come together to plan for a new future. In Annapolis, for example, the clergy met on 13 August 1783 and agreed 'A Declaration of Certain Fundamental Rights and Liberties of the Protestant Episcopal Church of Maryland (heretofore denominated the Church of England, as by law established)'.[8] The 'Rights and Liberties' included the right to organize as a Church, to maintain the three Orders of ministry, to insist on episcopal ordination, to hold a synod and to revise the liturgy.[9]

Approximately nine months later, on 25 May 1784, the clergy of Pennsylvania, together with lay delegates met and also agreed a similar set of 'Fundamental Rules or Principles'.[10] Clearly, unless 13 separate Anglican Churches were going to emerge, some co-ordinating structure was going to be necessary. The decision was therefore taken to hold a 'General Convention' to which representatives of the former Church of England in all the states would be invited. The convention took place later that year – on 6 and 7 October 1784 – but, in the event, only 7 of the 13 states were represented.[11] The Convention was presided over by the Revd William Smith of Maryland. Among other items of business it drew up seven 'Fundamental Principles' on which a constitution was to be created.

Materially and in terms of manpower, the Church was weak. Paul Zahl, Dean of Birmingham Cathedral, Alabama, writes that 'rural Virginia and Maryland, for example, were dotted with old brick churches dating from the late seventeenth and early eighteenth centuries. They stood empty. To the mind of the majority of Americans, these church buildings symbolized England and the autocracy of king and prelate.'[12] Clearly a major work of reconstruction was going to be necessary if the Anglican tradition was going to survive in the new republic.

William White

At this point it may be helpful to look at one of the most significant figures of this period of American Church history – William White. The son of an Englishman who had emigrated in 1720, White was born about 1747 and was educated at the Academy and College of his native Philadelphia. As a young man he was influenced 'by the preaching of Whitefield who, as an old man, on his last visit to Philadelphia, preached in Christ Church once more'.[13] White sailed to England in 1770 where he was ordained deacon in the Chapel Royal at St James's Palace by the Bishop of Norwich on 27 December 1770. He remained in England, living with his father's sisters at Twickenham, until after his ordination as a presbyter on St Mark's Day (25 April) 1772. White may have heard Whitefield, but he had not adopted Whitefield's theology. On the contrary, he was, like many of the clergy (especially in the southern states) Latitudinarian in his views. Guelzo goes so far as to say that 'he denied the central tenet of Protestant theology, justification by the imputed righteousness of Christ; he spoke of the Bible as "merely . . . containing credible history, transmitted, like other histories, by those who were the subjects of them respectively" . . . and freely suggested that the Nicene Creed and other anti-Arian documents in the prayer book were "calculated rather to obscure than to elucidate the truths of Scripture"'.[14] Given such views it is understandable that White took a 'relaxed' attitude to the question of providing episcopal oversight for the former Church of England parishes in the newly independent territories. In a set of proposals entitled *The Case of the Episcopal Churches in the United States* published in 1782 he suggested that (failing the obtaining of the historic succession from England) a candidate might be elected at a convention and consecrated by the other presbyters. Such bishops would be the *officers* of the Church, not its rulers. Such a concept clearly had many parallels with the emerging federal constitution of the United States. It also bears many similarities to the almost exactly contemporary solution reached by John Wesley for providing a ministry of oversight for the remaining Methodists in the former colonies.[15]

The Consecration of Samuel Seabury

In the light of William White's liberal theological views and readiness to abandon catholic order, the actions of the clergy of Connecticut become easier to understand.[16] In this northern state the Church of England had been very much a minority and so was used to defending itself against non-episcopal ecclesiologies. Faced now with the undermining of their long-fought-for position by their southern brethren, 10 of the remaining 14 presbyters met on 25 March 1783 and elected one of their number, Samuel Seabury, as their bishop. Seabury sailed for England with the request of the Connecticut clergy that he be consecrated by the Archbishop of Canterbury. This the Archbishop was unable to do, not least because of the legal requirement that any candidate take the oath of allegiance to George III, which Seabury could not now do. Faced with Archbishop Moore's inability to act, Seabury made enquiries about other sources of consecration. At one stage the bishops of Denmark were briefly considered, but rejected due to the break in the historic succession in that country.[17] Eventually, on the advice of Martin Routh of Magdalen College, Oxford,[18] Seabury turned to Scotland where the successors of the bishops dispossessed in 1689 had maintained their succession and a small flock in the face of draconian penal laws enacted against them (substantially as a result of their adherence to the Jacobite cause). 'If they consent to impart the Episcopal succession to the Church of Connecticut,' wrote Seabury, 'they will, I think, do a great work, and the blessing of thousands will attend them. And, perhaps for this cause, among others, God's Providence has supported them, and continued their succession under various and great difficulties, that a free, valid, and purely ecclesiastical Episcopacy may from them pass into the western world.'[19] The Scottish bishops were already aware of the possibility of this request. In 1782 the idea had been suggested to them that they might consecrate one or more missionary bishops for America. They had, however, felt unable to act without an explicit request from the Church in the ex-Colonies (and for fear of reprisals against them by the British Government).[20]

Interestingly, there was a precedent. In 1715, 1716 and 1725 the Scottish bishops had consecrated bishops for *England*. These were for Non-Juring communities, whom the 'older race' of Scottish bishops saw as the true Church in England, the Established Church being 'schismatical'.[21] By the time of Seabury's application the majority of Scottish bishops held more moderate views, though one bishop refused to participate in Seabury's consecration on the grounds that Seabury's existing Orders derived from the Church of England.[22]

In the event, on 14 November 1784 the Bishops of Aberdeen (Robert Kilgour), Moray, Ross and Caithness (Arthur Petrie) and John Skinner (Coadjutor of Aberdeen) consecrated Samuel Seabury in an upstairs chapel in Long Acre, Aberdeen. The following day Seabury signed a concordat with his consecrators, which included the commitment on his part to seek to introduce the Scottish Communion Service into America. This was to have a direct bearing on events nearly ninety years later.

Seabury returned to a rather confused situation. In his absence the meetings of the clergy of Maryland and Philadelphia mentioned above had taken place and other states were organizing similar gatherings. The relationship between the Churches in the various states (including Connecticut with its new bishop) needed to be defined as a matter of urgency. Equally pressing was the issue of Prayer Book revision.

The Prayer Books of 1785 and 1789

In view of the fact that, as will be shown below, the 1785 Prayer Book was part of the rallying cry of the Reformed Episcopal Church in the 1870s, and was sufficiently important to be mentioned in its Declaration of Principles (where it is still named), it is necessary to explore its genesis and eclipse in some detail.

In September 1785 a Convention was held in Philadelphia. Seabury declined to attend and only the southern states were represented. The Convention appointed two main subcommittees, one to work on a Constitution,[23] the other to revise the Prayer Book. Initially, only such adjustments as were necessary in the changed political situation were envisaged, but rapidly other proposals were made.[24] Some of these were of an anti-Trinitarian nature, such as the removal of the Athanasian and Nicene Creeds. Others reflected anti-hierarchical concerns in the new republic – 'minister' was substituted for 'priest' throughout, a change 'common to Latitudinarian revisions'.[25] Also removed was the phrase 'He descended into Hell' in the Apostles' Creed. Some passages of Scripture were removed from the lectionary as 'inexpedient to be read in mixt assemblies'.[26] In the Baptismal Service the rubric stating that baptized infants are 'undoubtedly saved' was omitted. So too, was the Black Rubric on eucharistic presence at the end of the Holy Communion service. A number of even more radical proposals failed to gain acceptance. In his sermon on 7 October, at a service when the new liturgy was used for the first time, Dr William Smith 'spoke in laudatory terms of the attempt of revision of 1689', many of the features of which had been adopted in the Proposed Book of 1785.[27] This had been an attempt (in England) to adapt the 1662 Prayer Book to satisfy some of the needs of Dissenters. It was never authorized in England, but exercised a fascination over the following two centuries for those wanting Low Church or Latitudinarian revisions of the 1662 Prayer Book.[28] Significantly, however, no one had ever seen the 1689 text. The only copy was kept in Lambeth Palace Library,[29] and publication of the entire text did not begin until the 1850s. Only 'garbled versions of the Commissioners' findings' were in the public domain.[30] The 'myth' persisted, however, that a Prayer Book which expressed many of the desires of Low Churchmen and Dissenters (and Latitudinarians) had been created and might do great good if made known and adopted. Despite its lack of availability, the 1689 Book nevertheless exercised a real influence. Hatchett traces its legacy and that of other sources, including the Church of Ireland Prayer Book and even the Non-Jurors, in the American revision.

The Proposed Book was actually published in 1786. Hatchett's judgment of it is that it was 'notably conservative and restrained' especially when compared with some other proposals around at the time.[31] Reaction to the book was mixed. There were those of a more strongly Latitudinarian disposition who would have preferred it to be less explicitly Trinitarian. In England (where the archbishops, galvanized by Seabury's consecration, were seeing through Parliament a Bill to enable them to consecrate without requiring an oath to the Crown) Churchmen were alarmed particularly at the removal of two of the three historic creeds and the deletion of a clause from the only one that remained. 'We cannot but be extremely cautious,' the Archbishops wrote, 'lest we should be the instruments of establishing an Ecclesiastical system which will be called a branch of the Church of England, but afterwards may possibly appear to have departed from it essentially, either in doctrine or discipline.'[32] There followed much correspondence, both between the states and with England. The American Churchmen were anxious to obtain the consecration of bishops from England, but unwilling to appear to be giving in to English demands. Eventually a convention of the southern states met at Wilmington from 10 to 11 October 1786 and voted to restore the Nicene Creed (but not the Athanasian) and to restore the deleted clause in the Apostles' Creed. In the meantime three presbyters had been elected by their state conventions for consecration as bishops. Two of these, William White for Pennsylvania and Samuel Provoost for New York sailed for England on 2 November 1786. They were received warmly at Lambeth Palace by Archbishop John Moore, who introduced them to King George III. On 4 February 1787 Moore, assisted by the Archbishop of York (William Markham), and the Bishops of Peterborough (John Hinchcliffe) and Bath and Wells (Charles Moss) consecrated White and Provoost in Lambeth Palace Chapel.

The Connecticut clergy had always argued that revising the liturgy and constitution should take place *after* there were bishops in office in North America. Now that this was the case, Seabury made contact with White and Provoost on their return from England. The result was that when the next General Convention took place (at Philadelphia in September 1789) not only was Seabury present, but so too were delegates from the northern states of Connecticut, Massachusetts and New Hampshire. From this time on, it was clear that there was only going to be one Protestant Episcopal Church in the United States. The first item of business was to amend the constitution to create a separate House of Bishops, which met on its own.[33] On 3 October committees were appointed to prepare new revisions of the liturgy.

To oversimplify, the Prayer Book created in 1789 undid some of the features of the Proposed Book of 1785. The word 'priest', for example, was restored in some places. The Nicene Creed was not re-inserted into the Eucharist, but a rubric permitted either it or the Apostles' Creed to be used there. Bishop White accepted the oblation and epiclesis from the Scottish rite saying, 'I can discover no superstition in them.'[34] The revised Communion rite was recommended to the House of Deputies by Dr William Smith, its chairman. The initial suspicion of some was apparently overcome by hearing it read magisterially by Dr Smith in his native

Scots brogue, and in the end the new Communion rite 'was accepted with acclamation'.[35]

The Baptismal service also underwent revision in a direction that would become highly relevant later. 'The Proposed Book [1785] had revised the rites of initiation in ways which edited out the doctrine of baptismal regeneration. Both White and Seabury explicitly taught this doctrine in their writings, and it was recovered in the 1789 book.'[36]

No attention was given to the revision of the Ordinal in 1789. This was not tackled until the General Convention of 1792, by which time the membership of the House of Bishops had risen to four, James Madison having been consecrated Bishop of Virginia by the English bishops in Lambeth Palace Chapel on 19 September 1790.[37] Once the text had been agreed (reluctantly by Seabury who did not like its Latitudinarian features) it was used immediately for the consecration of Thomas Claggett as Bishop of Maryland. At this, the first consecration of a bishop on American soil, all four of the bishops consecrated in Britain took part, thus uniting the Scottish and English successions. It is this united succession that is continued in the Free Church of England today.

It has been necessary to outline the above events in some detail as the interpretation of them was crucial in the events that were to take place in the early 1870s.

The Evangelicals in the Protestant Episcopal Church

George Whitefield may have been God's instrument in the 'awakening' of tens of thousands in North America in the mid eighteenth century, but his poor organizational skills meant that, as in England, it was not the Church of England that benefited from his ministry, most of his American converts ending up in Congregational, Presbyterian or Baptist Churches.[38] This meant that the Evangelical presence in the newly emerging Protestant Episcopal Church of the USA (PECUSA) was surprisingly weak, the Church being polarized between Latitudinarians and High Churchmen. (Zahl goes so far as to say that Evangelicals in the Episcopal Church 'were nonexistent before independence'.[39]) All this was to change in the early years of the nineteenth century. Traditionally dated to the ordination of William Meade and the consecration of Alexander Griswold in 1811, a substantial revival spread through the Protestant

Episcopal Church, resulting in approximately half a century of rapid growth in membership, clergy and dioceses.[40] The growth, says Guelzo, was 'nothing short of breathtaking . . . It was the Evangelicals who first carried the Episcopal banner over the Appalachians into what became the Evangelical bastion of Ohio in 1817, and by 1830 the Evangelicals had blazed the trail into Kentucky . . . Louisiana . . . Indiana, Illinois, and Iowa.'[41] Furthermore, to a greater extent than in the Church of England, Evangelicals were elected bishops and as the years passed, some dioceses had known no other type of bishop. One result of this revival was the eclipse of the Latitudinarian tradition, only the old High Church tradition survived, differing not so much in theology but in emphasis. The High Churchman took the externals of the faith, including the official definitions of its boundaries, very seriously; the Evangelical placed greater stress on inward experience and was more prepared to recognize and make common cause with those who shared a similar experience, but were outside the Episcopal fold.

From time to time the two traditions within PECUSA clashed. Perhaps the most significant of these clashes for the present story was in October 1853 when a 'Memorial' was presented to the House of Bishops by 12 presbyters. Their leader was William Augustus Muhlenberg and his influence can be seen in the Free Church of England down to the present day.[42]

William Augustus Muhlenberg 1796–1877

The Muhlenbergs were a prominent ecclesiastical dynasty. William's great grandfather had come to the British Colonies from Germany in 1742 to work among German and Swedish Lutherans. One of 'patriarch' Muhlenberg's sons, Peter, was ordained presbyter in England together with William White. The young William Muhlenberg was ordained deacon on 18 September 1817 to serve at Christ Church, Philadelphia, as chaplain to Bishop White. He was ordained presbyter on 22 October 1820.

Muhlenberg was what was then a rare type of churchman – a committed Evangelical who did not believe that Evangelical faith could only be expressed in a starkly Protestant ecclesiastical culture. At the Church of the Holy Communion in New York, of which he was rector from 1844 to 1877, 'Muhlenberg introduced weekly communion services, organized a sisterhood for social service, put away his preaching gown in favor of exclusive use of the surplice, and erected an altar with crosses, candles, flowers and incense.'[43] Muhlenberg's vision was of an 'Evangelical Catholicism' that would marry the fervour of Evangelical faith to Catholic Church order. For a few years he produced a journal called *The Evangelical Catholic*. In it he defended his chosen nomenclature: 'we believe in Christianity, not as an abstraction, but as an institution – a divine institution, adapted to all mankind in all ages; in other words, the Catholic Church. This we declare in calling ourselves Catholics.'[44] The word 'Catholic', however, had become identified with Rome:

> Speak of *Catholics*, and not one in a hundred would suppose you mean any others than members of the Roman Church. If we will have the name, and surrender it we can not, we must qualify it, we must explain it . . . therefore we style ourselves Gospel, that is *Evangelical Catholics*.[45]

This, for Muhlenberg, was the distinguishing mark of the episcopal communion he believed in – 'we go at once to the Gospel, and assert ourselves Gospel (i.e. Evangelical) Catholics'.[46] Moreover, it was a concept with a long and distinguished history. This, argued Muhlenberg is what the Reformers were, Gospel Catholics, helping the Catholic Church discover its Gospel roots.

But Muhlenberg was not exclusivist in his views. On the contrary, his complaint against the High Church bishops was that a narrow interpretation of the Protestant Episcopal Church's canons denied non-episcopalians access to the riches of Gospel Catholicism in its episcopal and liturgical fullness. In 1836 Muhlenberg wrote *Hints on Catholic Union*.[47] The keynote is Christ's words, 'that they all might be one . . . that the world might believe' (John 17.21). Muhlenberg argued for unity in doctrine, ministry (to be episcopal) and worship. Seventeen years later, in October 1853, Muhlenberg sought to put his vision of Christian unity into effect by, along with a number of other presbyters, presenting a Memorial to the House of Bishops of the Protestant Episcopal Church.[48] The Memorial drew the bishops' attention to 'the divided and distracted state of American Protestant Christianity, . . . the consolidated forces of Romanism, . . . and ignorance'. The Protestant Episcopal Church as presently constituted 'is not sufficient to the great purposes [of addressing these issues and dispensing the Gospel to the nation)'.[49] The 1853 Memorial sought to achieve this by making three basic recommendations:

1. That 'a wider door must be opened for admission to the Gospel ministry' by making episcopal ordination available to men 'among the other bodies of Christians around us, who would gladly receive ordination at your hands, could they obtain it without that entire surrender which would now be required of them, of *all* the liberty in public worship to which they have been accustomed . . .'.[50]
2. That the requirements of conformity to the Book of Common Prayer be eased, to prevent the Protestant Episcopal Church 'reject[ing] all laborers but those of one peculiar type'.[51]
3. That the bishops give the lead in achieving 'greater concert of action among Protestant Christians than any which yet exists'.[52]

The first clause prefigures remarkably closely Archbishop Geoffrey Fisher of Canterbury's appeal to the English Free Churches in 1946 to consider 'taking episcopacy into their system' as part of a process of 'growing alike'.[53] Muhlenberg was proposing that men might be episcopally ordained while remaining in their existing denomination, and able to use parts of the Prayer Book without being committed to unvarying use of the whole. In mid-nineteenth-century North America the High Church bishops were 'aghast at Muhlenberg's proposals' – 'How could it have entered into the mind of man to conceive of such a thing?' protested one.[54] Extending the blessings of episcopacy to those who were not prepared to submit to its discipline was unthinkable. The official 1856 response to the Memorial loosened some of the restrictions on liturgical usage, and set up a Commission on Christian Unity, but nothing came of the latter.

Forgotten as it is today, the Muhlenberg Memorial was nevertheless formative in the coming into being of the Reformed Episcopal Church for two principal reasons. First, it raised the possibility of an episcopal Church becoming the nucleus around which other Churches might unite. Secondly, the Memorial was accompanied by a brief doctrinal test which would be taken up a generation later. Muhlenberg had followed up the Memorial with a range of pamphlets expanding its themes. Some of these concentrated on loosening the canonical regulations concerning worship.[55] In another – 'An Exposition of the Memorial', published in November 1854 – he proposed that:

> when promising opportunities occur for admitting men to Holy Orders who would desire to receive them without being obliged to relinquish all

their existing ecclesiastical relations, let them be ordained on conditions like the following:

1. That they declare their belief in the Holy Scriptures as the word of God, in the Apostles' and Nicene Creeds, in the divine Institution of the two sacraments, and in the 'doctrines of grace' substantially as they are set forth in the Thirty-Nine Articles.

2. That in the stated service of the Lord's Day, they will use the Lord's Prayer – one of the creeds, or the Gloria Patri, or the Gloria in Excelsis, certain forms equivalent to the prayer 'for all sorts and conditions of men' and 'the general thanksgiving' . . . and further that in the essential parts of the administration of the Holy Sacraments, they will use unvarying forms, tantamount to those in the Book of Common Prayer . . .

3. That they will make report of their ministry once, at least, in every three years to the bishop or some approved ecclesiastical tribunal.[56]

This text was to form the starting point for the Declaration of Principles of the Reformed Episcopal Church and hence of the present-day Free Church of England.[57]

The balance between the Evangelical and High Church parties in the Protestant Episcopal Church was to be destroyed by the arrival of the Tractarian movement from England. This was to create a third grouping – the Anglo-Catholics – whose vision of the Church was, as seen in Chapter 2, inspired by different models. As in England, the chief battle-ground was the conduct and ethos of worship. Crosses and incense, which had been used 'innocently' by Muhlenberg, were introduced 'aggressively' by Tractarians as part of their attempt to de-Protestantize the Protestant Episcopal Church. Again, as in England, the Prayer Book was given an exclusively 'catholic' interpretation ('priest' meant 'sacerdotal figure', not 'presbyter', for example). Evangelical responses focused on attempts to revise the Prayer Book so as to exclude Anglo-Catholic interpretations, but no decisive action was taken by the General Convention. Frustration and despair increased in Evangelical quarters.

Thus, by the dawn of the 1870s, the Protestant Episcopal Church was in turmoil. The spread of Anglo-Catholicism seemed unstoppable, aided by a Prayer Book apparently capable of an anti-Protestant interpretation. The Church was becoming more and more exclusive, tending increasingly to 'unchurch' non-Episcopalians. What many longed for was a truly Protestant Episcopal Church, worshipping with a purified Prayer Book, and around which all Evangelical Christians could unite, in fulfilment of Muhlenberg's vision.

Eventually a bishop arose who was prepared to try and make the vision a reality.

George David Cummins 1811–1876

Cummins is, naturally, a pivotal figure in the story of the Reformed Episcopal Church and the present-day Free Church of England for it is from him that these communities derive the historic episcopal succession. But that is far from being the total of Cummins's legacy. On the contrary, he was to bequeath to the movement a vision which still challenges it to the present day. Like the leaders of the Countess of Huntingdon's Connexion and the growing number of 'Free Church of England' congregations coming into being across the Atlantic (of which he seems to have been unaware) he saw himself as a preserver and restorer, not an innovator. Cummins was anxious to rescue and maintain an episcopal and liturgical heritage which was coming under threat. Furthermore, he believed passionately (more so, probably, than his English contemporaries) that such a Church had a crucial ecumenical role to play. The evidence shows that 'the guiding star in [his] mind . . . was clearly Muhlenberg's model of "Catholic Evangelicalism"'.[58]

George Cummins was born in 1811. His father's family were Episcopalian, but his mother's were Methodist. Cummins's father died when his son was only three, and his mother married a Methodist preacher; it was therefore inevitable that the young Cummins grew up in the Methodist Episcopal Church. As a young man he felt a call to the ministry and in 1843 became an itinerant preacher 'preaching by day from tree stumps and fence rails and sleeping by night in the rain and heat, throughout eastern Maryland and northern Virginia'.[59] In 1845, however, he rejoined the Protestant Episcopal Church, was confirmed, and ordained deacon on 26 October of that year.[60] Cummins was a committed Episcopalian, deeply attached to liturgical worship. He was ordained presbyter in July 1847 and held a number of parochial appointments, being loved for his deep pastoral concern and his clear and moving preaching ministry. A rising star of the Evangelical world, he soon received invitations to speak in other places.

In 1863 Cummins became Rector of Trinity Church, Chicago, where he came into contact with the Rector of Christ Church in that city, Charles Edward Cheney. Cheney had built up his congregation from humble beginnings and was a stalwart Evangelical. Uncomfortable, like most Anglican Evangelicals, with the doctrine of baptismal regeneration, he had quietly ceased to use the word when conducting the baptism service. Reported to his bishop, Cheney was tried in the Church courts and formally deposed in 1871 (though the validity of the deposition was not upheld by the State Court). In practice this meant little, for he remained at Christ Church and continued to minister there with the support of his congregation. For Cummins, however, this treatment of his former neighbour was unjust and unsettling. Equally unsettling was the apparent silence of the Evangelical bishops in the face of the persecution of a fellow Evangelical for believing what they too believed. It was to add to his growing sense that the Protestant Episcopal Church was beyond rescue.

All of this lay in the future, however, when, in 1866 Cummins was elected Assistant Bishop of the Diocese of Kentucky. In human terms Cummins' election was not due simply to his success as a parish minister. An important corrective to the post-1873 view of Cummins as an uncompromising rebel is the fact that Cummins had in fact a reputation as a reconciler. He had shown this in his speech to the General Convention in 1865 on the receiving back of the dioceses of the defeated Confederacy. He had worked peaceably under High Church bishops. Such were his credentials in this regard that he was elected 'as the candidate most satisfactory to both High Churchmen and Evangelicals'.[61] He was popular and well received.

George Cummins's consecration as a Bishop in the Church of God took place on 15 November 1866 at Christ Church, Louisville, Kentucky. The chief consecrator was the Presiding Bishop of the Protestant Episcopal Church, John Henry Hopkins, Bishop of Vermont. Hopkins was nearing the end of his life (he died less than two years later). He himself had been consecrated back in 1832 by William White, then in his eighties. Thus, remarkably, there was only one consecration between that of Cummins and the events in Lambeth Palace Chapel seventy-nine years earlier. The other consecrating bishops were Benjamin Smith of Kentucky (Cummins's Diocesan), John Kerfoot of Pittsburgh, Charles Quintard of

Tennessee, Joseph Talbot of Indiana, Henry Lee of Iowa and Robert Clarkson of Nebraska.

Cummins's episcopal ministry began well. In 1868, however, developments which hitherto had taken place outside Kentucky, reached the diocese – a parish 'went Ritualist'. It was followed by others. It is important to understand Cummins's reaction. He clearly was not aesthetically comfortable with the externals of Anglo-Catholic worship (and in this probably differed somewhat from Muhlenberg). Far more importantly, the doctrines which the externals purported to teach were to Cummins irreconcilable with the plain teaching of Scripture and seemed to detract from the all-sufficiency of Christ's unrepeatable work on the Cross. Furthermore, the 'unchurching' of non-episcopal ministries was slamming the door in the face of other Christians. It was not just that Cummins found Anglo-Catholic practices unpleasant. For him Tractarianism was not simply *distasteful*, it was *wrong*; as well as obscuring the all-sufficiency of the Cross, it threatened to prevent the Protestant Episcopal Church ever fulfilling her destiny as the home for all Evangelical Christians. If Ritualism won control of PECUSA, Muhlenberg's vision could never be fulfilled.

Cummins's confidence in the Protestant Episcopal Church was further undermined in 1868 by the tract *Are There Romanising Germs in the Prayer Book?*[62] by Franklin S. Rising, secretary of the American Missionary Society of PECUSA. Rising's argument was that words like 'priest' and phrases like 'Receive the Holy Ghost . . .' in the Ordinal, together with references to the Apocrypha, contain the 'germ' of 'certain seminal doctrines, which, being implanted and taking root, in due time spring up and bear Romanism as their fruit'.[63] Up to this point Cummins had believed that Tractarianism 'was not a growth developing from seeds within the [Anglican] system, but a parasite fastening upon it from without and threatening its very life'.[64] Rising's work convinced Cummins that the problem in fact lay within. The Reformers' work 'begun so nobly under Edward VI' had been frustrated, not least by the suppression of the Proposed American Book of 1785 by that of 1789. 'The plain, literal meaning of the words of that [i.e. the 1789] book' were, Cummins now believed, on the side of the Anglo-Catholics.[65] Consequently, Cummins became, in his own words, 'an earnest advocate of revision'.[66]

> We asked but three things, the use of an alternative phrase in the baptismal
> office for infants, the repeal of the canon closing our pulpits against all non-

Episcopal clergymen, and the insertion of a note in the Prayer-book, declaring the term *Priest* to be of equivalent meaning with the word Presbyter. We were met by an indignant and almost contemptuous refusal. . . . The door was closed in our faces . . . The burden was indeed intolerable.[67]

Faced with such rejection, Cummins gradually came to believe that the liturgical solution lay in a return to the 1785 Prayer Book, free from the Scottish and other additions made in 1789. In his mind it came to be associated with a 'purer' form of episcopalianism in North America. Its 'Low Church' language, though originally, as seen above, inspired by Latitudinarian concerns, looked comfortingly 'Evangelical'. Its association with Bishop White (who was seen as 'Protestant' in comparison with 'Catholic' Seabury) increased its standing even further.

Thus, by about 1870, Bishop Cummins increasingly found himself ministering in a Church which bore less and less resemblance to the Protestant Episcopal Church as created in the early days following Independence from Great Britain. Cummins was not, of course, alone in his views. Evangelical laity, clergy and bishops had joined with him in his attempts to halt the creeping change coming over PECUSA. In many quarters there was a growing sense of frustration that nothing could be done within the structures of the ironically named *Protestant* Episcopal Church.

What finally prompted Cummins to take decisive action was the issue of Christian unity. In October 1873 the Evangelical Alliance met in the YMCA hall in New York. This international gathering included The Very Reverend Robert Payne Smith, Dean of Canterbury, bearing a letter of greeting from his Archbishop. On Sunday 5 October Payne Smith assisted at a celebration of Holy Communion at Madison Square Presbyterian Church and himself received the Sacrament from the pastor, Dr William Adams. No doubt encouraged by this example, Cummins himself accepted the invitation of Dr John Hall of Fifth Avenue Presbyterian Church to do the same the following Sunday. Cummins joined Hall and Scottish Free Presbyterian William Arnot at the Communion Table and himself administered the cup, with a great sense that the service was a foretaste of 'that eternal union in the House not made with hands'.[68]

The following day the *New York Tribune* carried a letter from William Tozer, retired Missionary Bishop of Zanzibar, to Horatio Potter, Bishop of New York, attacking Payne Smith's involvement in the

Presbyterian Communion Service on 5 October. Appalled, Cummins wrote to the *Tribune*. In his letter he denied emphatically that either he or the Dean of Canterbury had violated Church order. Cummins's letter 'brought down a hail of abuse, printed and otherwise, onto Cummins' unrepentant head'.[69] Words like 'apostate', 'perjurer' and 'fallen bishop' were used. There were calls for him to be tried. It was difficult to see how he could again minister with authority in Kentucky.

Muhlenberg supported Payne Smith and Cummins. He was one of the appointed speakers at the Conference, but abandoned his published subject to speak on 'The Lord's Supper in relation to Christian Union'. In it he argued passionately for what he called 'Representative United Communions'. After attacking the way that the Sacrament, intended as 'a bond of brotherhood', had become a wall of separation, and condemning over-zealous attempts (by Presbyterians and others) to 'hedge the Table', Muhlenberg argued for special united acts of Holy Communion of a 'pre-ecclesiastical' nature – marked by the simplicity of the apostolic age and blessed by the Holy Spirit. There was nothing in Scripture or the laws of PECUSA, Muhlenberg asserted, to forbid what Payne Smith and Cummins had done. On the contrary, he concluded, 'intercommunion among Christians, to be exercised on their own private judgement, is one of their inalienable rights'.[70]

Extremely welcome though Muhlenberg's support no doubt was, it did little to ease Cummins's situation. Over the next two weeks he consulted with colleagues. By the end of October he had decided that he could not return to his diocese. He spent a great deal of time talking to Muhlenberg. Finally, on 10 November 1873, he wrote to Boswell Smith, his Diocesan and the Presiding Bishop:

> Right Reverend and Dear Bishop: Under a solemn sense of duty, and in the fear of God, I have to tell you that I am about to retire from the work in which I have been engaged for the last seven years in the Diocese of Kentucky, and thus to sever the relations which have existed so happily and harmoniously between us during that time . . .

Cummins's chief reasons for this decision were the conviction that there was no possibility that the 'system of error, now prevailing so extensively' would be eradicated by the Church authorities, and the impossible position in which the reaction to his involvement in the Presbyterian eucharist had placed him.

> I therefore leave the Communion in which I have laboured in the sacred ministry for over twenty-eight years, and transfer my work and office to another sphere of labour. I have an earnest hope and confidence that a basis for the union of all Evangelical Christendom can be found in a communion which shall retain or restore a primitive Episcopacy and a pure scriptural liturgy, with a fidelity to the doctrine of justification by faith alone . . .[71]

From 11 November Cummins stayed at the home of Marshall Smith, where he spent long hours in discussion, including with Colonel Benjamin Aycrigg, Smith's father-in-law. By the morning of 13 November the decision hinted at in Cummins's resignation letter had become a fact – Cummins would lead the restoration of a purified episcopal community.

It is important to see Cummins in a wider context than simply that of North America. The formation of new independent episcopal jurisdictions was already taking place elsewhere. The late 1860s and early 1870s were dominated internationally by the debates leading up to, and the consequences of the First Vatican Council with its claims for immediate, universal ordinary jurisdiction for the Pope and his *ex cathedra* infallibility. Throughout the Roman Catholic world there were numerous protests and a number of breakaway movements. Some of these, after 1870, were to become organized as the 'Old Catholics'. Others looked to the Anglican Communion for assistance. Thus, in 1868 there had begun the movement which was to lead to the formation of the Spanish Reformed Episcopal Church. Initially looked after by the Bishop of Mexico (himself consecrated by PECUSA bishops) and for many years under the pastoral care of bishops of the Church of Ireland, the Spanish Reformed Episcopal Church is today an extra-provincial diocese (with its own bishop) under the metropolitical authority of the Archbishop of Canterbury.[72] The existence of such Churches is a reminder that around 1870 there seemed to be a substantial degree of 'realignment' taking place in the Western Church. Cummins was aware of this. His letter of resignation to Boswell Smith actually mentioned the Old Catholics and the Mexican Church. Ecclesiastical arrangements were clearly not as fixed in stone as they appeared.

One further event took place in 1873 which electrified the Christian world and may well have encouraged Cummins to take decisive action. In August of that year the Bishop of Deventer in the Netherlands (the sole surviving bishop in the Utrecht succession) consecrated Josef Reinkens as bishop for the 'Old Catholics' of Germany. Here were groups of people leaving the Church of Rome in protest against its increasingly extreme teaching and being provided with a bishop (by a single bishop consecration) to enable them to continue to live as episcopal communities. Why should not a parallel situation be possible in the United States? If groups of people were to withdraw from PECUSA in protest at *its* 'extreme teaching', why should they not be allowed to continue as episcopal communities under the oversight of bishops in the historic succession? The widespread acceptance of the validity of Reinkens' consecration may have shown Cummins that he did not need to persuade other bishops to join him in forming a new community.[73] One bishop was sufficient.

Aware that the hand of history was upon him, on 13 November 1873 Cummins drafted his 'Call to Organise':

> Dear Brother:- The Lord has put it into the hearts of some of His servants who are, or have been, in the Protestant Episcopal Church, the purpose of restoring the old paths of their fathers, and of returning to the use of the Prayer Book of 1785, set forth by the General Convention of that year, under the special guidance of the venerable William White, D.D., afterwards the first Bishop of the same Church in this country[74] . . . [There then follows a brief summary of the main features of the 1785 Book.] On Tuesday, the second day of December 1873, a meeting will be held in Association Hall, corner of Twenty-third Street and Fourth Avenue, at ten o'clock a.m., to organise an Episcopal Church on the basis of the Prayer Book of 1785: a basis broad enough to embrace all who hold 'the faith once delivered to the saints,' as that faith is maintained by the Reformed Churches of Christendom; with no exclusive and unchurching dogmas towards Christian brethren who differ in their views of polity and Church Order.

> This meeting you are cordially and affectionately invited to attend. The purpose of the meeting is to organise, and not to discuss the expediency of organising . . .[75]

A number of themes stand out. This is not to be a new Church – there is simply to be a restoring of old paths, a return to an earlier form of Anglicanism. The community is to be *episcopal*; there is no suggestion of exploring other polities. It is to be *liturgical*; the *lex orandi lex credendi* theme is very strong. It is to be ecumenically open. In his detailed analysis of Cummins's thinking at this time, Guelzo notes that what Cummins proposed 'was a much more complicated affair than even later Reformed Episcopalians have been inclined to admit'.[76] 'What really moved Cummins over the brink' (to use Guelzo's phrase) was not the traditional Evangelical protests against Ritualism, but

> the question of ecumenicity . . . That, together with Cummins's attachment to William Augustus Muhlenberg, links Cummins's attachment far more closely to the ambitious ecumenical interests of Muhlenberg, Stanley and Arnold than even to most of [his] fellow Evangelicals . . . In that light, Cummins was more than just a narrow-gauge Protestant reactionary.[77]

Printed copies of the Call reached the public from 18 November. Across the Protestant Episcopal Church there were broadly three reactions. There were those who rejoiced that a bishop had at last taken a stand, and prepared to join Cummins. There was, predictably, a great deal of denunciation from Anglo-Catholic quarters. More surprisingly, and most hurtful to Cummins, was the lack of support from the Evangelical bishops and clergy. Cummins had done what some of them had been advocating for a number of years. Many now dissociated themselves from him publicly; others simply kept their distance. Guelzo suggests that it may be that, in their eyes, Cummins had chosen the wrong issue on which to take a stand. They might have joined him on sacramentalism; Christian unity, however, was not a cause worth resigning over.

A fourth reaction was an official response from the American House of Bishops. In his own mind Cummins had transferred his work and office to another sphere of labour. The Protestant Episcopal Church felt it had to do something to mark Cummins's departure. A trial might well have backfired. It was decided to depose Cummins under the canonical process for dealing with one who has 'abandoned the Communion of this Church'. The problem was that the procedure required a six-month period in which the person in question could reconsider and return to the fold. During that period any ministerial acts would have to be conceded by PECUSA to be valid. Cummins's publicly declared intention 'to organise an Episcopal Church' therefore produced great alarm. The day before the Association Hall meeting the Presiding Bishop issued a proclamation declaring any episcopal act of Cummins 'null and void'. The proclamation failed in its intention. It was criticized in the press for making the Presiding Bishop 'appear at once both impotent and vindictive'.[78] It was ignored by Cummins.

The 2 December 1873 is a date equivalent in some ways to 24 June 1863. On both those days Anglican episcopal communities were formally constituted. Both, as has been shown, were the culmination of earlier movements. Both saw themselves as restoring a purer version of the English branch of the Catholic Church as reformed in the sixteenth century.

By contrast with the clergy of the Countess of Huntingdon's Connexion who had met at their annual Conference in midsummer 1863, the 1873 meeting, on a snowy, bitterly cold day, was composed of large numbers of people – clergy and lay – who had never come together before. The YMCA Hall was packed. After opening devotions Bishop Cummins read the 'Call to Organise', then Colonel Aycrigg took the chair. Cummins next introduced the Declaration of Principles which he had shared with the committee the previous evening.[79] These were committed by the meeting for review by a committee, which met in a twenty-minute break. On returning, the committee recommended a formal resolution to the meeting:

> That we whose names are appended to the call for this meeting, as presented by Bishop Cummins, do here and now, in humble reliance upon Almighty God, organize ourselves into a Church, to be known by the style and title of The Reformed Episcopal Church, in conformity with the following Declaration of Principles, and with the Right Reverend George David Cummins, D.D., as our Presiding Bishop.[80]

The resolution was passed unanimously by the clergy and laymen present and Aycrigg declared the Reformed Episcopal Church to be in existence, before yielding the chair to Cummins. In his first address as Presiding Bishop, Cummins stressed the continuity of the new community with 'our fathers' and beyond: 'we claim an unbroken historical connection through the Church of England with the Church of Christ, from the earliest Christian era'.[81] Having next spoken about the 1785 Prayer Book, Cummins went on to speak of a wider Christian union as the ultimate goal. The meeting broke into the singing of the *Gloria in excelsis*.

The rest of the meeting (which continued in the afternoon and designated itself the First General Council) was taken up with two main items of business. The first was structural organization. Various committees were formed, and the new Executive Committee charged with the task of drawing up a constitution.[82] The second was the election of one or more bishops. It is clear from the surviving accounts that Cummins wished to propose Muhlenberg himself, but Muhlenberg was not present at the meeting and in fact did not join the Reformed Episcopal Church.[83] In the event the meeting elected Charles Cheney, Cummins's former colleague from his Chicago days, and an enthusiastic supporter of the movement from the beginning.

Cheney's consecration took place at 10.00 a.m. on Sunday 14 December 1873 at Christ Church Chicago; Cummins, robed in rochet and chimere, presided, using an order of service slightly adapted from that of the Protestant Episcopal Church.[84] He preached a long sermon entitled 'Primitive Episcopacy'.[85] In it he denied the exclusivist 'pipeline' theories of episcopacy, and claimed instead to be returning to 'the true, simple Episcopacy of the Second Century, the period immediately succeeding the decease of the Apostles of our Lord'.[86] After the presentation, interrogations, litany and *Veni Creator*, Cummins laid his hands upon Cheney with the words: 'Take thou authority to exercise the office and work of a Bishop in the Church of God, now committed unto thee by the imposition of our hands; in the name of the Father and of the Son and of the Holy Ghost. Amen.'[87]

Thus was Cheney consecrated to 'a primitive episcopacy, the development of the practice and custom of the Apostles'.[88] A major step had been taken in the creation of a 'Gospel Catholicism' around which the separated Churches could unite.

Notes

1. Allen C. Guelzo, *For the Union of Evangelical Christendom* (Pennsylvania, Pennsylvania State University Press, 1994), p. 24.
2. A sense of this was brought home to the present writer when, at a Eucharist in Annapolis, Maryland, the chalice used in the administration bore the Royal Arms of William III and had been a gift from the King to the Governor of the Colony in 1696 (along with a Bible, Prayer Book and surplice). The Governor had presented them to St Anne's Church in 1704. Gifts of plate from the Crown to Royal Governors for use in their churches or private chapels were not uncommon. (I am grateful to Canon Pierce Middleton and Geoff Thomas for confirming these details.)
3. Thomas Bray (founder of the Society for Promoting Christian Knowledge (SPCK) and the Society for the Propagation of the Gospel (SPG)), for example, went to Maryland in 1699 as commissary to the Bishop of London.

4. The lack of bishops in North America was not the fault of the English bishops, some of whom even left bequests for the financial support of North American bishoprics. Throughout the eighteenth century the British Government was reluctant to act, for a variety of reasons including strenuous opposition from Dissenters in Britain and in the Colonies. Wand states that in 1722 an English Non-Juror bishop consecrated two bishops for America, but gives no source for this statement (J. W. C. Wand, *The High Church Schism* (London, The Faith Press, 1951), p. 47).

5. Mark A. Noll, *A History of Christianity in the United States and Canada* (London, SPCK, 1992), p. 150.

6. Guelzo, *For the Union*, p. 25.

7. The adjective 'Protestant' was dropped as recently as 1979.

8. Quoted in William Stephens Perry, *Historical Notes and Documents Illustrating the Organisation of the Protestant Episcopal Church in the United States of America* (Claremont, NH, Claremont Manufacturing Co., 1874), pp. 24f. This is possibly the first use of what was to become the name of the whole Anglican jurisdiction in the United States. It was clearly chosen to replace the former name of 'The Church of England'.

9. The significance of these early constitutional and doctrinal statements for the present-day Free Church of England will be discussed more fully in Chapters 9 and 10.

10. Perry, *Historical Notes*, p. 27.

11. Perry, *Historical Notes*, p. 3. Guelzo says that 9 states were represented, *For the Union*, p. 24.

12. Paul F. M. Zahl, *The Protestant Face of Anglicanism* (Grand Rapids, MI, William Eerdmans, 1998), p. 62.

13. Charles C. Tiffany, *A History of the Protestant Episcopal Church in the United States of America* (New York, Charles Scribner's Sons, 3rd edn, 1907), p. 297. White delighted in Whitefield's elocution, but was distrustful of the emotions raised in the crowd, and feared that many conversions would be short-lived. See Walter Herbert Stow (ed.), *The Life and Letters of Bishop William White* (New York, Morehouse Publishing Co., 1937), pp. 15ff.

14. Guelzo, *For the Union*, p. 27.

15. See Rack, *Reasonable Enthusiast*, pp. 506ff. and James Lewis, *Frances Asbury: Bishop of the Methodist Episcopal Church* (London, Epworth Press, 1927). The first ordinations of the Countess of Huntingdon's Connexion also took place at this time and were based on a similar understanding of New Testament texts.

16. It must also be remembered that the states were separate bodies with their own legislatures. Similarly (as White's use of the plural *Churches* in 1782 shows) the State Churches were inclined to see themselves at this stage as independent entities, not merely dioceses of a larger whole.

17. See Anglican–Nordic/Baltic Lutheran Conversations, *Together in Mission and Ministry. (The Porvoo Common Statement with Essays on Church and Ministry in Northern Europe)*, (GS 1083, hereafter cited as Porvoo Common Statement), (London, Church House Publishing, 1993), pp. 85ff.; Lars Osterlin, *Churches of Northern Europe in Profile* (Norwich, The Canterbury Press, 1995), pp. 83ff.

18. Routh (1755–1854) was later President of the College. An old-fashioned High Churchman, his patristic scholarship (and great age) made him an object of veneration to the early Tractarians.

19. Seabury to Dr Myles Cooper in Edinburgh, dated 31 August 1784; William Walker, *The Life and Times of John Skinner, Bishop of Aberdeen* (Aberdeen, Edmond & Spark, 1887), pp. 31f. See also Frederick Goldie, *A Short History of the Episcopal Church in Scotland* (Edinburgh, St Andrew Press, 1976), pp. 66f.

20. Walker, *John Skinner*, pp. 18ff.

21. Ibid., pp. 41ff.

22. Ibid., p. 30.

23. See Chapter 9.

24. See Marion J. Hatchett, *The Making of the First American Book of Common Prayer* (New York, Seabury Press, 1982), for a detailed account of the process.

25. Ibid., *op.cit.* p. 56.

26. Ibid., p. 76.

27. Ibid., p. 56.

28. For a full examination see Timothy J. Fawcett, *The Liturgy of Comprehension 1689: An abortive attempt to revise the Book of Common Prayer* (Alcuin Club Collection 54, Southend-on-Sea, Mayhew–McCrimmon, 1973).

29. Lambeth MS 2173.

30. Fawcett, *Comprehension*, p. 46. The aims of the 1689 Book have always been attractive to the Free Church of England tradition.

31. Hatchett, *The Making*, p. 85. For a summary of eighteenth-century Church of England suggestions for revising the Prayer Book, see R. C. D. Jasper, *Prayer Book Revision in England 1800–1900* (London, SPCK, 1954), pp. 1–5.

32. Quoted in ibid., p. 93.

33. At this Convention it consisted only of White and Seabury, as Provoost was ill. White yielded the presidency to Seabury on the grounds of seniority of consecration.

34. Quoted in Hatchett, *The Making*, p. 111.

35. Ibid. Hatchett makes is clear that a number of prominent people favoured the Scottish structure. Seabury alone does not have the credit for its acceptance.

36. Ibid., p. 124.

37. The English bishops had also begun to make episcopal provision for loyalist Anglicans in North America. On 12 August 1787 they had consecrated Charles

Inglis, who had fled from his New York parish to Canada at the Revolution, as Bishop of Nova Scotia.

38. Noll, *History*, p. 92.

39. Zahl, *Protestant Face*, p. 61.

40. The story is told in some detail in Guelzo, *For the Union*, pp. 32ff. and Zahl, *Protestant Face*, pp. 62ff. and the sources cited there.

41. Guelzo, *For the Union*, pp. 42f. Zahl adds Massachusetts, Pennsylvania and Rhode Island to the list of Evangelical dioceses created by 1850; *Protestant Face*, p. 65.

42. The eminent English liturgist, Ronald Jasper, called Muhlenberg 'saintly' and 'an outstanding figure and a conciliating influence'. R. C. D. Jasper, *The Development of the Anglican Liturgy 1662–1980* (London, SPCK, 1989), p. 66.

43. Guelzo, *For the Union*, p. 62.

44. Quoted in Anne Ayres, *The Life and Work of William Augustus Muhlenberg, DD* (New York, Thomas Whittaker, 1894), p. 238.

45. Ibid., p. 242.

46. Ibid., p. 240.

47. New York, Protestant Episcopal Press, 1836.

48. The full text of the Memorial, together with a wide range of documentation and the official response, can be found in Alonzo Potter (ed.), *Memorial Papers: The Memorial, with Circular and Questions of the Episcopal Committee* (Philadelphia, E. Butler & Co., 1857).

49. Text in Ayres, *Life and Work*, p. 266.

50. Ibid., p. 265.

51. Ibid.

52. Ibid., p. 267.

53. See Edward Carpenter, *Archbishop Fisher – His Life and Times* (Norwich, The Canterbury Press, 1991), pp. 309ff. for a full discussion of the context and reactions. Fisher's invitation to the Free Churches did not require them to surrender their denominational identity as a precondition for receiving the historic episcopate. The 'loosening up' envisaged in the second clause has been to some degree effected in England by the provisions of the Ecumenical Relations Measure and the Church of England's Ecumenical Canons. The request for stronger ecumenical ties has been met in Britain in a variety of ways over the twentieth century, culminating currently in the ecumenical 'Instruments' Churches Together in Britain and Ireland, and Churches Together in England.

54. Guelzo, *For the Union*, p. 64.

55. For example, *What the Memorialists Want: A Letter to the Rt Rev Bishop Otley, Chairman of the Commission* (New York, R. Craighead, 1854).

56. 'An Exposition of the Memorial' (November 1854), in Anne Ayres (ed.),

Evangelical Catholic Papers: A Collection of Essays, Letters and Tractates from the Writings of Rev. William Augustus Muhlenberg (New York, Thomas Whittaker, 1875), pp. 140f.

57. It is likely that other attempts to define an ecumenical consensus also influenced Cummins. See Chapter 10.

58. Guelzo, *For the Union*, p. 156f.

59. Ibid., p. 90.

60. Ibid. Guelzo suggests that the split within the Methodist Episcopal Church over the issue of slavery might have been a contributory factor to his decision to return to the Church of his birth.

61. Ibid., p. 106.

62. The text can be found reproduced in Vaughan, *History* (2nd and 3rd edns) pp. 157–70.

63. Quoted in Vaughan, *History*, p. 158.

64. Quoted in a letter to Cheney in 1875, reproduced as an Appendix in Vaughan, *History* (1st edn) pp. 176–86. This quotation is from p. 178.

65. Ibid., p. 181.

66. Ibid., pp. 182f.

67. Ibid.

68. Quoted in Guelzo, *For the Union*, p. 127.

69. Ibid., p. 133.

70. Quoted in Ayres, *Life and Work*, p. 458.

71. Full text in Vaughan, *History*, (1st edn), pp. 44–47.

72. See Charles Long (ed.), *Who are the Anglicans?* (Cincinnati, Forward Movement Publications, 1988), p. 63, and the Anglican Communion website.

73. Like many others at the time, the 1878 Lambeth Conference saw great hope in the secessions from the Roman Catholic Church: 'The fact that a solemn protest is raised in so many Churches and Christian communities throughout the world against the usurpations of the See of Rome, and against the novel doctrines promulgated by its authority, is a subject of thankfulness to Almighty God'; *The Five Lambeth Conferences* (London, SPCK, 1920), p. 94. By 1888 the next Lambeth Conference was explicit in it hopes for Bishop Reinkens and his people: 'For ourselves we regard it as a duty to promote friendly relations with the Old Catholics of Germany . . . in thankfulness to God, who has strengthened them to suffer for the truth . . .' (ibid., p. 163).

74. Cummins ignores Seabury. He also seems to have been rather naive about White's theology, confusing his Low Church Latitudinarianism with Evangelicalism.

75. Vaughan, *History* (1st edn), pp. 49f.

76. Guelzo, *For the Union*, p. 149.

77. Ibid. Arthur Stanley had been made Dean of Westminster in 1863 and had

horrified Anglo-Catholics by inviting the team of scholars working on the Revised Standard Version of the Bible – including Methodists, Baptists, Congregationalists and Presbyterians – to a joint Communion service in the Abbey in 1870. Thomas Arnold, Headmaster of Rugby, argued for the inclusion of Dissenters in a revivified National Church.

78. Ibid., p. 155.
79. See Chapter 10 for a detailed commentary on the Declaration of Principles.
80. Quoted in Vaughan, *History*, (1st edn), p. 60.
81. Quoted in Guelzo, *For the Union*, p. 159.
82. See Chapter 9.
83. This must have deeply disappointed Cummins. Muhlenberg himself was to state: 'I have always maintained that [Cummins's grievances] could have been relieved by another than the sad alternative which he has adopted.' Quoted in Ayres, *Life and Work*, p. 460.
84. There was no Ordinal in the 1785 Prayer Book. See Chapters 11 and 12 for details of the changes.
85. The text is reproduced in Vaughan, *History*, (1st edn), pp. 132–58. It must have taken over an hour to deliver.
86. Ibid., p. 142. At times Cummins seems to echo the 'free, valid and purely ecclesiastical episcopacy' phrase used by Seabury.
87. Quoted in H. Bower, *The Orders of the Reformed Episcopal Church Examined* (Malvern, The Advertiser Office, 1884), p. 34.
88. The words are from Cummins's sermon; Vaughan, *History*, p. 155. It is not relevant to trace the further history of the Reformed Episcopal Church in any detail. Cummins consecrated one further bishop, William Rufus Nicholson, on 24 February 1876. At this consecration he was assisted by Cheney and Bishop Matthew Simpson of the Methodist Episcopal Church, whom Cummins invited as proof of his ecumenical commitment, rejoicing that 'No such scene has been witnessed for centuries in the Episcopal Church' (quoted in Guelzo, *For the Union*, p. 212. Simpson's involvement (and that of his fellow Methodist bishop, Carman, who participated in Cridge's consecration (see below) interestingly united the succession derived from John Wesley's consecration of Coke with that derived from Wesley's contemporary, John Moore, Archbishop of Canterbury. Today the Reformed Episcopal Church has about a dozen bishops, one of whom acts as Presiding Bishop in addition to his diocesan responsibilities. See the Church's website: *www.recus.org*

CHAPTER 5

Transatlantic Union and the Historic Episcopate 1873–1877

Just three days after the consecration of Cheney, contact was established between the Free Church of England and the Reformed Episcopal Church. On 17 December 1873 Merryweather wrote to Bishop Cummins. Merryweather had read of the New York meeting of the 2 December 'from a short newspaper report'[1] and had concluded that 'the ground you desire to take is exactly the ground we occupy'.[2] These providential events, Merryweather suggested to Cummins, 'may be the means for effecting a powerful Protestant Union for the maintenance of Evangelical Church Principles in both Countries'.[3] He sent a collection of documents describing the principles and work of the Free Church of England.

Two days later the other great contender for the Free Church of England, Thomas Thoresby, also wrote to Bishop Cummins. Thoresby paid tribute to the new movement as preserving the principles of the original founders of the Episcopal Church in America. 'Your platform and ours are *nearly* identical,' he continued. 'We offer you the right hand of fraternal salutation. We are willing to take counsel together and to cooperate on the grounds of perfect equality, in pursuit of the great object for which we ecclesiastically exist.'[4] Thoresby, too, sent documents to Cummins, including the Prayer Book then in use.

Merryweather and Thoresby had written in a private capacity. Official contact did not commence until 10 February when the Council of the Free Church of England, at its quarterly meeting, asked Price as Bishop Primus to write on its behalf. The Council, too, believed that a union between the two Churches was the desirable way forward. Price seems to have been a little more cautious. His official letter was not written until a month later (10 March) and does not itself mention the possibility of union. In it Price states that he and others had some inkling of developments in the United States, 'but I was not prepared for the bold course which, by God's grace you have been able to take'.[5]

Despite the caution of Price and others, events moved swiftly. The Secretary of the Executive Committee of the Reformed Episcopal Church, the Revd Marshall Smith, replied to Bishop Price on 2 April 1874, stating that the committee unanimously approved of union, and that resolutions to effect it were being drawn up. At the second General Council of the Reformed Episcopal Church a plan of union was proposed by Marshall Smith and adopted, the decision being telegraphed to England on 23 May 1874.[6]

The scheme was actually a 'Federal Union', the differences between the constitutions of the two Churches, legally registered in two different countries, making what Vaughan calls 'organic union'[7] not possible. The proposals agreed in America were subsequently accepted by the Convocation of the Free Church of England on Tuesday 23 June 1874 at Spa Fields, and signed on 17 November that year. The terms of the Federal Union were:

1. Delegates might be sent to each other's Convocation or General Council;
2. In consecrations of bishops and ordination of ministers, bishops and ministers of each Church should be entitled to participate;
3. The clergy of each Church would be eligible to minister, temporarily or long term, in the other;
4. Communicants of each Church could be received by the other, on letters of dismissal;
5. Congregations of either Church might transfer their connection to the other on agreed terms;
6. The two Churches pledged each other their mutual co-operation, sympathy and support.[8]

At this distance in time, the articles are a little puzzling. Why, in particular, was it felt necessary to make provision for congregations to transfer from one Church to the other, particularly when the two bodies did not exist on each other's side of the Atlantic? The surviving sources do not seem to shed any light on this, nor does it seem to have been a major consideration at the time. Colonel Benjamin Aycrigg, a leading layman of the Reformed Episcopal Church greeted the union: 'This practically makes the two bodies one.'[9] And from the English side things were buoyant: 'the decisions of the FCE were being made from the standpoint of success, for it was in fact gaining members and building more churches each year'.[10]

The next few years were to be critical in the history of the Free Church of England. For all its Anglican roots and aspirations, it had developed for eighty years outside the Established Church in an atmosphere of English (and Welsh) Nonconformity. Its constitution explicitly spoke of Congregational and Presbyterian elements. Many of its ministers were not episcopally ordained. By contrast, the Reformed Episcopal Church seemed to have sprung into existence 'ready-made' with a bishop in the historic succession, a ministry composed entirely of episcopally ordained men, all organized according to a constitution and body of canons. for many in the Free Church of England (a good number of whose members still held dual membership in the Connexion) the American model was exactly what they had longed for. For others, it has to be admitted, a traditionally organized episcopal Church was *not* their vision.

Richard Fenwick traces carefully the tensions and trends of this time.[11] What is clear is the desire of some leading figures that the Free Church of England should be remodelled on the Reformed Episcopal Church pattern: 'Again and again it is seen that the theological and canonical boundaries of the FCE were to be extended *to match what Thoresby and others evidently considered a stronger system* . . . it might well be necessary to go *beyond* the confines of the Poll Deed.'[12] Thoresby's involvement is significant. It was he, after all, who had laboured for 14 years to produce the Consititution enshrined in the Deed Poll. It seems, however, that he saw in the Reformed Episcopal Church a better model than that which he had himself created.

A central area where some 'remodelling' was felt to be needed was the ministry. A series of articles in the *Free Church of England Magazine*, while continuing to attack sacerdotal pretensions, pointed out that the Free Church of England 'has established the principle by the election of its President Bishop, but left the further development of the Episcopate until the organisation of the church had become more complete'.[13] Thoresby himself wrote articles on 'Orders in the Free Church of

England' in which he argued that, while appointment to a particular 'district or diocese' might be elective or temporary, the candidate, once ordained, 'does not need re-ordination'.[14] This is moving towards a concept of the indelibility of orders – once a bishop, always a bishop – theologically undergirding what was by this time true in practice in the Free Church of England, for Benjamin Price had been repeatedly re-elected Bishop Primus since 1866.

It was not just the episcopate that was being reviewed. The diaconate in the Free Church of England, which had been a 'portmanteau' of lay ministries, was modified by the proposal that 'FCE deacons might take part in preaching and evangelising by special licence, and that a special service might be used for that purpose'[15] – in other words, that they be ordained to a litugically based ministry of outreach.

Despite misgivings in some quarters, the Free Church of England did indeed change its constitution. At a meeting of the Council at Westminster on 13 April 1875 the resolution was passed that 'the Constitutions and Canons of the Reformed Episcopal Church of America be recommended to Convocation for adoption as the bye-laws of the Free Church of England'.[16] The proposer and seconder were Thoresby and Merryweather, both rooted in the Countess of Huntingdon's Connexion. The April resolution was accepted almost unanimously at the Quarterly Meeting of Council, held on 11 May 1875 at Spa Fields. The modifications regarding the ministry were further reinforced in a 'Declaration Explanatory of the Constitution of the Free Church of England' issued by authority of Convocation following its June 1876 meeting. In relation to the diaconate it was stated that: 'The title of Deacon shall include licensed Evangelists and Probationers for the office of Presbyter; and such Probationers may be made Deacons of the Church according to the form set forth in the Second General Council of the Reformed Episcopal Church.'[17] Deacons were now, in effect, a distinct order. So, too, were bishops: 'For the due and solemn setting apart or consecration of Presbyters to the office of Bishop, the Free Church of England adopts the form used in the Consecration of Bishops, as revised and set forth by the Second General Council of the Reformed Episcopal Church.'[18] There was now an ordination service for each of the three traditional orders of catholic Christianity – deacons, presbyters and bishops. Furthermore, it was reported in the March edition of the *Magazine* that at the February Council meeting it had been agreed that at future Free Church of England consecrations, 'a consecrated Bishop or Bishops, and three or more Presbyters be invited to conduct the ceremony of Consecration'.[19]

The purpose of the modifications to the Free Church of England was twofold. First, to reconstitute it as a traditionally organized episcopal Church within the Anglican heritage; and secondly, to enable the Free Church of England to receive the historic episcopate from its federative partner.

This second goal had been envisaged by some within the Free Church of England ever since they heard of the existence of the Reformed Episcopal Church. The Honorary Secretary, J. R. Lumley, wrote in the June 1874 *Magazine* of how not just the Free Church of England, but all English Nonconformists would find their position transformed by receiving the historic episcopate from Cummins and Cheney:

> This would give the Nonconformists a status, which could not be denied by the haughtiest and stiffest of our Anglican Prelates. The Wesleyans, the Presbyterians, and others would all have an Apostolic Succession, which Anglicans, upon their own principles, must admit to be as valid as that of . . . the Archbishop of Canterbury.[20]

Such a scenario bears remarkable parallels to the extension of the episcopal system envisaged by Muhlenberg. All sorts of new possibilities were being raised. The April 1875 *Magazine* contained the quotation: 'A Ritualist clergyman was known to say that the Ritualists dreaded the Free Church of England, but if ever their Bishops received consecration through Bishop Cummins they would dread it still more.'[21]

From around the country the pressure was growing for the acquisition of the historic succession from the Reformed Episcopal Church. The Eastern District of the Free Church of England in its report to the quarterly meeting of Council on 11 May 1875 wished 'to impress upon the Council the importance of active steps . . . to secure the consecration – through the American bishop or other recognised Protestant Episcopalians – of bishops into the Free Church of England'.[22] The minutes further report that 'until late in the evening . . . the council were discussing the matter of the Constitutions, but especially the general desire existing for a more pronounced Episcopacy . . .'.[23] A year later the Northern District was urging the amending of the Deed Poll to make the diaconal and episcopal elements more distinct.[24] Despite considerable unease in some quarters, the tide was generally running strongly in favour of receiving the historic succession from the American partner Church.

The hope all along had been that Bishop Cummins himself would come to England, but Cummins was in poor health and died suddenly on 26 June 1876. The following day Convocation, meeting in England, agreed the Declarations Explanatory referred to above and instructed Council to make the necessary preparations for the visit of a bishop of the Reformed Episcopal Church.

The Consecrations of 1876

The bishop who was to come was Edward Cridge. Cridge was an Englishman, born in Bratton Fleming in Devon in 1817 and educated at Cambridge University. Ordained in 1848 he went out to the Canadian Pacific Coast in 1854, starting as a chaplain to the Hudson Bay Company post in Victoria and minister of the District Church there. Following the creation of the Diocese of British Columbia in 1860, the District Church was elevated to cathedral status, with Cridge as Dean. Although described as 'gracious and self-effacing to a fault',[25] Cridge took a stand in 1872 against Ritualist practices being introduced with the support of his bishop. Approximately three-quarters of the congregation supported Cridge and, after an acrimonious dispute with the Bishop, they and Cridge formed a new congregation, protesting that it was the Bishop and not they who were seceding from Anglicanism. In November 1874 Cridge learned of the Reformed Episcopal Church, which was already establishing congregations in eastern Canada. He and his congregation were gladly received by Cummins. At the Third General Council of the Reformed Episcopal Church in May 1875 Cridge was elected a Missionary Bishop for Canada.[26] He was consecrated on 17 July 1876 in Emmanuel Church, Ottawa by Bishop Charles Cheney, the newly elected Presiding Bishop (following the sudden death of Cummins just three weeks earlier) assisted by Bishops Nicholson (the second bishop consecrated by Cummins) and Carman (of the Methodist Episcopal Church). The General Council then authorized him to travel to England with the express intention of taking part in episcopal consecrations there. Cridge sailed from Quebec on 22 July on the *Moravian*, reaching Liverpool on 1 August.

Two weeks later the Convocation of the Free Church of England assembled at Christ Church, Teddington (the first time it had not met at Spa Fields) with Bishop Cridge present. The main business was to prepare for the consecrations that were to take place. On 15 August John Sugden, the Minister of Teddington, was elected and commended to Convocation for consecration as bishop. Sugden was a native of Kingstown (Dun Laoghaire) in Ireland. Following graduation from the University of London he had trained for the Bar, but on conversion instead spent many years as a missionary in India. He had gone as minister to Teddington in 1865.

For Cridge to consecrate Sugden would be straightforward, but would raise an anomaly: what would then be the status of Benjamin Price? Price had been functioning as Bishop Primus for ten years, but did not of course stand in the historic succession. This question had obviously exercised many minds, not least that of Price himself. Faced with the opportunity of acquiring what 'in the estimation of the Ritualists themselves, would be considered a *valid Ministry* . . . I was pressed on all hands to avail myself of it', he was later to write.[27] Price was a man of integrity. Simply to allow himself to be consecrated would not only appear to invalidate all the 'episcopal' acts (dedication of churches, ordinations, etc.) that he had hitherto performed, but would look like a 'sell out' to the doctrine of Apostolic Succession which, in its Tractarian interpretation, the Free Church of England had fought against for decades. Price needed biblical and theological justification for such a step. He found it. However imprecise the New Testament might be on some aspects of ministry, what *was* clear was that laying on of hands with prayer was a normal way of signifying the Christian community's setting aside of a person for a particular ministry, and of seeking God's blessing and empowering for that ministry. Price had merely been *elected* Bishop Primus, there had been no laying on of hands and prayer:

> This had been either neglected or overlooked in my case at my appointment . . . I felt therefore it was open to me, if it was thought desirable, to supply the omission by a renewed dedication to the office, on the occasion of a visit of a Bishop of the Reformed Episcopal Church . . . and thereby perhaps strengthen our movement.[28]

Price had therefore written to Bishop Cridge as soon as the latter had reached London. He explained the dilemma and suggested some slight modifications to the Consecration Service which might solve it. These were that in the Litany, into the petition 'that he may duly execute the office . . .' be inserted the words 'as in the past so in the future'; and that at the laying on of hands instead of '*Take* thou authority . . .' be substituted 'We confirm the authority to execute the office and work of a Bishop in the Church of God, committed unto thee . . .'.[29] Cridge's reply reveals that the problem had indeed occurred to him and to others in North America and states that he most readily concurred with Price's suggestions.

This issue having been amicably solved, Convocation, on the same day that it elected John Sugden, resolved that 'a special Consecration Service for Bishop Price (confirming all his episcopal and ministerial acts, in the past) be held this evening before the Ordination of Deacons'.[30] That Tuesday evening at 6.30 p.m. in Christ Church, Teddington, Benjamin Price was presented to Bishop Cridge by the Revds Thomas Dodd and Thomas Thoresby and, in Price's words, 'I was therefore duly and canonically consecrated Bishop of the Free Church of England.'[31] Also during the service, which took place in the context of Holy Communion, one man was ordained presbyter and five were ordained deacons.

The following Sunday afternoon, at 3.00 p.m. on 20 August at Christ Church, Westminster Bridge Road, Lambeth, John Sugden was 'solemnly consecrated to the Episcopal office' using the ordinal of the Reformed Episcopal Church.[32] The sermon was preached by Thoresby, who then, together with Alfred Richardson, formally presented Sugden to Bishops Cridge and Price. Merryweather, as Registrar, read the Testimonials. After the Litany, prayers and interrogations, the *Veni Creator Spiritus* was sung. ('It will be long before we forget the singing of *Veni Creator* at Christ Church Lambeth.'[33]) Cridge, assisted by Price and several presbyters, consecrated him 'a Bishop in the Church of God in the Free Church of England'.[34] Thus 'the solemn act was accomplished'. A congregation of several hundred then 'partook of the Lord's Supper'.[35] Within a mile of Lambeth Palace Chapel, where Archbishop Moore and his companions had consecrated White and Provoost, the succession inaugurated in 1787 had returned to England.[36]

Reaction to the consecrations was predictable. The editor of the denomination's *Magazine* enthused that these events 'mark, we verily believe, the commencement of a new era in the life of the Free Church of England'.[37] 'The Ritualistic papers', wrote Price, 'were furious in their denunciations and sought to repudiate the Orders thus conferred, but . . . our Orders were proved to be not only valid in historical grounds, but likewise from a strictly Church point of view, such as even High Churchmen themselves could but acknowledge.' Price's satisfaction is evident in his conclusion: 'Evidence was overwhelming that the Orders of the Free Church of England were equal to those of the Established Church of England as both derive from the same source – the See of Canterbury.'[38]

Everything was done to make the record of the consecrations as secure as possible.[39] Although Letters of Orders are not usually given to bishops, Cridge nevertheless drew up Deeds of Consecration which traced the Reformed Episcopal Church's episcopate to the consecrations of White, Provoost and Maddison by the Archbishop of Canterbury 'by which solemn acts of consecration the Protestant Episcopal Church in the United States of America became possessed of the same Episcopal succession as the United Church of England and Ireland'; Price's Deed concludes:

> NOW WE, Edward Cridge, by the grace of God, Bishop of the Reformed Episcopal Church, administering consecration, by the assistance of Almighty God, on Tuesday, the Fifteenth day of August in the year of our Lord 1876, at Christ Church, Teddington, in the County of Middlesex, did rightly and canonically consecrate our beloved Brother in Christ, Benjamin Price (Minister of Christ Church, Ilfracombe in the County of Devon) to the office of Bishop in the Free Church of England, according to the form and manner duly prescribed by the convocation of the said Church.[40]

'Thus,' wrote Vaughan in his official history, after recounting the events at Teddington and Lambeth, 'the ancient British Episcopate, whatever its content and meaning may be, was received by the youngest daughter in the family of Episcopal Churches . . .'[41]

The dreams of many sincere Churchmen and women had come true. Years of preparation had gone into bringing into being a Christian community characterized by its allegiance to the historic heritage of English Christianity, and now that community was headed by a bishop indisputably in historic succession from the See of Canterbury – from the throne of St Augustine himself. There was now, on the very doorstep of a greatly troubled and changed Church of England, a true alternative, a Church that held to all that was good in the Mother Church, but with a purified ministry and Prayer Book. Surely the faithful of England would now rally around her.

Seldom can such high hopes have remained so cruelly unfulfilled.

THE FREE CHURCH OF ENGLAND

Notes

1. Letter quoted in Vaughan, *History*, (1st edn), pp. 66f.
2. Ibid.
3. Ibid.
4. Ibid., p. 68.
5. Quoted in ibid., p. 69.
6. See Fenwick, *Thesis*, p. 112. The first General Council had been the inaugural meeting on 2 December 1873.
7. Vaughan, *History*, (1st edn), p. 70.
8. Quoted in ibid.
9. Benjamin Aycrigg, *Memoirs of the Reformed Episcopal Church* (New York, 1878), p. 44.
10. Fenwick, *Thesis*, p. 113.
11. Fenwick, *Thesis*, pp. 113–21.
12. Ibid., p. 117. Italics in the original.
13. *FCE Magazine*, February 1874, p. 31.
14. Ibid., January 1875, p. 4.
15. Ibid., May 1875, p. 85.
16. Ibid., pp. 83f.
17. Quoted in Price, *Organisation of the Free Church*, p. 15.
18. Ibid. This particular proposal had been passed by the Council meeting on 8 February 1876.
19. *FCE Magazine*, March 1876, p. 49.
20. Ibid., June 1874, p. 116.
21. Ibid., April 1875, pp. 66f.
22. Reported in ibid., June 1875, pp. 108f.
23. Ibid.
24. Fenwick, *Thesis*, p. 120.
25. Guelzo, *For the Union*, p. 213.
26. The term was widely used before the creation of a diocesan structure.
27. Price, *Organisation of the Free Church*, pp. 29f.
28. Ibid. The 1863 Deed Poll made provision for the choosing of a bishop, but said nothing about prayer and the laying on of hands or any other form of commissioning.
29. Ibid. The full text of Price's letter and Cridge's reply may be found here.
30. *FCE Magazine*, September 1876, p. 162.
31. Price, *Organisation of the Free Church*, pp. 31f. Rather surprisingly, Price speaks of his consecration in absolute, rather than confirmatory terms.
32. The occasion is described in *FCE Magazine*, September 1876, p. 172.
33. Ibid.

34. Price, *Organisation of the Free Church*, p. 31. The phrase is used to this day: a man is consecrated a bishop in the Church of God, *in* or *for* the Free Church of England. It is interesting that Price, despite his Calvinistic Methodist background, deliberately uses a form of words indicative of the catholicity of the episcopate. It is probable that Cridge rather than Price presided at Sugden's consecration to ensure that no objections could be raised to it on the grounds of the modifications used in Price's own case.

35. *FCE Magazine*, September 1876, p. 172.

36. It is possible that the choice of venue was influenced by precisely this consideration. Teddington (Sugden's church) was the more obvious choice. Convocation was meeting there and Price's own laying on of hands had taken place there just a few days earlier. Why move the entire Convocation for Sugden's consecration? It is difficult to avoid the conclusion that the symbolism of holding the first unambiguous consecration at *Lambeth* had proved irresistible. The succession which had left England *from* Lambeth was now pointedly returning to England *at* Lambeth. There seems to be something of a challenge to the Archbishop and Established Church implicit in the venue.

37. *FCE Magazine*, September 1876, p. 161.

38. Price, *Organisation of the Free Church*, p. 32. See Chapter 12 below for a fuller discussion of FCE Orders.

39. There is an interesting parallel with Matthew Parker who ensured that his own consecration as Archbishop of Canterbury in December 1559 was meticulously documented. See V. J. K. Brook, *A Life of Archbishop Parker* (Oxford, Clarendon Press, 1962), pp. 84ff.

40. The full text is in Price, *Organisation of the Free Church*, pp. 32f.

41. Vaughan, *History* (1st edn), p. 72. Cridge sailed for New York on 31st August, where he reported to the Standing Committee of the Reformed Episcopal Church. He continued to minister as bishop in Canada until his death in 1913. A number of organizations which he helped to found continue to the present day.

CHAPTER 6

Division, Subdivision and Confusion 1877–*c.*1893

It is perhaps the greatest tragedy in the life of the young episcopal Church that, at the very time when it was poised to offer a home to many who felt alienated in their parish churches, it descended instead into a series of fragmentations. By the time these were healed the focus of religious concern had to a large extent moved on, and the Free Church of England had, in human terms, 'missed the tide'.

The events were extremely complex and it is impossible to recount them in detail here.[1] All that can be done is to show the main trends, with a greater focus on certain critical events.

Separation from the Countess of Huntingdon's Connexion

'The most significant result of the consecrations,' concluded Fenwick, 'was the fact that it made the progress of break-up in the federative relationship with the Connexion irreversible.'[2] By accepting (indeed, welcoming) the historic succession the Free Church of England had chosen a different ecclesiology from the Connexion which had brought it into existence. It was a difficult time for all concerned. There were many who argued that the fault lay, not with the Free Church of England for moving in an increasingly Anglican direction, but with the Connexion for drifting inexorably away from its own Anglican identity and towards Congregationalism. The strain was particularly great on those whose roots were deep in the Connexion. Thoresby himself, architect of the original constitution of the Free Church of England, resigned at one stage, but was persuaded to reconsider and in fact, as has been seen, presented Price and Sugden to Bishop Cridge for consecration. His latter years were, sadly, marred by a bitter and public correspondence denouncing the direction that the movement had taken. Thoresby lived until 7 March 1883, dying at Spa Fields Parsonage (where Lady Huntingdon had also died). With him died one of the strongest links between the Free Church of England and its parent denomination. Despite the later difficulties, the *Free Church of England Magazine* carried a substantial tribute to him.[3]

Both parties were the poorer for the separation. The Connexion lost an opportunity to expand its work and continued to decline, having just 24 chapels in 2001.[4] The Free Church of England lost sight of its heritage of revival and evangelism, becoming substantially *negative* and anti-Tractarian.

For another half-century several attempts were made to unite the Connexion and the Free Church of England, particularly in the early 1880s, following the establishing of the Reformed Episcopal Church in Britain (see below) but the differences were now too great and no progress was made. The nature of the ministry, and particularly of the episcopal office continued to be a major area of disagreement. With the deaths over time of the generation of clergy who had been committed to *both* the Connexion *and* the Free Church of England the ties inevitably loosened rapidly. The Connexion increasingly shed its Anglican identity and was to become in effect a Congregationalist Connexion.[5] After 1875 Conference and Convocation never met together again. In the event, though, the final separation did not take place until the second decade of the twentieth century.

The Establishment of the Reformed Episcopal Church in the United Kingdom

It is important to remember that, at the end of 1876 the Free Church of England as an organized body with its own consititution had only been in existence for 13 years. It was now composed in the main of congregations that had left the Church of England (with a few remaining of Connexional origin). Although there was a common theme to their reasons for leaving – a refusal to accept Ritualism – there were neverthe-less many different local factors which affected expectations. The clergy of the Free Church of England were drawn from various sources – the Connexion, the Church of England and from Nonconformity. The body was simply too young and too heterogeneous to have a single settled iden-tity. There was inevitably a tendency to polarization. To oversimplify, there were those who *loved* the Church of England, grieved over what she had become, and sought to perpetuate her in an unsullied form in the Free Church of England. Then there were those who *hated* the Church of England and for whom the Free Church of England was a credible base from which to attack her and her perceived corruptions. The former group was, naturally, deeply committed to an Anglican style and polity. The latter group 'sat light' to such things and saw Nonconformity as the natural ally of the Free Church of England.

These tensions were to plunge the small Church into the most chaotic years of its existence, and finally tear it apart.

What is surprising is just how soon after the 1876 consecrations it had become clear to some members of the Free Church of England that, even with the historic episcopate, the denomination did not fulfil their vision. It was still *semi*-Anglican. The Reformed Episcopal Church, on the other hand, was *pure* Anglican – coming directly out of Anglicanism, complete with bishops, clergy, Prayer Book, constitution, canons and an Anglican 'mindset', it seemed just what they were looking for. It was only natural that they should gravitate towards it.

So, at the Quarterly Meeting of the Free Church of England Council on 13 February 1877, the Revd Philip Norton formally proposed a motion for 'the establishment of a distinct branch of the Reformed Episcopal Church' in the United Kingdom. The motion was lost. Also lost was a motion by the Revd Philip Eldridge to alter the title of the denomination.[6] This setback seems to have spurred the 'episcopal party' into action. Presumably despairing of the Free Church of England moving fast enough in what they considered to be the right direction, a number of people, as private individuals, in April 1877 petitioned the Reformed Episcopal Church in North America[7] to establish a branch in the United Kingdom. The petition was signed by a number of prominent people, including the peer Lord Ebury who, although never a member of the Free Church of England, was nevertheless prominent in the Protestant cause (and in particular that of Prayer Book reform) in the latter part of the nineteenth century.[8] The petition went so far as to recommend a candidate for consecration as bishop to lead this new venture. The name suggested was that of Thomas Huband Gregg.

Fenwick devotes many pages to the character and activities of Gregg, whose legacy can still be found in the Free Church of England today. A brief summary must suffice here. Huband Gregg was born in 1840 at Ballymahon in County Longford, Ireland. His father was the Rector of Ardargh in the Church of Ireland. After graduating from Trinity College, Dublin, he was ordained in 1863 in the Diocese of Salisbury in England. From 1869 to 1877 he was Rector of Harborne near Birmingham (then in the Diocese of Lichfield). Fenwick describes Gregg as 'strange, complex and brilliant',[9] with the restlessness that often goes with such a character. Alongside his parish work he studied for and obtained qualifications in medicine and surgery. He also gained a doctorate in Divinity. As well as a plethora of theological tracts, he wrote treatises on the climate of New Zealand and how to look after babies. Gregg was also very ambitious. He seems to have started to attend Free Church of England functions in 1876 and finally resigned his Church of England parish in May 1877. He clearly made a strong impression on those members of the Free Church of England and their associates who were now petitioning the Reformed Episcopal Church across the Atlantic.

At this distance in time, it seems amazing that, despite its existing federative union with the Free Church of England, the Fifth General Council of the Reformed Episcopal Church, meeting from 9 to 15 May 1877 in Philadelphia, agreed to form a branch in the United Kingdom. Even more surprisingly, they elected Gregg (who was not present) to be its bishop. Guelzo suggests that the actions are explicable in view of the fact that the Reformed Episcopal Church was beginning to pick up strong anti-American feelings from prominent members of the Free Church of England, whose Treasurer is said to have declared at a Council meeting that, 'we were not going to have an American Church brought over here'.[10] On the other side of the Atlantic there were certainly those who had always had doubts about the true Anglican nature and intention of the Free Church of England.

Whatever the reasons, the decision was made and Gregg was informed of his election by telegram. He immediately set sail for America, arriving in New York on 19 June. The following day at the First Reformed Episcopal Church on the corner of Madison Avenue and 55th Street, New

York, he was consecrated by Presiding Bishop Samuel Fallows, assisted by Bishops Charles Cheney and Rufus Nicholson. Three days later Bishop Gregg, accompanied by Fallows, embarked for England again.

The Free Church of England had obviously got wind of things for its Convocation, meeting on 26 June 1877 expressed its unhappiness at the idea of the Reformed Episcopal Church establishing itself in Britain as it 'deeply deplores even an appearance of division and rivalry'.[11] Fenwick sees Fallows's accompanying of Gregg to England as an olive branch by the Reformed Episcopal Church following its recent actions.[12] Fallows certainly held meetings with members of the Free Church of England, but nothing came of them and he sailed back to the United States on 18 August. The federative union between the American and British Churches was in effect at an end.

The next six months saw a substantial realignment of congregations and clergy. About nine clergy and the same number of congregations transferred from the Free Church of England to the British jurisdiction of the Reformed Episcopal Church. The process had already begun in June 1877 with Gregg's church at Southend leading the way. By the end of the year most of the decisions had been made and the new Church which had been created by vote of the General Council in May was a reality. The most prominent transfer was Bishop John Sugden who, just twelve months before, had been consecrated as Price's assistant. He was now assistant bishop to Huband Gregg.

The Free Church of England had split. The Reformed Episcopal Church had not been created *alongside* it, but from *within* it, with the more Anglican-orientated clergy and congregations transferring to the new body.

There was, understandably, a great deal of sorrow and bitterness, not least because some building projects which had begun under the auspices of the Free Church of England transferred to the Reformed Episcopal Church. For a brief moment the idea of joint membership seems to have been explored, along the lines of the precedent set between the Free Church of England and the Countess of Huntingdon's Connexion, but it was soon abandoned. By the end of 1877 there were *two* small episcopal Churches in Britain: the Free Church of England presided over by Bishop Benjamin Price, and the Reformed Episcopal Church presided over by Bishop Gregg, with John Sugden as Assistant Bishop.

The first General Synod[13] of the Reformed Episcopal Church in the United Kingdom met in June 1878. It devoted much of its time to revising its constitution and canons, a task which it continued at its September meeting. Authority to do so had been given by the General Council in North America the previous month. This was in response to vigorous representation from Bishop Gregg who maintained that some adjustments were necessary 'to avoid the name of "Yankee Church" in "conservative England"'.[14] Comparison of the revised form with the American original shows that the UK jurisdiction had taken as their model the Constitution of the Church of Ireland, sections of the Preamble and Declaration of which were added to the Declaration of Principles drafted back in 1873 by Bishop Cummins. The choice was an obvious one. The Church of Ireland, whose reform in 1833 had helped to bring the Oxford Movement into being, had been finally disestablished by an Act of Parliament passed in 1869. The following year a General Convention assembled in Dublin, composed of the archbishops and bishops, together with clerical and lay representatives, had approved a number of foundational documents. Thus for the first time an episcopal Church in the British Isles had comprehensively had to define itself and its basic tenets. Furthermore, the Church of Ireland had always been seen by members of the Free Church of England as a natural ally – a Protestant bulwark against popery – and no attempt was ever made to establish a Free Church of England or Reformed Episcopal congregation in Ireland. Both Merryweather and Price actually use the name 'The Free Church of Ireland' of the recently disestablished body.[15] For Price in particular the Irish Church was becoming the very model of Reformed Anglicanism: 'The Free Church of Ireland has entered on its new career of freedom . . . It has risen to the greatness of the occasion, and has been found equal to the crisis.'[16] The very form of the Church of Ireland – covering the whole nation, though spread very thinly in places – was one that the Reformed Episcopal Church could be envisaged as taking in Britain. With the promising example of the *Free* Church of Ireland before them, it is not surprising that the members of the General Synod of the Reformed Episcopal Church should look to it as their model. On a personal level, both Gregg and Sugden were from Ireland and would be familiar with the situation there. For Bishop Gregg in particular, anxious both to distance the Reformed Episcopal Church in the UK from its North American parent, and to assert its antiquity, assimilation to the model of the 'Ancient

Catholick and Apostolick Church of Ireland'[17] would have been highly desirable. The assimilation was made, and much of it survives in the Declaration of Principles of the united Church today.[18]

The Formation of the Reformed Church of England

Had the reforms stopped there, all might have been well. Gregg, however, had greater ambitions. As early as September 1877 it was becoming clear that he was unhappy with his position as a 'Missionary Bishop' answerable to the Presiding Bishop in America. He clearly wished to lead an independent Church. In June 1878 he had written to the Convocation of the Free Church of England, sending 'affectionate greetings', but signing himself 'Primate'. This adoption of a title hitherto reserved in England for the Archbishops of Canterbury and York suggested to the leaders of the Free Church of England precisely that concept of prelacy against which they were protesting. It helped ensure that tentative proposals for dialogue between the two bodies came to nothing.

If relations with the Free Church of England were strained by Gregg's action and style, the same was even more the case with the Reformed Episcopal Church in the United States and Canada. A flurry of correspondence sought to restrain Gregg, who, in about mid October 1878 simply wrote to Presiding Bishop Samuel Fallows requesting Letters Dimissory in order that he might act independently of the North American authorities. Even worse, Gregg stated that if the letters were not received within 30 days, he would act as if they *had* been received. Having issued an ultimatum, Gregg then proceeded to ignore it himself. On Tuesday 5 November 1878 in Trinity Church, Southend, Thomas Gregg single-handedly consecrated the Revd Nicholas Toke, formerly Vicar of Knossington in Leicestershire, a Bishop for the United Kingdom.

Gregg's action not only cut him off from the Church in America; it also split the infant Reformed Episcopal Church in the United Kingdom. Bishop John Sugden and at least nine other clergy and congregations withdrew from Gregg. On behalf of them Alfred Richardson, in his capacity as Secretary to the General Synod, made a public statement to the press: 'It is right that you should know officially that Bishop Gregg has severed his connection with the Reformed Episcopal Church, deeming it wiser, for reasons of his own, to form a separate sect.'[19] On 22 November the Executive Committee of the Reformed Episcopal Church in America 'resolved, that this Executive Committee recognize Bishop John Sugden and the Synod acting with him, as the Ecclesiastical Authority of the Reformed Episcopal Church in the United Kingdom'.

Gregg refused to be cowed. He claimed that he alone represented the true English Reformed Episcopal Church, and that the congregations now presided over by Bishop Sugden constituted a 'foreign jurisdiction'.[20] At the new denomination's General Synod in July 1880 the title 'The Reformed Church of England' was formally adopted, though the name 'Reformed Episcopal Church' continued to appear in the constitution. For the sake of clarity, only the name 'Reformed Church of England' will be used here. The name 'Reformed Church of England' had sometimes been used descriptively of the Established Church itself (e.g. E. Cardwell's *Documentary Annals of the Reformed Church of England*, Oxford, 1839). This may have influenced Gregg's choice of name.

So, only four years after the 1876 consecrations, about which such high hopes had been entertained, the whole enterprise was now in tatters. The Free Church of England was not only well into the process of an irrevocable separation from the Countess of Huntingdon's Connexion, but had split into two. That section which had reorganized as the Reformed Episcopal Church in the United Kingdom had itself been torn apart by the high-handedness of Thomas Gregg. Instead of a single episcopal Church around which Churchmen could unite, there were three tiny bodies, struggling to maintain a credible Christian witness amidst squabbles and further tensions.

From this point the tangled relationships between the three episcopal bodies becomes extremely complex. For the sake of clarity a brief overview of each will be given separately.

The Reformed Church of England 1878–1892

For all his manifest weaknesses, Bishop Gregg was an immensely able man. With great energy he set about organizing and expanding the community under his jurisdiction. His own church at Southend had to be enlarged twice to accommodate a growing congregation. From this strong base (where he had the benefit of a curate) Gregg had organized 6 congregations by April 1879.[21] By the end of the following year this number had risen to 16 – with 12 in England, 3 in Wales and 1 in Scotland.[22]

Amazingly, 5 more were added in the next year and a further 14 by 1891. In all, Gregg founded 29 churches in the UK, though some of them survived for only a few years.[23] Indeed, for much of the 1880s Gregg had more churches than the official Reformed Episcopal Church in the United Kingdom.

Nor were Gregg's activities confined to the United Kingdom. Since the beginnings of the Reformed Episcopal Church in North America there had been tensions between the Canadian and American parishes. Eventually some of the former applied to be under Gregg's jurisdiction and Gregg himself visited Canada for the first time in 1879. By 1885 there were 22 churches in Canada under the jurisdiction of the Reformed Church of England. For a short time Bishop Toke had them under his pastoral care, but he separated from Gregg in 1891. On 19 June 1892 Gregg consecrated Brandram Ussher as bishop for the Canadian parishes. Under Ussher, and with Gregg's approval, the rift between the Reformed Church of England and Reformed Episcopal Church congregations in Canada was healed.[24]

Bishop Gregg's vision was of a national episcopal Church identical in virtually every respect to the Church of England, but free from its Ritualist corruptions. In June 1881 his General Synod approved a plan for dividing England and Wales into 14 dioceses: Verulam, Selsea, Dumnoc, Caer Mephric, Caer Leirion, St Germans, Caerleon, Pengwern, Wyke, Hexham, Menevia, Margam, Alaunum and Clausentium. The names, interestingly, are in the main pre-Norman and demonstrate the appeal to Gregg of the ancient Celtic and Saxon Churches prior to the excesses and errors of the High Middle Ages. Gregg himself took the title of Bishop of Verulam, and Sugden that of Selsea, but after the split between them neither of the two bishops who subsequently worked with Gregg were given territorial titles.

The style of the Reformed Church of England was also modelled on that of the Establishment. Gregg sought to restore the sixteenth-century Reformers' ideal of frequent Communion and insisted upon the celebration of the Sacrament at least twice monthly. At times this meant granting faculties for deacons to preside in the absence of sufficient presbyters. It was a departure from catholic norms that Gregg did not like, but it demonstrates the importance of Holy Communion in his ecclesiology.

Bishop Gregg pursued his vision aggressively. From time to time he wrote provocative letters to bishops of the Church of England, pointing out that he too was an Anglican bishop. In 1887, to his delight, he was invited to Queen Victoria's Golden Jubilee service in Westminster Abbey as the 'Bishop of Verulam'. This he took as giving him the official State recognition he craved and he made much use of it in his correspondence and writings. Simultaneously, for much of the 1880s he campaigned to be recognized as the true Reformed Episcopal Church in the United Kingdom, claiming that he had not seceded in 1878. Sadly, this campaign often took the form of 'rubbishing' the UK branch of the Reformed Episcopal Church under the jurisdiction of Bishop John Sugden (and later Alfred Richardson). Surprisingly, Gregg had an ally in Bishop Cheney, perhaps because, as a strong Episcopalian himself, he supported Gregg's stance on the need for a truly *Anglican* Church. In the event, however, Gregg embarrassed Cheney by making public confidential correspondence between them, making any rehabilitation impossible. In 1889 the General Council in America finally reaffirmed its recognition of the Church presided over by Bishop Richardson (see below) as the official branch of the Reformed Episcopal Church in the United Kingdom.

This blow broke Gregg. His physical and mental health, already weakened by his incredible workload, began to deteriorate rapidly, a process hastened by the death of Gregg's father in July 1890 and by an accusation (which was never brought to court) of improper conduct towards a female member of his congregation. By the end of 1891 he was in an asylum and was registered insane in March 1892. He lived on until March 1896, but never recovered his sanity. He was only 56 at the time of his death.

The fate of what remained of the Reformed Church of England will be examined in the next chapter.

The Reformed Episcopal Church in the United Kingdom 1878–1892

The authorities of the Reformed Episcopal Church in North America were saddened and angered by Gregg's unilateral actions at the end of 1878. At the request of English Churchmen they had in good faith formally established a branch of the Reformed Episcopal Church in the United Kingdom and had consecrated as bishop the man recommended to them. Now the man on whom they had bestowed episcopal orders had declared his independence of them and had alienated his co-workers in Britain. As noted above, recognition was immediately given to Bishop Sugden and the clergy and congregations associated with him. This was ratified by the Seventh General Council meeting at Christ Church, Chicago from 28 May to 3 June 1879. The same meeting also recognized Sugden as the 'Presiding Bishop' of the Reformed Episcopal Church in the United Kingdom.[25] The General Council meeting was attended by the Revd Alfred Richardson, Secretary of the British jurisdiction. He had been sent both to give an account of the events in the UK and also to be consecrated bishop, to which position he had been elected by the British Synod on 26 November 1878. The election was confirmed by the General Council and Richardson was consecrated in St Paul's Church, Philadelphia on 22 June 1879 by Bishops William Nicholson and Samuel Fallows. Once back in England, Richardson assisted Sugden in the consecration of the Revd Hubert Bower (like Richardson, a former Connexional minister) at Littlehampton on 19 August 1879.

The Reformed Episcopal Church in the United Kingdom therefore had three bishops and was well set to expand. The country was divided into two dioceses – north and south of the rivers Thames and Severn – with Bishop Sugden in charge of the south and Bishop Richardson of the north. Bishop Bower had no territorial jurisdiction. The hoped-for growth was extremely slow. Sugden's health was poor (he resigned his position at Teddington in December 1880[26]) and he was unable to provide strong and effective leadership. Richardson proved to be an increasingly patronizing and abrasive character, not well suited for the task of building up the small denomination. Even so, by 1880 the Reformed Episcopal Church had 16 Churches, to which a further 12 had been added by 1891.

The governing body was the General Synod which had a Standing Committee and four other committees: Doctrine and Worship; Constitution and Canons; Finance; and Trustees of the Sustentation Fund. At its October 1882 meeting the General Synod passed the resolution:

> That, in view of the peculiar difficulties of the work of the Reformed Episcopal Church in Great Britain, and the great distance and consequent difficulty of communication between this country and America, this General Synod feels the imperative necessity of an immediate independent existence, with full communion with the General Council . . .[27]

Once again the American authorities were faced with a request for independence from a British offspring. Perhaps fearing a repeat of the Gregg scenario, the Ninth General Council granted the request at its 1883 meeting. Fenwick suggests that there was a degree of embarrassment and despair in relation to the situation in Britain.[28] For some in America it is likely that granting independence to the daughter Church was little more than cutting their losses.

These were difficult years. By 1884 Gregg was claiming that the Reformed Episcopal Church was breaking up.[29] This was an exaggeration, and it has to be conceded that Gregg's own animosity towards Richardson (which was reciprocated) did nothing to help. Gregg's view was communicated to Cheney who, in a letter dated 28 January 1889, wrote: 'All I learn from England convinces me more and more that Richardson is an exceedingly dangerous man; that he is not a Reformed Episcopalian at heart, but a scheming fellow . . .'[30]

Though clearly maligned, Richardson, who became Presiding Bishop in 1885 on the retirement of John Sugden, was undoubtedly a disaster. His abrasive, high-handed manner unilaterally wrecked proposals for closer relations with the Free Church of England and called forth the statement from Thoresby: 'The conduct of the few gentlemen forming the branch in this country of the Reformed Episcopal Church of America has been so extraordinary that we do not wish a closer union with them.'[31] Fenwick concludes that 'there was bad blood between Richardson and Price'.[32]

Things went from bad to worse. Despite Sugden's retirement, Bishop Bower does not seem to have taken on any particular responsibilities in the denomination. He assisted Richardson at the consecration of Thomas Greenland at Christ Church, Carlton Hill on 11 June 1888, but thereafter seems to have left the Reformed Episcopal Church. Incredibly, Bishop Greenland himself resigned on 1 January 1889, less than six months after his consecration. The reason seems to have been a breakdown in relationships both with Richardson and other clergy over a range of issues.[33] Other clergy left, some to the Free Church of England, the Reformed Church of England and to the Church of England itself, others to independent chapels.

At this low point Richardson unwisely got involved with other ventures. For the only time in the history of the Free Church of England or its constituent bodies one of its bishops took part in the consecrations of what are known as *episcopi vagantes*.[34] In late 1887 or early 1888 Richardson seems to have consecrated one James Martin for the 'Nazarene Episcopal Ecclesia', a small sect based in south London. Subsequently, on 4 May 1890 Richardson assisted at the conditional consecration of the Armenian Leon Chechemian for the 'Ancient British Church'. Both Martin and Chechemian were to be involved in a number of increasingly exotic and insubstantial bodies. As Fenwick says, 'This was all a far cry from the sternly "correct" and protestant Reformed Episcopal Church.'[35] These unauthorized actions seem to have resulted in a decision to take action against Richardson by the Reformed Episcopal Church.[36] Before canonical action could proceed, however, Richardson had resigned. The reason was money.

Financially, the Reformed Episcopal Church was in a worse condition than either the Free Church of England or the Reformed Church of England. It could not afford to print its own Prayer Books, using instead Church of England copies, with amendments written in. Nor could it afford a regular magazine. Many of the costs were borne by the clergy out of their own pockets. In such a climate, Richardson made some poor business decisions. He became involved in a company which ran into legal difficulties, and a sale of church buildings held in his own name fell through. He was declared bankrupt in June 1892.[37] As Fenwick puts it, 'Both the REC and the FCE were then, and remain today, rigidly and utterly "correct" in the expectations placed upon the conduct of life and business affairs of their clergy. As an undischarged bankrupt, Richardson could not continue in office with the REC.'[38] Bishop Richardson resigned and went to live in France, where he died in 1907.

The Reformed Episcopal Church was left in disarray, without an active bishop.

The Free Church of England 1878–1896

The secession of Bishop Sugden, Huband Gregg and others to the newly founded Reformed Episcopal Church in 1877–8 was a serious blow to the Free Church of England, which had managed to maintain its unity since being incorporated fifteen years previously. The destabilizing effect of the secession was to continue and very nearly produced a further division.

The records of the June 1878 Convocation show that a resolution was presented by a 'Provisional Council of the (Episcopal) Free Church of

England'. This advocated both the addition of the word 'Episcopal' to the official title of the denomination, and the adoption of 'the Declaration of Principles and Constitution, as set forth in the Circular of the Free (Episcopal) Church of England'.[39] The resolution was moved by no less a person than F. S. Merryweather. It seems that, even after the departure of the more Anglican-minded members to the Reformed Episcopal Church, there still remained in the Free Church of England a body of people who wished for a more explicitly episcopal identity and style and who had already organized themselves into a distinct group to press for changes in the direction they desired. An amendment moved by Thoresby, seeking to move the denomination in precisely the opposite direction by revising the Canons (which had been adopted wholesale from the Reformed Episcopal Church in 1876) was narrowly passed by three votes. Convocation was clearly split down the middle. Bishop Price, having consulted with 'the Episcopalian members of the Convocation', announced that he must stand with the post-1876 Declarations and Canons – despite his own origins he believed it would be wrong to renege on the agreement which had secured the historic succession for the Free Church of England. The denomination prepared for division. At a meeting on 26 June 1878 the principles and constitution of a body to be called 'the Episcopal Branch of the Free Church of England' were agreed and an executive Council appointed.[40] By September the 'necessary steps for the election of two Bishops at the ensuing Convocation were discussed and arranged'.[41] At its meeting in October, however, Convocation, having looked into the abyss, drew back. The *Magazine* reported that, 'The feeling was general, that the points of difference were so unimportant, that anything like separate action would be both unwise and unnecessary.'[42] A special committee was formed to draw up a definitive settlement of all questions affecting the harmony of the Church. The committee met on the morning of 12 November 1878, and a reconvened Convocation assembled that after-noon. Convocation re-affirmed the unity of the denomination. The records speak of the Church 'placing her truly Scriptural Episcopacy on a more solid basis than ever'.[43] In practice, it seems as though the status quo was maintained – neither Merryweather's strengthening of the episcopal element, nor Thoresby's watering down of it in the direction of the orig-inal Deed Poll.

Having weathered this crisis the Free Church of England continued its work. The episcopate was increased by the consecration of Frederick

Newman of Christ Church, Willesborough, Kent on 2 July 1879. Bishop Price was assisted at the consecration by Bishop Sugden, which says much for the relations between the two men. Sugden himself justified his action to the General Council of the Reformed Episcopal Church in North America by speaking of the need 'to throw away petty jealousies . . . keeping the unity of the Spirit in the bond of peace'.[44] Four years later a further bishop was consecrated: Henry Orion Meyers. For some reason Newman, rather than Price, was the main consecrator, assisted by Sugden. It may be that Price was unwell. He was 79 by this time and Meyers was being consecrated as a 'Missionary Bishop' – in other words, to assist Price. The arrangement does not seem to have worked, for between approximately 1890 and 1897 Meyers lived in Melbourne, Australia.

By 1880 the Free Church of England was by far the largest of the three episcopal bodies that had resulted from the events of 1877–8, with 39 churches served by 35 clergy.[45] The churches were divided into six 'Districts or Dioceses': London, Northern, Eastern, Western, Midland and North and South Wales.[46] The names are less romantic than those of Bishop Gregg's dioceses, but, unlike them, represent genuine working areas. Each had a President, Treasurer and Secretary. The Council continued to meet quarterly and Convocation annually, except in emergencies such as that which had arisen in 1878.

Despite an episcopal team and a settled organized structure, the Free Church of England did not prosper. The 39 churches of 1880 had shrunk to 22 by 1895, and the six districts had been reduced to two dioceses. There seem to be many reasons for this. Price himself laid some of the blame on 'the want of cohesion among us [which] has paralysed some of our most promising efforts'.[47] Continual theological wrangling was preventing visionary work from being carried out. Inevitably, too, the Free Church of England suffered from association with the Reformed Episcopal Church and the Reformed Church of England whose very bitter disputes sketched above were taking place all too publicly.

A major cause of failure was simply the lack of money. The support of moneyed aristocrats or industrialists was drying up. All the money had to come from the members of the congregation. Vaughan summed up very bluntly the scenario in all too many places:

> Groups of Church people, caught in a wave of Protestant enthusiasm . . .
> secured land, and built a Church, often on a Mortgage and always from

outside sources, for there were no central funds. All went well for a while, then, a quarrel in the congregation, or some blunder by the minister split the church and those remaining had difficulty in supporting their minister and paying off the Mortgage: the inevitable happened: the Mortgage was foreclosed and the remaining group scattered.[48]

The surviving magazines and circulars of the period contain constant appeals for money. Giving was clearly unrealistic, even by the standards of the day. Withholding of promised giving was an all too common protest when individuals did not get their own way. There was simply no possibility of building up central funds that could be used to help weaker churches in times of difficulty. Congregations had to stand or fall by their own unity, vision and generosity.

Interestingly, Price began to realize that the movement needed to re-examine its very *raison d'être*. It was no longer enough for the Free Church of England to be *against* something – Ritualism; it needed to be *for* something – the saving of souls. 'It would be a blessing, at least, to be imbued with the spirit of this evangelism, and be not only a protesting, but also a working Church . . .'[49] Price's choice of words is revealing: it looks as though he was having doubts about the negative ethos of the denomination, and now felt it was time to be doing some *positive work* for the Kingdom. With his roots in Welsh Calvinism and the Connexion, Price no doubt remembered the desire of Whitefield, Rowland, Harris, Haweis and their fellow-evangelists to bring the *joy* of the Gospel (rather than carping Protestantism) to those who had not yet experienced it.

Towards the end of the 1880s attempts to reunite the Free Church of England with the Reformed Episcopal Church in the United Kingdom (under Richardson) were made. The pre-existing 'federative union' with the Reformed Episcopal Church in North America (which was described as 'mischievous' and 'a deep root of bitterness'[50]) had been formally terminated by Convocation in 1882. Six years later, however, the time was clearly believed to be right to heal the breach between the two Churches in the British Isles. Indeed, on 10 October 1888 it was believed by many that union had been achieved. A meeting took place at which 'the fusion of the two bodies (always one in heart and principle) was carried by acclamation. Henceforth we shall be known as "The Free Reformed Episcopal Church of England" . . . Good Bishop Price was in the chair, supported by Bishops Richardson, Sugden, Meyers and Greenland.'[51] The rejoicing was premature. In fact nothing came of the supposed union. It looks as though insufficient preparatory work had taken place, not least in relation to the legal steps needed to effect such a union. From the Reformed Episcopal point of view, the American authorities do not seem to have been consulted, and were not at all supportive. It may be that rumours had reached them of Bishop Richardson's involvement with the 'Nazarene Episcopal Ecclesia'. Another attempt at union was made in December 1890. This too, got bogged down with legal problems and theological differences. It looks as though a major sticking point was Richardson's insistence on the episcopal re-ordination of Free Church of England ministers who had been presbyterially ordained in the Connexion. The parity of presbyters had always been a fundamental point with the Free Church of England, and negotiations foundered.

By this time the Free Church of England was facing its own leadership crisis. Bishop Newman had died in October 1887. Bishop Meyers was now living in Australia. Bishop Price was nearly 90 and failing. In 1889 he and Meyers had consecrated Samuel Dicksee and William Baker, but, as events were to show, these two were unable to work together. The end of an era came on the Feast of the Epiphany – 6 January – 1896 when Benjamin Price died at the age of 91.

Price's contribution to the development of the Free Church of England is unique. In his own person he encapsulated the transformation undergone by the denomination as a whole. His origins lay in the Calvinistic wing of the Evangelical Revival brought into being by Whitefield, Howell Harris, Daniel Rowland and their associates. He ministered in the Countess of Huntingdon's Connexion in the semi-Anglican state that Haweis's oversight had preserved. Deeply opposed to Roman Catholicism and Tractarianism, he had been a collaborator with Thoresby, Merryweather and others in the attempt to convert the Connexion into a Protestant episcopal alternative to the Established Church. He allowed his own office to evolve from President to Bishop Primus and received the sign of the historic succession. He lived to transmit the episcopal office to others. The surviving evidence suggests that Price's integrity and the respect in which he was held enabled others – and hence the community as a whole – to make the journey with him. Without him the transition from Connexion to episcopal Church is unlikely to have taken the form it did. His passing took the denomination into uncharted waters.

Thus, the early 1890s saw each of the three small denominations come to a point of crisis. For the Reformed Church of England it was the mental incapacity of Huband Gregg in 1891, leaving his congregations without a bishop. For the Reformed Episcopal Church it was the indiscretions of Alfred Richardson, leading to his disgrace and resignation in 1892, leaving his Church, too, without an active bishop. For the Free Church of England it was the increasing incapacity and death of the venerable Benjamin Price, whose wise hand had guided the Church since its earliest days. An objective observer would very reasonably have expected the entire movement to die out by the end of the decade.

It did not.

Notes

1. They occupy over 150 pages in Richard Fenwick's thesis.
2. Fenwick, *Thesis*, p. 125.
3. *FCE Magazine*, April 1883, pp. 67–85. The Vicar of Clerkenwell, whose predecessor's actions against Haweis and Glaswell had forced Spa Fields Chapel into Dissent back in 1782, actually took part in the funeral service.
4. Cook, *Selina*, p. 440.
5. Fenwick, *Thesis*, pp. 298–326 surveys the changing relationship.
6. *FCE Magazine*, March 1877, pp. 42f.
7. The term 'North America' is more accurate, as by this stage the Reformed Episcopal Church was composed of bishops, clergy and congregations in both the USA and Canada.
8. Ebury's support for the Free Church of England in the context of Prayer Book revision is discussed in Chapter 11.
9. Fenwick, *Thesis*, p. 134.
10. Guelzo, *For the Union*, p. 227.
11. *FCE Magazine*, August 1877, p. 149.
12. Fenwick, *Thesis*, p. 145.
13. Interestingly the term 'General Synod' was adopted by the Church of England for its central representative body 92 years later.
14. Aycrigg, *Memoirs*, p. 315. A. E. Peaston says of the UK branch that 'The Reformed Episcopal Church, despite its nomenclature, was a thoroughly English institution'; *The Prayer Book Revision in the Free Churches* (London, James Clarke & Co., 1964), p. 76.
15. Merryweather, p. 188; Price, *Opening Address at the 9th Annual Assembly or Convocation*, in *FCE Magazine* July 1871, p. 170.

16. *FCE Magazine*, p. 170.
17. The phrase is from the Church of Ireland's *Preamble and Declaration*.
18. The development of the Constitution and Declaration of Principles will be discussed further in Chapters 9 and 10.
19. Letter reproduced in the *Southend Standard*, 22 November 1878, p. 4, col. 6.
20. The text of a postcard by Gregg in which this phrase occurs is published in the *Episcopal Gazette*, November 1879, p. 14.
21. Fenwick, *Thesis*, p. 166.
22. Ibid., p. 168.
23. Ibid., pp. 187f.
24. The story of the enterprise in Canada would merit a separate study of its own. Fenwick, *Thesis*, pp. 169f. and 188ff. describe the events in more detail.
25. Fenwick, *Thesis*, p. 166.
26. Sugden's position at Teddington was anomalous. It was a *Free Church of England* congregation, yet from 1877 Sugden had been a bishop of the *Reformed Episcopal Church*! Vaughan later confessed himself unable to understand how the situation had continued to exist ('Memories and Reflections of Forty-Five Years in the Ministry of the Free Church of England', n.p., 1949, p. 8).
27. Quoted in Fenwick, *Thesis*, pp. 230f.
28. Ibid.
29. Ibid., p. 206.
30. Quoted in ibid., p. 213. The original letter is held at the Reformed Episcopal Seminary, Philadelphia.
31. *The Rock*, 15 August 1879.
32. Fenwick, *Thesis*, p. 181.
33. Ibid., pp. 236ff. Fenwick's list includes finance, styles of worship and strategies for expansion. For a couple of years Greenland organized what he called 'The Free Protestant Church of England Mission' before retiring to Bournemouth. He maintained good relations with some former Reformed Episcopal Church colleagues, including Philip Eldridge, at whose consecration in 1892 he assisted (see below). Greenland died on 9 May 1904.
34. *Episcopi vagantes* – 'wandering bishops' – were in the early and medieval Church bishops who, for one reason or another, found themselves without a jurisdiction. Some literally 'wandered' and interfered with regular diocesan administration. In the twentieth century the term came to be used of individuals claiming a tactile succession of consecration (and hence arguably valid episcopal Orders) from a bishop of one of the historic Churches of Christendom. Their following is usually tiny, or may even be non-existent. The standard works on *episcopi vagantes* are H. R. T. Brandreth, *Episcopi Vagantes and the Anglican Church* (London, SPCK, 2nd edn, 1961) and P. F.

Anson, *Bishops at Large* (London, Faber & Faber, 1964). Brandreth (p. 2) says of them: 'some are honest and believe they have a genuine vocation to guide, in isolation from the rest of Christendom, the small handful of people which acknowledges their claims; some others are clearly not honest, and use their supposed episcopal status as a means of personal enrichment . . . others again are mentally unbalanced.' Examples of sexual misconduct can also be found. Brandreth believed all *episcopi vagantes* to be ecclesiastically in error and found particularly painful 'that light-hearted trafficking in holy things, which characterizes so many of [them]' (p.xiii). In 1985 there were estimated to be over a thousand such persons, the majority of them in America; Alan Bain, *Bishops Irregular* (Bristol, published by author, 1985), p. 12.

35. Fenwick, *Thesis*, p. 243. See pp. 242–46 for the details. Brandreth notes Richardson's involvement (*Episcopi Vagantes*, pp. 79, 84n), as does Anson (*Bishops at Large*, p. 219). Neither classes the Reformed Episcopal Church or the Free Church of England as an *episcopus vagans* organization (see list in Brandreth, pp. 120–22).

36. Vaughan, 'Memories', p. 19.

37. See Fenwick, *Thesis*, pp. 247ff. for the details.

38. Ibid., p. 249.

39. *FCE Magazine*, August 1878, p. 149.

40. Ibid., p. 154.

41. Ibid., October 1878, p. 191.

42. Ibid., November 1878, p. 201.

43. Ibid., December 1878, pp. 221ff.

44. *Report of the Eighth General Council of the REC (USA)*, 26–30 May 1881, Second Day, pp. 48f.

45. See Fenwick, *Thesis*, p. 181, for a list of the churches.

46. Ibid., p. 287 for a list of the areas covered by the dioceses.

47. *FCE Magazine*, June 1881, p. 122; July 1881, pp. 123ff.

48. Vaughan, 'Memories', p. 17.

49. Quoted in Fenwick, *Thesis*, p. 327.

50. *FCE Magazine*, September 1882. The words are those of the Revd G. Hugh Jones, secretary of the Council.

51. Letter from the Revd W. H. Simms, dated 11 October 1888. Published in the *Episcopal Recorder*, 25 October 1888.

CHAPTER 7

Reuniting the Strands *c.*1892–1927

The young denomination had shared the fate of many reforming movements – it had suffered severe fragmentation. On a much larger scale this had been true of the sixteenth-century Reformation itself: the movement intended to cleanse and renew the Western Church had not only split that Church but had then itself subdivided into a variety of confessional bodies. The Free Church of Scotland, whose success had so heartened Merryweather and his contemporaries in the 1840s, was also to suffer a series of secessions. On a scale even closer in size to the Free Church of England, the Non-Jurors had split into at least two groups (Usagers and Non-Usagers); a division which had seriously weakened the movement and contributed to its extinction. In recent years the so-called 'Continuing Churches' that have come into existence in various parts of the Anglican Communion have also displayed a tendency to fissure.

Remarkably, the movement for a reformed episcopally ordered community recovered. On the human level it is a tribute to the patient labours of Church leaders and to the faithfulness of congregations. The gospel was preached, the Sacraments administered, the faithful were pastored and catholic order was maintained. Throughout the sad divisions and their slow healing the twofold continuity identified in Chapter 1 – in apostolic faith and in a structured Christian community – was maintained. The road to unity was a long one, slowly travelled and with various setbacks, but the end result was (as is so often the case in ecumenism) a Church enriched by its constituent traditions.

The Re-uniting of the Reformed Church of England and the Reformed Episcopal Church

As might be expected, the crisis caused by Bishop Gregg's collapse into insanity severely damaged the Reformed Church of England. Over half of Gregg's congregations failed almost immediately, leaving only about nine.[1] The General Synod survived as the Church's principal executive body, but there was no obvious successor to Gregg, and the Reformed Church of England seems to have been in effect paralysed.

The Reformed Episcopal Church, on the other hand, was better placed to weather its moment of crisis. Following Richardson's resignation Bishop John Sugden came out of retirement and took up office again as Presiding Bishop. A godly, eirenic and much-respected man, he immediately provided *continuity*, not just with the pre-Richardson era, but with happier days of great hope when he had been consecrated by Bishops Cridge and Price back in 1876.

The May 1892 meeting of the General Synod of the Reformed Episcopal Church confirmed Richardson's resignation, appointed Sugden as Presiding Bishop, and proceeded to elect Philip Eldridge and James Renny to the episcopate. They were consecrated on 24 June 1892 by Bishop Sugden, assisted, interestingly, by Thomas Greenland (whose brief episcopal ministry in the Reformed Episcopal Church had been brought to an end by the breakdown of his relationship with Richardson) and William Baker, one of the two recently consecrated bishops of the Free Church of England. Twelve months later Sugden graciously retired once more from the office of Presiding Bishop and Eldridge was elected as his successor, thus beginning a long and valuable ministry.

Fenwick believes that from the beginning of his episcopate Eldridge was in contact with the Revd Frank Gregg, son of Bishop Gregg, and one of the remaining clergy of the shattered Reformed Church of England.[2] No records survive of the negotiations, but they were clearly successful. On Tuesday 15 May 1894 the General Synods of the Reformed Church of England and the Reformed Episcopal Church met together at Balham and a vote to unite was passed unanimously. An indication of the degree of harmony is evidenced by the fact that it was Frank Gregg who proposed Eldridge as Presiding Bishop of the united Church.[3] Because of legal problems surrounding the trusts the official name of the new denomination was 'The Reformed Episcopal Church in the United Kingdom of

Great Britain and Ireland, otherwise called the Reformed Church of England' – a formula that was to be used again in 1927.

The thoroughly Church of England style that Gregg had required of his churches was preserved by a resolution to the effect that 'in the manner of performing public worship, the customs and use at present prevailing in the several congregations in union with this Church, shall be allowed . . .'.[4]

The united Reformed Episcopal Church now had 17 congregations.[5] Sixteen years of unnecessary division had been healed and the bitter memories created by Gregg's actions could now begin to fade. The General Council in North America was so moved by news of the union that it rose to sing the Doxology.[6]

Sadly, soon after these events, the Church was deprived of Bishop Renny's ministry, for he died in July 1894. A former schoolmaster, he had devoted himself to the training of the clergy and at one point had eight students in residential training.[7] His death brought to an end what might have been an extremely valuable contribution to the denomination.

Two years later again, Bishop Gregg died, never having recovered his sanity. His passing was not noted in the denominational magazine. By contrast, the death of John Sugden in June 1897 was marked by many tributes.[8]

The years following 1894 seem to have been good ones for the Reformed Episcopal Church. In his 1900 report to the General Council in America Eldridge records how well things had worked out:

> During the six years which have elapsed, and in which I have had the honour to preside over the United Church, no disagreement of any kind has existed amongst us, to weaken our councils and hinder our work. Every trace of past estrangement has long since faded from view, and today no one could tell that we had ever been so sadly divided.[9]

These years also saw some modest growth, with the number of churches rising to 21. By May 1900 (when Eldridge made his report already quoted) the ministry consisted of 1 bishop, 24 presbyters, 1 deacon and 3 licensed Readers. Easter communicant figures were estimated at 1,500, with 2,580 children in the denomination's Sunday Schools, served by 256 teachers.

Eldridge was forward-looking. Interestingly, like Bishop Price before him, he was coming to see that the movement needed a cause other than the opposing of Ritualism. Like Price, Eldridge too saw evangelism as the activity where efforts should now be directed. The rapidly growing cities and towns, where spiritual provision was often inadequate, were where the new priority should lie, 'apart altogether from the question of ritualism'.[10] Sadly, there are few signs that the Reformed Episcopal Church and the Free Church of England heeded the prophetic words of Eldridge and Price in this regard. It is arguable that the failure to shift from a negative to a positive focus has been one of the major factors isolating and inhibiting the denominations in the century that was to follow.

The Episcopacy Crisis in the Free Church of England 1896–1901

For 30 years Benjamin Price's statesmanlike guidance had done much to hold the Free Church of England together, not least after the loss of clergy and churches to the Reformed Episcopal Church in 1877. He had the trust of both 'wings' – he was a Calvinistic Methodist in origin, but was also a bishop consecrated in the historic succession. The removal of his restraining hand in 1896 (and that of most of the first generation of 'Founding Fathers' at about the same time) ushered in a short turbulent period for the Free Church of England, which went through its 'identity crisis' at the very time that the Reformed Episcopal Church and the Reformed Church of England were harmoniously recovering from theirs.

The tensions that emerged following the death of Price focused mainly on the nature of the episcopal office and have been referred to in the previous chapter. On 30 June 1896 Samuel Dicksee was elected Primus of the Free Church of England. He and Baker were now the only two bishops of the denomination resident in the UK: Meyers was living in Australia at this time. Dicksee and Baker were very different in churchmanship and in them the polarization within the Free Church of England was made visible. William Baker was very much in the Anglican mould while Dicksee was of a far more radical Protestant persuasion. In brief, Dicksee used his position as Primus to make a number of statements about the episcopal office which Baker took to be an attack on himself (which they probably were). Eventually, on 5 November 1897 William Baker resigned as Bishop of the Northern Diocese and from the Free Church of England. Dicksee was now virtually unchallenged, for, although Bishop Meyers had returned from Australia by this date, he seems to have kept his distance.

Dicksee was, sadly, very much in the Alfred Richardson mould. His surviving Addresses show him to be 'dogmatic and lacking in tact'[11] with an aggressively militant style. He seems, moreover, to have sought to abandon 'the careful protestant via-media that had been nurtured by Price and Newman in former days'.[12] By 1900 it was clear that Dicksee was trying to change the ministry of the Free Church of England. Following the resignation of Baker there was no attempt to elect and consecrate a bishop for the Northern Diocese. The Revd William Troughton, Minister of Emmanuel, Morecambe, was elected 'President of the Northern Synod' only. There seems also to have been a deliberate shift in the terminology used of the ministry – presbyters were spoken of as 'admitted' rather than 'ordained'. It looks very much as though Dicksee was trying to take the Free Church of England back to its pre-1876 state. His reasons for this are not entirely clear, but Fenwick is inclined to see a parallel in the 'spiritualization' movement active in Congregationalism at this time.[13]

The crisis came to a head at Convocation in June 1901. Dramatically, however, Dicksee himself had died just a few months previously and it was left to his remaining supporters to move the following motion on 25 June:

> That in future Presidents of the Northern and Southern Dioceses respectively be elected, that they be given the New Testament title of Bishop, that they be NOT consecrated, and that they wear no other dress than the ordinary Ministers of the Free Church of England.

The situation envisaged is reminiscent of that of the early days of Benjamin Price, when he was annually elected President of the joint meeting of the Connexional Conference and Convocation. The title 'bishop' is related solely to the New Testament and not to the historic order transmitted down the centuries and carefully passed on by George Cummins and his successors. The reference to dress presumably means the use of the surplice, rather than rochet and chimere, but could also refer to frock coat, apron and gaiters which the bishops were wearing at the time, identical with those of the Church of England.

The radicals did not, however, have the support that they believed. The original motion was never voted on, being overtaken by an amendment 'that the Bishops of the Free Church of England be Consecrated as heretofore' which was carried by 15 votes to 5.

It was, as Fenwick rightly identifies, a 'watershed' in the history of the Free Church of England.[14] From June 1901 onwards the traditional three-fold ministry in historic succession was secure. 'By the same token, the more Calvinistic and radically protestant influence was ended.'[15] A theological strand, going back in effect to the time of George Whitefield himself, had been broken. The Free Church of England was now no more Calvinistic than the Thirty-Nine Articles. Further, had the changes desired by Dicksee and his supporters come into effect, it is highly likely that the Free Church of England would have followed the path taken by the Countess of Huntingdon's Connexion and would have drifted into Congregationalism. It is likely that, by jettisoning the more radical element, the 1901 Convocation saved the Free Church of England and thus ensured the continuation of its heritage into the present-day denomination.

However, even after the historic vote of 25 June, the Free Church of England was still facing a crisis. Henry Meyers was now the only surviving bishop and his health was failing rapidly – he was too ill to attend the meeting of Convocation. He was, nevertheless, elected Primus. Troughton was elected Bishop of the Northern Diocese and the matter of his consecration was referred to the Northern Synod. A specially convened meeting of that Synod met on Tuesday 23 July at St John's Tottington. It is clear that not all the controversy had died down. The Secretary 'explained the position of affairs with reference to the Bp's consecration and read extracts from correspondence relating thereto'. It was only after 'prolonged deliberation' that the following motion was moved: 'That the "Act" of Consecration on Bp Troughton take place at Hounslow at as early a date as the Northern Secretary can arrange.' This was followed by a further motion: 'That the public consecration service be held at Morecambe on a day suitable to the Northern brethren and that the actual date be left for the Bp & Secretary to arrange.'[16]

Troughton was thus to have two services – the actual consecration by Bishop Meyers which, by virtue of the latter's failing health was going to have to take place at Hounslow where he lived, and a public 'inauguration of ministry' service at Troughton's own church at the heart of the Northern Diocese. The latter service was agreed 'unanimously'; the former only 'Nem.Con': it looks as though some present were not entirely happy with the arrangements, though this may have related to the particular circumstances created by Meyer's health, rather than to the concept of consecration as such.[17]

Just 12 days later William Troughton was consecrated a Bishop in the church of God by Henry Meyers. This is the only consecration in the official list not stated to have taken place in a church. Fenwick suggests that it was probably performed in a 'nearby chapel'.[18] In view of Meyer's state of health – he would be dead within weeks – it is more likely that it took place at Meyer's home, with one of the rooms presumably being furnished as a chapel. Meyers was assisted by 'several presbyters'. It is the only 'private' consecration in the entire history of the Free Church of England and Reformed Episcopal Church.

The succession was preserved and by the end of 1901 William Troughton was elected Bishop Primus of the Free Church of England.[19] Thus both the Free Church of England and the Reformed Episcopal Church in the United Kingdom began the twentieth century as conventionally ordered episcopal Churches on the Anglican model.

Both denominations also entered the twentieth century maintaining their claim to represent the true Church of England tradition. For the Free Church of England Bishop Troughton could claim in his Presidential Address to Convocation in June 1903: 'But *we* are *not dissenters* from the worship and teaching and doctrines of the dear old Church of England . . . and . . . we hold dear that historic succession that we have from the church of this dear land of ours.'[20] Similarly, Bishop Eldridge ended his booklet *The Origin, Orders, Organisation and Worship of the Reformed Episcopal Church in the United Kingdom* with the claim: '. . . it is the Ritualist priest, and not the Reformed Episcopal minister, who is the real Dissenting parson . . .'.[21]

It was the very claim and polity of the two Churches that was to contribute greatly to their isolation for much of the twentieth century. The Church of England refused to take seriously Churches whose very existence were a rebuke to what she had allowed herself to become. At the same time, the Nonconformist traditions, while they might admire the preaching ministry of some Free Church of England and Reformed Episcopal Church figures, were not interested in exchanging their own structures and traditions for a set virtually indistinguishable from those of the Established Church. The result was a reflection in microcosm of the position of the Church of England, which also claimed to bridge an ecclesiological divide: neither bank was sure that the bridge actually reached it.

Now that the Free Church of England had passed through its moment of crisis, attention could turn once again to the issue of reuniting the two denominations. In order to understand the process, it may be helpful to present a brief 'snapshot' of the two bodies as they were in the first two decades of the twentieth century.

The Reformed Episcopal Church 1901–*c.*1922

In 1900 the Reformed Episcopal Church had 21 congregations; by 1914 this had risen to 26, though had declined slightly to 24 by 1922. It is perhaps surprising that the decline was not greater, given the massive disruption caused by the Great War. Some churches in sensitive areas were required to close 'for the duration'. Working patterns – and hence church-going patterns – were disrupted. Some clergy left their congregations to serve as chaplains to the Armed Forces. Shortages of materials such as paper affected the production of magazines and newssheets. On top of all this the Reformed Episcopal Church (and of course the Free Church of England) shared in the massive loss of men in the carnage of the trenches. Churches to this day still have their 'rolls of honour' of the fallen. The loss was serious enough in large denominations; in small Churches like the Reformed Episcopal and the Free Church of England the loss of significant numbers of young men from their membership was potentially catastrophic.

Up until 1913 Philip Eldridge was the only bishop, presiding over the whole denomination as a single unit. There had been several attempts to elect additional bishops, but these had either failed to produce the necessary majority or the chosen candidates had declined the office. Eventually cautious steps were taken to restore the two-diocese structure set up in 1881, but which seems to have collapsed due to Bishop Richardson's inability to work with colleagues. A first step was the setting up of a 'Diocesan Association of Northern Churches' in 1909. The intention was to provide 'a support, administrative and information network'[22] for the congregations in northern England and Scotland. As Eldridge lived in Brighton there was a clear need to provide structures of oversight and communion between the widely scattered congregations. The Secretary of the new Diocesan Association was the Revd Frank Vaughan, Minister of Warrington Church.

Vaughan is one of the giants of the Reformed Episcopal/Free Church of England story and deserves a study in his own right. Originally from Bristol, he had run away from home after an unhappy childhood and eventually joined the army, rising to the rank of sergeant in the Grenadier Guards. Returning to civilian life he was for a time a Stipendiary Lay Reader in the Church of England Diocese of Liverpool before joining the Reformed Episcopal Church in 1904. He was a man of strong character and good at achieving practical results.

It is therefore no surprise to find that, shortly after Vaughan moved to be minister of the church in Harlesden, a similar Association of Southern Churches was formed in 1912. The two embryo dioceses become formally constituted dioceses by act of the General Synod in June 1915. Each had its own Diocesan Synod and officers. Their boundaries were explicitly to follow those of the Provinces of Canterbury and York in the Church of England.[23] Vaughan had been consecrated bishop by Eldridge and Richard Brook Lander of the Free Church of England on St Mark's Day (25 April) 1913. His initial ministry had been 'Assistant Bishop to the Presiding Bishop'. Following the creation of the two dioceses in 1915, it emerged that neither bishop wanted to take the Northern Diocese. In the end Eldridge agreed to become Northern Diocesan, initially as a temporary measure. In fact he remained in the post (and as Presiding Bishop) until his death in 1921.

Eldridge was, however, worn out and in failing health. He was of a much more pro-Church of England mind than Vaughan, who seems to have been reacting against his Church of England past. Their personalities, too, were very different. The differences between them were to delay the road to unity.

The Free Church of England 1901–c.1921

Like the Reformed Episcopal Church, the Free Church of England actually grew in the early years of the twentieth century from 20 congregations in 1901 to 28 by 1913. The Great War only reduced the number by one, leaving 27 in 1920.[24] Before the War there were four churches in Glasgow, largely serving Church of Ireland families who had come to live and work in that city. Some of the denomination's churches were strong enough to run Day Schools for local children.

Following his consecration in 1901 William Troughton was the sole bishop in the Free Church of England until he consecrated Richard Brook Lander in October 1904. Lander took charge of the Southern Diocese, a position which he held until the union. Troughton was Northern Diocesan and Primus (and Minister of Emmanuel, Morecambe) until his death in 1917. Curiously, no new bishop was then consecrated for the Northern Diocese, which was adminstered by the Revd A. V. Bland (also from Morecambe) as President of the Northern Synod until 1927.

An event of great historical significance for the Free Church of England took place the year before the commencement of the Great War: the last church – Worcester – to have dual membership of both the Countess of Huntingdon's Connexion *and* the Free Church of England withdrew from membership of the latter. This final parting followed the death of the minister, the Revd E. J. Boon, on 27 November 1913. His successor and the Vestry did not wish to continue the link. Prior to this there had in fact been a modest amount of increased contact between the two denominations. In 1911 Bishop Troughton in his presidential address at Convocation had expressed his support for a union of the Free Church of England with both the Reformed Episcopal Church and the Connexion, and some meetings of representatives took place.[25] In June 1913 the 50th anniversary of the legal inauguration of the Free Church of England was marked by Convocation meeting at Spa Fields Chapel, where the crucial resolution had been passed by the Connexional Conference. Despite these attempts to maintain links the relationship unravelled. The final break between the Connexion and the Free Church of England seems to have been precipitated by disagreements over shared work in the Sierra Leone Mission. By 1919 'the last possible hope for a union between the FCE and the Connexion had vanished'.[26] The separation symbolized by Worcester's departure marked the end of the dream cherished by Thoresby and others that the Free Church of England would absorb the Connexion of which it was the true fulfilment. In practical terms it meant that the Free Church of England no longer had to retain a 'Connexional perspective' as it increasingly moved on from its semi-Anglican past, not least in the unity discussions with the Reformed Episcopal Church. So complete was the break that the Free Church of England members of the delegation helping to draw up the 1927 Constitution felt no need to ask for joint membership with the Connexion, such as had been provided for in 1863.[27]

Unity Talks

The final severing of the links between the Connexion and the Free Church of England cleared the way for what would now be called a 'bilateral' scheme of union between the Free Church of England and the Reformed Episcopal Church (which had never been totally comfortable with the Connexion's increasingly non-Anglican identity). There had been a number of abortive initiatives in the first decade of the twentieth century, but no real progress. In later years Vaughan identified the attitude of the bishops as a significant reason: 'Bishop Eldridge was strongly opposed to it, on legal grounds. Bishop Troughton was not interested, Bishop Lander, only languidly so . . .'.[28] The bishops' lack of enthusiasm seems to have been reflected in a coolness between the two Churches in general. There was at this period the occasional transference of congregations from one to another (made possible by the vesting of properties in local trusts). This no doubt engendered some ill-feeling. Personalities and differences in ethos no doubt played their part.

Things began to change from about 1914. It seems that much of the credit for this, humanly speaking, must go to Frank Vaughan, for whom the uniting of the two Churches was a priority. In this he had an ally in the Revd William Young, General Secretary of the Free Church of England. With their encouragement a Joint Committee produced by 1917 a unity scheme to bring into being a united denomination to be called 'The Episcopal Free Church'. The scheme did not, however, have the support of the Bishop Primus of the Free Church of England (Troughton) or the Presiding Bishop of the Reformed Episcopal Church (Eldridge) and 'definite opposition, some in pamphlet form, was disseminated among the Churches'.[29] Discussions limped along and a draft Constitution was discussed clause by clause by the Free Church of England Convocation in June 1919. Interestingly, the name 'The Episcopal Free Church' had now been dropped and it was proposed that the united denomination be named 'The Free Church of England otherwise called the Reformed Episcopal Church'.[30] This was the name that was to be used when union did at last take place in 1927.

Shortly after this, however, the whole process came to an abrupt halt.

The Impact of the Lambeth Appeal to All Christian People

The reason for the sudden cessation was that, for about half of the Reformed Episcopal Church (including its Presiding Bishop) an alternative ecumenical possibility had taken precedence – that of uniting with the Church of England.

On 7 August 1920 the bishops of the Anglican Communion, gathered in the Lambeth Conference, issued an 'Appeal to all Christian People'. In this they were reflecting a growing Christian awareness of the need for the Church to lead the way in healing a world that had just emerged from an immense global conflict by healing its own divisions. What many would see as a response to the prompting of the Holy Spirit was seen across Christendom – from the Patriarch of Constantinople to the Methodist Connexions.

The text of the Lambeth Appeal had been prepared over several months, significantly, in consultation with other Churches. It was therefore very much in the public domain. Bishop Eldridge does not seem to have been part of the formal consultation process but was certainly in touch with it. It looks as though some years previously Eldridge had come to believe that the Reformed Episcopal movement was not going to succeed and that the best course of action would be to negotiate reception into the Church of England under terms that guaranteed the Evangelical nature of the congregations. From 1919 he had been in contact with Chavasse, Bishop of Liverpool, who consulted the archbishops of York and Canterbury. On 28 February 1920 Eldridge met a group of Church of England bishops at Chichester. At that meeting Eldridge seems to have agreed to re-ordination of Reformed Episcopal clergy, re-confirmation of those laity who wished it and the placing of the congregations into an Evangelical Church of England patronage trust.

Not until this stage did Eldridge inform his fellow-bishop, Vaughan, of what had been provisionally agreed. Understandably, Vaughan was appalled and called the terms that Eldridge had agreed to, 'unconditional surrender of all we claimed to stand for since 1873'.[31] At Vaughan's insistence the proposals were put to the Diocesan Synods. The Northern Diocese (Eldridge's) accepted them by a majority of 11 to 7. The Southern Diocese (Vaughan's) passed instead an alternative set of terms and sent it to the Archbishop of Canterbury and every Diocesan Bishop of the Church of England. The terms were that the Reformed Episcopal clergy be received in their Orders and that the Declaration of Principles and Prayer Book be accepted unaltered.

In an attempt to salvage something from the situation Eldridge actually went to Lambeth Palace to meet Archbishop Davidson on 18 June 1920. Davidson was impressed by Eldridge and liked him, but by this stage the Unity Committee of the Lambeth Conference was formally 'processing' the Southern Diocese's resolution. The committee contained two PECUSA bishops who were no doubt well aware of their Province's violent repudiation of Bishop Cummins back in the 1870s. The chairman was A. C. Headlam, Bishop of Gloucester, whose ecumenical commitment to overseas Churches (such as the Baltic Lutherans) was not mirrored by his attitude towards an episcopal community on his own doorstep. Nor are his recorded remarks about the Reformed Episcopal Church in the spirit of the Appeal to all Christian People: 'It is a body of malcontents and we feel that the only way forward is to deal with individuals. . . . I need say no more.'[32]

The Reformed Episcopal Church's approach to the Church of England had been brutally rejected. Archbishop Davidson tried to make amends by sending Eldridge a signed copy of the Conference Report and writing, 'I cannot help hoping that we may by degrees bring to an end the division which ought not I think to continue in existence amongst us.'[33]

Not surprisingly, there were repercussions for the Reformed Episcopal Church. Several clergy left and joined the Church of England.[34] A small schism took place in the Northern Diocese: five Churches left the Reformed Episcopal Church and organized themselves as the 'Evangelical Church of England', appointing two of their presbyters as 'bishops'.[35] But, amazingly, the Reformed Episcopal Church survived the trauma. In March 1921 Bishop Eldridge took a period of leave and sailed from Tilbury to visit his daughter who was a missionary in South Africa. The strain of the preceding months took its toll. Off the coast of Africa he suffered a stroke and died. He was buried at sea.

Tying the Knot 1921–1927

Back in England Vaughan was elected Presiding Bishop (he was the only bishop) and immediately resumed the interrupted task of uniting the Reformed Episcopal Church with the Free Church of England. Within four months of Eldridge's death the Report of the Joint Committee of Reformed Episcopal and Free Church of England representatives was received by the General Synod and the resolution put that: 'a Union of Co-operation and Fellowship should be forthwith established between the FCE and the RCE'. It was carried unanimously.

The resolution was received cautiously but positively by the

Convocation of the Free Church of England. The courtship began in earnest.

The image of 'courtship' was used frequently over the next few years. Alongside the formal meetings and reports there was a deliberately planned 'growing together' process. At this distance in time it is difficult to appreciate how necessary this was. Vaughan states that the two Churches were 'never in close fellowship, each jealous of its own position, and perhaps a little scornful of the other side'.[36] Yet the Churches shared a virtually identical theological position, used substantially the same Prayer Book and had structures and administrative procedures that mirrored each other very closely. Clearly there were important differences of style and self-image. In particular, though the Free Church of England was no longer *semi*-Anglican as it had been in the 1860s and 70s, it was still not quite *pure* Anglican in the same sense as the Reformed Episcopal Church.[37] Both Churches might see themselves as purified versions of the Church of England, but their visions of what that meant differed subtly. Such differences, combined with inevitable personality differences within the leadership, necessitated a slow, gentle approach.[38]

A regular feature of the courtship was the holding of a number of 'united Conventions' of members of both Churches. The first took place at Emmanuel, Morecambe in autumn 1921 and was followed by others. These helped build up a degree of enthusiasm for unity, especially in the north where both denominations had the greatest concentration of Churches.

By 1924 things were sufficiently far advanced for Convocation and General Synod to meet simultaneously at St John's, Tottington (Free Church of England[39]). The business meetings were separate, but acts of worship and social activities were joint. The two bodies sent a joint Loyal Address to the King. The arrangement worked so well that it was agreed to continue the pattern for the next three years. And so the process continued – too slowly for some, too rapidly for others. At times the Reformed Episcopal Church seemed the more enthusiastic partner, with the Free Church of England dragging its feet; at others the reverse seems to have been true.

There seems to have been a 'cool' period in the process in 1925, for Bishop Lander did not invite Vaughan to join in the consecration of William Young, but by the time General Synod and Convocation met jointly in 1926 things were much more positive. The outward signs were the joint Loyal Address (once more) and the commitment to a joint Year Book. Inwardly, clearly the psychological moment for commitment had arrived. On the morning of Tuesday 1 June Convocation and General Synod each passed motions committing themselves to unity with the other and nominating members to a Joint Union Committee which was to finalize the process. There then followed what must have been a moving piece of symbolism. The Convocation resolution was carried to the General Synod by the Revd Donald Thompson who had left the Reformed Episcopal Church and joined the Free Church of England at the time of the 1920 Lambeth Appeal. The General Synod resolution was carried to Convocation by the Revd George Forbes-Smith who had left the Free Church of England for the Reformed Episcopal Church in 1920. For a tradition not given to 'grand gestures' it was an imaginative act.

Thus encouraged, the Joint Union Committee approached its task. It was wisely decided to make sure that all the local congregations 'owned' the union, so the proposed Preamble and Constitution were sent to every one of the churches of both denominations, for approval by clergy and people. In addition, members of the Union Committee visited several congregations, explaining issues and calming fears. The proposals were examined by solicitors acting for each denomination and Counsel's opinion sought. Everything possible was done to make the outcome 'watertight'.

The title of the united Church was to be 'The Free Church of England otherwise called the Reformed Episcopal Church', a decision influenced by the need to carry the various trusts into the new body. Understandably some Reformed Episcopal Church congregations would have preferred the order of names to be reversed, but the final sequence was defensible on the grounds that, as distinct bodies, the Free Church of England was indisputably older than the Reformed Episcopal Church. Fenwick is inclined to see the Free Church of England as 'winning' the tussle over the new Constitution. In fact, a closer examination does not really bear this out. In the new Constitution the *vocabulary* is often that of the old Free Church of England, but the *substance* is predominantly that of the Reformed Episcopal Church. 'Primus' and 'Convocation' may win over 'Presiding Bishop' and 'General Synod', but the strucure and polity is unequivocally episcopalian. The ordained ministry is the three-fold one of catholic order. Gone is the reference to the Fifteen Articles of the Countess of Huntingdon's Connexion, found in the 1863 Constitution. Gone, too, is any provision for joint membership of that body.[40]

After months of intensive work and a vote in favour of union on the basis of the proposed Constitution from every congregation, the courtship was (in the language used at the time) finally consummated in June 1927. Convocation and General Synod met at Christ Church, Liscard (on the Wirral) from 13 to 16 June. The crucial acts took place on the 14th.[41] The two bodies met separately but transacted identical business. In each the report of the Joint Union Committee was presented, then the official resolution to unite the Churches was put.[42] The Union Committee report recited the origin of the Free Church of England in 1844[43] and that of the Reformed Episcopal Church in 1873 led by 'the Right Reverend George David Cummins, D.D., a duly consecrated Bishop of the Church of God, and in episcopal succession from the ancient See of Canterbury'. The recital continues with the giving of the succession to the Free Church of England, the similarity of character and government between the Churches, their agreement on the Declaration of Principles and the unanimous vote in favour of union. It continues:

> We, the signatories, unanimously recommend (1) That on and after the fifteenth day of June 1927, the Free Church of England and the Reformed Episcopal Church shall unite as one Church; the United Church to be known as 'The Free Church of England, otherwise called the Reformed Episcopal Church in the United Kingdom of Great Britain and Northern Ireland.'

The report went on to name the agreed Constitution and Canons and provided for the administration of the various trusts by a Central Board. It was accepted unanimously by both Convocation and General Synod.

The next morning, 15 June, at 10.30 a.m. 'the First Annual Convocation' of the united church convened with Bishop Lander in the Chair. The Revd A. V. Bland of Morecambe reported the previous day's Convocation vote, and the Revd J. C. Magee reported the decision of the General Synod. There then followed further legal business after which the Convocation of the United Church formally adopted for itself the Constitution and Canons agreed by its predecessor bodies. The new legal basis was duly enrolled in the Chancery Division of the High Court on 10 December that year, thus superseding the 1863 Constitution over which Thoresby had laboured for so many years. The 1927 enactments are the legal basis of the denomination to the present day. The united Church was now well and truly in existence.

In North America the General Council of the Reformed Episcopal Church approved the union, rose and sang the *Te Deum* on hearing the news, and voted a grant of $1,000 to the united Church.

Fenwick comments on how little attention the union received in the various histories of the local congregations.[44] It seems to have passed unnoticed, too, in the wider Christian community. Various other contemporary unity schemes – from the Methodists to the Church of South India – have been well researched and published, but nothing appears to have been written on the union of these two episcopal Churches until Richard Fenwick's pioneering work.[45]

From the 1780s the vision had been formed of a Church 'essentially one with the Church of England' – but clearly Gospel-based, purged and free – with its marks of catholicity and apostolicity stretching back through English history and the patristic era to the original apostolic community. The fulfilment of that vision had been prevented by the sad and traumatic divisions of the 1870s, 80s and 90s. But now those divisions had been healed. Against all the odds the movement had survived, with its essential characteristics – evangelical, episcopal, liturgical – intact. The united Church, having been tested in the fires, could now take its place among the Christian communities of England.

Notes

1. Fenwick, *Thesis*, p. 224.
2. Ibid., pp. 252f.
3. *Minutes* of the united Synod, 1894, p. 1.
4. Quoted in Fenwick, *Thesis*, p. 253.
5. These are listed in ibid., p. 254.
6. *Proceedings of the Fourteenth General Council . . .* p. 77.
7. Vaughan, 'Memories', p. 7.
8. See Fenwick, *Thesis*, pp. 256ff.
9. *Proceedings of the Sixteenth General Council . . .*, May 1900, pp. 58ff.
10. Ibid.
11. Fenwick, *Thesis*, p. 317.
12. Ibid.
13. Ibid., pp. 321–24.
14. Ibid., p. 299.
15. Ibid.

16. Free Church of England: Minute Book of the Northern Synod (1901–1923); Meeting of 23 July 1901.
17. The description of the public service as a 'consecration' suggests there was unease at the private nature of the laying on of hands by Bishop Meyers. The records do not show whether the possibility of asking bishops of the Reformed Episcopal Church to act was considered.
18. Fenwick, *Thesis*, p. 325.
19. The death of Bishop Meyers was recorded with 'deepest sympathy with Mrs Meyers and her family' at the meeting of the Northern Synod on 27 November 1901.
20. *FCE Year Book 1903–4*, p. 3.
21. Published London, 1910. The contents were reprinted as an Appendix to the first edition of Vaughan's *History* in 1936. The quotation is from p. 266 of the latter.
22. Fenwick, *Thesis*, p. 356.
23. The Free Church of England had adopted the same two-diocese structure in 1889, but seems to have, characteristically, defined the boundary in less ecclesiastical terminology as the River Trent.
24. It should be pointed out that these were not necessarily the *same* congregations throughout the period. Churches joined or were started; others left the denomination or failed. The same is true of the Reformed Episcopal Church.
25. The Reformed Episcopal Church did not share Troughton's enthusiasm for the Connexion and asked for it to be excluded from the talks. Fenwick, *Thesis*, p. 385.
26. Ibid., p. 382.
27. From the Connexion's side it seems as though painful memories have led to the Free Church of England being 'air-brushed' out of the Connexion's memory. Given the vast amount of debate and activity devoted to the Free Church of England in the nineteenth century and its relevance to the Connexion's very identity, it is extraordinary that there is no mention of it in, for example, either Cook, *Selina*, or the first edition (1972) of Kirby, *Elect Lady*. Kirby's revised edition (1990) contains the sentence: 'During the course of its history the Connexion has had tenuous links with the Free Church of England and at one time the possibility of actual union was considered but nothing came of this in spite of the fact that a trust deed setting forth terms of union was enrolled in Chancery in 1863' (pp. 57f.). It seems that the memory of the actual relationship has been lost in the Connexion.
28. Vaughan, 'Memories', p. 10.
29. Vaughan, 'Memories', p. 11.
30. *FCE Year Book 1918–19*, pp. 2, 4, 18.
31. Vaughan, 'Memories', p. 13.

32. 1920 Lambeth Conference Papers, vol. 108, fols 240–43 (Lambeth Palace Archives.
33. Quoted in Fenwick, *Thesis*, p. 422.
34. Vaughan, who was very bitter about the whole incident, uses the emotive phrase 'made their submission'; 'Memories', p. 14.
35. See Fenwick, *Thesis*, pp. 358, 423, 439. Some of these returned after 1927, see Chapter 8.
36. Vaughan, 'Memories', p. 5.
37. As an example of deviation from this Anglican 'purity' Vaughan cites the occasional installing of deacons as incumbents by the Free Church of England, and the laying on of hands by presbyters at the ordination of a deacon, 'Memories', p. 5.
38. Fenwick mentions in particular the different origins of the two bodies of Canon Law, and the issue of trusts as significant differences. The personal relationship between Vaughan and Lander was not very close. *Thesis*, p. 446.
39. It was at the opening of this church that Benjamin Price had first been unambiguously described as 'Bishop'.
40. The Constitution will be considered in more detail in Chapter 9.
41. Perhaps fittingly, the date is that of the commemoration of 'Richard Baxter, Puritan Divine'.
42. The full text of the resolutions is printed in *The Constitution and Canons Ecclesiastical* (1983 edn) published by the denomination.
43. The eighteenth-century heritage referred to in the Preamble to the 1863 Constitution is ignored. Given the final separation from the Connexion that had recently taken place, perhaps this was inevitable.
44. Fenwick, *Thesis*, p. 468.
45. Had the two branches of the Non-Jurors reunited it would no doubt have been exhaustively studied.

Eighteenth-Century Roots

George III, who is reputed to have said that in his judgment the Wesleys, 'George Whitefield and the Countess of Huntingdon have done more to promote true religion in this country than all the dignified clergy put together'

George Whitefield, 1714–1770. 'The pioneer of the Evangelical Revival.' Appointed Chaplain to the Countess of Huntingdon in 1748. The FCE is part of Whitefield's legacy

Selina, Countess of Huntingdon, 1707–1791. Her 'Connexion' of chapels forms one of the oldest strands in the history of the Free Church of England

Thomas Haweis, 1734–1820, whose 1795 declaration that the movement was 'essentially one with the Church of England' was accepted as authoritative by the Free Church of England at the inauguration of its Constitution in 1863

The Nineteenth-Century Context

Queen Victoria receiving Holy Communion from Archbishop Howley at her Coronation in 1838 – just six years before the second group of Free Church of England congregations began to leave the Established Church

Edward Adolphus, 11th Duke of Somerset, 1775–1855, who allowed his chapel at Bridgetown to leave the Church of England in 1844 and thus become what is mistakenly viewed as the first 'Free Church of England' congregation

The Revd James Shore, 1844. Minister of Bridgetown Chapel, whose treatment by the Bishop of Exeter encouraged other congregations to seek to form 'a Free Church of England'

John Moore
Consecrated 12 February 1775;
Archbishop of Canterbury 1783–1805

William White
Consecrated 4 February 1787;
Presiding Bishop of PECUSA
1795–1836

John Hopkins
Consecrated 31 October 1832;
Presiding Bishop of PECUSA
1865–1868

George Cummins
Consecrated 15 November 1866;
Presiding Bishop of REC 1873–1876

The Succession – 2

Charles Cheney
Consecrated 14 December 1873;
Presiding Bishop of REC 1876–1877,
1887–1889

Edward Cridge
Consecrated 17 July 1876;
Bishop of REC (Canada) 1876–1913

John Sugden
Consecrated 20 August 1876;
Presiding Bishop REC (UK)
1878–1885, 1892–1893

Philip Eldridge
Consecrated 24 June 1892;
Presiding Bishop REC (UK) 1893–1921

The Succession – 3

Frank Vaughan
Consecrated 25 April 1913;
Presiding Bishop REC (UK) 1921–1927
Primus 1930–1962

Thomas Cameron
Consecrated 21 September 1950;
Primus 1962–1975

Cyril Milner
Consecrated 29 August 1973;
Primus 1975–1998

Kenneth Powell
Consecrated 1 October 1986;
Primus 1998–2000, 2003–

Significant Figures

William Augustus Muhlenberg whose
ecumenically orientated 'Evangelical
Catholicism' inspired Bishop
Cummins

Benjamin Price who led the transformation from a Connexion of Chapels
into a fully constituted episcopal
Church

Thomas Huband Gregg who ensured
a robustly Anglican identity to the
British REC

John McLean
Successor to Troughton and Vaughan
at Emmanuel, Morecambe; Bishop of
the Northern Diocese 2003–

CHAPTER 8

The United Church 1927–2004

With hindsight it can be seen that it was not until 1927 that the concept of a free Church of England reached a mature, stable expression. The process of blending the eighteenth-century Evangelical Revival tradition, as represented by the Countess of Huntingdon's Connexion, with post-1844 anti-Tractarian secessions from the Church of England, and with the North American-derived ecumenically inspired Reformed Episcopal Church had been tortuous and painful. But compared to the century or so leading up to 1927, the years that have elapsed since have been remarkably stable. There have been all the problems and challenges that beset any group of sinful men and women trying to maintain a Christian witness during the accelerating change of the twentieth century. But the fact that the Free Church of England[1] weathered them is an indication of its maturity. There were important issues and difficulties, but such traumas as have occurred have not been on the scale that the earlier years had seen.

Part of the reason for this is no doubt simply that by the early twentieth century many congregations were long-established and composed of second- and third-generation members. These were people who had grown up in the Free Church of England or Reformed Episcopal Church and for whom its ways were 'normal' – not ideals to be fought for in the teeth of fierce opposition, as had been the case for earlier generations. Indeed, for the years since 1927, the focus should really be on the individual congregations and the clergy that ministered in them, for it is here that the task of simply 'being the Church' has been carried out. The present chapter, however, makes no attempt to chart the multifaceted work of evangelism, teaching and pastoring in the congregations scattered throughout Britain. Some individual churches have published their own histories over the years, and what in many ways is the most important part of the story of the Free Church of England can be found there. Here it is only possible to summarize briefly significant events and trends in the life of the Church as a whole.

1927–1945

The first years of the united Church were marked by growth. The denomination had a new sense of confidence and was clearly looking more attractive than the old Free Church of England and Reformed Episcopal Church had done. New congregations were formed in places as far apart as Lancashire and Kent. Furthermore, some of the churches which had left the Reformed Episcopal Church following the events of 1920 to form the Evangelical Church of England now returned to the fold.[2] By the summer of 1939 the Free Church of England had 50 churches.

Among the many 'normal' activities undertaken by the congregations during these years was the support of overseas missionary work. This included not simply financial giving, but the departure of several members of the denomination to work overseas. This was a tradition that stretched back to the eighteenth century – Thomas Haweis's passion for overseas mission has already been noted. In 1785 an African American, John Marrant, was ordained into the Connexional ministry by Thomas Wills, and subsequently built up a number of black congregations in Nova Scotia. Some of these eventually transferred to Sierra Leone, where a number of 'Huntingdon Churches' exists to the present day.[3] These were supported by the Free Church of England until the split with the Connexion became definitive in about 1920. After that date the denomination transferred its main missionary interest to the China Inland Mission for a number of years. In October 1889 the Reformed Episcopal Church in North America established a mission at Lalitpur, in the Upper Punjab in India, with a church, hospital and orphanage. The Lalitpur mission continues to the present day and is regularly supported by the British denomination.

The pattern of growth within the UK continued even during the early years of the Second World War. Gradually, however, the effects of wartime conditions began to make themselves felt. Some churches in the south-east were forced to close 'for the duration'. Some were damaged by bombing. Two – Exeter and Clydebank, Glasgow – were destroyed by enemy action. The general dislocation of life and social patterns once again took its toll, as it had in the Great War.

Confidence was further eroded by an internal dispute that led to the resignation of one of the bishops and at least one presbyter. The subject of the dispute was Freemasonry. In the 1940s many in leadership positions in the Free Church of England (like the Church of England) were Freemasons. At the time Masonic membership and Christian commitment were not seen with the same degree of incompatibility as later generations have viewed them. Within the Free Church of England it was common knowledge that Bishops Vaughan, Young and Magee were Masons. The fourth bishop, Donald Thompson, was not, and felt Freemasonry to be incompatible with Evangelical principles. Eventually, after some exchanges with Bishop Vaughan, Thompson resigned over the issue.[4]

Thompson's loss in 1942 was particularly serious as, from his rectory in Putney, he was running a training scheme for the denomination under the name of 'The Bishop Cummins Theological College'. Plans were in hand to enable students to read for an Oxford degree. On Thompson's resignation the training scheme folded.

In his letter of resignation Thompson had also expressed his unhappiness at the suppression of the Central Diocese, which had taken place earlier in 1942 by vote of Convocation 'for reasons of economic expediency'.[5] Others beside Thompson were unhappy with some of the trends in the Church. In normal times such difficulties might have been quickly forgotten, but exaggerated by the strains of wartime living, they brought to an end the period of optimism and growth that the events of 1927 had created. The tide turned and steady decline set in.

1945–1975

There have been many attempts to analyse, interpret and explain the post-war decline in the practice of Christianity in Britain. The Free Church of England has undoubtedly shared in that decline, though, statistically, probably to a lesser extent than some other Churches, including the Church of England. Proportionately, however, the decline has been serious in such a small community.

Put briefly, the 47 churches that had survived the war had dwindled to 39 by 1960, and 29 by 1975. Fenwick catalogues the fate of the congregations.[6] In most cases the reason was simply the inability of a small congregation to maintain its building. The situation highlights the poverty of the Free Church of England and its total lack of central resources to assist struggling congregations through 'a bad patch'. Furthermore, lack of resources meant that there was no chance of building new churches in the new housing developments that were springing up all over Britain.

In addition, many of the congregations were eclectic, rather than community-based. Their congregations travelled in to worship, rather than being drawn from the immediate locality. As infirmity, death and social mobility reduced the congregations, there were simply not enough 'locals' to replace them and to work to keep the church open. When the nature of a church's neighbourhood changed, there were no resources to enable the congregation to 'relocate' to a more suitable area.

Undoubtedly, the Free Church of England's isolationist stance was one of the main reasons for its decline. Despite the commitment to 'maintain communion with all Christian Churches' explicit in its Declaration of Principles, the Free Church of England at this period was as anti-ecumenical as the contemporary Roman Catholic Church. Both had great difficulty in recognizing any other body as a true Christian Church and both feared that they would be compromised and polluted by involvement in the search for Christian unity.

In 1951, as part of the festivities to mark the Festival of Britain, the denomination sponsored a stand at the United Exhibition in Central Hall, Westminster, along with approximately 160 Evangelical societies and organizations. As a photograph shows,[7] the stand featured the denomination's 'coat of arms', which seems to have been adopted around that time. The shield bears a St George's Cross, surmounted by a jewelled crozier and an open Bible. The heraldic supporters are a turbaned Middle Eastern shepherd holding a lamb in the folds of his robes, and an early nineteenth-century presbyter in frock coat and holding a Bible. The shield (though not the supporters) is still used on Free Church of England stationery and publications.

Some attempts were made to reach out to other Christian communities. One of the earliest of these seems to have been with the Moravians. The details of the contact remain to be explored, but they appear to have been initiated by the pre-union Reformed Episcopal Church, for, in 1921, Vaughan invited Moravian Bishop Herbert Mumford to take part in the consecration of Joseph Fenn. Further involvement in episcopal consecrations took place in 1938, 1950 and 1963.[8] The contact was understandable. Both the Moravian Church and the Free Church of England were Protestant episcopal Churches with an Evangelical piety and liturgical worship. As seen in Chapter 1 the two bodies shared a common heritage in the events of the Evangelical Revival. Indeed, given the fact that several of the Moravian congregations had been founded by Whitefield's lieutenant, Cennick (and others by Ingham), both the Moravians and the Free Church of England could be said to share a substantial common ancestry in the Whitefieldite section of the Revival. As recently as the 1960s Moravian representatives regularly attended Convocation. After that decade the contact seems to have been lost, perhaps partly because the Moravians began to move into mainstream ecumenical co-operation (for example the Covenant for Unity) where the Free Church of England did not follow.

In the 1960s tentative conversations also took place with the Wesleyan Reform Union, the Independent Methodists and the Countess of Huntingdon's Connexion. Representatives were sent to each other's annual meetings and pulpit exchanges took place. Attempts at actual union failed, chiefly because the other bodies 'did not desire Episcopacy'.[9] There were also doctrinal problems. As Ward put it: 'Within our ranks we had some who were opposed to Wesley's doctrine and were strongly for Calvinism and this upset the Wesleyan Reform Union and caused strained relationship.'[10]

The surviving Calvinism mentioned by Ward was strongest in the Southern Diocese at this period, and Richard Fenwick attributes to it the fact that more churches failed in the south than in the less doctrinally narrow north. Theological attitudes inhibited the development of a wider social and community life, the lack of which contributed to the demise of congregations.[11]

One practical consequence for the Free Church of England of this aloofness from ecumenical contact was that it was unable to take advantage of the sharing of church buildings and other facilities that was enabling other denominations to renew their work in existing areas and move into new ones. A further consequence was that the Free Church of England was denied access to grants or other funds that might have been available from ecumenical sources. It was not until 1954 that the Church joined the then Free Church Federal Council, after an earlier abortive attempt and much soul-searching.

An additional significant factor in the decline was the age of the leadership. Retirement from the ministry of the Church of England did not become compulsory until 1974, and then only applied to those appointed to office after that date. Compulsory retirement of Church officers at 75 has only just (2002) been introduced in the Free Church of England. One consequence of this has been good men staying in post after their powers have waned and they are no longer able to equip others to meet new challenges. A further factor is the canonical requirement for bishops not to be 'in any secular avocation or employment' (Canon 21), which, given the very small stipends available, has tended to restrict the office to men who have retired from other work. In the 68 years between the retirement of Bishop Lander in 1930 and the death of Bishop Cyril Milner in 1998 there were only three Bishops Primus. The problem is seen clearly with Frank Vaughan. As one of the denomination's greatest bishops he gave strong leadership throughout the first half of the twentieth century. But by the end of the Second World War he was 76, with failing hearing. He continued as Primus until his death in September 1962 at the age of 93 – greatly respected and loved by many, but unable to lead the Church in responding to a society changing out of all recognition.

Vaughan's successor as Primus, Thomas Cameron, was 73 when he took over. The other bishops were of similar age and, though often godly and much-loved pastors, were simply not capable of providing a clear vision, energy and strong leadership. Fenwick concludes of the bishops of this period: 'Most were . . . too elderly or too uncertain in health to have undertaken the office of Bishop with success when they did.'[12]

In the mid 1960s Bishop Burrell is reported as telling the denomination that it faced a choice between 'change and decay'.[13] By refusing the former, the Free Church of England chose the latter.

As a result of all these factors, 'from 1946 to 1975 the FCE was a "surviving Church" – but barely so'.[14]

1975–1997

By 1978 the entire previous generation of bishops was dead. Their place was taken by two men in their 50s who, though very different in many ways, were nevertheless to provide the denomination with a period of stability, halt the decline and even begin to encourage it in new directions.

Cyril Milner (1916–1998) had, after leaving school, been a member of the Methodist Church Mission in London. He joined the Free Church of England and was ordained deacon in 1945 as curate to Ambrose Bodfish at Saltley, Birmingham. In 1947 he became Rector of St Paul's Fleetwood where he was to remain until his death. He was involved in the wider community, and even served on the Lancashire Education Committee.[15] On 29 August 1973 Milner was consecrated by Cameron, Burrell and Watkins as assistant to Bishop Burrell in the Northern Diocese. Within a month Burrell was dead and Milner succeeded him. In 1975 he was elected Primus in place of Cameron who was 86. Within a year Watkins (the southern Diocesan) was seriously ill with Parkinson's disease, Forbes-Smith had died, and Cameron was incapable of anything but the lightest duties. Convocation therefore elected the Revd Arthur Ward to the episcopate.

Ward had been a commissioned Salvation Army officer and had joined the Free Church of England in 1957. After ordination he served at Bexhill-on-Sea, Exmouth and Teddington. He proved a competent and respected leader.[16] Ward's consecration took place on 11 September 1976. It was a historic event. For the first time a bishop of the Reformed Episcopal Church crossed the Atlantic to participate in the consecration of an English bishop.[17] The Presiding Bishop, Theophilus Herter, took the opportunity to strengthen the links between the sister Churches. Also taking part in the laying on of hands was Bishop Russell White, retired Bishop of Tonbridge in the Church of England Diocese of Rochester. White, who was an old friend of Ward, brought into the Free Church of England episcopate not only the nineteenth- and twentieth-century Church of England successions, but those of the Old Catholics and Swedish Lutherans.

By the end of the year Ward had succeeded Watkins as Southern Diocesan. Cameron died the following April. There were thus only two functioning bishops in the denomination. In view of the accelerating decline in membership experienced by all mainline denominations in the 1970s and 80s, it is remarkable that, under Milner and Ward, so many

Free Church of England congregations managed to keep functioning. Inevitably there were some losses. One of the most symbolic was perhaps Gregg's old church at Southend, which closed in 1980. Some of the rest were reinforced by people seeking an alternative to the liturgical upheavals then taking place in the Church of England. Some congregations had strong youth work attached, which helped keep numbers up. Hardly any were touched by the Charismatic Movement.

In 1986 Convocation elected another younger man to the episcopate. Kenneth Powell was a third-generation member of the denomination, based at Emmanuel, Saltley, near Birmingham. Alongside his work in sales marketing he had been ordained deacon in 1977 and presbyter in 1979. For three years after his consecration he was assistant to Ward, succeeding him as Diocesan in 1989. One of those laying on hands at Powell's consecration was the Revd Rowland Graves, President of the Wesleyan Reform Union, perpetuating the older contact.

The Ward–Milner years saw the coming into existence of two areas of work outside the UK which still exist. One is in New Zealand where, having started in 1983, six affiliated congregations had been formed by 2002. Opposition to liberal theology and the ordination of women seem to have been substantial motivating factors.[18] More surprisingly, was the request in 1989 by a number of Russians in St Petersburg (then Leningrad) for liturgical worship in an episcopal framework. Having been turned down by the Church of England Diocese in Europe (whose policy was not to encourage the formation of indigenous Anglican congregations) the group turned to the Free Church of England. After a visit by Bishop Powell it was accepted as bona fide and organized as a congregation. It uses a Russian translation of the denomination's Prayer Book with a few indigenous features. The presbyter is a physician who was ordained in 1993.

This modest overseas expansion (and the exotic experience of having a bearded Russian presbyter at Convocation) helped bolster the confidence of the denomination. Many churches were weak, but there was a growing feeling that they might have survived the worst. In 1994 the denomination celebrated the 150th anniversary of the 'freeing' of the Bridgetown Chapel with a series of events including a Special Service and celebratory dinner in May. The service was attended by the Bishop of Lewes (Ian Cundy) representing the Archbishop of Canterbury (see below). Another event was a 'Fun Day' held at Dudley Zoo on 2 July, attended by 1,000 members of the denomination. Under the realistic and trusted leadership of Milner, Ward and Powell the Free Church of England dared to consider new possibilities. In his Convocation Charge of that year Milner told the assembled delegates, 'It is . . . of paramount importance that we set in motion a pattern of growth within the church', though he acknowledged that 'congregations do not grow easily numerically'.[19] Poignantly, however, Milner also revealed that his primary 'model' was centred on the erection of church buildings, as it had been in the nineteenth century: 'I think we have to accept the fact that as conditions are at this present time we as a denomination have little or no opportunity of building churches in new areas. If that is a correct assumption then it is of paramount importance that we keep the churches we have.'[20]

In 1994, however, Milner's attention was elsewhere.

Conversations with the Church of England 1992–1997

As long ago as 1867 Bishop Price had spoken of the Free Church of England as 'possessing more sympathy with the Church of England, and from our position more ready to extend the right hand of fellowship, than some Christian bodies . . .'.[21] In practice, as has been seen, Price's attitude was not reflected in the denomination as a whole. Locally, matters were complicated by the fact that Free Church of England, Reformed Episcopal Church and Reformed Church of England congregations were deliberately planted in Anglo-Catholic parishes. There was inevitably little local sympathy or desire for rapprochement.[22] In 1946 a motion had been brought to Convocation, encouraging moves towards the Church of England (and, interestingly, pre-dating Archbishop Fisher's appeal to the Free Churches of November that year), but it had been soundly defeated.

In the late 1980s informal contact was established between the Free Church of England and the Church of England as part of Archbishop Robert Runcie's commitment to 'all-round ecumenism'. A number of initiatives flowed from this.

The May 1991 Convocation asked the Evangelical Alliance to sponsor the gazetting of the denomination under the Sharing of Church Buildings Act. This allows the Free Church of England to share premises (under agreed conditions) with other Churches that are similarly gazetted. The same Convocation also voted to request the Archbishops of

Canterbury and York for 'designated status' under the Ecumenical Relations Measure.[23] This was duly done on 28 January 1992. This means that under the Ecumenical Canons of the Church of England (B43 and B44), Church of England clergy and laity may, subject to a number of provisos, lawfully perform within the Free Church of England (at the request of the appropriate denominational authorities) a range of liturgical functions that they are permitted to perform within the Established Church. Similarly, Free Church of England clergy and laity may be invited to perform equivalent functions in Church of England worship. Apart from making possible sharing in each other's worship on an occasional or regular basis, the provision would also allow Free Church of England congregations without a minister to seek help from Church of England clergy. Were the two Churches ever to be members of a Local Ecumenical Partnership (LEP), even closer reciprocity would be possible.

The following year, in May 1992, Convocation accepted a Council recommendation to request conversations with the Church of England with a view to establishing closer fellowship. The motion, proposed by the Revd John Knight and seconded by Dennis Harvey, the Registrar, was carried by 48 votes to 28.[24] Following the vote, Milner, as Primus wrote to Archbishop Carey on 6 July 1992 informing him of Convocation's request. Representatives from the two Churches met three times between December 1992 and December 1993, the meetings being chaired by Bishop Milner and the Bishop of Lewes, the Rt Revd Ian Cundy.[25] The outcome was a recommendation to both Churches that a small group work on the theological issues that were perceived as dividing the Churches. This was put to Convocation in May 1994 and the motion, proposed by the Registrar, Dennis Harvey, that talks should continue, was carried.[26] With this mandate the nominated group met during 1995 and 1996, drawing up a draft report similar in format to those agreed between the Church of England and other Churches. After an Introduction and Historical Outline of the Free Church of England, the three main sections were entitled 'Our Common Calling to Full Visible Unity', 'What We Can Now Agree in Faith' and 'Next Steps'. The methodology was to draw where possible on existing ecumenical agreements to try and achieve consistency with other dialogues.

The draft report was presented in May 1997 to Convocation, the membership of which had changed significantly since 1994. Bishop Ward had died in August 1995. He had been a strong supporter of the

Conversations, having told Convocation, 'If we do not move forward with these unity discussions, then, ultimately, we will die.'[27] A number of new men of very different views to Bishop Ward had joined the denomination. On 2 September 1994 Arthur Bentley-Taylor, formerly a member of an independent Presbyterian Church in Wales, had been ordained deacon to serve at Emmanuel, Workington, and was made a presbyter the following year.[28] On 29 April 1995 the Revd Dr Barry Shucksmith was received as a presbyter from the Church of England by Bishop Powell, and was licensed as Curate to Emmanuel Church, Farnham, where he was installed as incumbent in July 1997.[29] Shucksmith had been ordained to a curacy in the Diocese of Southwark in 1968, but 'it was not long before I fell foul of the Bishop of Southwark, and had to exercise my ministry at home in Independent Churches, and overseas in the Church of England in South Africa, in order to be faithful to the Lord'.[30] After a spell as a Royal Navy chaplain, Shucksmith became incumbent of St Mary's Broughton in the Diocese of Lincoln, but resigned 'as a Priest of the Established Church' on 22 February 1994, following the promulgation of the Canon permitting the ordination of women as priests in the Church of England.[31] His convictions that 'God is about to judge the Established Church of England, for its unfaithfulness to Him, in a way that we have not seen for centuries' and that 'I do not believe that the Church of England will ever again do good to our Nation'[32] inevitably made him an immediate opponent of the Conversations. At Convocation on 22 May 1996, just over 12 months since he had been licensed in the Free Church of England, Shucksmith was elected a bishop (with responsibilities as Assistant Bishop in the Southern Diocese and for the Churches Overseas). His consecration took place at Christ Church Teddington on 16 October of that year.[33]

When in May 1997 Convocation came to discuss the Report of the Conversations with the Church of England, it was also circulated with a paper by Bentley-Taylor, entitled 'Analysis and Assessment of "A Report of the Free Church of England and the Church of England Informal Conversations 1992–96"', running to four closely typed A4 sheets.[34] The *Analysis* asks some fair questions of the Report, but also betrays some fundamental misunderstandings and a mindset seriously inimical to ecumenical endeavour. Within the first 12 lines it informs Convocation that accepting the Report would commit them 'to courses long since repudiated by the founders of the FCE' and that 'the Report commences a transformation of the FCE from a Protestant and Evangelical cause into a pre-Reformation, Sacramental Church'.[35] Two fundamental concerns seem to lie behind Bentley-Taylor's arguments. The first is his conviction that the Church of England is no longer a Gospel Church, being riddled by 'hypocrisy of the worst kind' which he sees in the formal consent to the Thirty-Nine Articles and Book of Common Prayer by Church of England bishops who 'thereafter proceed to write books denying them'.[36] The second is the belief that 'some members of the FCE are aware that the ecumenical movement has long since become an interfaith movement'.[37]

Bentley-Taylor rightly points out that the roots of the Free Church of England 'long pre-date the ritualist movement of the 19th century'. He protests most strongly, however, at the description of the nineteenth-century founding fathers as 'anti-ritualists'.[38] This position appears extraordinary in the light of his own subsequent calls for the denomination to remain firmly 'anti-Tractarian', and Shucksmith's recommendation in his paper 'Agenda For Renewal 2002–2012' that the Free Church of England needs to re-emphasize that it is 'evidently anti-tractarian'.[39] Bentley-Taylor's words about members of the Free Church of England not being 'nervous and emotional reactionaries'[40] have a curious ring to them.

At points the *Analysis* simply misunderstands what the Report is saying. The reference to 'baptism inseparable from faith and conversion'[41] is *not* saying that 'every baptized person, irrespective of age or conviction, is by baptism constituted a converted believer'.[42] It is in fact saying precisely what the Free Church of England has always said about baptism, namely that baptism needs to be accompanied by faith and conversion if a person is to become a member of the *koinonia* 'grounded in the life of the Holy Trinity'.[43] The *Analysis* reading of the text here and in other places seems to be perverse.

The foregoing examples should suffice to give a flavour of the type of arguments presented against the Report. Bentley-Taylor, in addition to theological opposition, was prepared to believe that bribery was involved: 'there are many rumours circulating to the effect that offers were made to the FCE representatives if they brought the FCE back into the Church of England'.[44] The idea that canonries and other preferments might be showered on the Free Church of England members of the Conversations if they 'delivered up' the Free Church of England indicates something of the thought-world that some of those opposed to the Report live in.

The Convocation Minutes record that after Bentley-Taylor had spoken to his *Analysis*, he 'was followed by seven other clergy, all of whom spoke passionately against the continuation of the Talks . . .'.[45] These were followed by the Revd Dr Mark Gretason, one of the delegates, 'with an eloquent and well-reasoned speech'. Of the remaining speakers 'six spoke in favour and eight against'. The final vote 'resulted in 61% being in favour of discontinuing the talks'.[46]

With hindsight, it can be seen that the Report failed to gain acceptance for three main reasons:

- Those in favour had little experience of bringing a document and issues of this kind to Convocation. There seem to have been no adequate attempts to educate the delegates in the issues and their implications in preparation for the debate.
- There was clearly a vocal and well-organized opposition.[47] Some of the motivation for this lay not simply in unease with the Report itself but with a passionate dislike of the Church of England and the perceived aims of the ecumenical movement. Doubt also seems to have been cast on the motives of the Report's authors.
- Many of the 'ordinary' members of Convocation were uncertain what the consequences of accepting the Report would be. In fact it would have done little more than authorize a further set of 'Formal Talks' and open up to the Free Church of England a number of resources, particularly in the area of ministerial training. Not all seem to have understood this, some apparently believing it would commit the Free Church of England to joining the Church of England. The language of Bentley-Taylor's paper evoked that of the nineteenth-century literature of the denomination, suggesting that it was again involved in a life or death struggle. It is not surprising that many 'waverers' voted against the Report, believing that they were benefiting the Free Church of England by doing so.

On the Church of England side, the decision of Convocation not to proceed with talks was noted with great regret. Mutual respect and friendships had grown up in an atmosphere very different to former times. The Conversations were noted as a sign of hope at the 1998 Lambeth Conference, but also as a reminder that reconciliation with bodies that had left the official Anglican Communion was not going to be easy.[48]

The Aftermath

The collapse of the talks with the Church of England in May 1997 in effect brought the Ward–Milner era to an end. In September 1997 Cyril Milner celebrated 50 years as Rector of St Paul's Fleetwood. Just over a year later, on 29 November 1998, he died aged 82. He had been Bishop Primus since 1975. The Bishop of Peterborough, who had been Milner's co-chairman in the Conversations, attended his funeral at Fleetwood.

Milner's death left Kenneth Powell as the only bishop in the denomination, as Shucksmith had written to tender his resignation with immediate effect on 19 November 1998. On 23 April 1999, however, Shucksmith wrote again, seeking now to withdraw his resignation. This change of mind may have been prompted by the election of Bentley-Taylor to be Bishop of the Northern Diocese in succession to Milner, by the Diocesan Synod on 24 March 1999. The obvious candidate had been John McLean of Morecambe, who had held a number of important posts at diocesan and denominational level, but he had been taken ill on the day of the election and would not allow his name to go forward. In the event, at Convocation in May 1999, McLean (now recovered) was elected a bishop (with 84 per cent of the vote). Bentley-Taylor's election as Bishop of the Northern Diocese was not in fact ratified by Convocation with the necessary two-thirds majority, but was allowed to stand following scenes of protest from Bentley-Taylor's supporters. The same Convocation referred the question of Shucksmith's status to Counsel's Opinion.

Prior to the consecration of McLean and Bentley-Taylor the English succession was nearly extinguished by the sudden illness of the new Primus, Powell, who required emergency surgery. His death would have left the denomination without a canonically active bishop. He recovered sufficiently to perform the consecrations at Christ Church Wallasey on 11 September 1999, assisted by two bishops of the Reformed Episcopal Church who came over from America.

The status of Shucksmith was handled by the May 2000 Convocation where it was reported that, 'It was Counsel's opinion that Bishop Shucksmith had effectively retired himself.'[49] Bentley-Taylor proposed that Counsel's Opinion be not accepted and that Bishop Shucksmith had not resigned. After debate Bentley-Taylor's motion was carried by 49 votes to 20, with 3 abstentions.

As an immediate consequence of this, Powell, who had found it virtually impossible to work with Shucksmith, announced that he would therefore not stand for re-election as Primus that year. The announcement clearly took everyone by surprise. The minutes record that 'Bishop Shucksmith indicated that he was not prepared to stand for election to that office. Bishop McLean declined the invitation extended to him, and at the invitation of the Chairman Bishop Bentley-Taylor agreed to his name going forward.'[50] As the only candidate he was duly elected, but not unanimously. Powell stood for Primus at Convocation in 2001, but was defeated by Bentley-Taylor. In 2002 he proposed Bentley-Taylor, who was elected unopposed. Bentley-Taylor was elected Primus for the final time in June 2003.

The last five years have thus seen the Free Church of England enduring a period of turmoil, where the dominant voices have been reminiscent of the era of Dicksee and Richardson, almost exactly a century before. There appear to have been deliberate attempts to dismantle some of the achievements of the Ward–Milner era. As in earlier episodes, much of the motivation seems to have derived from a deliberate misunderstanding of the intrinsic rationale of the denomination which an official tract produced in the 1950s summed up thus: 'Ours is a broad, comprehensive and evangelical basis of fellowship.'[51] Instead of this generous, unthreatened sense of identity, there have been moves to create a narrow, more restrictive body. This has been seen most particularly in the sphere of relations with other Churches. The transformation of the Free Church Federal Council into the Free Churches Group within Churches Together in Britain and Ireland has prompted calls (as might be expected given the attitudes recorded above) for the Free Church of England to cease its membership. Bentley-Taylor's proposal to that effect was however defeated by 17 votes to 1 at Council in March 2002. The denomination remains in the Free Churches Group, but only, bizarrely, 'as a stand against Churches Together in England'.[52]

Slight progress is being made in a number of other areas, such as the agreement of a retirement date of 75 for executive officers[53] and the permitting of the New International Version as an authorized version of the Bible for use in church (along with the Authorised Version, Revised Standard Version and New King James Version).[54]

In practice, however, much of this feels like 'arranging the chairs on the deck of the Titanic'. The seventy-fifth anniversary of the creation of the united Church, found the denomination in some turmoil, racked by acrimonious dispute, dubious conduct and completely at a loss where to go. Vaughan's words of 1944 had returned with a vengeance: 'Time and time again [the little Church] was betrayed from within; often it had to prune its branches and re-group its forces; at times it seemed likely that it would destroy itself.'[55]

Convocation in June 2003 achieved little. Bentley-Taylor was re-elected as Primus, but only by a majority of 6 votes over Powell. Shucksmith's 'Agenda for Renewal 2002–2012' was not adopted as the way forward for the denomination, but was referred to a committee. A motion requiring tighter adherence to the Canons and Bye-laws regarding the admission of clergy from other denominations, and ordination was not put to Convocation by Bentley-Taylor (who was soon to be formally accused of abuses in these areas), but referred to a committee. Nothing was achieved towards uniting the denomination around a common vision.

This unsatisfactory state of affairs reached a head in July 2003. Earlier in the year complaints had been made to the Charity Commissioners about some of Bentley-Taylor's activities, and eventually a series of formal Accusations were made against him under the Disciplinary Canons. Shucksmith resigned from the denomination in protest.[56] In an attempt to prevent Bentley-Taylor standing trial a number of his supporters called a Special Convocation, which was held on 4 October 2003. At that meeting, however, Bentley-Taylor announced his resignation as Primus and Diocesan Bishop with effect from the end of the month. A fortnight later, at the Northern Diocesan Synod on 22 October, he announced that he was withdrawing from the Free Church of England. On 15 November 2003 the Council confirmed Bentley-Taylor's resignation and ordered that a Letter Dimissory be sent to him. At the same meeting the Council appointed Powell as Primus. McLean was appointed Bishop of the Northern Diocese and was confirmed in that office by the Diocesan Synod on 24 March 2004. A number of clergy and laity who refused to accept the jurisdiction of Bishops Powell and McLean were ruled by the denominational solicitors and by a special convocation held on 6 March 2004 to have placed themselves outside the Free Church of England.

The resignations of Shucksmith and Bentley-Taylor and the withdrawal from the denomination of their closest supporters hopefully begins to draw a line under what has been a very unhappy period in the life of the Free Church of England. The episode has highlighted a number of issues which are discussed more fully in Chapter 13. Clearly some difficult decisions lie ahead, but recent developments raise the possibility of a new start for the Free Church of England. Much will depend on the leadership given by Powell and McLean, and whether or not the denomination is capable of learning the lessons of its past. The words of Bishop Eldridge in 1901 have a new relevance: 'We cannot erase the past; what we have written we have written; but we need not write again the same sad story of failure and sin.'[57]

Notes

1. The name 'Free Church of England' is used for convenience of the post-1927 united Church. The correct legal name is of course 'The Free Church of England otherwise called the Reformed Episcopal Church'.
2. Including Emmanuel, Workington and St David's, Preston.
3. See Kirby, *Elect Lady* (2nd edn), pp. 59ff. for a brief account of the Sierra Leone Mission.
4. For details see Fenwick, *Thesis*, p. 483.
5. Ibid., p. 478.
6. Ibid., pp. 483ff. and 489ff.
7. See the photograph in Vaughan, *History* (2nd edn) facing p. 109.
8. See the official list of consecrations in the Year Book. Curiously, there is no memory or record of Free Church of England bishops taking part in Moravian consecrations; see the Moravian list of consecrations published in J. T. and K. G. Hamilton, *The History of the Moravian Church* (Bethlehem, PA, 1967), pp. 645–53.
9. Letter from The Rt Revd Arthur Ward to the present writer, dated 9 April 1991.
10. Ibid.
11. Fenwick, *Thesis*, pp. 492, 618.
12. Ibid., p. 494.
13. Quoted in *Reformed Episcopal Viewpoint: An Independent Forum for Friends of the Free Church of England* (No. 2, Winter 1996).
14. Fenwick, *Thesis*, p. 494.
15. Milner's obituary can be found in the *FCE Year Book 1999–2000*, p. 7.
16. A brief summary of Ward's ministry can be found in the insert to the *FCE Year Book 1995–96*.
17. The reverse had happened. Vaughan, for example, had taken part in conse-

crations in America.

18. A similar affiliated movement in Australia did not survive. In 2003 the organization in New Zealand was downgraded to 'Scattered Members'. The 2003–2004 *Year Book* describes the situation in New Zealand as 'very desperate', p. 63.

19. *FCE Year Book 1994–95*, p. 12.

20. Ibid. Milner's approach was criticized in the periodical *Reformed Episcopal Viewpoint* (No. 2, Winter 1996), which pointed out that other Churches had experienced growth without having to have a building first.

21. *FCE Magazine*, July 1867, p. 198.

22. It had been policy from the first not to initiate a work in Evangelical parishes (Merryweather, p. 86).

23. Minutes of Convocation, *FCE Year Book 1991–92*, p. 45.

24. Minutes of Convocation, *FCE Year Book 1992–93*, pp. 50f.

25. Bishop of Peterborough from 1996.

26. Minutes of Convocation, *FCE Year Book 1994–95*, p. 47.

27. Quoted in Fenwick, *Thesis*, p. 507.

28. *FCE Year Book 1995–96*, p. 25; ibid. *1996–97*, p. 27.

29. Ibid., *1996–97*, p. 36; ibid., *1998–99*, p. 27.

30. J. B. Shucksmith, *Honest For God* (Cosham, J & B Books, 1996), p. 11.

31. Ibid., p. 59.

32. Ibid., pp. 30, 11.

33. *FCE Year Book 1996–97*, p. 50.

34. Hereafter, cited as *Analysis*. I am grateful to Bishop Bentley-Taylor for providing me with a copy. Convocation Minutes state that the paper was by Shucksmith, but Bentley-Taylor assured the present writer that it was his work.

35. *Analysis*, p. 1.

36. Ibid.

37. Ibid., p. 2.

38. Ibid.

39. For example, Bentley-Taylor asks whether the Free Church of England 'intends to remain faithful to . . . its anti-Tractarian stance' in his report as Primus. *FCE Year Book 2002–2003*, p. 20. 'Agenda for Renewal 2002–2012', p. 2.

40. *Analysis*, p. 1.

41. *Report*, para. 39.

42. *Analysis*, p. 3.

43. *Report*, para. 39.

44. Letter to the present writer, dated 9 October 1999.

45. Minutes of 1997 Convocation, *FCE Year Book 1997–98*, p. 46.

46. Ibid.
47. Anecdotal evidence suggests some co-ordination of speakers.
48. Dyer *et al.*, *Conference Report*, p. 228.
49. Convocation Minutes, *FCE Year Book 2000–2001*, p. 48.
50. Ibid.
51. To Introduce and Welcome You to the Free Church of England, FCE New
    Series p. 1(b).
52. Council Minutes; see *FCE Year Book 2002–2003*, p. 21.
53. The same as in the Roman Catholic Church.
54. For the text of these new bye-laws, see *FCE Year Book 2002–2003*, p. 91.
55. Vaughan, *Prospect and Retrospect: the Centenary Charge* (printed by Wallasey
    and Wirral Newspaper Co., 1944), p. 6.
56. 'Kindly receive this letter as my resignation from Farnham and the
    Denomination,' he wrote to Powell, his Diocesan, on 24 July 2003. In the same
    letter Shucksmith also stated that he could 'no longer with good heart and
    conscience commend the Free Church of England, as it is at the present time,
    to my flock, friends or the general Christian public'. The comment was made
    that Shucksmith's statement might actually benefit the Free Church of
    England by deterring from joining it the sort of people who had caused so
    much trouble in recent years. Shucksmith's resignation from the denomin-
    ation was formally ratified by Council at its meeting on 8 October 2003.
57. 'Christmas and New Year Message' in *Work and Worship* (January 1901), p. 43.

CHAPTER 9

Constitution and Organization

The present-day Free Church of England is organized and functions in accordance with the 'Constitution and Canons Ecclesiastical' drawn up preparatory to the union of 1927.[1] The current version, incorporating some minor subsequent amendments, is dated 1983. As the name suggests, this corpus is intended to fulfil much the same function as the 'Constitutions and Canons Ecclesiastical' of 1604 did for the Church of England prior to the promulgating of a new set between 1964 and 1969.[2] The Free Church of England corpus does not, however, derive from that of the Church of England. As might be expected from the Church's history, it derives from two main sources: the Countess of Huntingdon's Connexion and the Protestant Episcopal Church in the USA.

The constitutional and canonical organization of Churches has until recently been a much neglected field of study. That is now changing with (in the Anglican world) the studies of Bray and Doe in particular.[3] In the absence of any existing study of the Constitution of the Free Church of England, it is helpful to trace its development in some detail. It is clear, however, that the subject would repay rigorous academic research.

The Development of the 1863 Constitution of the Free Church of England

As noted in Chapter 2 in particular, the first Constitution of the Free Church of England under that name was adopted by the Conference of the

Countess of Huntingdon's Connexion on St John the Baptist's Day 1863 and enrolled in a Deed Poll in the High Court of Chancery. That Constitution was not, however, a *de novo* creation; rather, it was the culmination of a process of development reaching back into the previous century.

The 'Plan' of 1790

Drawing up sets of rules for Christian communities was very much a feature of the eighteenth-century Evangelical Revival. Zinzendorff had drawn up Statutes for the Herrnhut community in 1727.[4] Daniel Rowland and John Wesley had done the same for their societies from 1742 and Ingham in the 1750s.[5] By comparison, the attempt to organize definitively Lady Huntingdon's followers came late in the day.

The 'Plan for an Association for Uniting and Perpetuating the Connection of the Right Honourable the Countess Dowager of Huntingdon' was issued on 3 March 1790 on behalf of the Countess in the name of her Secretary, George Best.[6] It had been drawn up by 'several ministers and laymen' at Lady Huntingdon's invitation and was submitted to her and to the congregations for consideration. The Plan in fact was little more than the regularizing of the system of itinerant preachers which the Countess had been running almost single-handedly up to this point. It divided England (including Monmouth, then part of England) into 23 Districts, listing the Chapels in each of them, together with any 'horse rides' – series of preaching stations visited on horseback. Each District was to have a Committee, consisting of the ministers with two laymen from each congregation.

The Committee for the District of London was to be known as the London Acting Association. This body was to exercise a supervisory role over the Districts, which were to send to it accounts of their quarterly meetings.[7] Once a year each District was to send one minister and two laymen to meet with the London Acting Association; this joint body, together with the Trustees of the College, was to constitute the General Association of the Connexion.[8] Its task was to have been to oversee the 'state and concerns' of the Connexion and to settle all disputed matters. Delegated power from the General Association was to reside in the London Acting Association.

A 'General Association Fund' was to be created and the members of the Societies 'invited to contribute an assistance of not less than a penny a week'. This was to be entrusted to District Treasurers who were to forward it to the Treasurer of the London Acting Association. The General Association was to decide how this money was to be spent 'for the benefit and sole use of the connection'. It was not, however, envisaged that this would be primarily on buildings. These were a local responsibility. Any General Association Fund money intended for 'new buildings or the erection of galleries' required a seven-eighths majority.

As seen in Chapter 1, the Plan was never adopted. On the Countess's death her ownership of the chapels passed to four Trustees, the senior of whom, Thomas Haweis, seems to have continued to run the Connexion as essentially a 'preaching agency', loosely affiliated (at least in Haweis's mind) to the Church of England.

The 1836 Constitution

With Haweis's death in 1820 the situation changed. From 1821 the Ministers of the Connexion began to meet annually and to elect one of their number as President of the meeting. (For 1823 and 1824 the President was a lay Trustee. From 1825 to 1829 the single lay Trustee was joined by a Minister. From 1829 only Ministers were elected President.[9]) By 1836 it was felt necessary to 'declare what persons are Members of the said Conference and how the Succession and Identity thereof is to be continued . . .'.[10] To that end it was declared that the 'Ordained Ministers of the said Connexion . . . together with the said Trustees of Lady Huntingdon's Connexion and also the Trustees of Cheshunt College . . . and the Elders Deacons and Managers of the respective Congregations of such Ministers do and shall constitute the said Annual Conference . . .'.[11]

The Regulations by which the affairs of the Conference were to be organized were set out in 11 clauses, which bear the marks of being developed from the 1790 Plan.

The name used for the national body that was to meet annually is 'Conference or Association'. It is clearly modelled on the Plan's 'General Association', though in practice only the name 'Conference' seems to have been used.

There is no provision for the division of the country into Districts. Presumably by this time the contraction of the Connexion had rendered this unnecessary. There is therefore no reference to reporting back to a central Committee, nor, indeed, is such a Committee provided for. Rather, the Conference members immediately upon assembling are to choose a President from among themselves. The President 'shall have and may exercise during his Presidency such powers privileges and authorities as the Conference or Association shall from time to time see fit to entrust into his hands' (clause 4). It is difficult to avoid the conclusion that Thomas Haweis had provided the model for this role in his twenty-nine years of oversight over the Connexion. The President is to have the support of a Secretary who is also to be appointed by Conference (clause 4).

All decisions require a three-quarters majority to become Acts of the Conference, so long as there is a minimum of 12 members present. The powers of Conference include those of being able to expel any who maintain doctrines contrary to the Fifteen Articles of Faith of the Connexion or are found guilty of immoral conduct (such a person is to be treated 'as if he were naturally dead' – clauses 5 and 7).

The 1836 Constitution also (unlike the 1790 Plan) makes provision for the increase of the ministry. Candidates for ordination are to serve as Probationers in the Connexion for at least six months after which they are to be examined by the Conference 'touching their doctrine, manner of life and usefulness' (clause 6). If approved by a three-quarters majority 'they are to be Ordained and admitted Ministers of the Connexion' (clause 7). The Minister's place of service is to be directed by Conference, subject to any local Deeds. Conference also has the power to expel from his charge any Minister guilty of unsound teaching (clause 9).

Conference 'shall and may from time to time make such Bye-laws, Orders and Regulations for the furtherance and execution of the objects and intents of these Presents . . . as they shall from time to time deem necessary' (clause 8). All such enactments 'shall be entered and written in the Journals to be kept for that purpose and, when entered, publicly read to the Conference or Association and then subscribed by the President and Secretary thereof for the time being during the time such Conference or Association shall be assembled' (clause 10). Only such publicly attested enactments are to have any force.

Should the membership of the Conference drop below 12 for three years running, 'the said Conference is to be extinguished' and all authority return to the Trustees of the properties (clause 11).

By comparison with the 1790 Plan, the Constitution of 1836 clearly shows a degree of development. There are now explicit rules for the admitting of new ministers and, significantly, an office of oversight or *episkope* is beginning to emerge. It is elective and usually annual (rather like the President of the Methodist Conference or the Moderator of the General Assembly of the Church of Scotland) but, like those offices, clearly has a role beyond the actual meeting of the Conference. Haweis's 'with us a few preside' has become 'with us *one* presides'.

The 1863 Constitution

When Thomas Thoresby sought to draw up for the Free Church of England a Constitution which he saw as fulfilling the intention of the Countess, it is clear that he had the 1790 Plan and the 1836 Constitution in front of him. Both, in fact, are mentioned in the Deed Poll of 1863. Significantly, there does not seem ever to have been any independent constitution or organizational structures for the post-1844 'Free Churches', despite the fact that they were at times spoken of as constituting a unit independent of the Connexion.[12] The only *institutional* continuity is that provided by the Connexion.

Like the 1836 Constitution, that of 1863 begins with a Preamble reciting the history of the movement back to the desire of Lady Huntingdon 'to assist in the Propagation of the Gospel', and the appointment of various Trustees in the intervening years. Reference is then made to the 1836 and 1790 arrangements. The latter is stated to have been 'only partially acted upon' and the former is clearly felt not to govern the Connexion 'in accordance with the original design of the said Countess'. Nevertheless, the verbal similarities between the 1836 and 1863 Constitutions in several places confirm the evolution of one from the other.

The annual 'Assembly' is now designated 'Convocation' to distinguish it from the Connexional Conference (whose members are also deemed members of Convocation – clause 7). The composition of the Convocation is refined from the 'Minister, Trustees, Elders, Deacons and Managers' of 1836 to 'all Bishops, Presbyters and Deacons of the Church' (clause 6). Presbyters include both Teaching and Ruling Elders, and Deacons include both Managers and Churchwardens, but the shift to traditional terminology is remarkable. There is no 'lay' representation as such.

Convocation is to have a 'President or Bishop Primus of the whole body', but the person may not be chosen from any of the members or ministers, rather he must be one of the Presbyters already chosen by his fellow-Presbyters and the Deacons to 'have the oversight for the common good of all the Congregations in a given District or Diocese' (clause 4). This is clearly highly significant. The division of England into Districts as envisaged in 1790 is to take place, but these are now to be known as Dioceses and each is to be under the oversight of an individual designated a 'Bishop'. Furthermore, only one of these Diocesan Bishops can become Primus. Clause 5 expressly declares that 'in the Free Church of England there are two orders of Ministers *videlicet* Bishops and Deacons', but the actual disposition of ministries moves in a much more hierarchical direction.

Bishop Price explicitly traced the origins of the District Meeting to the 1790 Plan, and referred to it as 'having in it the nature of a Diocesan Synod'.[13] Price saw the District Meeting as 'the keystone of the arch' and gave directions for its profitable use.

Just as the 1836 Constitution allowed Conference to define the powers of the President, so that of 1863 directs that 'Convocation shall from time to time prescribe and declare the duties of the Bishop Primus and the Diocesan Bishops respectively and the period of time for which they shall remain in Office' (clause 17). The latter provision suggests that a period of exercise of *episkope* longer than one year is being envisaged.

Clause 10 of 1863 requires the appointment of a Secretary in language virtually identical with the earlier Constitution.

Similarly, clauses 12 (the power of Convocation to make bye-laws, etc), 13 (the requirement that all enactments be recorded, read and signed in the presence of Convocation in order to have effect) and 15 (concerning the six-month probationary period of candidates for the ministry and the need for them to be approved by three quarters of Convocation) reproduce almost verbatim clauses 8, 10 and 6 of 1836.

By comparison with the earlier Constitution, that of 1863 lays much more emphasis on the importance of ordination, clauses 19 and 25 in particular stressing its necessity before any pastoral appointment is entered into. Curiously, nothing is said about the minister or place of ordination. Presumably Thoresby intended that the Connexional practice of ordination by senior ministers would evolve naturally into ordination by senior Presbyters/Bishops. Convocation (like Conference before it) is to appoint the Ministers to 'the several Churches or Chapels forming the Free Church of England' or, significantly, 'shall direct the manner and conditions of such appointments' (clause 18). In practice, the appointing of clergy to their charges was to pass from Convocation to the bishops. Convocation may expel any member for maintaining Doctrines contrary to the Thirty-Nine Articles or proven guilty of immoral conduct 'or who shall refuse to conform to the usages of the Free Church of England' (clause 11). This last provision has no counterpart in 1836 and suggests a desire to prevent the diversity of worship styles and dress spreading in the Connexion.

The doctrinal basis of 1836 was the Fifteen Articles (there is no mention of them in the 1790 Plan). In 1863 the basis is 'the Bible' (clause 2). Also accepted 'as in accordance with the Bible' are the Thirty-Nine Articles and Rubric of the United Church of England and Ireland. The Fifteen Articles are treated 'as included in the said Thirty-Nine Articles'. The doctrinal affirmation required of all members of Convocation, clergy and office bearers is: 'I do believe the Holy Scriptures of the Old and New Testament to be the Word of God and to contain all things necessary to Salvation and I do sincerely engage to conform to the Doctrines and Worship of the Free Church of England.' Interestingly, this does not derive from the Subscription required by clergy of the Church of England. It is, however, identical with that devised in 1789 for the Protestant Episcopal Church in the USA (see below). If Thoresby himself was not aware of the situation in PECUSA, some of the Church of England clergy whom he consulted probably were. The formula was no doubt attractive because of its uncompromising statement that the Old and New Testaments are the Word of God. There is no such statement prescribed in 1836, though subscription to the Fifteen Articles is essential. Given the doctrinal controversies (both of the previous century and currently raging), it is remarkable that the declaration is not more narrowly defined.

The 1836 Constitution had no need to make provision for the ownership and trusteeship of property and chapels as this was already provided for in the terms of the Countess's will. By contrast, the 1863 Constitution has three clauses (21, 22 and 23) devoted to the matter, requiring, among other things, that all Trustees be 'Communicants and Members of the Free Church of England'.

Unlike the 1790 Plan, there is no provision for district/diocesan committees. This is perhaps surprising, but it must be remembered that there were no Diocesan Synods in the Church of England at this time, to suggest such a structure. It would not have been part of the experience of the 'evangelical Churchmen' whom Thoresby consulted. Nor is there any equivalent of the London Acting Association, either in 1836 or 1863. It may be that the creation of the role of 'President' or 'Bishop Primus' was felt to render such a corporate body unnecessary. Alternately, some provision may have been made in the bye-laws (the earliest of which do not seem to have survived).

The three Constitutions of 1790, 1836 and 1863 thus show a clear evolution. From the 'preaching agency' envisaged by the dying Countess can be seen developing an ecclesiology which is moving in the direction of that of traditional catholic Christendom. The Free Church of England is to be a unified body, controlling its own property, served by a ministry broadly grouped into Bishops, Presbyters and Deacons and governed by a representative body. The anomalies of the Connexion, not least the separation of the Ministers from the two groups of Trustees, are removed. Even so, many of the more Anglican-minded members of the movement were unhappy with it, and a desire for a full-blooded Anglican Constitution was to be a significant factor in the setting up of the Reformed Episcopal Church in the UK in 1877.[14]

As an independent corpus the 1863 Constitution was to be short-lived. Although it survived formally until 1927, most of those years were spent in the shadow of another constitution whose origins were very different.

The Development of the 1877 Constitution of the Reformed Episcopal Church

Ironically, less documentary evidence seems to have survived concerning the creation of the Constitution of the United Kingdom branch of the Reformed Episcopal Church, than of the chronologically earlier Constitution of the Free Church of England. Although the process is less well chronicled, what is clear is that the Reformed Episcopal Constitution is essentially a modification of that of the Protestant Episcopal Church in the USA. To understand it, therefore, it is necessary to look at the origins of that document.

The formation of the Protestant Episcopal Constitution

Chapter 4 has already provided a brief glimpse at the reconstruction work necessary if a Protestant Episcopal Church was to survive American

independence from Britain. There were no bishops, no diocesan structures (such as there was had nominally been part of the Diocese of
London), no Convocations or Synods, no clear notion of where ultimate
ecclesiastical authority rested.

It soon became clear that the challenge was to bring together the
'proto-constitutions' being drawn up by such groups as the clergy of
Maryland (August 1783), the clergy and laity of Pennsylvania (May 1784)
and the clergy of the southern states who met in New York (October 1784).
This last gathering had produced seven 'Fundamental Principles' which
were to be used as the basis for a constitution. The following year – in
September 1785 – the first General Convention, meeting at Christ Church,
Philadelphia, appointed a committee to produce a draft Constitution.
The author was William White: 'The constitution was drafted by [myself]
in a sub-committee; part of a general committee, consisting of a clergyman and a layman from each state.'[15] This draft – anticipated in some
respects in the 1784 'Fundamental Principles' and modified before its final
adoption in 1789 – was, nevertheless, 'the root out of which the constitutional system of the Church has grown'.[16] For former members of the
Church of England in the 13 Colonies, 'the adoption of the constitution
created a Church, as the simultaneous adoption of the Constitution of the
United States created a nation'.[17]

There seems to be no evidence that Bishop Cummins had any
major objection to the PECUSA Constitution,[18] other than a frustration
in using it to control growing Anglo-Catholic practices. On the contrary,
its association with Bishop White and the earlier, 'purer' days of the
Protestant Episcopal Church no doubt made it attractive in his eyes. In all
events, he and his General Council modelled the first Reformed Episcopal
Church constitution upon it.

Further influences on the Constitution of the Reformed Episcopal Church

It is important to see Cummins's constitutional work in its wider context.
In the mid nineteenth century constitutional issues were a very real
concern in the growing Anglican Communion. As new territories were
opening up (both as a result of emigration from the British Isles and missionary work among indigenous peoples) it was becoming apparent that

the diffuse constitutional arrangements that obtained in the Church of England could not easily be adapted to such situations. A radical new approach was pioneered by, among others, Bishop George Selwyn of New Zealand. 'Selwyn sought to create a church unambiguously apostolic with appropriate lay participation. In 1842 he refused government assistance for buildings and stipends, arguing that the early church had depended on the gifts of the faithful. He wished to do the same.'[19] Two years later he called a synod without royal approval – something not possible to this day in the Church of England – 'insisting that episcopal authority was sufficient'.[20] From such beginnings Selwyn and the New Zealand Church developed a Constitution including Diocesan Synods and a General Synod, all with lay representation. Its form was 'on the lines of that of the American Episcopal Church'.[21] Selwyn's work is particularly important in the context of the Free Church of England as it was explicitly acknowledged by the Church of Ireland as having influenced its own Constitution in the late 1860s.[22] Those drawing up the Constitution of the newly disestablished Church of Ireland also had in their hands a collection of documents compiled in 1870 by the Revd W. Sherlock entitled *Suggestions towards the Organization of the Church of Ireland based on that of the Reformed Episcopal Churches abroad.* The title intriguingly suggests that the designation 'Reformed Episcopal Church' was in currency in the late 1860s and early 1870s.

Ecclesiastical Constitutions also dominated the agenda of the first Lambeth Conference in 1867. The bulk of the Committee Reports address such issues as Diocesan and Provincial Synods, schemes for electing bishops, and the constitution of the Court for the trial of a bishop.[23]

All of this would have been known to Cummins. The 1867 Lambeth Conference (which took place the year after his consecration) had been attended by Presiding Bishop John Hopkins, together with Bishops Lee, Quintard, Talbot and Kerfoot from among Cummins's consecrators, and 13 other PECUSA bishops. In 1873 Cummins approached the task of creating a Constitution for the Reformed Episcopal Church well aware of developments throughout the Anglican Communion.

The details of Cummins's work remain to be explored, and it is not clear to what extent various intermediate texts have survived in the archives of the Reformed Episcopal Church. It is quite possible that further research will reveal not just the record of the adaptation of PECUSA's Constitution into that of the Reformed Episcopal Church, but the subsequent modification of the American recension by the British branch of that Church.[24]

The Conjunction of Constitutions

The 1863 and 1873 Constitutions first came together in 1875 when, as noted in Chapter 5, the Council of the Free Church of England passed the resolution that 'the Constitution and Canons of the Reformed Episcopal Church of America be recommended to Convocation for adoption as the bye-laws of the Free Church of England'.[25] This must have produced something of a chimera. The older corpus now had a very different Constitution – different in structure and content – as its bye-laws. Little evidence seems to have survived as to how this worked in practice, though further research may shed more light on this. Note has already been taken of how the understanding of the ministry in the Free Church of England was being modified simultaneously in a more traditional threefold direction. Presumably a sense of urgency in acquiring the historic succession made a more leisurely integration of Constitutions impracticable. Nor does there seem to be any evidence as to the status of the Reformed Episcopal Church Constitution within the Free Church of England once the Reformed Episcopal Church had been constituted as a separate body in England in 1877. The continuing 'Establishment' nature of the Free Church of England suggests that the anomalous 'bye-laws' may not have been repealed. In the run-up to the union of 1927 there is little indication that the Free Church of England was operating on a substantially different basis to the Reformed Episcopal Church, which would have been the case if it had reverted completely to the 1863 Constitution alone. This is reinforced by the fact that the 1927 Constitution is not in fact a hybrid composed of equal amounts of the former Constitutions, but is in structure and content substantially that of the Reformed Episcopal Church, with 1863 elements and vocabulary integrated. Such an outcome would have been easier to achieve if the Free Church of England negotiators were already familiar with the Reformed Episcopal Church Constitution.

This raises the further question as to which form of the Reformed Episcopal Constitution (if any) was accepted as authoritative by the Free Church of England. The version adopted as the bye-laws in 1875 was obviously the 'American' version created by Bishop Cummins and the General

Council on the basis of that of the Protestant Episcopal Church. By 1878, however, there also existed a 'British' version, containing the amendments made by Bishops Gregg and Sugden and their Synod, taking the recent Constitution of the Church of Ireland as their model. The most important difference was the additions to the Declaration of Principles.[26] Further amendments were of course made by the Reformed Church of England when it broke away under Gregg, though the basic American form is unchanged. This is all the more noteworthy given Gregg's desire to distance himself from the 'Yankee Church'.[27] Technically, the Free Church of England was presumably bound to the American version, but it must obviously have been aware of the British version and it is, significantly, the British Declaration of Principles rather than the American one that appears in the post-1927 Constitution.

In the event, as can be seen, elements from sources as disparate as the First General Convention of PECUSA in 1789 (together with later additions), the Countess's failed Plan of the following year, the 1836 Connexional Constitution, the labours of Thoresby, Selwyn, the Church of Ireland, Cummins and Gregg all found their way into the 1927 Constitution.

The Present Constitution – a Brief Analysis

The fact that the present Constitution of 'the Free Church of England otherwise called the Reformed Episcopal Church' is in fact based substantially on that of the Protestant Episcopal Church in the USA and the Church of Ireland makes it relatively straightforward to undertake a comparative study between it and other Anglican Constitutions. Ironically, this is the aspect of the Free Church of England which is least like the Established Church, though this is due to the peculiar constitutional arrangements of the latter, and not of the Free Church of England.[28] The content is first examined, then, for convenience, a brief structural summary is appended.

Content

The corpus of material falls into three parts: a Constitution consisting of 18 Articles; 126 'Canons of the Convocation'; and 26 'Bye-laws, Orders, Regulations and Injunctions of Convocation'.[29] This division is itself 'mainstream Anglican', all but two of the independent Provinces of the Anglican Communion having a *constitution* ('a body of primary or fundamental law') and a body of *canons* ('binding domestic law which is made for the Church by itself') created according to procedures laid down in the Constitution.[30] The Free Church of England's bye-laws find their equivalent in the various bodies of 'other species of laws . . . broadly inferior, and made as the result of delegated powers'[31] found in most parts of the Anglican Communion. There is quite a lot of duplication of content between the Constitution and Canons in the Free Church of England corpus, some sections (for example Article XIII and Canon 124, Article XIV and Canons 94 and 95) being virtually identical.

The Constitution

Article I is the Declaration of Principles, the content of which will be discussed in the next chapter. Derived as a concept from early American and contemporary Anglican models, this, too, is characteristically Anglican: '*fundamental declarations* or *fundamental principles*' are incorporated into or accompany the Constitution in a number of Anglican Provinces.[32] Such principles are usually only capable of being amended by especially rigorous procedures. The Churches of Australia, Canada and New Zealand, like the Free Church of England, prohibit any alteration of their Fundamental Declarations or Provisions.[33]

All other Articles of the Free Church of England Constitution may be altered by a three-quarters majority of members present and voting in Convocation,[34] provided that the change is ratified by a similar majority in the next Convocation, which must take place not less than three months after the first (Article XVI).

Articles II to IV deal with the powers, meetings, membership and convening of Convocation, which is stated in Article II to have 'chief legislative power and jurisdiction'. This whole Article is in fact virtually identical with Clause IV of the Preamble and Declaration of the Church of Ireland from which it is clearly derived.[35]

All members of Convocation are required to make a declaration before they take their seat. This declaration for the clergy is the one laid down in the 1863 Free Church of England Constitution (see above) with the addition of the words 'so long as I shall continue a Minister thereof' from the Reformed Episcopal Constitution. To this is added:

I believe the Doctrine of the said Church, as set forth in the Declaration of
Principles thereof, to be agreeable to the Word of God, and in Public Prayer
and Administration of the Sacraments, I will use the Forms canonically
prescribed and none other, except so far as is or shall be ordered or permitted by lawful authority; and further, I will pay true and canonical obedience to the lawful authorities of the said Church. (Article IV)

This is clearly a re-working of the Declaration of Assent and Oath of
Canonical Obedience of the Church of England. Doe considers the
phrase 'agreeable to the Word of God' to be rare in Anglican formularies
and almost certainly derives from the Church of Ireland where it is also
found.[36]

For the laity the declaration reads:

I, MN, a Representative of . . . do solemnly declare that I am a
Communicant of the Free Church of England, otherwise called the
Reformed Episcopal Church, and I do solemnly promise and engage to
conform to the Doctrine, Discipline and Worship of the said Church as set
forth by the authority of Convocation thereof.

The second half of this is found only in PECUSA and the Churches
(Brazil, Mexico and Chile) which derive their Constitution from it.[37]

Convocation is to be presided over by the Bishop Primus who is to
be chosen annually by that body from among the bishops. The Primus is
also ex officio Chairman of all committees and has jurisdiction over all
Congregations and Ministers for which other canonical oversight is not
provided (Canon 20).

Convocation's legal continuity with its pre-1927 predecessors is
safeguarded in the full title of the body. That for 2001, for example, is
described in the Minutes as 'The 74th Convocation of the Free Church of
England, otherwise called the Reformed Episcopal Church, being also the
138th Annual Convocation of the Free Church of England, and the 124th
Annual Synod of the Reformed Episcopal Church in England'.[38] The
main reason for this seems to be to safeguard the various Trusts in which
the pre-union properties are vested.

Articles IX and X deal with Trusts and are modelled on those of the
1863 Constitution. As in that document, Trustees must be Communicants
of the Free Church of England. Properties already held in trust are to be
administered by 'the Free Church of England Central Trust', an important

body in the life of the denomination. Properties acquired subsequently are to have as their legal basis the Model Trust Deed drawn up by Convocation. Not all the current properties used by the Free Church of England are in fact vested in Central Trust. In some cases the local Trustees have the power, should they so wish, to take their building out of the denomination.[39]

The current liturgical provision is stated in Article X which requires the 1956 revision of the Book of Common Prayer.[40] This has been modified by a bye-law (III.12) passed in 1998 and called 'The Alternative Services Measure'.[41]

Internal Discipline is provided for by Articles XIV and XV, by which bishops, clergy and laity 'shall be liable to trial and discipline' for a variety of offences, principally teaching contrary to the doctrinal standards, 'a walk or conversation unworthy of a Christian Profession', and refusal to obey the regulations and ordinances. The precise procedures are set out in Canons 93 to 122. There are various kinds of 'court' for the different categories of accused.[42] Sentences for a clergyman can be 'either reprimand, suspension or displacement from all his ministerial functions in this Church'. For a layman it is deposition 'from any office he may hold in the parish, until such time as due penitence shall be manifested' (Canon 111). There is a right of appeal to Convocation sitting as a Court of Appeal (Canons 114 to 122). The whole process follows closely Anglican Communion models.[43] The disciplinary procedures are seldom used, but were invoked in 2003 against Bishop Bentley-Taylor . Following the resignation from the denomination of Bentley-Taylor, the formal Accusation against him was dropped and the matter did not proceed to a formal trial.

Concerning the Ministry, the Constitution declares the Church's belief that the Episcopate is 'an office proceeding from the Presbyterate:- *primus inter pares* and not an order in succession to the Apostolate' (Article V).[44] Ordinations and consecrations are to be according to the order contained in the Prayer Book (Article V). Candidates for ordination as deacons are to serve for at least six months as Readers, after which they may be recommended to Convocation which must approve them for ordination by a three-quarters majority (Canon 39).[45] The canonical ages for ordination are the same as those in the Book of Common Prayer (Canon 38).

Bishops are to be chosen or received 'agreeably to such rules as shall be fixed by Convocation' (Article VI). The relevant rules are set out in

Canons 21 to 25. Election is either by a Diocesan Synod, which must be confirmed by Convocation, or directly by Convocation. Voting is by Houses (the bishops and presbyters forming one House, the deacons and laity the other) and the name of the candidate obtaining a clear majority of the votes of each House is presented to Convocation (or Diocesan Synod) when a two-thirds majority is required.[46] A Certificate of Election and a Certificate of Good Life and Learning must be presented before the candidate can be consecrated (Canons 25 and 26). The text for the latter is set out in Canon 25 and is identical with that required by the PECUSA canons in the 1870s. A candidate for the episcopate may not be in secular employment (Canon 21), though, out of necessity, this is permitted for presbyters and deacons (Canon 42). As Eldridge explained in his 1910 publication, the whole process is similar to that of the Church of Ireland, though without the veto of the House of Bishops.[47]

As in 1836 and 1863, the 'jurisdiction, powers, and duties' of a bishop are to be defined by Convocation and no bishop may perform an episcopal act outside the Free Church of England without the consent of the Bishop Primus and Council (Article VI). The Canons require each bishop to visit every church in his jurisdiction once in every three years.

Among the remaining Articles of the Constitution Article XIII is particularly significant as it states that 'Except where otherwise canonically specified, or where contrary to Evangelical or Protestant Principles, this Church conforms to the ancient laws and customs of the Church of England.'[48] The provision is clearly in line with the consistently expressed intention that the Church believes itself to be in direct continuity with the ancient Church of this land. Further, it confirms the intrinsically Anglican identity of the denomination. Interestingly, this Article has been interpreted recently as tying the Free Church of England not just to the model of *past* Church of England laws and customs, but to *present* ones.[49] This raises some interesting possibilities.

Article XVII of the Constitution provides that 'Convocation shall adopt and publish Canons for the government and administration of this Church.' To be binding any Canon must be passed by a three-quarters majority of Convocation and ratified by a similar vote at the ensuing Annual Convocation, which shall take place not less than three months after the first.

The present Canons[50]

It is far beyond the scope of the present work to offer any kind of analysis of the 126 Canons of the Free Church of England. It may, however, be helpful simply to list the categories into which they are grouped and to give an indication of the numbers in each category.

Of Convocation

Organization and Duties	1–17
Of Diocesan Synods	18–19

Of the Ministry, Doctrine and Worship

A. Of Bishops[51]	20–37
B. Of presbyters and deacons	38–43
C. Of Lay Readers	44–45
D. Of Ministerial Appointments and Duties	46–61
E. Of Congregations	62–70
F. Of Parish Meetings and Officers	71–80
G. Of The Book of Common Prayer	87–91
H. Of Discipline	92–122

Miscellaneous Provisions   123–26

Printed with the Canons are a number of other items, including the 'Form of Request for a Faculty' and 'A Draft Agreement for an Incumbency'. There are also a number of 'Canonical Forms' covering a range of matters such as Annual Returns, Letters of Orders, Certificate of Reception of a Presbyter and a model Deed of Covenant for constituting a new congregation.

Much of this would be very familiar to anyone accustomed to Church of England (and general Anglican) usage.

The Bye-laws, Orders, Regulations and Injunctions of Convocation[52]

This is a collection of Convocational acts from 1927 onwards. They are arranged broadly thematically in three sections, with the year of enactment alongside.

Part I – Administration
This contains miscellaneous statements including the requirement for all properties to be insured, the setting up of a 'Home Mission Fund', the diocesan boundaries, the appointment of a Central Board of Examiners and the necessity to send letters through 'the proper channels'.

Part II – Financial
This includes the setting of the minimum stipend for clergy in full-time incumbency (£4,000 in the year 2000) and the requirement for congregations to pay the costs of their representatives at Convocation.

Part III – Doctrine, Worship, etc.
A range of provisions including the authorizing of a hood for non-graduate presbyters, the wearing of a blue scarf by Readers, the need for a resolution of Council or Convocation before a man ordained in another Church is received, and minor amendments to the Litany.

A brief summary of probable sources in relation to the structure of the corpus

(i) To commence with a Declaration of Principles follows mainstream Anglican Communion practice. In 1927 the immediate influence was obviously the Reformed Episcopal Constitution, itself influenced (in its British recession) at this point by the Preamble and Declaration of the Church of Ireland.

(ii) A division into a Constitution and a separate body of Canons is, again, characteristic of many Anglican Provinces. The 1863 Constitution had no such division. The source once again is the Reformed Episcopal Church, following the pattern established in 1789 by PECUSA.

(iii) The sections into which the Canons are divided resemble those of the Reformed Episcopal Church and PECUSA, though the name 'Title' for each has been abandoned. Unlike the American models, however, the 1927 Canons begin with a section on Convocation and Diocesan Synods, rather than the ministry. This closely parallels the Church of Ireland sequence. The 1863 Constitution does not address Convocation until Clause 6, so is unlikely to be the main influence here.

(iv) Unlike the Reformed Episcopal Church the 1927 Constitution does not place the Canons 'On Discipline' in a separate section, but includes them under 'Ministry, Doctrine and Worship'.

(v) For the majority of Canons the primary textual source is the Reformed Episcopal Constitution, though with some 1863 Free Church of England 'blocs' and a preference for Free Church of England terminology.

(vi) The 1863 Constitution has no specified 'Canonical forms' appended. Those in current use derive from Reformed Episcopal models, often (for example in the case of Letters of Orders) closely following Church of England usage.

(vii) The provision of Bye-laws, Orders, Regulations and Injunctions seems to be the most significant structural element to survive from the 1863 Constitution. The Reformed Episcopal Constitution has no equivalent.

The Life of the Church

Within this framework of Constitution, Canons and Bye-laws (of which, as in any Church, many of the laity are blissfully unaware) the congregations function very much as congregations of the Church of England. A chief difference is of course that the parishes are not geographical, but consist of persons enrolled as Communicants who contribute to the support of the parish. Communicants are defined as 'persons who shall partake of the Lord's Supper in some Congregation of this Church, at least three times in the year, of which Easter shall be one, or whose names shall appear in the Roll of Communicants . . . or . . . upon the Roll of Scattered Members' (Canon 66).

Churchwardens and Delegates to Diocesan Synod and Convocation are elected at the Annual Congregational Meeting at which is presented the Minister's Report and the Accounts in the form required by the Charities Act 1993. There is no archidiaconal Visitation to admit the elected officers. Instead the names are sent to the Diocesan Bishop who admits them for the following year by issuing a certificate (Form F) to each and entering the names onto a prescribed form over his hand and seal, a copy of the document being returned for display in the church.

The Annual Congregational Meeting also elects a Church Council which is to assist the churchwardens in the discharge of their duties when desired to do so (Canon 76). The remit of the Church Council is more limited than that of a Parochial Church Council (PCC) in the Church of England, its responsibilities being substantially limited to the property of the Church.[53] If a minister wishes to have lay advisers to assist him 'in the Spiritual government of the Parish' he may nominate two or more such persons to constitute a 'Parish Council' (Canon 85).

The Synods of the present two dioceses usually meet twice a year. The membership is made up of all the ministers ecclesiastically resident within the limits of the diocese 'and duly licensed to officiate therein', together with the churchwardens and two delegates from each congregation. Each diocese has its own Secretary and Treasurer.

Fellowship is clearly important in a small Church composed of scattered congregations, and both dioceses from time to time organize occasions such as Teaching Days and social events. Occasionally these may take place on a national basis, the most recent examples being gatherings to celebrate the 150th anniversary of the 'freeing' of Bridgetown Chapel in 1994 and the Millennium. On both occasions Family Days were organized. A congregation hosting a diocesan event usually provides substantial refreshments, this being particularly necessary as some participants will have travelled long distances.

Convocation usually meets in May. For the 25 years up to and including 2002 meetings had been held at Sunbury-on-Thames, though the older pattern had been to alternate between the two dioceses. In 2003 the venue moved to the Hayes Conference Centre at Swanwick.

At meetings of Convocation the Bishop Primus takes the chair. Convocation appoints a Secretary, who is also the General Secretary of the denomination, for which he receives a small honorarium. The post is in some respects equivalent to that of the Secretary General in the Church of England.

It is still a requirement that 'All Canons, Bye-laws, Regulations, Resolutions, Injunctions and Acts whatsoever of Convocation shall be entered in the Minute Book . . . and when entered, shall be confirmed as correct during the time such Convocation is assembled. They shall then be subscribed by the President and Secretary . . .' (Canon 6). The arrangement has continued from the original 1836 Constitution of the Countess of Huntingdon's Connexion and is perhaps especially important for a small denomination whose representatives are widely scattered. There is probably also an egalitarian principle involved: it is Convocation, not the Primus, which 'has chief legislative power and jurisdiction' (Article II).

Convocation is also required to appoint a Registrar, usually a solicitor, whose presence in gown and bands is visible on formal occasions. He is to keep the official records of the Church, including the details of the participants at episcopal consecrations (Canon 9). The Registrar also offers legal advice to the denomination, recourse also being made to the denominational solicitors for more serious matters.[54]

The third officer appointed by Convocation is the Treasurer, who must be a layman and who handles denominational finances (Canon 10).

The Secretary, Registrar and Treasurer, with the Bishops, Diocesan Secretaries and Diocesan Treasurers, are ex officio members of the Council, together with between eight and ten others appointed by Convocation. The Council, which usually meets twice a year, has full *ad interim* power and jurisdiction between Convocations (Article II). Its actions do not require subsequent authorization by Convocation (Bye-law 1.12). To Council also is delegated 'such administrative powers and functions as Convocation shall from time to time resolve' (Article II). It is in effect the permanent executive body of the denomination, dealing on a regular basis with a wide range of matters. Because of the scattered nature of the Free Church of England, the Council usually meets residentially. Its membership and position make it in some respects analogous to the Archbishops' Council in the Established Church.

The Year Book

Throughout its existence the united Church has produced an annual Year Book, as did its predecessor bodies.[55] This is currently published in about September and contains the official lists of the office holders, clergy and congregations. It also includes the bishops' reports and those of various officials; the annual accounts of the Church; and the Minutes of Convocation held earlier that year. An invariable feature is the definitive list of episcopal consecrations, going back to John Moore, Archbishop of

Canterbury. There is also a list of the serving bishops of the Reformed Episcopal Church in the USA and Canada. It is usual for the Bishop Primus's Convocation Charge and for sermons delivered at Convocation to be printed for the benefit of the other members of the denomination. The diocesan reports provide invaluable 'snapshots' of the state of the individual congregations.

This all-too-brief look at a hitherto neglected aspect of the Free Church of England thus reinforces two important characteristics of the denomination's identity. The first of these is its structural continuity with the family of congregations organized by the Lady Huntingdon and her co-workers in the second half of the eighteenth century. The claim to continuity made in the Preamble to the 1863 Resolution is confirmed by the clear dependence of the 1863 Constitution on that of 1836 (which itself looked back to the 1790 Plan). This continuity of *structure* obviously indicates a continuity of personnel, worship and witness. This finding helps correct the excessive claims made about 1844 and the anti-Tractarian context as the origin of the denomination.

The second finding to emerge from this study is the mainstream Anglican character of the Constitution which the Reformed Episcopal Church bequeathed to the united Church in 1927. The modern Free Church of England's Constitution is of a structure characteristic of many Provinces of the Anglican Communion and deserves to be studied along with them. Should the Free Church of England ever contemplate constitutional reform this family likeness means that there are a number of close parallels from which lessons might be learned.

Notes

1. For at least one Church of England priest the Constitution was a significant factor in his decision to join the denomination on resigning his benefice: 'Only the Free Church of England offers a settled Constitution, an historical platform, and is a tested vehicle . . .'; Shucksmith, *Honest for God*, p. 141.
2. The Latin and English text of the 1604 canons can be found in J. V. Bullard, *Constitutions and Canons Ecclesiastical 1604* (London, Faith Press, 1934). For a brief summary of the process leading to the new Church of England canons see G. Bray, *The Anglican Canons 1517–1947* (London, Boydell Press/Church of England Records Society, 1998), p. lxxxvii.

3. N. Doe, *The Legal Framework of the Church of England* (Oxford, Clarendon Press, 1996); hereafter cited as *Framework*. N. Doe, *Canon Law in the Anglican Communion* (Oxford, Clarendon Press, 1998), hereafter cited as *Canon Law*.

4. Podmore, *Moravian Church*, p. 6.

5. Evans, *Daniel Rowland*, pp. 175ff.; Rack, *Reasonable Enthusiast*, pp. 237ff.; Pickles, *Benjamin Ingham*, pp. 60ff. Further research into the mutual inter-dependence of these and those of Lady Huntingdon's Connexion may be instructive.

6. The full text is in Cook, *Selina*, pp. 448–53.

7. An abstract of the monthly meetings of the Welsh Methodists was to be sent to their General Association (Evans, *Daniel Rowland*, p. 224).

8. 'Association' was the name used by the Welsh Methodists as well, perhaps to distinguish themselves from Wesley's 'Conference' (ibid., p. 223).

9. See the list in J. B. Figgis, *The Countess of Huntingdon and her Connexion* (London, Partridge & Co., 1891), p. 207 and Appendix 4.

10. The full text of the 1836 Constitution can be found in the *Evangelical Register*, 1854, pp. 180–83. The quotation is from p. 181.

11. Ibid.

12. See Chapter 2.

13. *FCE Magazine*, July 1867, p. 224.

14. See Guelzo, *For the Union*, p. 253.

15. *Bishop White's Memoirs*, pp. 99ff., quoted in Perry, *Historical Notes*, p. 210.

16. Tiffany, *History*, p. 347.

17. Ibid., p. 348.

18. The version Cummins knew contained a number of modifications incorporated since 1789. For the text see *Digest of the Canons for the Government of the Protestant Episcopal Church in the United States of America . . . together with the Constitution* (Printed for the Convention (no place given) 1875).

19. Ian Breward, *A History of the Church in Australasia* (Oxford, Clarendon Press, 2001), p. 99.

20. Ibid. The Church of Ireland historian C. A. Webster called Selwyn's synod '. . . the first experiment of the kind which the Anglican Communion had tried since Convocation was silenced in England in 1717' ('The Reconstruction of the Church' in Walter Alison Phillips (ed.), *History of the Church of Ireland from the Earliest Times to the Present Day* (London, OUP, 1933), vol. III, p. 363).

21. Ibid.

22. Ibid.

23. *Five Lambeth Conferences*, pp. 58–73.

24. Guelzo indicates something of the constitutional battles that broke out in the Reformed Episcopal Church following the death of Cummins, but does not treat of the main Constitution in detail (*For the Union*, pp. 247ff.).

25. *FCE Magazine*, May 1885, pp. 83f. In 2002 the General Council of the Reformed Episcopal Church in the USA and Canada approved a thorough overhaul of its Constitution and Canon Law.

26. This will be discussed more fully in Chapter 10. Like Cummins, Gregg and Sugden were clearly aware of developments in other parts of the Anglican world.

27. See Chapter 6. The text of the Reformed Church of England Constitution can be found in *Constitution and Canons of the Reformed Episcopal Church . . . otherwise called the Reformed Church of England* (London, E. Marlborough & Co., 1883). The word 'Title' is still used for the divisions within the corpus of canons (printed in the same Gothic Black Letter as in the PECUSA text) and the names of the sections are identical with the American ones, though the order of two of them is reversed.

28. See Doe, *Framework, passim*.

29. See *Constitution and Canons Ecclesiastical* (1983 edn) published by the denomination. The current edition of the bye-laws is dated 1999.

30. The definitions are from Doe, *Canon Law*, p. 21. The two Anglican Churches which do not have a written Constitution in a single document are England and Scotland

31. Ibid.

32. Ibid., pp. 21, 26.

33. Ibid. The relevant Free Church of England Article is XVIII.

34. The same majority as required in the 1790 Plan.

35. See, for example, *The Constitution of the Church of Ireland: Being Statutes passed at the General Convention 1870* (Dublin, Hodges, Foster & Co., 1870), p. 5. The text may also be found on the Church of Ireland website.

36. Doe, *Canon Law*, p. 207.

37. Ibid.

38. *FCE Year Book 2001–2002*, p. 49.

39. One of the present congregations, Willesborough in Kent, has moved between the Free Church of England and the Church of England on more than one occasion.

40. See Chapter 11 for a discussion of the Church's worship.

41. See Chapter 11. The name has obviously been adopted from the Church of England statutory provision of that title.

42. See Bray, *Anglican Canons*, pp. xcii–cxii for a convenient discussion of the concept of ecclesiastical courts.

43. See Doe, *Canon Law*, pp. 80ff.

44. See Chapter 12. Similar views can be found on the website of the *Reform* network within the Church of England.

45. This aspect is the same as in 1836 and 1863. In practice today candidates are approved at meetings of the Council.

46. See Doe, *Canon Law*, pp. 109ff. for Anglican Communion parallels.
47. See Vaughan, *History* (1st edn), p. 257. Reflecting on the system, Vaughan considered one of the weaknesses of election the fact that many of the electors 'cannot possibly be in a position to judge the suitability of candidates for the episcopate' ('Memories', p. 26). The history of the denomination has often borne out Vaughan's observation.
48. Canon 124 repeats this requirement.
49. In a letter to Bishop Kenneth Powell, dated 21 March 2002, Bishop Shucksmith quotes the *modern* Canon C1.2 of the Church of England as committing the Free Church of England to a doctrine of the indelibility of Orders.
50. See Bray, *Anglican Canons*, pp. xxi–xxxiv for a discussion of the concept of canon law in general, and pp. xxxiv–xci for Anglican canon law in particular.
51. The 1927 Canons reverse the order of ministers as found in the Reformed Episcopal and PECUSA Constitutions which begin with candidates for ordination then go on to deacons, presbyters and bishops.
52. The first three categories are the same as those of the 1836 Constitution. In 1871 a set of bye-laws drafted by Council were brought to Convocation for approval, along with revised Articles and Catechism (*FCE Magazine*, July 1871, p. 180).
53. Historically, this difference is no doubt due to the fact that the Free Church of England and Reformed Episcopal Church had separated from the Church of England prior to the passing of the 1919 Enabling Act which brought PCCs into existence and defined their duties and powers.
54. Doe, *Framework*, p. 237 gives a summary of registrars' duties in the Church of England.
55. As noted earlier, lack of funding prevented this on some occasions.

CHAPTER 10

The Faith of the Church

Three times every year – at Convocation and Diocesan Synod – the clergy and lay delegates of the Free Church of England declare their assent to the doctrinal basis of the Church. Compared with the Church of England (where clergy only declare their assent on changing post, and most of the laity not at all) this is a high degree of doctrinal awareness.

The reasons for this doctrinal prominence are not difficult to understand, given the history of the Church. The eighteenth-century Evangelical Revival stressed the objective and subjective importance of the doctrines of grace in a context of latitudinarianism, deism and indifference. The nineteenth-century 'second strand' remonstrated against the undermining of the Established Church's biblical and Reformation basis by the 'romanizing' of the Tractarians. (In the twentieth century this was extended to doctrinally liberalizing trends in the Church of England and elsewhere.) In addition, the post-1927 united Church has remained a small body in the British Isles and therefore has retained a stronger sense of doctrinal identity among its members than might otherwise have been the case. Minorities tend to be acutely aware of what makes them different from the majority.

At its best, the Free Church of England's concern for doctrinal correctness is not just a *polemical* one (though some of its members have behaved as if that were the case), but a *soteriological* one. The gospel is about God's offer of salvation, and people need accurate information if they are to 'access' it. Doctrine matters, therefore, because people's eternal salvation depends on it.

The Declaration of Principles

Some background to the concept of a Declaration of Principles and an indication of the various strands that have come together to form the present-day text are set out in earlier chapters. The full text of the Declaration of Principles of the present-day Free Church of England is set out in Appendix 1 and should be referred to in conjunction with the commentary below. The sources are indicated by the use of different type to facilitate the following commentary, which is not intended to be exhaustive, but merely to highlight something of the historical context and modern points of contact.

Commentary

It is immediately obvious that the core of the Declaration is the text drafted by Cummins and presented to the steering committee of what was to become the Reformed Episcopal Church, shortly before the meeting of 2 December 1873.[1] It contained, in Guelzo's opinion, 'surprisingly little that was radical'.[2] Vaughan wrote of them: 'They contain no new truth, no startling setting forth of belief: they are but the voices of the past re-echoing in the present.'[3] This basic text was adapted by the UK branch of the Reformed Episcopal Church in 1877 and 1878.

A *Preamble*

This does not form part of the UK Reformed Episcopal Church text, nor that of the Reformed Church of England. It was probably drafted in 1927. The clause recognizes and stresses the fact that the denomination is part of a larger whole – 'a branch of the Holy Catholic Church'. (The phrase is probably based on that in the Nicene Creed as it appears in the Book of Common Prayer, with the original 'one' missing.) The emphasis is strengthened by the declaration of 'essential unity' with all others who are united with Christ by a like faith. The retention of the word 'Catholic' is noteworthy, given the strong anti-Roman stance of many in the denomination. The description of Christ as 'Head over all things' (deriving from Ephesians 1.22f.) is found in the Church of Ireland Preamble and Declaration, but also in other similar statements.

B *Sources of the faith*

This section is clearly Cummins's reworking of Muhlenberg's Exposition of the Memorial of 1853, and it is significant that it was to this document that he turned when looking for a starting point for his all-important doctrinal statement. Cummins has added 'once delivered unto the saints' (Jude 3) strengthening the continuity with the apostolic deposit of the faith. This way of defining the faith was clearly important to him, for he included it in his 'Call to Organise' of 13 November 1873. Cummins has defined 'the Holy Scriptures' as the Old and New Testaments, possibly to exclude the Apocrypha. His description of the Scriptures as 'the sole rule of faith and practice' is paralleled by their description in the Lambeth Quadrilateral (see below) as 'the rule and ultimate standard of faith'.

Quite why Cummins has omitted Muhlenberg's reference to the Nicene Creed is not clear, especially as he had regretted its omission from the 1785 Prayer Book.[4] It was generally less used, and therefore less well known than the Apostles' Creed. One possible reason is the view current at the time that the Apostles' Creed was a sufficient statement of faith for the laity, while the clergy needed the Nicene Creed as well.[5]

The phrase 'Divine Institution', both reaffirms the Divinity of Christ and the fact that the sacraments are not merely 'helpful' human ordinances. They are commanded of God and are defined in Article 19 as one of the marks of the Church. As the Anglican Evangelical Tim Bradshaw puts it, 'The sacraments are vital for the Church, being ordained by the Lord himself.'[6]

'Doctrines of grace' was a semi-technical phrase in the Reformation tradition for 'the human experience of God's free, gratuitous, salvific activity'.[7] Theological writers (often leaning heavily on Augustine) have produced many categories – prevenient, common, special, assisting, etc. For the Declaration of Principles, however, the guiding framework is the Thirty-Nine Articles. The addition of 'substantially' is noteworthy. There had always been some misgivings about the Thirty-Nine Articles even within the Episcopal Church in North America. The 1785 Convention had revised them.[8] They had not been printed in the 1789 Book of Common Prayer.[9] This seems to be reflected in the qualification, which goes right back to Muhlenberg. Given the ecumenical origin of his 'Exposition' the intention seems to be to allow non-Anglican understandings of grace to a certain degree. If the Memorial had been accepted, non-episcopalians would not have been required to subscribe to an exclusive set of 'doctrines of grace' as long as their theological position was 'substantially' in agreement with that of the Articles. This would appear to have the result of binding the present-day Church to the *substance* of the Articles, but not necessarily to every letter of them. The Articles will be discussed more fully below.

C *Episcopacy*

This clause stands in the post-1927 text exactly as drafted by Cummins. Its wording reflects the language of the issue raised so forcibly by the Tractarians – do bishops exist by divine right (*iure divino*) or human (*iure humano*)?[10] For some Anglo-Catholics episcopacy was as much instituted and commanded of God as baptism or the Eucharist, 'to be perpetually and universally observed without exception'.[11] This interpretation, with its consequent unchurching of non-episcopal bodies, is obviously rejected by the clause. This is in line with the position generally taken by sixteenth- and seventeenth-century Anglican Divines:

> if by *jure divino* you understand a law and commandment of God, binding all Christians universally, perpetually, unchangeably, and with such absolute necessity, that no other form of regiment may in any case be admitted, in this sense neither may we grant it, nor yet can you prove it to be *jure divino*.[12]

There was, however, another sense of the term *ius divinum*, relating to 'such things as have authority and warrant from the institution, example or approbation either of Christ himself, or his Apostles and have . . . been held by the consentient judgement of all the Churches of Christ . . .'.[13]

This position seems to be that of Cheney, whose essays on the Reformed Episcopal tradition are still viewed as authoritative. While denying explicit divine institution of the episcopal office ('. . . not as of Divine Right'), Cheney saw no problem in the denomination accepting that even a *iure humano* episcopacy had apostolic 'approbation': 'The Reformed Episcopalian cannot believe that within thirty years of the death of the last Apostle, the universal government and polity of the Church could have become episcopal if such a system had been repugnant to the Apostles' own teaching and practice.'[14] Like Cheney, Bradshaw sees no contradiction between a human development and the will of God. For him, Evangelical ecclesiology's 'view of episcopacy regards the institution to have arisen naturally in the providence of God'.[15]

By describing episcopacy as 'desirable' the clause in effect says that while bishops are not of the *esse* of the Church, they are of its *bene esse*.[16] This is made explicit by Cheney: 'While maintaining that the episcopate is not essential to the "being" of the Christian Church, may we show that it can be for the "well being" of the Church.'[17] Some members of the denomination would probably say *optime esse*. Again, this is in line with the authorities quoted by Bell. Bradshaw unconsciously echoes the language of this clause in his assertions:

> The evangelical claims to stand in the mainline tradition of Anglicanism, for the majority of its post-Reformation existence, in holding the view that the episcopal form of church government is *ancient*, with a proven track record, and not to be abandoned. . . . The Anglican heritage of the Reformation, claimed by evangelicals, regards episcopacy as *desirable* for the order of the church, but not constitutive of the church.[18]

It is difficult to imagine a clearer restatement of the position of the Declaration of Principles.

In the Reformed Church of England under Gregg this clause was expanded by a recognition of 'the ecclesiastical parity of Presbyters, whether canonically received from other Churches, or Episcopally Ordained in this Church' and a statement that 'the Episcopate is an office proceeding from the Presbyterate . . . and not an order in succession to the Apostolate'. This expansion has been redrafted and included in Article V of the 1927 Constitution. The statement about the origin of the episcopate from the presbyterate is consonant with Lightfoot's classic conclusion that 'the episcopate was formed not out of the apostolic order by localisation but out of the presbyteral by elevation: and the title, which originally was common to all, came at length to be appropriated to the chief among them'.[19] Significantly, this conclusion, which would once have been fiercely resisted in parts of the Church of England, is accepted in the report *Episcopal Ministry* which concludes that in some New Testament communities, 'among a group of "presbyter-bishops", one became distinct as presiding bishop without losing the sense of fully sharing a common pastorate and liturgical duty with his presbyteral colleagues, sitting with them in common council much like the twenty-four elders of the Revelation of John of Patmos (Revelation 4.4)'.[20]

Viewed together, clauses 1 and 2 of the Declaration of Principles (**B** and **C**) are very similar in content to the Lambeth Quadrilateral, the four-fold basis for ecumenical discussion, formally adopted at the Lambeth Conference of 1888 and still authoritative within the Anglican Communion. The similarity is probably no accident. The Quadrilateral is generally believed to have been first formulated in a work entitled *The Church-Idea: An Essay Towards Unity*, published in 1870 by William Reed Huntington, Rector of All Saints, Worcester, Massachusetts.[21] Huntington, like Muhlenberg before him, was searching for 'the absolutely essential features of the Anglican position' which could form the basis of what he called 'a Church of the Reconciliation'. These essentials Huntington defined as:

1st. The Holy Scriptures as the Word of God.
2d. The Primitive Creeds as the Rule of Faith.
3d. The two Sacraments ordained by Christ himself.
4d. The Episcopate as the key-stone of Governmental Unity.[22]

Various influences on Huntington have been traced, including the English Churchman F. D. Maurice.[23] One acknowledged influence is Muhlenberg 'whose work [along with that of J. H. Hopkins, Cummins's consecrator] forms a bridge to Huntington's "American Church" idea'.[24] Cummins must have known of Huntington's work as it predated his leaving of PECUSA by three years. The two clearly shared some of the same influences, together with a belief that the Protestant Episcopal Church had the potential to be at the heart of reuniting fragmented North American Protestantism. Cummins differed from Huntington, however, in his commitment to the doctrinal and liturgical aspects of Anglicanism. For him the Thirty-Nine Articles and the (1785) Book of Common Prayer were essential. For Huntington the Articles should not continue to be considered one of the essentials. Liturgical uniformity, while it had strong arguments in its favour, was not a feature of the Early Church and should not therefore be 'among the first principles of Church unity'.[25] On the episcopate, Huntington's position was similar to that of Cummins: he claimed for it no more than that it 'has a strong historical presumption in its favour, – a presumption which nine-tenths of contemporary Christendom respect'.[26] Huntington's work thus sheds light on what Cummins meant by 'desirable' in relation to episcopacy. Not only is it a *good* form of government – tried and tested through many centuries in a wide range of situations – but it also offers the structure most likely to be able to unite the Churches. At no point does Cummins ever seem to have considered abandoning episcopacy. It was simply too precious an inheritance.

The contrast between Cummins and Huntington is instructive. The latter drew a distinction between 'the Anglican *principle*' and 'the Anglican *system*', which he saw as 'two very different things'.[27] The 'system' included the externals of worship and structure – 'the picturesque costume which English life has thrown around it'. This he wanted to strip away. Cummins, on the other hand, was much more anxious to retain a great deal of the 'system' as well as the 'principle'.

The evidence therefore suggests that Cummins's Declaration of Principles shares a common origin with the Lambeth Quadrilateral. Both emerged from the same North American search for a framework for unity. Paradoxically, Cummins's vision of a united Church was more strongly Anglican than that of Huntington, whose formula was to become official policy for the whole Anglican Communion.

D *The 1785 Prayer Book*

This clause has its origins in Cummins's reluctant conclusion that 'romanising germs' did indeed exist in the 1789 Book of Common Prayer and that a return to the 'purer' 1785 version was essential. In the United Kingdom this provision seems to have been a dead letter. As the next chapter will show, the evidence suggests that from the beginning versions of the Church of England's 1662 Book of Common Prayer were used by the Free Church of England, Reformed Episcopal Church and Reformed Church of England.[28]

There then follow five 'erroneous and strange doctrines' to be rejected and condemned. These are, as Guelzo observes, 'carefully worded to exclude only the most extreme ultras among the Anglo-Catholics'.[29] All the assertions against the cited doctrines can be supported from within the Anglican tradition.

E *Ecclesiastical Polity*

The question as to whether the Church can exist in more than one polity is a post-Reformation issue. Prior to the sixteenth century the Church, in both East and West, existed only as an episcopally ordered body (with the exception of a few very small groups such as the Waldensians). The failure of most Western European bishops to support and lead the Reformation meant that alternative structures of oversight and government had to be created on the Continent. Those Churches which did maintain the historic episcopate (principally England, Ireland and Sweden) had to make a judgment on the status of such structures and the ecclesiality of the communities which created them. The sixteenth- and seventeenth-century Church of England had accepted these communities as true members of the Church of Christ. Episcopacy is the best form of government, but if 'in a disturbed Church' it cannot be had, then '. . . if orthodox Presbyters be compelled to ordain other Presbyters that the Church may not perish, I could not venture to pronounce Ordination of this kind null and void . . .'.[30] Anglo-Catholicism denied this. The motivation behind the inclusion of this clause is clearly Cummins's desire for fellowship – including sacramental fellowship – with fellow-Christians in other Churches. For him it was self-evident that such communities were true Churches.

Today the Church of England also explicitly acknowledges once more that the Church of Christ does not simply exist in only one form of ecclesiastical polity, and, significantly, has applied that principle not just to 'foreign' Churches, but to non-episcopal bodies in the British Isles. In recent years the Church of England has made the statement that 'We acknowledge one another's churches as churches belonging to the One, Holy, Catholic and Apostolic Church of Jesus Christ . . . [and] . . . one another's ordained ministries as given by God and instruments of his grace . . .' in partnership with the Evangelical Church in Germany (including both Lutheran and Reformed polities), with the Lutheran and Reformed Churches of France, with the Moravian Church and with the Methodist Church of Great Britain.[31] The Established Church now endorses this clause of the Declaration of Principles.

F Priesthood

The 'priesthood' of presbyters and bishops has been, and continues to be, a source of division between Churches. The context of this clause is of course the claim that the presbyterate was 'a sacrificing priesthood'. It was precisely the lack of such a concept of priesthood in the Church of England formularies that was to lead Pope Leo XIII to pronounce

Anglican Orders as 'absolutely null and utterly void' in *Apostolicae Curae* in 1896.

The Anglican–Reformed International Commission recognized that 'the word "priest", used of an ordained minister, has acquired overtones which render it unacceptable to many Christians'.[32] Even so, the Report stated:

> We are . . . agreed that since it is acknowledged that the whole Church is called to be in Christ a priestly body (1Peter 2:5, 9), and since ministers are called to lead, enable and equip the Church for this priestly office, the priestly nature of the ministry cannot be denied . . . Ordained ministers are related, as are all Christians, both to the priesthood of Christ and to the priesthood of the Church.[33]

The Declaration of Principles seems consistent with this. It relates ministerial priesthood to the 'royal priesthood' bestowed by God on those who are in Christ. As the authors of *Growing Into Union* put it: 'an ordained man does not cease to be a member of the royal priesthood of the Church'.[34] The Free Church of England merely denies to the ordained ministry 'another sense' of priesthood which is not related to that possessed by the body.

Significantly, the Church of England has itself refused to commit itself to a precise doctrine of ministerial priesthood. As recently as 1986 the General Synod declined to welcome the conclusions of the Board of Mission and Unity Report *The Priesthood of the Ordained Ministry*[35] as 'a contemporary Church of England expression of the Anglican understanding of the priesthood of the ordained ministry' but simply as 'a stimulating contribution towards the development of' such an understanding. Synod's misgivings arose largely out of a belief that the conclusions were insufficiently true to the whole of the Anglican tradition and not adequately based on the evidence of the New Testament.[36] Given this reticence on the part of the Established Church, it is highly unlikely that the Free Church of England's position could be judged to be outside acceptable Anglican teaching on this subject.

G The Lord's Table

The sixteenth-century repudiation of 'the sacrifices of Masses, in which it was commonly said that the Priest did offer Christ', as 'blasphemous fables and dangerous deceits' (Article XXXI) was reflected in the terms used for the ecclesiastical furniture at which the Eucharist took place. In the 1549 Prayer Book it is called both 'the Altar' and 'God's Board'. By 1552 it is still referred to as 'God's Board', but more usually as 'the Table', and this terminology continues until the revision that brought the 1662 text into existence. Here 'God's Board' is no longer used, but the Table is now usually described as 'the Lord's Table' and as 'the Holy Table'. These three terms (Table, Lord's Table, Holy Table) are used in the current Free Church of England Prayer Book. The *Handbook for Ministers* contains a brief order for the 'Dedication of a Communion Table', which contains the phrase, 'To the glory of God and in memory of . . . we dedicate this Holy Table . . .'.[37] Clearly it was the Tractarian attempt to revert to the pre-Reformation term 'altar' to accompany an enhanced doctrine of eucharistic sacrifice that made necessary the denial 'that the Lord's Table is an altar on which the oblation of the Body and Blood of Christ is offered anew to the Father'.

Such a statement finds support from what might be considered an unexpected source. Canon VII of the proposed Canons of 1640 'which represented the summit of Laudian schemes for the Church of England'[38] makes the same point. Commenting on the placing of the Table against the East wall, it states, 'And we declare that this situation of the holy table, doth not imply that it is, or ought to be esteemed as a true and proper altar, whereupon Christ is again really sacrificed . . .'.[39]

H *Eucharistic Presence*

The denial that Christ is present 'in the elements of Bread and Wine' in the Lord's Supper is simply a restatement of the teaching already set forth in the 'Black Rubric' of the 1662 Book of Common Prayer of the Church of England. Speaking of the Eucharist, the rubric states plainly that 'the natural Body and Blood of our Saviour Christ are in Heaven, and not here . . .'. Therefore, states the rubric, 'no Adoration is intended, or ought to be done, either unto the Sacramental Bread or Wine there bodily received, or unto any Corporal Presence of Christ's natural Flesh and Blood . . .'. Given that this assertion was not preventing the veneration of the consecrated elements in the Established Church, the Free Church of England strengthened the wording by adding 'real and essential' from the text of the rubric as it appeared in the 1552 Book of Common Prayer to the 'corporal' of 1662. It also adds a further sentence: 'The act and prayer of

Consecration do not change the nature of the Elements, but only set them apart for a holy use.'

In its clear condemnation of any 'localizing' of the presence of Christ, the Free Church of England Declaration is consistent with 'classical' Anglicanism. Canon VII of 1640, for example, commends the practice of bowing on entering and leaving a Church, but

> not with any intention to exhibit any religious worship to the communion table, the east, or church, or anything contained in so doing, or to perform the said gesture in the celebration of the holy eucharist, upon any opinion of the body of Jesus Christ on the holy table, or in mystical elements, but only for the advancement of God's majesty . . .[40]

As Buchanan comments, even these Laudian compilers 'guard their eucharistic doctrine against anything that smacks of Rome'.[41] Today, Rome herself is prepared to use language not inconsistent with that of the Black Rubric. The Anglican–Roman Catholic International Commission, for example, could say in one of its *Elucidations*: 'Becoming does not here imply material change . . . . It does not imply that Christ becomes present in the eucharist in the same manner that he was present in his earthly life'.[42] This seems consistent with the Free Church of England (and Church of England) denial of the presence of Christ's 'natural body'.

Nevertheless, there *is* a doctrine of consecration in the Free Church of England. The addition to the Black Rubric just quoted speaks of an 'act and prayer of Consecration'. After the administration the minister is to place upon the Lord's Table 'what remaineth of the consecrated Elements, covering the same with a fair linen cloth'. Any left over is not to be thrown away or given to the minister's use (as in 1552) but is to be 'reverently' eaten and drunk by the minister and such communicants as he shall invite. As the *Handbook for Ministers* puts it, 'The elements have been solemnly dedicated and used for the most sacred purpose known to men: they should be disposed of in a suitably reverent manner.'[43]

The Sacrament, rightly received, is a real means of grace. That this is intended to be central to the experience of the tradition as well as a formal item of doctrine is perhaps best illustrated by the following quotation from Whitefield:

> On receiving the holy Sacrament, especially before trials, I have found grace in a very affecting manner, and in abundant measure, sometimes

imparted to my soul, – an irrefragable proof to me of the miserable delusion of the author of that work called *The Plain Account of the Sacrament*, which sinks that holy ordinance into a bare memorial . . .[44]

Further examples from other leaders of the Evangelical Revival could be added. The desire of the English Reformers and the founding fathers of the Reformed Episcopal Church and Free Church of England to avoid the excesses associated with certain doctrines of eucharistic presence should not be taken as a denial on their part of a *spiritual* presence of Christ in the Eucharist. The official booklet by F. H. Easton, published in 1964, actually accepts the term 'Real Presence', stating it to be 'a spiritual presence in the hearts of His people'.[45] The denomination's sacramental theology will be discussed further in Chapter 11.

I *Baptismal Regeneration*

The concept of baptismal regeneration, of which most members of the Church of England are probably unaware, still excites some interest in Free Church of England circles. In the middle of the nineteenth century it was one of the most hotly debated of controversies and resulted in numbers of people leaving the Established Church – to Rome, to Baptist affiliation, and to the Free Church of England. In view of its historic and continuing significance, it is necessary to set out something of the background.

In the 1840s, at the same time that he was taking action against James Shore, Bishop Henry Phillpotts of Exeter was also at issue with another presbyter. George Cornelius Gorham had come to Phillpotts's notice by advertising in 1846 for a curate 'free from Tractarian error', and thus, like Shore, became a marked man. Phillpotts's opportunity came in 1847 when the Lord Chancellor presented Gorham to the living of Bampford Speke near Exeter. Phillpotts refused to institute Gorham until the latter had satisfied him on the soundness of his doctrine, particularly in relation to baptism. In brief, Phillpotts declared Gorham's baptismal doctrine unsound. Gorham appealed to the Court of Arches, which found for the Bishop. Gorham then appealed to the Judicial Committee of the Privy Council which, on 8 March 1850 reversed the decision of the Court of Arches. Like the Shore case, the scenario was not in fact a straightforward Evangelical/Tractarian clash, but 'the Judgement of the Privy Council was an important event in the life of the nation: by some it was regarded as a blow to traditional orthodoxy, by others as a vindication of the very principles for which the Church of England stands'.[46]

The central point in the controversy was 'whether all infants lawfully baptised were regenerated'.[47] Gorham had argued that the apparently categorical statements to this effect in the Baptismal Service were to be interpreted in the light of the Thirty-Nine Articles. Article XXV clearly states that the sacraments only 'have a wholesome effect or operation' on those who 'worthily receive the same'. Gorham was prepared to concede that 'when the[se] conditions are fulfilled, regeneration does actually take place *in* Baptism . . . it being impossible that such dispositions and fruits should exist, except where the Holy Ghost has imparted a new nature; which he may do *before* Baptism, *in* Baptism, or *after* Baptism "as he listeth"'.[48] The Privy Council summarized Gorham's position as follows:

> That Baptism is a Sacrament generally necessary to salvation, but that the act of regeneration does not so necessarily accompany the act of Baptism that regeneration invariably takes place in Baptism; that the grace may be granted before, in, or after Baptism; that Baptism is an effectual sign of grace, by which God works invisibly in us, but only in such as worthily receive it, – in them alone it has an wholesome effect . . .[49]

Concerning these views the Judicial Committee declared itself 'unanimously agreed in opinion that the doctrine held by Mr. Gorham is not contrary or repugnant to the declared doctrine of the Church of England . . .'.[50] This ruling, seen as upholding the precious doctrine of justification by faith, was greeted with joy by Evangelicals. It prompted a number of Anglo-Catholic secessions from the Church of England on the grounds that a secular body had in effect removed a clause from the Creed ('I acknowledge one baptism for the remission of sins.').

Suppported by this ruling, Evangelicals such as J. C. Ryle, Bishop of Liverpool continued to use and understand the categorical statements of the Prayer Book Baptismal Service in a sense of 'charitable supposition'. In a context of virtually indiscriminate baptism this was too much like special pleading for Cummins and many other Evangelicals both in North America and in England. They agitated for the removal from the Baptismal Service of the offending phrases (see Chapter 11). Cheney, as has been seen, suffered legal action for refusing to use them. The issue was therefore a priority in the drawing up of the doctrinal basis of the Reformed Episcopal Church.

Clause I is therefore no more than a slight reworking of Gorham's vindicated position. Regeneration *is* connected with baptism, but not inseparably so. It does not automatically take place when baptism is administered; it *may* take place then in some instances, but it may also precede or follow the act of baptism.[51] Cummins and Cheney would presumably have taken for granted, as Ryle and Gorham did, that regeneration may also not take place at all in the lives of many baptized persons – there is only an effect 'in such as worthily receive it'. This position was given immediate liturgical expression when the Reformed Episcopal Church 'struck out the assertion which made baptism with water the unfailing channel of regeneration. It made its message, reiterated every time the sacrament is performed, a clear enunciation of the truth that baptism is a *sign and seal* of spiritual regeneration, but not that regeneration itself.'[52]

The current *Common Worship* Baptismal Rite of the Church of England avoids the term 'regeneration' and uses imagery of baptism as the beginning of a *process* or *journey*. Like the Prayer Book, it uses the language of 'charitable supposition' and, from a Free Church of England perspective, is somewhat ambiguous in places. It would not, however, seem to be inconsistent with this statement in the Declaration of Principles.

J *The 1662 Prayer Book*

As noted above, the 1785 Prayer Book, which meant so much to Cummins, seems never to have been used in the UK. Both the Reformed Episcopal Church and the Free Church of England used their revisions of the 1662 Book of Common Prayer. This will be discussed in more detail in Chapter 11.

The use of 1662 seems to stem both from a conviction that it was a truly Reformed liturgy (once the 'romanizing germs' had been removed) and in order to make it easier for members of the Church of England to transfer to the rival denominations. The intention was to offer Prayer Book worship as it had been before the incursions of the Tractarians. The logic of the Free Church of England's constitutional position and intent would appear to be that it should now be using *Common Worship*, with any 'sacerdotal doctrines and practices' removed.

There now follow Sections K and L which have no North American equivalent and which derive almost *verbatim* from the 'Preamble and

Declaration' of the Church of Ireland. As seen in Chapter 6 they were almost certainly added to Cummins's Declaration of Principles under the influence of the Irishmen Gregg and Sugden in an attempt to root the UK branch of the Reformed Episcopal Church more firmly into the indigenous Churches of the British Isles. The sequence of the two is the same as in the Church of Ireland document, but in that text they are separated by a clause stating the Church of Ireland's approval of the Thirty-Nine Articles and the 1662 Book of Common Prayer. In the Declaration of Principles these have already been dealt with in B, D and J, and so the Irish clause has been omitted here.

K *Witness against obscuring the Primitive Faith*

This clause was in the draft text read by the Bishop of Cork to the united General Convention of the Provinces of Armagh and Dublin (consisting of both clergy and laity) on 20 February 1870 in St Patrick's Cathedral, Dublin. It is consistent with the Church of Ireland's understanding of itself not as 'a new Communion' but as 'one of the most ancient Churches in Christendom'.[53] This sense of continuity within the Anglican Churches of the British Isles had been vividly expressed by John Bramhall, Bishop of Derry 1634–61, and Archbishop of Armagh 1661–63: 'The Church of England before the Reformation and the Church of England after the Reformation are as much the same Church as a garden before it is weeded and after it is weeded, is the same garden . . . '.[54] Merryweather's image of the stream still flowing even if its banks need clearing of weeds from time to time makes the same point.[55]

Clause **K** is therefore a commitment to a constant vigilance against 'weeds' in the context of a strong sense of continuity with the primitive faith and the pre-Reformation Church. The Free Church of England version differs from the Irish only in substituting 'were disowned and rejected' for 'this Church did disown and reject'; a change made necessary by the fact that the Reformed Episcopal Church did not exist as a distinct body in the sixteenth century. The primitive faith has not been lost, it has merely been 'from time to time defaced or overlaid' by 'innovations in doctrine and worship'. For the modern Church of Ireland it is this 'constant witness' against such defacing that renders its members '*Protestant* or *Reformed* Catholics'.[56]

L Ecumenical Commitment

This also derives from the Church of Ireland Preamble and Declaration, but has been significantly altered. The clause did not form part of the draft text presented to the Convention in 1870, but was added during the debate following the reading of the draft.[57] The Irish version reads: 'The Church of Ireland will maintain Communion with *the sister Church of England, and with* all *other* Christian Churches *agreeing in the principles of this Declaration*; and will set forward, so far as in it lieth, quietness, peace and love among all Christian people.'

The words in italics have been omitted in the Free Church of England version. The removal of the reference to 'the sister Church of England' is understandable; the recent secession (in 1877/8) of members of the Reformed Episcopal Church from the Established Church made it impossible to claim to be in communion with that body. In addition to the Church of England, the Irish Church is only committed to maintaining communion with 'all other Christian Churches agreeing in the principles of this Declaration'. In 1870 that could only have meant Churches of a Reformation heritage, as other Churches (Rome in particular) could presumably not agree to the assertion that the Scriptures contained all things necessary for salvation, and that the Primitive Faith had been 'defaced or overlaid' by innovations in doctrine and worship. The Reformed Episcopal Church Synod, however, removed this limitation. There is, therefore, no restriction on the Churches with which the Free Church of England is committed to 'maintaining communion'. What had happened between 1870 and 1877 to prompt such a change? The answer is almost certainly the consecration of Josef Reinkens as bishop for the 'Old Catholics' in Germany on 11 August 1873 by the Bishop of Deventer, and of Edward Herzog as bishop for the Old Catholics of Switzerland on 18 September 1876 by Reinkens. As noted in Chapter 4, the breaking away of communities from the Roman Catholic Church following the First Vatican Council had caught many people's imaginations and opened up new possibilities. Even Bishop Cummins, in far-off America, had expressed 'an interest in the Old Catholic movement as a basis for Christian unity'.[58] By 1881 Reformed Episcopal apologists were citing Reinkens' consecration (which was widely accepted as valid, despite there being only one consecrating bishop) as evidence for the validity of Cheney's consecration only four months later.[59] Cummins's interest in the

Old Catholics would obviously be known in the Reformed Episcopal Church. In the UK Gregg in particular seems to have been attracted by the possibility of contact with the Old Catholic movement.[60] This is almost certainly the motivation behind the removal of the Church of Ireland restriction, which the Old Catholics might have found difficult to accept. Though not sharing the same Protestant identity, they were determinedly anti-Roman Catholic, and must have seemed like obvious allies. By removing the restrictive clause the way was (and is) opened for the Reformed Episcopal Church and its successor, the present-day united denomination, to 'maintain Communion' with Churches that do not necessarily share the same Reformation heritage or the same theological and liturgical tradition. The foresight of the 1877/8 Synod has freed the hands of the modern Free Church of England to engage in wide-ranging ecumenical contact.

M *The location of authority*

This clause does not form part of the Declaration of Principles, but is included here as its parent text *is* part of the Preamble and Declaration of the Church of Ireland, occurring immediately after the Irish version of L. Both versions place 'chief legislative power' in a body representing all the orders of the Church. A definition of this kind is particularly relevant in the British context where the 1604 Canons stated that 'the King's power . . . is the highest power under God'.[61] For the Church of England 'chief legislative power' lay (and still lies) with Parliament (in relation to Measures) and the Crown (whose assent is still required before Canons can be promulged).

In summary, it can be seen that the Declaration of Principles contains nothing that has not legitimately existed historically in the Anglican Tradition or in the present-day Anglican Communion. The *tone* of the Declaration, with its use of words like 'condemns', 'rejects' and 'repugnant', while uncomfortable to many modern Christians, is nevertheless no more aggressive than that found elsewhere in classic Anglican formularies.

Beneath the language is a set of theological positions which seemed under dire threat in the 1870s, but are now widely accepted in the Anglican (and wider Christian) world. The Church of England, for example, does not now 'unChurch' non-episcopal communities, but acknowledges them to be members of the One, Holy, Catholic and Apostolic Church. General Synod has drawn back from committing the Established Church to a particular doctrine of ministerial priesthood. The tide of Anglo-Catholicism, which seemed about to sweep away the whole Reformation heritage, has receded considerably. Many of the fears of the nineteenth-century leaders of the movement did not come to pass.

The Thirty-Nine Articles

The Declaration required of clergy and laity of the Free Church of England does not explicitly refer to the Thirty-Nine Articles, but the 'Doctrine of the said Church, as set forth in the Declaration of Principles thereof' is stated to be agreeable to the Word of God, and an undertaking is given to 'conform to the Doctrine, Discipline, and Worship' of the Church.[62] As noted above, this doctrinal deposit includes the Articles. The 1863 Constitution stated that the Articles were part of the doctrinal basis of the Free Church of England, though certain sections were placed in parentheses, and subscribing clergy might omit these. The text, with the brackets inserted, is printed by Merryweather.[63] No bracketed sections appear in the current text.

There is no need here to discuss the history of the Articles in any depth.[64] The Reformers in both England and Continental Europe tended to draw up Confessions of Faith to state their distinctiveness from the teachings of Rome. Such confessions frequently related to each other, and this is true of the English Articles which 'are often identical with those of Augsburg'.[65] At the same time the sacramental doctrine enshrined in the Articles has consistently been of the Reformed tradition, though no direct textual dependence on any of the Reformed Confessions is discernible.[66]

Commentary

All the Thirty-Nine Articles of the Free Church of England are identical with the 1571 Church of England text, with the following exceptions, which are briefly noted below.

XXXIII Of Excommunicate Persons; XXXV Of the Homilies

These do not appear in the Free Church of England text. The place of the first of these is taken by an Article on Auricular Confession which describes the practice as 'a human invention' with 'no sanction in the word of God'. The second is replaced by an Article on Apostolical Succession. This is defined as the teaching 'that the Ministry in the Christian Church must be derived through a series of uninterrupted ordinations from the Apostles themselves' without which 'there can be no Christian Church, no valid ministry, and no due ministration of Scripture'. Such a doctrine is said to have 'no foundation in Scripture, and is productive of great mischief'. Both these Articles are inserted so as not to disturb the overall sequence of numbering.

VI Of the Sufficiency of the Holy Scriptures

This does not list the Apocryphal books and states that they 'are not to be used to establish any doctrine; nor are they to be publicly read in Church'.[67]

XIII Of Works before Justification

The statement that such works 'are not pleasant to God' is replaced by 'are not of saving efficacy'. The reference to the Schoolmen is removed, together with the declaration that 'we doubt not but that they have the nature of sin'.

XVI Of Sin after Baptism

This is titled 'Of Sin after Conversion', and the word 'conversion' is also substituted for 'baptism' in the body of the Article. The adjective 'deadly' relating to sin, is removed (it was bracketed in Merryweather's text).

XVII Of Predestination and Election

Perhaps surprisingly, in view of the impression of a strongly Calvinist stance in the Free Church of England, this Article is identical with its 1571 equivalent (as is the text given by Merryweather[68]). The recent

Anglican–Methodist *Common Statement* acknowledges that this Article, and the other historic formularies were 'certainly shaped by the Reformed theological tradition (as well as by Lutheranism), and teach the doctrine of God's electing grace. However, they are careful not to go beyond the patent sense of Scripture and they discourage speculation about the hidden purpose of God or the destiny of individuals.'[69] The *Common Statement* also points out that the Anglican formularies 'do not support either the doctrine of reprobation (predestination to perdition) or Pelagianism (the view that we can be saved through moral regeneration in our own strength)'.[70]

The virtually exclusive association of the doctrine with the name of Calvin is unfortunate. As Griffith Thomas points out, 'It must never be forgotten that the Reformers taught predestination long before the time of Calvin . . . Luther was as dogmatic as Calvin himself. It was Melanchthon, not Calvin, who first gave predestination a formal place in the Protestant system.'[71] The Free Church of England therefore stands with the broad consensus of sixteenth-century Reformers in teaching 'God's electing grace', but is not committed to the various derivative doctrines (reprobation, double predestination, preterition, etc.) which have been deduced from it.

XIX Of the Church

The 1571 text is prefaced by the following sentence: 'The Holy Catholic Church is "the blessed company of all faithful people", who, united to Christ by Faith, and made partakers of the Holy Ghost, are the "Spouse and Body of Christ"'.

XXI Of the Authority of General Councils

The statement that Councils 'may not be gathered together without the commandment and will of Princes' is omitted.

XXV Of the Sacraments

As might be expected, this has been more substantially reworked, though the basic form is still the 1571 text. The Sacraments are now described as 'certain sure witnesses *to Divine truth*'. The adjective 'effectual' before 'signs of grace' is removed. God still 'strengthens and confirms our faith in him' by the Sacraments, but the statement that he 'doth work invisibly in us and quicken' our faith by them is removed. Clearly the intention is to remove the possibility of an *ex opere operato* interpretation, but it is arguable that the Article now says less than Whitefield and his contemporaries would have wished, and less than the liturgical text (certainly of the Eucharist) actually says (see Chapter 11). Arguably, too, it says less than Calvin: 'God therefore accomplishes what he promises in the symbols, and the signs are not without their effect in showing us that the author of them is true and faithful.'[72]

XXVI Of the Unworthiness of the Ministers

The title is changed to 'Of Unworthy Persons ministering in the Congregation'. This is shortened by the removal of the statements that 'we may use their ministry' and 'nor is the grace of God's gifts diminished from such as by faith and rightly do receive the Sacraments ministered unto them'. Again, the real concern seems to be a fear of allowing a 'mechanical' view of the Sacraments, though the amended Article still states that the believer 'is not deprived of the benefits of God's Ordinances'.

XXVII Of Baptism

Contrary to what might be expected, the Free Church of England version agrees with that of 1571 in calling baptism, 'not only a sign of profession, but . . . also a sign or symbol, of Regeneration or new Birth'. However, 'the promises of forgiveness of sin, and of our adoption to the sons of God by the Holy Ghost' are said to be 'visibly set forth', rather than 'visibly signed and sealed'. In view of the strength of the Baptismal Controversy, it is remarkable that the Article has not been more substantially reworked. The baptism of young children is said to be 'not contrary' rather than 'most agreeable' to the institution of Christ.

XXVIII Of the Lord's Supper

Most of this is identical with the 1571 version, including the statement that 'to such as rightly, worthily, and with faith receive the same, the Bread which we break is a partaking of the Body of Christ; and likewise the Cup of Blessing is a partaking of the Blood of Christ'. The only difference is that, after the repudiation of transubstantiation, is inserted: 'Consubstantiation (or the doctrine that Christ is veiled under the unchanged Bread and Wine) is utterly without warrant of Scripture, and is productive, equally with transubstantiation, of idolatrous errors and practices.' Griffith Thomas describes consubstantiation as 'difficult to define' and relates it to Luther's doctrine of the ubiquity of Christ: 'as He is everywhere He must be given with the bread and wine'.[73] Griffith Thomas argues that Article XXVIII (in the 1571 form) and Article XXIX ('Of the Wicked which eat not the Body of Christ in the use of the Lord's Supper') show that 'this Lutheran doctrine is no part of the English teaching'.[74] The Free Church of England addition is thus merely making explicit what is already taught in the Articles.

XXXVI Of Consecration of Bishops and Ministers

The difference here is merely that the reference to the Ordinal 'set forth in the time of Edward the Sixth, and confirmed at the same time by the authority of Parliament' is replaced by 'set forth by this Church'. Those ordained by the book are decreed 'to be rightly, orderly, and lawfully consecrated and ordered'.

XXXVII Of Civil Magistrates

This retains the teaching of the 1571 text, but removes the reference to the Elizabethan Injunctions as irrelevant in the denomination's context.

In conclusion, then, it is remarkable how conservative the revision of the Articles has been. As with the liturgical forms (see Chapter 11) the only significant redrafting (and that of a minimal nature) has been in relation to statements which were being interpreted by Anglo-Catholics in a manner contrary to their original intention. The real difference between the Free Church of England and the Church of England regarding the Thirty-Nine Articles, however, lies not so much in their text, but in their authority. The Anglican–Methodist *Common Statement* concedes that 'in practice both churches permit a range of emphases' and 'the way in which the terms of subscription to the formularies are expressed softens the impact of underlying historical controversies'.[75] The Free Church of England would not consider it legitimate to use such latitude so to interpret the Articles as to nullify totally their original intention.

Thus, as has been shown, the faith of the Free Church of England is defined in exclusively Anglican terms. Its formularies reflect the issues that seemed under particular threat in the nineteenth century, but are relatively restrained in their attempts at restatement.

Notes

1. Guelzo, *For the Union*, p. 155.
2. Ibid., p. 156.
3. Vaughan, *History*, (1st edn), p. 63.
4. Guelzo, *For the Union*, p. 159.
5. This was argued by, for example, William Reed Huntington (see Michelle Woodhouse-Hawkins, 'Maurice, Huntington and the Quadrilateral' in J. Robert Wright (ed.) *Quadrilateral at One Hundred* (Cincinnatti, Forward Movement Publications, 1988), p. 71.
6. T. Bradshaw, *The Olive Branch: An Evangelical Anglican Doctrine of the Church* (Carlisle, Paternoster Press, 1992), p. 179.
7. Donald K. McKim (ed.), *The Westminster Handbook to Reformed Theology* (Louisville, Westminster John Knox Press, 2001), p. 97.
8. See Hatchett, *The Making*, pp. 56, 77.
9. Ibid., p. 133.
10. For a brief introduction to this debate see Richard A. Norris, 'Episcopacy' in Stephen Sykes and John Booty (eds), *The Study of Anglicanism* (London, SPCK, 1988), pp. 296–309.
11. G. K. A. Bell, *Christian Unity: The Anglican Position* (London, Hodder and Stoughton, 1948), p. 23.
12. Francis Mason (1566–1621) quoted in Bell, *Christian Unity*, p. 25. Bell quotes passages from a number of authors to the same effect.
13. Bell, *Church Unity*, pp. 23f.
14. Charles Edward Cheney, *What Reformed Episcopalians Believe* (Philadelphia, The Reformed Episcopal Publication Society, 1st edn 1888, 1978), p. 66.
15. Bradshaw, *Olive Branch*, p. 169.
16. As Guelzo says, this, 'actually pegged Cummins higher on that point than some of his Evangelical brethren were interested in going'; *For the Union*, p. 156.
17. Cheney, *What Reformed Episcopalians Believe*, p. 66.

18. Bradshaw, *Olive Branch*, pp. 175, 177.
19. J. B. Lightfoot, *The Christian Ministry* (London, MacMillan & Co., 1901), p. 25.
20. *Episcopal Ministry: The Report of the Archbishops' Group on The Episcopate* (London, Church House Publishing, 1990 (GS 944)), para. 36, p. 17. The report believes that in other NT communities (particularly those mentioned in the Letters to Timothy and Titus) the 'bishop' carried more of a sense of apostolic delegate.
21. See J. Robert Wright, 'Heritage and Vision: the Chicago–Lambeth Quadrilateral' in Wright (ed.) *Quadrilateral at One Hundred* (Cincinnati, OH, Forward Movement Publications, 1988), pp. 8–46, for a discussion of the genesis of the Quadrilateral.
22. W. R. Huntington, *The Church-Idea*, (1870, 1st edn), pp. 155–57.
23. See Woodhouse-Hawkins, 'Maurice, Huntington and the Quadrilateral', pp. 61–78. Maurice listed six 'signs', counting baptism and Eucharist separately and adding 'forms of worship'.
24. Charles P. Price, 'Whence, Whither and What?' in Wright, *Quadrilateral*, p. 84.
25. Huntington, *Church-Idea*, p. 203.
26. Ibid., p. 195. Sixteen years later, in 1886, the PECUSA bishops were to adopt a much 'higher' view and describe the episcopate as part of the sacred deposit 'committed by Christ and his Apostles to the Church unto the end of the world, and therefore incapable of compromise or surrender'. Text in Wright, *Quadrilateral*, pp. vii–viii.
27. Ibid., p. 156.
28. The Reformed Church of England Constitution omits this clause as irrelevant to its situation.
29. Guelzo, *For the Union*, p. 156.
30. John Davenant (1572–1641) Bishop of Salisbury. Quoted in Bell, *Church Unity*, p. 25.
31. *The Meissen Declaration* (London, Council for Christian Unity, 1991), p. 2; *The Reuilly Common Statement* in *Called to Witness and Service* (London, Church House Publishing, 1999), p. 36; *The Fetter Lane Common Statement* in *Anglican–Moravian Conversations* (London, Council for Christian Unity, 1996), pp. 30f.; *Affirmations* in *An Anglican–Methodist Covenant* (London, Methodist Publishing House/Church House Publishing, 2001), pp. 60f.
32. *God's Reign and our Unity* (London, SPCK/Edinburgh, The St Andrew Press, 1984), p. 50.
33. Ibid.
34. C. O. Buchanan, E. L. Marshall, J. I. Packer, Graham Leonard, *Growing Into Union: Proposals for forming a United Church in England* (London, SPCK, 1970), p. 86. See Chapter 13 for a summary of *Growing Into Union*.

35. GS 694.

36. *General Synod: Report of Proceedings*, 17.3 (November 1986), pp. 743–88. The report is, however, quoted as though authoritative in *An Anglican–Methodist Covenant*, pp. 47f.

37. *The Free Church of England otherwise called the Reformed Episcopal Church Handbook for Ministers* (1st edn 1927, reprinted by authority of Council 1989), p. 228; hereafter cited as *Handbook for Ministers*. It is not entirely clear whether 'in memory of . . .' refers to the donor of the Holy Table or the saint in whose name the Church is dedicated. The former seems the more likely.

38. Colin Buchanan in *News of Liturgy*, September 2002, No. 333, p. 4.

39. Text in Bray, *Anglican Canons*, p. 570.

40. Ibid., p. 571.

41. Colin Buchanan in *News of Liturgy*, September 2002, No. 333, p. 5.

42. *The Final Report* (London, SPCK/Catholic Truth Society, 1982), p. 21. This is not to say that the Free Church of England would endorse everything in the ARCIC reports.

43. *Handbook for Ministers*, p. 238.

44. *Journals*, p. 56.

45. F. H. Easton, *Know Your Church* (London, FCE, 1964), p. 29.

46. J. C. S. Nias, *Gorham and the Bishop of Exeter* (London, SPCK, 1951), p. 9.

47. Ibid., p. 13.

48. Quoted in ibid., p. 15.

49. *The Judgement of the Judicial Committee of the Privy Council, delivered March 8th 1850* (London, Seeleys, 1850), p. 9.

50. Ibid., p. 20. Queen Victoria approved and confirmed the report at a meeting of the Privy Council on 9 March 1850.

51. Cheney actually echoes the words of the Gorham Judgement in his statement that the Holy Spirit 'might regenerate the soul in the hour of the baptismal rite, or before, or afterwards'; *What Reformed Episcopalians Believe*, p. 16.

52. Ibid., p. 18.

53. The phrase is from a resolution passed by a united meeting of Provincial Synods on 14 September 1869. Quoted in E. A. Webster, The Reconstruction of the Church', in W. A. Phillips (ed.), *History of the Church of Ireland from the Earliest Times to the Present Day* (London, OUP, 1933) vol. III, p. 364.

54. *A Just Vindication of the Church of England from the Unjust Aspersions of Criminal Schism*, (London, 1654); quoted in G. R. Evans and J. R. Wright, *The Anglican Tradition* (London, SPCK, 1991), p. 221. Bramhall's name is familiar to members of the Free Church of England as it appears annually in the Year Book as an authority for the validity of consecration by a single bishop.

55. Merryweather, p. 2.

56. *www.ireland.anglican.org/geninfo/pandc.html*. The Church of Ireland official

website (14 October 2001) (italics in original). Note the similarity to Muhlenberg's term *Gospel* Catholics.

57. Webster, 'Reconstruction', p. 368.

58. Guelzo, *For the Union*, p. 169.

59. H. Bower, *The Orders of the Reformed Episcopal Church Examined* (Malvern, The Advertiser Office, 1881), p. 25

60. Fenwick is inclined to believe an allegation made in 1879 that Gregg had actually been in contact with the Church of Utrecht, *Thesis*, p. 138.

61. Bullard, *Constitutions and Canons*, pp. 2–4. Compare the modern Canon A7: 'We acknowledge the Queen's excellent Majesty, acting according to the laws of this realm, is the highest power under God in this kingdom, and has supreme authority over all persons in all causes, as well ecclesiastical as civil.'

62. Article IV.

63. pp. 165–80. The bracketed Articles are III, VIII, XIII, XX (part), XXIII, XXXV, XXXVI. The relevant clause of the 1863 Constitution is 2.

64. For a detailed account and commentary, see W. H. Griffith Thomas, *Principles of Theology* (London, Church Book Room Press, 1945). The first version appeared in 1553, believed to be substantially the work of Cranmer and Ridley; they were reworked by Archbishop Matthew Parker in 1563 and finally edited by Bishop Jewel in 1571 when, by Act of Parliament, all clergy were required to subscribe to them.

65. Thomas, *Principles*, p. xxxiii. The Confession of Augsburg of 1530 ('the Augustana') 'is the classic statement of Lutheran doctrine' (p. xxx).

66. Thomas, *Principles*, p. xxxiii.

67. Interestingly, Whitefield did not share this aversion to the Apocrypha: 'Reading afterwards in the Book of Maccabees, and thinking of my present situation, this verse was pressed with unspeakable comfort on my soul: "After this they went home, and sung a song of thanksgiving, and praised the Lord in Heaven". I hope my friends will take care to fulfil this when we meet together on shore', *Journals*, p. 172 (Monday 30 October 1738).

68. The Spanish Reformed Episcopal Church, under the metropolitical jurisdiction of the Archbishop of Canterbury, omits this Article entirely.

69. Anglican–Methodist, *Common Statement*, para. 115, p. 38.

70. Ibid., para. 114.

71. Thomas, *Principles*, p. 242. 'It was a necessary and wholesome reaction against the papal doctrine of human merit. It was . . . death to all pride and self-righteousness' (p. 243).

72. Calvin, *Institutes*, 4, 14, 17.

73. Thomas, *Principles*, p. 397.

74. Ibid., p. 398.

75. Anglican–Methodist, *Common Statement*, para. 117, p. 38.

CHAPTER 11

Worship

Like so much else in the life of the Free Church of England, the denomination's worship is constitutionally tied to that of the Church of England. Canon 87 requires that the Free Church of England's Prayer Book 'shall agree with the Book of Common Prayer of the Established Church, as far as may be consistent with the Evangelical Principles of this Church'.[1]

This has been the consistent situation since the eighteenth century. Unlike the Scottish Episcopal Church, for example, the Free Church of England has never had a time in its history when its worship was anything other than liturgical.[2] The leaders of the Evangelical Revival had no quarrel with the Book of Common Prayer: 'I have no objection against, but highly approve of the excellent Liturgy of our Church,' wrote Whitefield.[3] There was no impetus to change it; indeed, the Holy Communion Order has been memorably described by the Anglo-Catholic liturgist Gregory Dix as 'the only effective attempt ever made to give liturgical expression to the doctrine of justification by faith alone'.[4] Blessed with a liturgy that taught the central doctrine of their preaching, Whitefield and his contemporaries gloried in its use.[5]

Within the breadth of Prayer Book liturgy, there was a special attachment to the service of Holy Communion. The Evangelical Revival had not just been about preaching. 'It is not so generally realised,' writes Skevington Wood, 'that the Evangelicals were equally concerned to restore this Sacrament to its rightful place in the life of the Church.'[6] Whitefield's *Journals* contain frequent references to his administering or helping to administer 'the blessed Sacrament' or 'the Holy Eucharist'. When on board ship in his frequent travels across the Atlantic he records how he had the Eucharist on Sundays and on the feasts of St Matthew and St Michael and All Angels.[7] In view of the later rather anti-sacramental attitude that would develop among many Evangelicals in reaction to Tractarianism, it is important to realize the importance of eucharistic piety to the earlier generations. Something of Whitefield's approach to the reality of feeding on Christ in the Sacrament has already been noted in Chapter 10. In 1739 he wrote: 'Received the Sacrament at Crooked Lane, but was a little dissipated; however, I found that I received Christ, and fed on Him in my heart by faith with thanksgiving'.[8] At times he could write that he 'felt great hungerings and thirstings of the blessed Sacrament'.[9] His frustration prior to his ordination as a priest has already been noted. Nor was Whitefield's approach to the Eucharist merely individualistic. There was also a communal (and at times an ecumenical) dimension: '. . . got Mr. T. to preach, who (though a Baptist Minister) joined with us in receiving the Sacrament, in the Church of England way. The King [i.e. Christ] was pleased to sit at His Table: He brought us into His Banqueting House, and caused it to be a feast of fat to our souls. Many, I believe, fed on Jesus in their hearts with thanksgiving'.[10]

Nor was Whitefield exceptional. John Wesley received Communion weekly whenever possible and some of his brother Charles's hymns are rich in eucharistic doctrine and imagery. Daniel Rowland, too, experienced the power of a sacramental ministry alongside that of the Word. At Abergorloch on 12 June 1742, '. . . the presence of the Lord so filled the place, in the sermon and the sacrament (which he administers there once a month) that . . . few were unaffected'.[11] Other examples can be found among the leaders of the Revival.

This attachment to the Prayer Book and a rich sacramental experience was carried over into the Countess of Huntingdon's Connexion after the formal break with the Established Church. Thomas Haweis, whose ministry of 'oversight' as Principal Trustee has been explored earlier, robustly asserted: '. . . nor is the Liturgy of the Church of England performed more devoutly in any church, nor the Scriptures better read for the edifying of the people, as those who attend our London congregations can witness'.[12] Among those London congregations was of course Spa Fields Chapel: 'Those who worshipped there,' asserted Merryweather, 'loved the Church of England with a tender and hallowed love. The services were conducted in Church order and in accordance with the Book of Common Prayer.'[13] The recent Anglican–Methodist *Common Statement* affirms that the Countess's Connexion, 'which gathered churches under the Calvinist influence of Whitefield . . . was even more insistent on the use of the Anglican liturgy than those associated with Wesley'.[14] As recently as 1964 four Connexional chapels were still using a version of the Book of Common Prayer, with the surplice being worn for Holy Communion in three of them.[15]

The events of the nineteenth century were to challenge the movement's unreserved devotion to the Prayer Book and to leave the legacies of an amended text and a subtly altered attitude in the modern Free Church of England. The full story of liturgical revision in the Free Church of England tradition is still waiting to be told. All that is attempted here is a brief look at a few significant events which have contributed to present-day practice.

As has already been seen, one of the basic methodologies of the Tractarian movement was to revive obsolescent practices sanctioned by the 1662 Book of Common Prayer, then to reinterpret much of the book in pre-Reformation and/or post-Tridentine terms. To maintain the true Protestant faith, the Book must therefore be revised to exclude any such practices or interpretations. Chief among the champions for such revision was Robert Grosvenor, third son of the first Marquess of Westminster. Created first Baron Ebury in 1857, he was to devote the rest of his life to furthering the cause. He was also well disposed towards the Free Church of England.

In 1859 Ebury founded 'The Association for Promoting a Revision of the Book of Common Prayer'. The aim was to remove 'a few relics of a Popish age', after which 'the Prayer Book will become a manual of devotion which cannot be surpassed, and a bond of union among the Reformed Churches throughout the world'.[16] Particularly striking is the similarity to the position to be taken just a few years later by Bishop Cummins on the other side of the Atlantic. The two men shared an ecumenical concern. Liturgical revision was not just about *excluding* Tractarians; it should facilitate the *inclusion* of Dissenters.

Any liturgical revision in the Established Church could only (at that time) be sanctioned directly by Parliament and to that end Ebury introduced Bill after Bill into the House of Lords. The Free Church of England, of course, suffered from no such restraints. The original 1790

Plan had made no mention of forms of worship, presumably because there was no question of anything other than the Book of Common Prayer being used. Nor is there any mention in the 1836 Constitution, though by this time it is almost certain that some chapels were abandoning liturgical forms and it may have been thought expedient to remain silent on the subject. The 1863 Constitution, however, declared that the ministers of the Free Church of England were 'free to employ whatever they deem valuable and to refuse what appears to them objectionable in the service of [the United Church of England and Ireland]'.[17] Clearly it was quickly felt necessary to bring some uniformity into the new denomination's liturgical practice and to make it even more attractive to other evangelicals. In June 1865, the *Harbinger* appealed for 'Ministers and members of Evangelical Churches . . . to meet from time to time to consider those passages in the Book of Common Prayer, to which Evangelical Nonconformists and many members of the Church of England entertain conscientious objections'.[18] The deliberations evidently produced a draft text, for in June 1867 Thoresby presented to Convocation a 'revised Prayer Book, which was carefully and accurately considered in detail, and referred for final approval to an able Revision Committee' charged with the task of removing sacerdotalism, baptismal regeneration, real presence teaching and priestly absolution.[19] The Baptism Service was ready for final approval in early 1868 and the Confirmation Service by August of that year.

The details of the changes made are described by Merryweather, though, curiously, no mention is made of the Communion Service, despite the fact that a revision had been promised in 1868, and in July 1869 the *Free Church of England Magazine* reported that it had been discussed and permission given to proceed to publication.[20] The attitude to the revision of the services had, records Merryweather, been cautious: 'Formularies of a thousand years ought not to be touched except with reverence.'[21] As well as removing a few items seen as unscriptural, the revision allowed a breadth of churchmanship by putting 'in brackets certain passages and words, about which difference of opinion is allowed by Convocation; which passages and words, enclosed by brackets, may be read or omitted, according to the conscience or discretion of the officiating minister'.[22] Bracketed sections include, for example, the words 'and hath given power and commandment to his ministers to declare unto his people being penitent the absolution and remission of their sins' in the

Declaration of Forgiveness in Morning and Evening Prayer; and, more surprisingly, the phrase 'He descended into Hell' in the Apostles' Creed. In the Baptism Service there are 'no vows, no sponsors, no sign of the cross, or predication of the effect of baptism. The child is dedicated to God, surrounded with the atmosphere of prayer, received into the visible Church, and then taken home to be trained in the nurture and admonition of the Lord.'[23] Merryweather ends his rather sketchy description by saying, 'It must not, however, be assumed that the work of Liturgical revision in the Free Church of England is either complete or final,'[24] which may explain the lack of a Communion Service. The identity of the chief compiler is revealed by the 1869 Convocation Minutes: 'As the Revd T. E. Thoresby had personally made the Revision . . . it was agreed unanimously that he should be allowed a royalty of ONE PENNY per copy . . .'[25] The book cost 2/6d, with a wholesale price of 1/6d to congregations.[26]

Vaughan seems to have been unaware of this work, for he explicitly says that 'the FCE did not produce a book of their own'.[27] Instead, he states, the Free Church of England used 'a shortened form' of a book produced in 1876 by Ebury's 'Prayer Book Revision Committee' 'for the use of the Free Church of England'.[28] Peaston states that this book 'was never in general use, probably owing to the cost of production'.[29] Vaughan possessed 'a copy of that book with that imprint' in his collection.[30]

By the second half of the 1870s the United Kingdom branch of the Reformed Episcopal Church had been founded.[31] It seems unlikely that it ever used the 1785 Prayer Book of its American parent.[32] Nor does there seem to have been much exploring of Muhlenberg's liturgical innovations. Vaughan states that Gregg produced a revision of 1662 'for the use of his Churches in England'.[33] This was apparently also used by some of the Reformed Episcopal Churches under Sugden's jurisdiction, though Vaughan states that not all of them did so.[34] Indeed, at one stage Gregg appears to have held the copyright in his own name, and reduced the official branch of the Reformed Episcopal Church in the UK to using the Church of England's Prayer Book with alterations pencilled in.[35] It appears that it was not until 1904 that a revision of the Prayer Book was produced for use of all the Churches in the Reformed Episcopal Church tradition. This was substantially Gregg's revision, 'but with still further approximations to the Anglican liturgy'.[36] Interestingly, in 1910 the Convocation of the Free Church of England gave its congregations permission to use this book if they so wished, and Young, the General

Secretary of the pre-union Free Church of England actually purchased and distributed copies to facilitate this.[37] It was this Reformed Episcopal Church version which was adopted without alteration as the official Liturgy of the united Church in 1927.

By the 1990s the denomination was becoming acutely aware that it needed to address the issue of its liturgical provision. Various modern-language versions of the 1662 have been discussed unofficially, in particular *The Prayer Book of the Church of England in South Africa* (1992)[38] and *An English Prayer Book*, edited by Roger Beckwith and published by the Church Society in 1994.[39] To date, however, the Church has not had the unanimity of mind, or the resources, to undertake a thorough revision of its liturgy. Instead, in 1998 Convocation adopted The Alternative Services Measure.[40] This states that the denomination's Prayer Book is invariably to be used at all diocesan, denominational and sacramental services, but allows a parish 'that desires to use an alternative form of worship during a main Sunday service' to apply to the bishop for authorization to do so. Permission can only be given subject to a number of 'conditions, restrictions and regulations' which, among other things, restrict the use of such an 'Approved Alternative Liturgy' (AAL) to no more than once a month (or twice if there are five Sundays) if the congregation has only one service on a Sunday. AALs should not be used in the same part of the day as a Prayer Book service (so as not to be in direct competition) and the bishop must be provided with a schedule of the congregation's worship pattern to help him be sure that the Prayer Book is not being afforded merely 'token' use. In some miscellaneous clauses the 'Measure' requires Holy Communion to be administered at a main service at least once a month; requires the use of 'proper grape wine . . . a fine vintage is preferred', but allows non-alcoholic wine as 'acceptable'; reminds congregations and clergy that the use of a common cup is the accepted denomination practice; requires the use of robes; and permits metrical psalms and traditional language canticles from the Church of England's *Alternative Service Book 1980*. The final clause states that the 'Measure' does not apply to such acts of worship as youth services, harvest festivals and carol services. Anecdotal evidence suggests that some of the denomination's churches have well-attended 'Alternative' services, with numbers considerably higher than when the Prayer Book is used.

The present Prayer Book

There is no space here for a detailed textual commentary on the liturgical texts of the denomination. All that can be done is briefly to draw attention to some basic diagnostic features.[41]

The form of the book

Perhaps the first thing that strikes someone attending a service for the first time is that the book handed to them looks identical to 1662 Prayer Books for congregational use in the Church of England. Measuring three and a half inches by six inches, with *Small Pica* as the font, it is only very close examination that reveals any difference. The edition currently in use is that of 1956, published by Marshall, Morgan and Scott.

The Preface

This states that, 'In making this revision of the Book of Common Prayer . . . it has been our express desire to follow, as closely as possible, the arrangements and language of the old Formularies of the Church of England, to which we, and the whole Christian Church, owe so much.' Other attempts at Prayer Book revision are acknowledged.

The ornaments rubric

Not surprisingly, the ambiguities surrounding the equivalent rubric in 1662 are removed. The minister is not to wear alb, vestment nor cope, but if a bishop, a rochet and chimere, while deacons and presbyters wear a plain surplice and a plain black scarf, with or without the hood of their degree. The rubric also forbids the use of any 'picture, cross, crucifix, incense, candles, molten, painted or graven images or images'. Interestingly, the prohibition on a cross is not unique to the Low Church tradition. No less a representative of the pre-Tractarian High Church school than Bishop Phillpotts himself argued that a cross or crucifix was inappropriate, particularly at the Eucharist. The Eucharist, he argued, 'is a pleading here on earth of Calvary as an actual, living, triumphant reality; the cross speaks of Calvary as an event, dead and past, and encourages people to think of the Eucharist as nothing more than a bare remembrance of what is past and gone.'[42]

The rubric concludes with the statement that 'In the conduct of Public Worship, the customs and usages of the Church of England shall be observed; except where otherwise specified in this Book, or where contrary to the Evangelical and Protestant Principles of this Church.'

Morning and Evening Prayer

These are virtually identical to 1662, the chief difference being the placing in brackets of the words 'and hath given power and commandment to his ministers . . .' in the Absolution (which is itself called 'The Declaration concerning the Remission of sins').

Holy Communion

The Order is preceded by the Collects, Epistles and Gospels exactly as in 1662. The opening rubrics are very similar to those of the Book of Common Prayer, with the addition of a rubric requiring the Table to be wood, devoid of cross or candles, and with a cover the colour of which is not changed to indicate the Church seasons. The minister is not to kneel or say any prayer with his back to the people.[43]

In some Churches the Ten Commandments are divided into two groups, with the response said or sung at the end of each. This arrangement is found in the Church of Ireland Prayer Book.[44]

Surprisingly, there are Gospel responses: 'Glory be to thee, O Lord' and 'Thanks be to thee, O Lord'. These are not in 1662 and it may be that their inclusion indicates their survival in popular usage.[45]

The Prayer for the Church Militant omits the reference to 'oblations', reflecting the view that the word might refer to the bread and wine.

Prior to the Third Exhortation and Invitation to Confession, there is inserted: 'Our fellow Christians of other branches of Christ's Church, and all who love our Lord Jesus Christ in sincerity, are affectionately invited to the Lord's Table.' This of course ran strongly counter to the practice of most of the Established Church until the mid twentieth century. The Absolution, like the final Blessing, is to be said by the Bishop ('being present'), rather than the presiding presbyter.

The Prayer of Humble Access is the same as that of 1662, save for the addition twice of the word 'spiritually': 'Grant us therefore, gracious Lord, so *spiritually* to eat the flesh of thy dear Son Jesus Christ, and so *spiritually* to drink his Blood . . .' The phrasing seems to be suggested by that of the Third Exhortation of 1662: 'for then we spiritually eat the flesh of Christ and drink his blood'. The same methodology is used in the Prayer of Consecration (which does not bear that name in the FCE rite, but is referred to as such in the Black Rubric). Here the central petition runs: 'grant that we receiving these thy creatures of bread and wine, according to thy Son our Saviour Jesus Christ's holy institution, in remembrance of his death and passion, may, *after an heavenly and spiritual manner*, be partakers of his most blessed Body and Blood . . .'. Here the source is clearly identifiable. Article XXVIII includes the sentence: 'The Body of Christ is given, taken and eaten, in the Supper, only after an heavenly and spiritual manner.' What is remarkable is the way the revisers have amended the text at these two sensitive places to clarify what they believed to be biblical doctrine, but have done so by using texts that were already authoritative in the Church of England. The result is impressive and, in its own terms, unanswerable.

The Prayer of Consecration is to be said by the presbyter 'standing at the North side of the Table' as in the Church of Ireland order.[46] At the utterance of the Dominical words, the manual acts are mandatory, as in 1662. The Words of Administration are the combined 1549 and 1552 form. Bye-law III.12.3.c states that 'The use of the common cup for the administration of consecrated wine to the people is the accepted practice in the FCE', and a note allows 'intinction' and, in extraordinary cases such as acute alcoholism, communion in one kind. The use of individual communion glasses was introduced into at least one congregation at the height of the AIDS scare, and has persisted since. The provision for Supplementary Consecration is the same as that in 1662. The word 'reverently' is omitted from the rubric requiring the minister to place upon the Table 'what remaineth of the consecrated elements, covering the same with a fair linen cloth'. Presumably 'reverently' was seen as potentially opening the door to a range of unacceptable devotional practices. The word remains in the rubric about the consumption of the consecrated elements that are left over.

The first Post-Communion Prayer asks God to 'accept this our *service* of praise and thanksgiving', instead of *sacrifice*; and the second Post-Communion prayer gives thanks 'for that thou has vouchsafed to feed us, who have duly received *this holy Supper* [not *these holy mysteries*], with the spiritual food of the most precious Body and Blood.'

The final rubrics are very similar to those of 1662. An additional rubric allows (with episcopal permission) for the Words of Administration to be said once only to each group of communicants, 'provided that the words shall be said separately to any Communicant so desiring it'. In some Churches the custom is to say the words to the whole rail, then *repeat* them to each individual. It does not seem to be what the rubric intends.

So few are the changes to the actual prayers of the Order that some churches actually use large print versions of 1662 (there being no 'Altar Book' versions of the Free Church of England rite) with the alterations marked.

The Public Baptism of Infants

The alterations to the service are relatively modest, being confined almost exclusively to the removal of references to regeneration and the blessing of the water. The signing with the Cross has also been deleted from the rite. Otherwise the text (including the requirement that baptism take place 'when the most number come together) is basically that of 1662, with little material added.[47]

Other services

All the 'lesser' services of the Prayer Book are present – Private Baptism, Confirmation, Churching of Women, Matrimony (including the words required by civil registration), Visitation and Communion of the Sick (without the provision for absolution), Accession Day, Commination (called 'A Penitential Service'), Forms for Use at Sea. There then follow the Psalms, divided for daily use, as in 1662.

Additional services are A Children's Service, which is mainly in versicle and response form, and A Thanksgiving for Harvest (including a Collect, Epistle and Gospel).

The Ordinal

This has its own title page and preface. In the latter it is stated that:

> It is evident that from the earliest times there have been these Ministers in Christ's Church; Bishops, Presbyters and Deacons. . . And therefore, to the intent that this Ministry may be continued, and reverently used and esteemed in the Free Church of England . . ., no man shall be accounted or taken to be a lawful Bishop, Presbyter or Deacon in such Church, or suffered to exercise any of the said Functions, except he be called, tried, examined and admitted thereto, according to the Form hereafter following, or hath had formerly Consecration, or Ordination.

The removal of the reference to the three Orders having existed in the time of the Apostles reflects both what is historically verifiable, and the desire not to see the episcopate as a continuation of the apostolate.

In the services themselves the bishops are addressed as 'Reverend Brother in Christ' ('Most Reverend' in the case of the Primus). Candidates for the episcopate are presented to be 'ordained and consecrated Bishop'.

The structure and text of all three services follows very closely that of 1662, though the Litany is not printed out, which has resulted in its omission on occasion. The formula at the laying on of hands for deacons is identical with that of 1662. *Veni Creator Spiritus* is sung in the rite for presbyters and bishops. For the former the words at the laying on of hands reflect both the conviction that only the Holy Spirit can make a man a minister of Christ, and the desire to remove the sacerdotal implications of John 20.23:

> Almighty God grant unto thee the gift of the Holy Ghost for the Office and Work of a Presbyter in the Church of God, now committed unto thee by the Imposition of our hands. And be thou a faithful Dispenser of the Word of God, and of his holy Sacraments; in the Name of the Father, and of the Son, and of the Holy Ghost. Amen.

For a bishop the first sentence is the same, with 'Bishop' substituted for 'Presbyter'. Then follows: 'And remember that thou stir up the grace of God which is given thee: for God has not given us the spirit of fear, but of power, love and soberness.'

The Ordinal also contains the forms for Receiving a Presbyter of Another Church, and the Installation of Ministers.

Additional considerations

Robes

As noted above, liturgical dress is cassock, surplice, scarf and hood for presbyters; rochet and chimere for bishops. Wearing of a black gown for preaching was once widespread (it was required by Bye-law 16, section 1 of the pre-1873 Free Church of England in Churches held under the Central Deed Poll Trust), but has not been the usual practice for many decades.[48] There is probably a continuous tradition of use of the surplice for the Eucharist, stretching back through Connexional days to eighteenth-century Church of England usage (though evidence suggests that the surplice was by no means universal in the Established Church at this period). Merryweather speaks of it as the normal vesture for 'the reading of the Liturgy', which suggests that it was worn for all services by 1873.[49] This presents an interesting contrast with the Scottish Episcopal Church, in which the black gown was the norm from the sixteenth to early nineteenth centuries, after which the surplice was encouraged, though fiercely resisted by both clergy and laity for some years.[50] In its consistent use of the surplice the Free Church of England (and its pre-1927 parent bodies) also presents a sharp contrast with the Reformed Episcopal Church in the USA. There, after years of bitter controversy, the use of the surplice virtually ceased and all clergy (bishops included) wore only the black gown, sometimes with a cassock. Only in the last few decades have surplice, rochet and chimere been restored.[51] Surprisingly, in view of the internal divisions it has suffered, the Reformed Episcopal movement in the UK seems to have escaped any major crisis over robes. The hood worn is either that of a graduate's degree or the Presbyter's Hood of the denomination, introduced in 1927.[52]

Bishops are clad in cassock and gown at the beginning of their consecration service,[53] then don the rochet, followed later in the service by 'the rest of the Episcopal habit' (i.e. chimere and scarf) as in the 1662 Ordinal. The episcopal chimere was black until the 1990s when scarlet chimeres began to make an appearance. They are now worn by both of the bishops on more 'festive' occasions. Some bishops now wear pectoral crosses and discrete episcopal rings. Bishops in charge of congregations will sometimes wear simply surplice, scarf and hood for 'ordinary' services in order to enhance a feeling of the 'special' on other occasions by wearing rochet and chimere. When ministering in other congregations, the use of episcopal robes seems to be universal. Mitres are obviously not worn, though they are used heraldically on bishops' seals.[54]

The current *Handbook for the Clergy* contains a section on 'Our Vestments, Ornaments and Architecture' in which a brief account of clerical dress is given.[55] It implies that the cassock was not generally worn in the earliest decades of the denomination's independent existence (as it was not by some Evangelicals in the Established Church in living memory), but judges it 'simple and harmless' and 'its adoption is more seemly than the appearance of half-covered legs'.[56]

Clerical dress is not restricted to worship. In the nineteenth century frock coats were the norm, with the bishops in 'aprons' and gaiters. As recently as the 1960s at meetings of Diocesan Synod the clergy wore cassocks and the bishop a frock coat. Nowadays a range of different coloured clerical shirts is the norm, though the bishops usually wear purple. No Free Church of England bishop has yet appeared in a purple cassock.

In relation to the laity, the once universal Church of England practice of female Confirmation candidates wearing white veils is retained in some Free Church of England congregations. Readers wear blue scarves over their surplices.[57] Choirs may wear robes (similar to academic gowns) but not surplices.[58] Churchwardens carry staves of office on formal occasions.

The appearance of the churches

Something has been said of this in Chapter 3. Many of the church buildings are handsome edifices, usually brick-built with stone doorways and windows. A few are more basic wooden frame constructions. Most have a hall alongside; some have quite extensive facilities. In the second half of the twentieth century several churches were rebuilt, usually with modern facilities adjacent.

The interiors are typical of Anglican 'Low Church' style. Bare wooden Communion Tables are common, despite the fact that the rubric presupposes a cover.[59] Pews and kneelers are the norm, though there is an increasing tendency (as in the Church of England) for congregations not to bother to kneel.

Some of the Churches have attractive woodwork and stained glass, though occasionally stained glass has been removed under the influence of a zealous minister who has taken objection to such 'popery'.

Liturgical style and ethos

The style of worship aimed at from the earliest days of the denomination's independent history is exactly summed up by the Second Vatican Council: 'The rites should be distinguished by a noble simplicity. They should be short, clear and free from useless repetitions. They should be within the people's comprehension, and normally should not require much explanation.'[60] Worship is generally dignified and devout, though occasional sloppy examples can be found, particularly where the minister has had little 'liturgical formation'. The *Handbook for the Clergy* contains a whole section on how to lead various acts of worship (including the arrangements for the consecration of a bishop), which concludes with nine pages dedicated to 'Deportment', including the warning that 'slovenliness or carelessness in deportment are not evidences of true Protestantism or of consecration of life'.[61]

Generally, the Free Church of England has not recovered the strong eucharistic devotion of its eighteenth-century founders and predecessors. This is no doubt due to the fear that any positive exploration of eucharistic teaching and piety will lead directly to full-blown Tractarianism. Holy Communion is still not the main service each Sunday within the denomination.

The whole Liturgical Movement has largely passed the denomination by. This is true not simply in terms of texts, but in relation to matters of approach to worship. There is, for example, little understanding of the concept of the liturgical presidency. The officiating minister is still described in eighteenth-century terms as 'reading the service'. Understandably, there is little interest in liturgical creativity. Thus, when in 1994 the denomination celebrated the 150th anniversary of the 'freeing' of the Bridgetown Chapel in 1844, it did so not with a specially constructed act of worship, but with a service of Evening Prayer. Nor has the musical tradition inspired in part by the Charismatic Movement made much headway, at least at official levels. The sense of 'freedom' which would permit, for example, the raising of hands in worship, has not yet arrived.

With most congregations quite small (quite a few are regularly under 20, some under 10) the denomination finds it difficult to cope with large numbers on the occasions when they are present. Uncertain what to do about administering communion to large numbers due to attend an episcopal consecration, the possibility was considered of restricting reception of the Sacrament to the clergy, the candidate's family and members of Council, effectively reducing approximately two hundred other people to non-communicating attendance! Fortunately wiser counsels prevailed. However, the habit of administering to one rail of communicants at a time, then dismissing that rail, makes the administration to large numbers intolerably long.[62]

There is no doubt that the majority of the membership of the Free Church of England is attached to its Prayer Book. Right up to the present the denomination continues to attract members of the Established Church who prefer 'the old services'. There is of course a painful inconsistency here. It is a fundamental Reformation principle (enshrined in Article XXIV) that worship must be in a tongue 'understanded of the people'. In defending its sixteenth-century texts, the denomination at times sounds like those who argue for the retention of Latin in the Roman rites – an irony which is lost on some of its members. As noted in the previous chapter, the logic of the Free Church of England's Canon and historic stance is that it should now use the *Common Worship* of the Church of England, modified in places according to the denomination's specific doctrinal stance. Quite apart from other considerations this would give it access to a modern-language text of the Prayer Book Communion rite. Whether this is a position the denomination would be prepared to adopt, and whether it has anyone capable of undertaking the task, remains to be seen.

Notes

1. The Declaration of Principles makes the same point: '. . . this Church accepts the Book of Common Prayer of the Church of England, with such revisions as shall exclude sacerdotal doctrines and practices'.
2. See Duncan Forrester and Douglas Murray (eds), *Studies in the History of Worship in Scotland* (Edinburgh, T&T Clark, 1984) for descriptions of episcopalian worship at various periods. Note, for example, the quotation from Sir George MacKenzie in 1691: 'The way of worship in our church differed

nothing from what the presbyterians themselves practiced (except only that we used the doxology, the Lord's Prayer, and in Baptism the Creed, all which they rejected)' p. 61.

3. *Journals*, p. 286 (6 June 1739).

4. Gregory Dix, *The Shape of the Liturgy* (London, Dacre Press, 1945), p. 672.

5. Whitefield and his contemporaries were also comfortable with what might be termed the 'High Calvinist' doctrines of the Prayer Book, particularly in relation to the Sacraments. See Bryan D. Spinks, *Sacraments, Ceremonies and the Stuart Divines* (Aldershot, Ashgate, 2002) for a recent treatment of this area.

6. Skevington Wood, *Thomas Haweis*, p. 65.

7. See, for example, *Journals*, pp. 334f.

8. *Journals*, p. 203 (Sunday 28th January 1739).

9. *Journals*, p. 41.

10. Ibid., p. 448 (Sunday 10 August 1740).

11. Quoted in Evans, *Daniel Rowland*, p. 232.

12. Quoted in Seymour, *Life and Times*, vol. 2, p. 521.

13. Merryweather, p. 49.

14. Anglican–Methodist *Common Statement*, p. 4.

15. Peaston, *Prayer Book Revision*, pp. 68f. The chapels were Basingstoke, Brighton, Worcester and Tonbridge Wells (which did not use the surplice). Worcester, it will be recalled, had only ceased to have joint membership with the Free Church of England in 1913. None of the Connexional chapels currently uses the Prayer Book or surplice.

16. *Special Address at the Council of the Association for Promoting a Revision of the Book of Common Prayer*, adopted May 1869; quoted in Jasper, *Prayer Book*, p. 50. See also Jasper, *Anglican Liturgy*, for accounts of eighteenth- and nineteenth-century attempts to revise the Prayer Book.

17. Clause 2.

18. *Harbinger*, June 1865, p. 161.

19. *FCE Magazine* July 1867, p. 210; the proposed changes to Morning and Evening Prayer and the Litany were also presented on this occasion, pp. 211–13. Merryweather, p. 156.

20. *FCE Magazine*, July 1869, p. 217.

21. Merryweather, p. 155; 'a thousand years' of course includes pre-Reformation usage.

22. Ibid., p. 156.

23. Ibid., p. 162. It will be remembered that Prayer Book revision in the United States in the 1780s had sought to remove this phrase from the Creed.

24. Ibid.

25. *FCE Magazine*, July 1869, p. 217.

26. Ibid., July 1871, p. 196.

27. Vaughan, 'Memories', p. 8.
28. Ibid., pp. 6ff.
29. Peaston, *Prayer Book Revision*, p. 72.
30. Ibid. There is no mention of an 1876 book in G. J. Cuming, *A History of Anglican Liturgy* (London, Macmillan, 1982, 2nd edn) or in Jasper's list of nineteenth-century publications – another curious example of the 'invisibility' of the Free Church of England. Vaughan claimed that his archive at Morecambe contained a copy of every edition of the Prayer Book since 1785 ('Memories', p. 28).
31. The Reformed Episcopal Church in North America was just as committed to liturgical worship as the Free Church of England. See Cheney's defence of the Book of Common Prayer in *What Reformed Episcopalians Believe*, pp. 69–76.
32. The Reformed Episcopal Church in North America itself began to move away from the 1785 Prayer Book surprisingly quickly (initial attempts to revise it beginning even while Cummins was alive). From 1912 it began to use versions closer to those of PECUSA (Guelzo, *For the Union*, pp. 232ff., 286).
33. Vaughan, 'Memories', p. 7.
34. Ibid.
35. See Guelzo, *For the Union*, p. 256.
36. Peaston, *Prayer Book Revision*, p. 74; Vaughan, 'Memories' p. 7.
37. Vaughan, 'Memories', p. 8.
38. Gillits, CESA, 1992.
39. With Oxford University Press.
40. The name is clearly copied from the 1965 Prayer Book (Alternative and other Services) Measure passed by Parliament to allow the Church of England an increased freedom to revise its own liturgical tradition. The Free Church of England 'Measure' forms Bye-law III.12.
41. A set of brief notes on the various services can be found in Peaston, *Prayer Book Revision*, pp. 80–87.
42. Quoted in G. W. O. Addleshaw, *The High Church Tradition* (London, Faber & Faber, 1941), p. 54.
43. Some Reformed authors have, on the contrary, argued that the minister *should* stand facing the same way as the people for acts of praise, confession and intercession, for in these he is one with them. See P. T. Forsyth, *Church and Sacraments* (London, Independent Press, 1917), p. 145.
44. See Bernard Wigan, *The Liturgy in English* (London, OUP, 1962), p. 28.
45. The pre-Gospel response is that of the 1549 Order. Similar responses are found in the Canadian and Scottish orders (ibid., pp. 29f.).
46. Ibid., p. 35.
47. The treatment of this rite is a good illustration of Peaston's observation that '. . . all Puritan and Evangelical amendments revisions [*sic*] are effected

almost invariably by way of omissions, and not by additions' (*Prayer Book Revision*, p. 80).

48. The pre-union Reformed Episcopal Church required the churchwardens to provide a gown as well as a surplice and scarf, but made no law as to its use. A note appended to current Bye-law III.12.3.c stresses that this is to be the proper vesture of the clergy 'at <u>all</u> ministrations of **public** worship' (bold type and underlining in original).

49. Merryweather, p. 96. The surplice, as noted above, was still used in three Connexional chapels as recently as 1964 (Peaston, *Prayer Book Revision*, p. 69).

50. See Walker, *For the Union*, pp. 275ff. For some staunch Episcopalians the surplice was a 'hated garment'.

51. See Guelzo, *For the Union*, pp. 257–67 for an account of the vestments controversy in the Reformed Episcopal Church. Currently the Church is in some places cautiously exploring the use of eucharistic vestments.

52. Bye-law I.1.

53. *Handbook for Ministers*, pp. 181f. This *may* reflect pre-nineteenth-century Church of England practice. In the 1662 Ordinal the bishop-elect is not required to wear his rochet until his presentation after the sermon (Matthew Parker wore a surplice throughout his consecration in 1559, but had worn academic dress for Morning Prayer which had preceded it; see Brook, *A Life*, p. 85). Deacons and presbyters (who are only required to be 'decently habited') were regularly ordained in black gowns in the Church of England until the mid nineteenth century. See the examples quoted in Alan Munden, *The History of St John's College Nottingham. Part 1: Mr Peache's College at Kilburn* (Nottingham, St John's College, 1995), pp. 6f.

54. These show an Agnus Dei on a shield, with a scroll beneath bearing the Latin *Deus providabit* (God will provide) alluding to Abraham's words in Genesis 22.8 – 'God himself will provide the lamb'. The shield and mitre are surrounded by the traditional vesica (pointed oval) of episcopal seals, with the words, 'The Seal of AB, Bishop in the Church of God' followed by the year of consecration. Bishops usually sign with their Christian name and surname, followed by 'Bp', though in recent years some have taken to placing a cross before their name instead of the suffix.

55. *Handbook for Ministers*, pp. 149–59.

56. Ibid., p. 155. Prior to the nineteenth century surplices were full-length garments. Their shortening, with consequent exposure of the legs, was a Tractarian fashion that the FCE clergy seem to have followed. The loss of the cassock seems to have been a temporary phase. Writing shortly after his ordination as a deacon, Whitefield describes how, 'as I passed along the streets, many came out of their shops to see so young a person in a gown and

cassock'; *Journals*, p. 77 (August 1736). Whitefield was 21 at the time. He also wore a clerical wig.

57. Bye-law III.10. As in the Church of England, this replaces an earlier ribbon and badge, and is a further example of the denomination altering its practice to keep up with changes in the Established Church.

58. Bye-law III.3.

59. Some churches remove the cover on Maundy Thursday, to leave the Table bare for Good Friday. The practice was certainly followed by Bishop Vaughan and may be an ancient survival of pre-Tractarian practice (Vaughan being unlikely to have borrowed an Anglo-Catholic custom).

60. *The Constitution on the Sacred Liturgy*, III.A.34. Text in Austin Flannery (ed.), *Vatican Council II: The Conciliar and Post Conciliar Documents* (Leominster, Fowler Wright Books, 1981), p. 12.

61. *Handbook for the Clergy*, p. 238. The section on leading worship occupies pp. 180–239.

62. The consecration of Bishops MacLean and Bentley-Taylor in 1999 (with perhaps three hundred communicants) took over four hours. A Church of England consecration or ordination with perhaps a thousand communicants usually takes less than half that time.

CHAPTER 12

Ministry and Orders

One of the striking features of many official publications of the Free Church of England and Reformed Episcopal Church in the late nineteenth and early twentieth centuries is the juxtaposition of a sometimes aggressive Protestant stance with a vigorous defence of the validity of its Orders on catholic terms. Thus, for example, the first edition of Vaughan's *History* contains 140 pages of Appendices of which nearly half are related to the question of Orders. Earlier, in 1881, Herbert Bower had published a 95-page work entitled *The Orders of the Reformed Episcopal Church Examined.*[1] This is reproduced in the current edition of the *Handbook for Ministers* (1989) of which it forms approximately one third of the text. All three editions of Vaughan's *History* contain as an appendix an article entitled, *Reformed Episcopal Orders Examined. Objections Answered*, published in Chicago in 1908. The anonymous author states that he is a member of 'the Anglican Church', presumably PECUSA. The question is clearly one of importance for the denomination and has been subject to much investigation.

The intention of the present chapter is not to re-examine the issue in the nineteenth-century terms which have dominated the debate hitherto, but to do so in the light of the wider ecumenical consensus that has emerged during the course of the twentieth century. The present-day climate is, in fact, one in which the Free Church of England can feel much more comfortable than it did a century ago.

The original context

When reading the publications of the denomination it is important to recognize the context in which a stand was being taken. In England and Wales (and Ireland) the experience of episcopacy was inextricably linked to prelacy. Bishops ranked high in the social order (between barons and viscounts – the archbishops outranked even dukes) and lived in considerable estate, with large numbers of retainers. However humble they might be as individuals (and some were), escape from their exalted status in the eyes of society was impossible. Moreover, until well into the nineteenth century bishops had the power, supported by the State, to enforce their will. Diocesan Courts touched many areas of ordinary people's lives, not least the sensitive area of proving a deceased person's will. The bishops did not look much like the successors of Galilean fishermen.

As the secular state of the English, Welsh and Irish bishops began to decline in the nineteenth century, increasing claims were made for their spiritual exaltation. For much of the late nineteenth century and the first half of the twentieth, the ecclesiology of the Church of England (and significant parts of the Anglican Communion) was dominated by a tradition that made the highest of claims for episcopally ordered ministry. Such a stance was usually accompanied by a rejection of the validity and fruitfulness of non-episcopal ministries. Thus, for example, Kenneth Kirk, Bishop of Oxford, could write:

> There are some results which no invalid ministry, however learned, pious, zealous, and edifying, can secure . . . The results we have in mind are the continuity and maintenance of the Church of the New Testament – the Church of the apostles – with its faith, its Scriptures, and its sacraments intact.[2]

For Kirk and many others:

> a valid ministry is one which, in accordance with primitive ordering, proceeds in due succession from the apostles by laying on of hands of the Essential Ministry; and that should such a ministry fail, the apostolic Church, which is the Body of Christ in space and time, would disappear with it . . . These things we do not say of non-episcopal ministries; for judged by scriptural and apostolic tests we find them to be invalid.[3]

In Churches without bishops, then, 'the Church of the apostles' has disappeared.

Such a conclusion, in direct continuity with the position of Newman in Tract 1 back in 1833, was unacceptable to Evangelicals within the Church of England and, of course, to the Free Church of England and Reformed Episcopal Church. For them a ministry was 'validated' by the marks of the Lord having blessed it. To Kirk signs of spiritual fruitfulness no more guaranteed that a ministry was 'valid' than domestic harmony guaranteed that a couple were lawfully married.[4] Given such a polarization, it is all the more remarkable that the movement fought so hard to maintain, defend and continue an episcopal ministry in the historic succession.

The present context

Historically the Reformed Episcopal Church and the Free Church of England have sought from Anglican Provinces an acknowledgment that their Orders are as valid as those of that Communion. This issue still has relevance today, not least because Free Church of England presbyters do, from time to time, apply to join the Church of England or the Episcopal Church in the USA and a decision has to be made about their Orders. More importantly, the issue will have to be definitively addressed if the two Churches are ever to 'normalize' relationships, either bilaterally or in a broader ecumenical context. The matter is also of importance for some of those considering joining the Free Church of England. Fortunately the climate has shifted considerably in the Free Church of England's favour since the first frosty exchanges in the last quarter of the nineteenth century.

In recent decades a great deal of ecumenical consensus has been reached on the place of the ministry in the life of the Church and in particular in relation to the apostolicity of the Church. Of particular importance for the Free Church of England are those statements agreed by the Church of England, for it is to that Church that the Free Church of England is historically and constitutionally most closely related. Much of the 'spadework' has however been done in an international context, most notably the seminal document *Baptism, Eucharist and Ministry* produced in 1982 by the World Council of Churches, which expressed a remarkable degree of consensus on the three areas.[5]

The Church of England's recent ecumenical 'methodology' has been to produce a series of agreed statements with dialogue partners. It is in these that current Church of England ecclesiology is expressed. Two important themes (among many) may be identified as of particular relevance here.

The first is the recognition by the Church of England of non-episcopal Churches and ministries.[6] Thus, for example, the Church of England (together with the other Anglican Churches in the British Isles) has said with the Reformed and Lutheran Churches of France:

> We acknowledge one another's churches as churches belonging to the One, Holy, Catholic and Apostolic Church of Jesus Christ . . . We acknowledge that in all our churches the word of God is authentically preached, and the sacraments of baptism and the eucharist are duly administered . . . We acknowledge that one another's ordained ministries are given by God as instruments of grace for the mission and unity of the Church and for the proclamation of the word and the celebration of the sacraments.[7]

Similar statements have been made with the Protestant Churches of Germany, the Moravian Church, the Nordic and Baltic Lutheran Churches, and the Methodist Church of Great Britain.

Such statements go a long way to suggesting that the British and Irish Anglican Churches have adopted the Free Church of England's position (which was also theirs in the sixteenth century) that the Church of Christ does not exist 'only in one order or form of ecclesiastical polity'.[8]

In a context where the episcopate is no longer seen as defining the 'validity' or otherwise of a Church, it has been possible to explore more openly the role of that ministry within the Church. The dominant motif used is that of *apostolicity*. The theological understanding is set out most fully in the House of Bishops Occasional Paper *Apostolicity and Succession*, which was drawn up as part of the theological preparation for the Porvoo Agreement with the Nordic and Baltic Lutheran Churches.[9] Briefly, apostolicity is defined in terms of mission – the sending of Christ by the Father, the sending of the Apostles by Christ, and the ongoing mission of all Christians. Apostolicity therefore is about both the origins and the continuity of the Church: 'The Church can be described as apostolic in two principal senses: on the one hand, it is historically founded and still rests upon the apostles Jesus sent and their witness to him. On the other hand it is itself "apostled" or "sent" in every generation.'[10] The apostolicity of the Church is shown by its bearing a number of 'marks' or characteristics. Quoting *Baptism, Eucharist and Ministry*, the House of Bishops lists these as:

> witness to the apostolic faith, proclamation and fresh interpretation of the Gospel, celebration of baptism and the eucharist, the transmission of ministerial responsibilities, communion in prayer, love, joy and suffering, service to the sick and the needy, unity among the local churches and sharing the gifts which the Lord has given to each.[11]

Significantly, 'the transmission of ministerial responsibilities' – including teaching and oversight – is only *one* of a range of marks of apostolicity. Historically, this transmission found expression in the development and continuity of the ministry of bishop. The bishop is to protect the apostolicity of the Church, but his 'pedigree' does not *guarantee* it. Apostolicity is located in the community, its life, teaching and witness, as well as in the bishop.

In the light of such theological thinking, it is now possible to look afresh at the Free Church of England.

A continuity of communities

The continuity within the Free Church of England tradition of communities holding the apostolic faith and living the apostolic life becomes particularly significant in the light of the broadening of the definition of apostolicity.

The earliest communities were the societies organized by Whitefield and his associates, and in particular by the Countess of Huntingdon. These consisted of men and women who saw themselves as simultaneously members of the Church of England, holding to its doctrinal tenets, receiving the Dominical sacraments, and using the historic creeds. In addition to these external marks they strove to live dedicated lives, governed by the standards of behaviour prescribed by the New Testament. They were apostolic, too, in the sense that they saw themselves as having a *mission* – they were scattered, like the earliest disciples, in order that through them the Word of God might reach more and more people.

As these earliest communities gradually (and unwillingly) separated from the Church of England, they took with them these marks of apostolicity. A continuity of intention to preserve the apostolic faith in its Anglican identity is identifiable from Haweis to Thoresby, as detailed in earlier chapters.

The same continuity is apparent in the second wave of congregations in the years following 1844. These, too, maintained the Creeds, sacraments, doctrinal and ethical teaching of the Church of England.

Nor was there any sense of a break with older continuities. On the contrary, the literature of the period shows a strong sense of identity with the historic Church in England. It is this legacy which was seen as being threatened by Tractarianism and which the Free Church of England movement sought to preserve. In the writings both of the pre-union Free Church of England and Reformed Episcopal Church, Archbishop Cranmer, the making of the Edwardine Prayer Books and the martyrs under Mary Tudor are part of *their* history – hence the sense of outrage when their memory and achievements seemed under threat. Nor is this continuity confined to the Reformation period. Merryweather's tracing of the community back through the Middle Ages and patristic times to the apostolic era has been noted in Chapter 1. For Merryweather the homilies of the Anglo-Saxon churchman Aelfric are 'another testimony to our ancient faith',[12] and executed Lollards are described as 'the martyred progenitors of the Free Church'.[13] Nearly one hundred years after Merryweather, in 1964, the Revd F. H. Easton, in an official booklet *Know Your Church*, written to teach younger members of the Free Church of England their heritage, sees the Celtic Church, too, with its independence from Rome's jurisdiction and errors, as a precursor to the Free Church of England. After the Saxon incursions, Iona and Bangor-is-y-Coed in North Wales are named as places where 'the light still continued to shine'.[14] The cover of the booklet shows the third-century mosaic of the head of Christ and the Chi-Rho from the Roman villa at Hinton St Mary in Dorset. The message is consistent and unmistakeable: We are in continuity with the earliest believers in Britain. It is a further important corrective to the tendency to see the Free Church of England as a body with an exclusively nineteenth-century self-understanding. It also provides a point of contact with the current interest in the Celtic and Saxon Churches and their spirituality.

The legitimacy of this sense of wider continuity is increasingly being acknowledged by other traditions. Thus, for example, the Orthodox bishop, Kallistos Ware, can write:

Need the apostolic succession be expressed always and everywhere under the same outward forms? ... The real question for us as Orthodox, then, is not simply: Does this other ecclesial body possess bishops as we do? We must also ask: how does this other body, as a total community, understand and live out its apostolic continuity?[15]

Measured by such criteria, even the pre-1876 Free Church of England could (and did) claim to be an apostolic community.

A continuity of oversight and episcopal intention

The communities formed in the eighteenth century and after 1844 lacked (in terms of the recent dialogues) *one* of the marks of apostolicity – a ministry of bishops in the historic succession – due to the refusal of bishops of the Established Church to ordain their candidates or give leadership to their cause. This does not mean, however, that they lacked a ministry of oversight or an orderly 'transmission of ministerial responsibilities'. At the first ordination in the Countess of Huntingdon's Connexion, Thomas Wills actually stressed the validity of his own (episcopal) ordination and that of William Taylor who was to join him in the act of ordination. As validly ordained presbyters he and Taylor had authority to ordain others, *presbuteroi* and *episcopoi* being the same office in the New Testament. The ordination prayer asked for the gifts and grace of the Holy Spirit for the candidates.[16] Over this newly independent ministry, after 1791 Thomas Haweis, as has been shown, exercised a ministry of *episkope* which was continued after his death by a succession of Presidents.

Even more significantly, the concept of episcopacy, far from being repudiated, was actually embraced and progressively strengthened. As early as 1795 Haweis could describe the mode of government as 'essentially episcopal – with us a few preside'. This was not simply a matter of convenience; Haweis believed the system of episcopacy to be the best, once shorn of its secular pomp:

> When I speak of episcopacy as most correspondent, in my poor ideas, to the apostolic practice and the general usage of the Church in the first and generally esteemed purer ages, let no man imagine I plead for that episcopacy which, rising very early on the stilts of prelatical pride and worldy-mindedness, has since overspread the earth with its baneful shadow ...[17]

Set free from such accretions, however, episcopacy was an attractive office of apostolic approbation.

Despite the drift of the Connexion away from Church of England norms in the early nineteenth century, this sense of episcopacy was not lost. Thoresby was able to look back and see the congregations of the Connexion 'subject to a general Conference of Presbyters, under the guidance of [a succession of] President Bishop[s]'.[18]

The year 1863 saw, as has been seen, the enshrining of the office of bishop – Diocesan and Primus – in the Constitution.

The situation, then, between 1791 and 1876 was of a Christian community that had lost the *sign* of the historic succession, though it had never denied the value of that sign, and had maintained a ministry of oversight and teaching defined in increasingly catholic terms. There are thus some parallels with those Nordic and Baltic Churches which lost the historic succession, but remained episcopally organized. Like them, the Free Church of England was free to 'embrace it without denying [its] own apostolic continuity'.[19]

Thus, when the Free Church of England received the sign of the historic episcopate in 1876, it was being consistent with its existing intention. As Chapter 5 shows, certain adjustments were necessary, but there was no need for the Free Church of England 'to take episcopacy into its system' – episcopacy already *was* its system.[20] It was simply strengthened by recovery of the sign of the historic succession.

With the Reformed Episcopal Church, both in North America and in Britain, the situation was very different. Here were communities bringing with them *all* the marks of apostolicity as found in Anglicanism, including the ministry of bishops in the historic succession. Indeed, one of the very first acts of the newly constituted Reformed Episcopal Church on 2 December 1873 was to elect a presbyter for consecration as bishop to assist Bishop Cummins in the ministry of oversight and 'to see the apostolic succession maintained'.[21] In his letter of resignation from the Protestant Episcopal Church on 10 November, Cummins had stated his 'earnest hope and confidence that a basis for the union of all Evangelical Christendom can be found in a communion *which shall retain or restore a primitive Episcopacy*'.[22] The 'Call to Organise' of 13 November 1873 had explicitly stated the intention 'to organize an Episcopal Church'.[23] At the inaugural meeting Cummins claimed for the new jurisdiction 'an unbroken historical connection through the Church of England with the

Church of Christ, from the earliest Christian era'.[24] Even Cummins's opponents conceded that he acted as though he believed himself to be possessed of an indelible episcopal character which he could transmit to others.[25]

Nor was Charles Cheney, the candidate elected on that occasion, in any doubt that everything the episcopate possessed in the Protestant Episcopal Church in the USA, it possessed in the Reformed Episcopal Church. 'The highest churchman in the land cannot deny the validity of the Episcopate of the Reformed Episcopal Church,' he told his congregation on 7 December 1873, a week before his own consecration.[26] To Episcopalians the Reformed Episcopal Church could say, 'Whatever you had in your mother Church, of historic value, you have here also. If your old Church claimed to give you an Episcopate historic beyond all question, so do we.'[27] Vaughan in England took exactly the same line. Writing of the 1876 consecrations, he claimed, 'Thus the ancient British Episcopate, whatever its content and meaning may be, was received by the youngest daughter in the family of Episcopal Churches.'[28] It is not a *different* episcopal office, it is the same. Cummins's transferral of his office was in some ways analogous with his being translated to another see. The ministry was the same, only the community in which it was exercised had changed. Moreover, the office went back to earliest times. For Cheney 'the New Testament hints at, if it does not clearly prove, the fact that overseers were appointed while the Apostles lived, to do precisely the work which bishops do in an episcopal Church of our own time'.[29] The official *Handbook for the Clergy* takes the same line, calling the 'historical succession' 'the faithful continuance of Apostolic Custom and Practice . . . the office and order conveyed from one group to its successors by the primitive and Apostolic means of the "Laying-on-of hands"'.[30] There is no mistaking the intention of the founders of the Reformed Episcopal Church to continue the office of bishop in the historic succession.

A continuity in the sign of the historic succession

All the consecrations in the Free Church of England and Reformed Episcopal Church in the UK have been attested public acts, usually attended by hundreds of people. The only exception to this is the consecration of Troughton by Meyers in 1901, due to the latter's ill health – and even here the private nature of the ceremony was sanctioned by resolution of the Synod of the Northern Diocese.[31] Indeed, the special arrangements indicate the denomination's resolve not to lose the sign of the historic succession.

In all cases the candidates had been elected by the canonical procedures then in force in the relevant body.[32] A Certificate of Election is required to be produced at the Consecration, together with a Testimonial as to the fitness of the candidate, signed by a number of presbyters. The date and place of Consecration, together with the names of the officiating bishops are recorded, usually with the phrase 'assisted by several presbyters' (sometimes the number is given). These records are held by the Registrar and appear annually in the Year Book. This may be a practice inherited from the Protestant Episcopal Church in the USA, which also publishes details of its episcopal consecrations (beginning with Seabury) in its Year Book. The Reformed Episcopal Church in the USA and Canada does the same.

The Year Book currently lists all successions from that of John Moore, consecrated in 1775, who as Archbishop of Canterbury was the chief consecrator of William White and Samuel Provoost in 1787. Moore also heads the list in Eldridge's *The Origins, Orders, Organisation and Worship of the Reformed Episcopal Church*, published in 1910, and reproduced as an Appendix in the first (1936) edition of Vaughan's *History*.[33] The 1960 and 1994 editions of the *History* preface the entries with a list of Archbishops of Canterbury from Matthew Parker to Moore.[34] A succession list by consecration from Parker (which is not quite the same sequence as holders of the office of Archbishop of Canterbury) hangs in some of the denomination's churches.

This commitment to retaining 'the sign of the historic episcopal succession'[35] understood not as by itself a guarantee of the fidelity of the apostolicity of the Church, but as one mark among several of such apostolicity, is fully consonant with the understanding of the episcopal office agreed by the British and Irish Anglican Churches and the Nordic and Baltic Lutheran Churches. As the *Handbook* declares, the Free Church of England has no intention of abandoning the historic succession: 'In this Church we guard the succession that we have received from the Anglican Church as one of our most valued possessions.'[36]

A continuity of 'sees'

An important dimension in current thinking about episcopacy is the concept of continuity in *office*. This relates to the emphasis on a continuity of communities discussed above and is much to the fore in the writing of contemporary Orthodox theologians. Bishop Kallistos Ware puts it particularly forcefully:

> The act of consecration, even when correctly performed by other validly consecrated bishops, is not by itself sufficient; it is also required that the new bishop shall be consecrated for a specific local church. Unless he succeeds legitimately to a throne, he has no true share in the grace of apostolic succession, but is merely a pseudo-bishop.[37]

Another Orthodox bishop and theologian, John Zizioulas, calls the consecration of titular and assistant bishops 'a violation of basic ecclesiological principles under the influence of a false notion of sacramentalism as a transmission of episcopacy from one individual to another'.[38] The argument is one that Bishop Cummins and his contemporaries would have no doubt warmly agreed with. To quote Zizioulas again: 'It is only when apostolic continuity is understood as a continuity of *structure* and as a succession of *communities* that the episcopal character of apostolic succession acquires its uniqueness.'[39] The ancient succession lists of, for example, Irenaeus or Hegesippus famously list not consecrators but occupants of the see.[40] In Canon Arthur Couratin's famous phrase, for the Early Church apostolic succession was not about hands on heads but about bottoms on thrones.

From this perspective, too, the Free Church of England and Reformed Episcopal Church practice is in line with traditional thinking. As the historical chapters above have shown, in all cases the community is prior to the bishop; in Ware's phraseology, there is a throne for him to succeed to. This can be seen in the inaugural meeting of the Reformed Episcopal Church in the YMCA Hall in New York on 2 December 1873 where the gathering *first* by resolution 'organise[d] ourselves into a Church, to be known by the style and title of *The Reformed Episcopal Church*' and *secondly* appointed 'the Right Revd Geo. David Cummins, DD. as our Presiding Bishop'.[41] The jurisdiction was created, then the bishop elected to it. The same pattern is found in the April 1877 petition from the United Kingdom to the General Council in North America. The

General Council was asked to establish a branch of the Reformed Episcopal Church in the UK, and, having done so, to consecrate Huband Gregg as its first bishop.

Clearly, in the case of the consecrations of Price and Sugden for the Free Church of England in 1876, the accepting community had long been in existence.

Once possessed of the historic episcopate in the UK, both the Free Church of England and the Reformed Episcopal Church established diocesan structures, which were generally maintained, despite the traumas and vicissitudes described above. In this the denominations differed from the Scottish Episcopal Church which for long periods had no dioceses and consecrated bishops to an 'episcopal college'. There have been 'Assistant Bishops' and 'Missionary Bishops' but these have always been in addition to a backbone structure of 'Diocesan Bishops'.

The dioceses themselves are now well established. If the continuity of the present Northern and Southern Dioceses be accepted from their creation by the Reformed Episcopal Church in 1881, then they are older than 16 (36 per cent) of the 44 present-day dioceses of the Church of England. The Free Church of England now has its own 'historic sees' to which it consecrates bishops.[42] A list of the diocesan bishops is found in Appendix 5.

Earlier Objections

It should be clear by now that current Anglican and wider ecumenical thinking about the nature of episcopacy is consonant with the understanding and practice of episcopacy in the Free Church of England. For the sake of completeness, however, the objections raised against the Orders deriving from Bishop Cummins will be briefly rehearsed, together with a summary of the answers that may be given against them. The first registering of any objection goes back to Presiding Bishop Boswell Smith's statement, in the days following Cummins's resignation, that any episcopal acts performed by him would be 'null and void'. That declaration was intended to head off any substantial secession from the Protestant Episcopal Church. Thereafter the American Church sought to persuade the rest of the Anglican Communion to take a similar line. Nothing explicitly relating to the issue appears in the Encyclical Letter and reports of the 1878 Lambeth Conference, though, at this distance in time, it is inter-esting to contrast the sympathy expressed towards the 'Spanish and Portuguese Reformed Episcopal Church' and other groups seceded from Rome with the hostility being enacted towards the American 'Reformed Episcopal Church'.[43]

By the 1888 Lambeth Conference the question of the Orders deriv-ing from Cummins was sufficiently pressing to require a statement to be made by the Presiding Bishop of PECUSA, John Williams.[44] This con-ceded that at the time of Cheney's consecration, 'Bishop Cummins had not been deposed, and therefore his act, however inconvenient, cannot, so far as he is concerned, be counted as having no force . . . The Consecration itself is, clearly, utterly uncanonical, though, of course, not, *per se*, invalid.' The statement then goes on to list a number of facts which, in the view of the majority of PECUSA bishops, rendered Cheney's consecration 'null and void'.[45] Interestingly, the Lambeth Conference Committee hesitated to repeat the judgment of the American bishops on the validity of Orders deriving from Cummins. The Committee Report simply reads:

> With regard to Orders alleged to be derived, though irregularly, through the American Church, it may be sufficient to say that the whole transaction is disallowed and regarded as null and void by the American Episcopate. This fact, in the opinion of the Committee, may be taken as a sufficient guide to all Bishops of the Anglican Communion.[46]

The main points put forward by the PECUSA bishops may now be briefly surveyed.

1) *Only one Bishop took part in the initial consecration (that of Cheney).* The requirement that three or more bishops (or two at the least) should take part in the consecration of a bishop derives from Canon 4 of the Council of Nikaia (Nicaea) in 325. The context, however, is about the desirability of involving other bishops of the province, rather than a conviction that, to put it crudely, a 'critical mass' of bishops needs to be assembled before enough radiation can be emitted to create a new bishop. In fact both the Eastern and Western families of Churches have accepted that consecration by a single bishop is valid. Cummins's supporters – and some who disapproved of his action – were able to produce many examples of this.

More recent ecumenical examples confirm the acceptance of single-bishop consecrations. Current Roman Catholic Canon Law requires three bishops for a valid consecration, but allows that one bishop may act alone if he has papal dispensation.[47] In 1944 Pope Pius XII made explicit the historic Roman Catholic position that a single bishop was sufficient for a valid consecration.[48] The Church of England and the Roman Catholic Church accept as valid Old Catholic Orders, which have passed on several occasions through a single-bishop consecration.[49] The Church of England also accepts as valid the Orders of the Church of Sweden, whose succession also on occasion passed through a single bishop, who was not the chief consecrator at the consecration in question.[50] Also accepted by the Provinces of the Anglican Communion is the succession of the Mar Thoma Syrian Church of Malabar which derives from a single-bishop consecration for the Diocese of Thozhiyoor.[51]

Free Church of England responses to this objection have tended to quote the letter of Pope Gregory to Augustine of Canterbury who had asked, 'If a long journey is involved, so that bishops cannot easily assemble, is it permissible for a bishop to be consecrated without other bishops being present?' Gregory's reply had been, 'In the church of the English where you are as yet the only bishop, you cannot do otherwise than consecrate a bishop without other bishops being present.'[52] The Year Book, at the end of the list of consecrations, also prints quotations from Bingham's *Antiquities of the Church*, by Archbishop Bramhall of Armagh and Canon Liddon in 1876 to the effect that consecrations by a single bishop are valid.

ii) *Cummins and Cheney were deposed at the time of Cheney's consecration in December 1873.*

As a matter of historical fact, Cummins had *not* been deposed by the Protestant Episcopal Church in the USA when he consecrated Cheney. The six-month period in which a bishop threatened with deposition could reconsider had only just begun by December 1873. Cheney's 'deposition' was that referred to in Chapter 4 in relation to his refusal to declare baptized infants regenerate. In 1874 the Circuit Court of Illinois found that irregularities in composition and procedure meant that the ecclesiastical tribunal which claimed to have deposed Cheney 'was not a court, according to the canons of the Protestant Episcopal Church' and that Cheney had 'never been lawfully deposed from the ministry of the Protestant Episcopal Church'.[53]

Apologists have argued that, even if Cummins and Cheney *had* been technically deposed by PECUSA, it no more invalidated their ministerial acts than the excommunications issued by Rome invalidated those of Anglican or Old Catholic bishops.

iii) *The sufficiency of the Order of Service.*

In their 1888 statement the American bishops stated, 'we know not what service was used'.[54] In fact the very pages used by Cummins survived and were still in existence in 1908. They are entitled, 'The Form of Consecrating a Bishop authorized for use in the Reformed Episcopal Church'.[55] Most of the debate has focused on the 'formula' used at the laying on of hands. It is now a commonplace of liturgical scholarship that the use of a formula of consecration is itself not the most ancient form of ordination, and that where a formula is used, it has varied from place to place and age to age. In this context the formula used by Cummins cannot be judged 'insufficient'.[56] Furthermore the rest of the service 'is not without prayers for the bestowal of the Holy Spirit upon the one about to be consecrated as Bishop'.[57] The Episcopalian author had no hesitation in concluding that, 'There can be no doubt whatever as to the full sufficiency of the Reformed Episcopal ordinal for a valid conveyance of the Episcopate.'[58]

iv) *The 'Intention'.*

It has been argued that Cummins's rejection of the claims made for episcopacy by Tractarianism meant that he did not 'intend' to make Cheney a bishop in a sense consonant with the intention of the catholic Church. Apologists point out that his actions in travelling several hundred miles to Chicago to lay hands on Cheney, together with his repeated remarks (some of them quoted earlier in this chapter) about continuity with the Reformers via the Church of England demonstrate that he 'intended to impart, at the desire of the church that had elected the new bishop, the episcopal character that he had himself received from the bishops of the Episcopal Church . . . and they from Dr John Moore, Archbishop of Canterbury, in 1787'.[59] Bower concludes his examination, 'Again and again [Cummins] affirmed that the orders given by himself were such as the most advanced Anglican would be compelled to acknowledge as valid. Certainly he did not err in "intention".'[60] The statements of Cummins and Cheney cited above (pp. 251–52) confirm this.

v) *The Involvement of Presbyters in the laying on of hands.*

This was a further objection adduced by the 1888 statement to the Lambeth Conference. This has been judged as 'so weak as to be no objection'.[61] There was no suggestion of any of the presbyters presiding at the consecration. None of them uttered the 'enabling words'. Their involvement has generally been seen as neither adding to nor subtracting from the act in any way. The parallel of the participation of presbyters at a presbyteral ordination has often been made – such an ordination would still be valid if conducted by a bishop without any presbyters present. Their involvement shows approval and acceptance.

There is also ecumenical precedent. In pre-Vatican II practice it was not uncommon for the two 'co-consecrators' at an episcopal ordination in the Roman Catholic Church to be in presbyters' Orders. Current practice in the Church of Sweden is to have presbyteral representatives of the diocese join in the laying on of hands of the new bishop.[62] The argument that the participation of presbyters detracts from the validity of the consecration cannot be sustained.

vi) *Some of those consecrated have not been episcopally ordained presbyters.*

While Cheney and Nicholson were in undoubted Anglican Orders at the time of their consecrations by Cummins, later candidates have not been, but have been accepted into the Reformed Episcopal Church (or Free Church of England) in their existing Orders. The response has usually focused on the *per saltum* consecrations of laymen and deacons to the episcopate in the Early Church, and on the consecrations of Scottish Presbyterians by the English Bishops in 1610. Modern examples may be adduced from, for example, the Church of South India.[63] Once again, the objection cannot be sustained.

Church of England approaches

Unlike the Protestant Episcopal Church in the United States of America, the Church of England has never declared the Orders of the Free Church of England and Reformed Episcopal Church 'invalid'. It has, however, been guided by the Lambeth Conference resolutions. That of 1888 has been noted above. Some 32 years were to pass before the matter was again considered by the Lambeth Fathers. The 1920 Lambeth Conference (which had caused such heartache in the Reformed Episcopal Church) while unable to accept the conditions that Vaughan's Diocesan Synod had laid down for re-union (see Chapter 7), nevertheless,

> recommends that, if applications for admission into the English Church are made by individual ministers of that Communion, such applications should be sympathetically received, and the ministers if in all respects equal to the standards and requirements of the Church of England, be ordained *sub conditione.*

Clearly the passage of time (and perhaps the respect in which the Archbishop of Canterbury and other bishops held Eldridge) had softened the official position. The tone is very different to that of 1888, and conditional ordination is very different to the 'null and void' of the earlier Committee report. It allows the possibility that the Orders already held may be valid.

In 1960 following 'several' approaches to diocesan bishops by 'priests of the Liberal Catholic Church seeking to be admitted to the ministry of the Church of England' and 'at least one' such approach by a minister of the Free Church of England, the Faith and Order Advisory Group (FOAG) drew up a report on 'Episcopi Vagantes and those ordained by them'. The report (most of which was concerned with the Liberal Catholics) contained a broadly accurate précis of the history of the post-union Free Church of England (paras 21 and 22). It then conceded that consecration by a single bishop could be valid, and that

> the grounds for rejecting FCE orders are somewhat uncertain, at least in respect of succession. Cummins was not a 'vagans' bishop in the usual sense. His occasion for schism was a misguided and premature ecumenism, and rather extreme Protestant views. Not heresy but schism is therefore the main issue if FCE members seek to enter our church's ministry.[64]

The Recommendations conclude that:

> It is clear that the orders of this Church derive from an Anglican bishop; and that its bishops have been consecrated in due succession and its priests

ordained with the use of the Anglican Ordinal, though in a slightly altered form . . . We cannot regard these alterations as being in themselves sufficient to call in question the validity of the ministry.[65]

The report does not, however, follow through the logic of its own arguments. It is clear that a number of FOAG members were anxious to find reasons not to admit the validity of the Free Church of England's Orders. In the event two areas are further explored in detail.

The first is that 'They hold regeneration to be not *in any way* dependent upon the act of baptism.'[66] Despite the fact that the relevant clause of the Declaration of Principles is then quoted, this is not of course the case. As seen in Chapter 10 the Free Church of England denies an *inseparable* connection between baptism and regeneration, but, in line with Gorham, allows that regeneration may precede, accompany or follow baptism (or may not take place at all). The group 'spent a good deal of time considering the case . . . about which many views are tenable in our Church',[67] but chose to see what it believed to be the Free Church of England position as 'most serious exaggerations'. Even so, FOAG recognized that

> if we are to be consistent with past decisions we cannot view the statement about baptismal regeneration as casting doubt on the validity of the FCE baptisms. Nor can we regard this exaggeration of view of baptism as in itself casting doubt on the validity of their ordination.[68]

The second area explored by FOAG was that of ministerial priesthood. It was conceded that by 'the careful retention of episcopal ordination and the use of the 1662 Ordinal' the Free Church of England expressed an 'intention' 'to continue the ministry which Christ instituted in his Church',[69] but wondered if this intention were vitiated by the statement in the Declaration of Principles and the removal of the Johannine commission to bind and loose from the formula of ordination? There were also fears that the Free Church of England statements might not be easily reconcilable with statements made by the Church of England in ARCIC and the Anglican-Methodist and Series 3 Ordinals. There is also a reference to *Apostolicae Curae*. This betrays the source of the underlying concerns. Ever since Pope Leo IX's condemnation in 1896 of Anglican Orders as 'absolutely null and utterly void' largely on the ground that the Anglican Ordinals do not contain the intention to create a priesthood identical to 'the "sacrificing priesthood" of the Roman Catholic Church',[70] Anglicans have been anxious to show that their presbyterate *is* a priesthood. The Free Church of England's protest against a crude understanding of this was naturally alarming in this context. As regards ministerial priesthood, stated FOAG, it 'may be saying that there is no such thing. This raises a serious question about the intention of the FCE in ordination, and where there is doubt in such a matter, the appropriate way of dealing with it is by conditional ordination.'[71] A Note appended to the report states that this is the course followed by PECUSA in relation to clergy from the Reformed Episcopal Church.

Several observations may be made. First, the whole debate was of course being conducted without any contact with the Free Church of England whatsoever. There was no thought of *asking* the denomination what its views were on this matter. Secondly, the FOAG report does not state what doctrine of ministerial priesthood it would have hoped to find in the Free Church of England. Thirdly, the statement in the Declaration of Principles manifestly does *not* say that there is no connection between 'Christian ministers' and priesthood. It merely denies that the ordained ministry possesses 'another sense' of priesthood than the 'royal priesthood' bestowed by God on whose who are in Christ. Fourthly, as seen in Chapter 10, when FOAG itself published a report on *The Priesthood of the Ordained Ministry* in 1986,[72] that report was not accepted by the General Synod but merely welcomed as a contribution to the debate. The Free Church of England had been condemned for not holding a doctrine about which the General Synod itself is unable to define its views.

To be fair to the compilers of the Episcopi Vagantes Report, it has to be remembered that they were making recommendations which would affect matters of public ministry and therefore were, in the circumstances, probably right to err on the side of caution. In a context of no contact between the two Churches and a broadly aggressive stance against the Church of England by the Free Church of England in 1960, the outcome was perhaps inevitable. In a different context it is doubtful if the same conclusion could be justified.

Significantly, Henry Brandreth (who worked with the Archbishop of Canterbury's ecumenical staff at Lambeth) in his 1961 work on *episcopi vagantes* noted in Chapter 6, did not class the Free Church of England or the Reformed Episcopal Church as such organizations. This is all the more remarkable as he *does* state that Bishop Fred Morris, former Bishop of North Africa who had accepted election as Bishop of the Church of England in South Africa (CESA), 'must now be reckoned as an *episcopus vagans*'.[73] (This decision was vigorously challenged by CESA. In 1966 the Lambeth Consultative Group reversed an earlier decision that CESA clergy be conditionally ordained on being received into a Province of the Anglican Communion. They are now simply received into the Province concerned.)

This view that however reprehensible its doctrines might be (and it is clear that many of those advising the archbishops had no sympathy with them) nevertheless the Free Church of England was a *bona fide* Church, seems to have been increasingly accepted. In 1963 Canon Herbert Waddams a former General Secretary of the Archbishop of Canterbury's Council on Foreign Relations (CFR) advised Archbishop Ramsey's Chaplain that 'so far as the Orders of the Church are concerned, they seem to be valid'.[74] This advice was passed on by the Archbishop in a letter: 'This little Church has Orders which are technically valid . . .'[75]. This does not, however, appear to have resulted in a change to the practice of conditional ordination.

Nevertheless, an increasingly sympathetic line has been adopted. In 1979 the Revd Christopher Hill of CFR[76] could write of the Free Church of England: 'there would appear to be no deviation from acceptable Anglican orthodoxy. It might even be argued that conditional ordination is inappropriate in this case as there has never been any dispute as to the episcopal succession of the Free Church of England.'[77]

Two developments have changed the situation even further. The first is the substantial theological shift away from locating 'apostolic succession' almost exclusively in the episcopate to locating it in a variety of places within the community. Something of this has been noted above. It is a development which has broken the theological logjam with relation to the Nordic and Baltic Lutherans. One of the first indications of it might be found in Resolution 54 of the 1958 Lambeth Conference which puts the inability to 'recognise the Churches of such Episcopi Vagantes as properly constituted Churches' *before* its inability to 'recognise the orders of their ministers'. The priority of the community is beginning to be recognized.

The second development was of course the opening of an official dialogue between the Free Church of England and the Church of England as described in Chapter 8. The draft agreed report makes no reference to any possible deficiency in the Orders of the Free Church of England. Regarding the ministry it simply states:

> Both our churches have a common ecclesiastical order focused in the three-fold ministry of bishop, presbyter and deacon . . . Within this threefold ministry the bishop signifies and focuses the continuity and unity of the whole Church. Continuity with the apostles' doctrine and teaching (Acts 4:42) and unity in both our churches is expressed in the consecration of bishops in the historic succession as is clear from the preface to the Ordinal in each Prayer Book . . . (para. 54)

> Both our churches are committed to the maintenance of the historic episcopate and in our age believe it to hold a necessary place in safeguarding the visibility of unity and apostolic teaching of the Church. The structure and distribution of oversight are essentially the same, though locally adapted. In both our churches consecration to the episcopate is normally for a diocese. (para. 55)

Paragraphs 58, 59 and 60 set out in further detail the ministries of bishops, presbyters and deacons.

The eirenic agreement is significant. As described above, the Conversations were not intended to produce a scheme for 'reconciling' the Churches. The tone of the report suggests that recognition by the Church of England of the Orders of the Free Church of England should not be a problem.

By way of postscript, an interesting unofficial 'snapshot' of current Anglican thinking about the validity of Orders is provided by reaction to the consecration in Singapore of two bishops to serve 'traditionalist' Anglicans in North America. In *News of Liturgy* February 2000 Colin Buchanan gave a 'checklist' against which to judge the consecrations. These may be reduced to four questions:

- Are they needed? (Free Church of England bishops are consecrated to minister to pre-existing congregations which will accept their ministry.)
- How are they chosen? (Free Church of England bishops are elected by a long-established canonical process involving clergy and laity.)
- Under what authority are they? (Free Church of England bishops are bound by the Constitution and Canons of the Church and

are answerable to the Primus, each other and the denomination as
a whole.)
- What was the status of the consecration service? (Free Church of
  England consecrations are public occasions, announced well in
  advance. Assent to the consecration is given in the election process.)

Buchanan argues that the Singapore consecrations fail all the above tests,
but is still unwilling to deny that the candidates are now 'true bishops'.
On such a basis it would be impossible to deny the same status to bishops
of the Free Church of England.

An Ecumenical Dimension

For the sake of completeness, it should be noted that the Orders of the Free
Church of England do not derive solely from Bishop Cummins. While studiously preserving its own episcopal continuity the Free Church of
England has a tradition of inviting men who exercise *episkope* in their own
Churches to participate in the laying on of hands at episcopal consecrations. This is in line with an acceptance of the ministries of other Churches
going back to the sixteenth century. Thomas Haweis in his turn believed
that a Swiss Protestant minister, the Archbishop of Uppsala, a Lutheran
superintendent and a Huguenot pastor were 'as truly ordained by Christ
and His Church as the Archbishop of Canterbury, or the Moderator of the
General Assembly'.[78] Interestingly, in the light of modern ecumenical consensus, Haweis also believed that many 'who renounced the name of episcopacy accepted the thing'.[79] The tradition of involvement goes back to
Bishop Cummins's invitation to Bishop Matthew Simpson of the (episcopal) Methodist Church (together with one Methodist minister and two
Presbyterian ministers) to join in the laying on of hands at the consecration of William Nicholson on 24 February 1876.[80] In recent decades in
England a representative of the Free Church Federal Council has usually
been invited to take part, with the result that, for example, the
'Presbyterian succession' has passed to the Free Church of England. On
four occasions in the twentieth century Moravian bishops have participated, providing a link with that ancient Protestant community.

On 11 September 1976 one of the consecrating bishops at the consecration of Arthur Ward was the Right Revd Russell Berridge White, the

retired Bishop of Tonbridge in the Diocese of Rochester. White himself was in both the Old Catholic and Swedish successions and through him these have passed, as a matter of historical continuity, into the Free Church of England (along with the more recent Church of England succession up to Geoffrey Fisher). It could be argued that there is now 'prudent doubt' about the invalidity of Free Church of England Orders even in Rome's eyes (to use the phrase employed by the Roman Catholic Church in the case of the conditional ordination of Graham Leonard).[81]

More healthily, perhaps, is the openness to other communities (and hence a sense of catholicity) that such participations indicate. Part of 'maintaining communion with all Christian Churches' must include a sharing of *episkope* and its transmission.

Ministry and Gender

The practice of the Free Church of England agrees with the position of the Orthodox and Roman Catholic Churches that 'only a baptised man can validly receive sacred ordination'[82] and that 'the minister of sacred ordination is a consecrated bishop'.[83]

There has been virtually no literature produced by the denomination during the past decades while the ordination of women debate has raged in the Anglican Communion. The assumption is clearly present however, that such a development would not be admissible. Indeed, the denomination has in recent years been joined by a number of Church of England presbyters who have resigned their benefices under the Ordination of Women (Financial Provisions) Measure.

Theological opposition would no doubt be expressed primarily in terms of *headship*. It is significant that the Free Church of England has never admitted women Readers. It is widely conceded that the primary context of certain New Testament texts differentiating the ministry of women is that of *teaching*. To admit women to a public teaching office (as the Church of England did when it allowed them to become Readers) is therefore to 'sell the pass' and to make it virtually impossible to resist calls for their ordination to a ministry of eucharistic presidency. If women can preach the Word, why can they not administer the 'visible Words' of the Sacraments? The Free Church of England position is therefore consistent.

Selection and Training

The Free Church of England has never been able to produce enough ordinands to meet all its ministerial requirements. It therefore has to resort to recruiting from outside its membership, with results that have not always been happy, though some very good men have exercised godly ministries for very little temporal reward. When a church falls vacant, advertisements are usually placed in a range of Christian publications. The successful candidate is usually required to be approved by both bishop and congregation, but the trust deeds of some churches reduce the bishop's role somewhat.[84]

Those already ordained in another Church require the unanimous consent of the bishops and a resolution of Council or Convocation before being admitted to the ministry of the Free Church of England.[85] Those episcopally ordained are received as presbyters.[86] With those who have exercised a presbyteral ministry, but are not episcopally ordained, a degree of discretion is exercised by the receiving bishop. Some such candidates are received into the ministry of the Free Church of England by being ordained to the presbyterate (without prior ordination to the diaconate), others are accepted in their existing Orders.[87] The practice is seen as consistent with the denomination's historical ecumenical stance on the parity of presbyters.[88]

Lay candidates for ordination, whether applicants from outside or internal candidates, are required to serve as Readers for a minimum of six months before being recommended by the bishop to Convocation, which is required to give a three-fourths majority in approval.[89] Once approved, the candidate has to obtain passes in a range of subjects from the London Bible College or other approved course prior to ordination.[90] There is a denominational Examinations Board and in recent years there has been a tendency to set examinations internally. The quality of these is patchy; some are genuine attempts to equip candidates for ministry, others appear merely to confirm stereotypes and prejudices.[91]

The Constitution requires a public announcement of the intended ordination – the *Si Quis* – a procedure abandoned in the Church of England in the 1970s. Ordinations are to take place in Advent, Lent and Trinity seasons.[92] Ordinations to the presbyterate are to be notified to Council by the bishop, but no further approvals are required. 'Certificates of Ordination' signed by the bishop, were issued by the Registrar in the pre-1873 Free Church of England.[93] These were replaced by Letters of Orders, virtually identical to those issued by the Church of England, signed by the bishop and bearing his seal.[94]

There are no archdeacons, deans or canons. Bishops may appoint a chaplain. Some clergy without congregations may be designated 'Diocesan Curates' and used by the Bishop to fill temporary vacancies.

Theology of the Ministry

Despite its repeated rejection of what it saw as unscriptural inflated claims for the ministry, both the pre-union Free Church of England and Reformed Episcopal Church traditions had a positive theological stance on the God-given nature of the ministry. Cheney may be taken as representative:

> Romanist and Protestant agree so far as this, that both confess that the Word of God authorizes the appointment of a class of men whose lives shall be wholly consecrated to the sacred ministry. There is substantial unanimity in acknowledging that our Lord himself appointed men to such an office . . .[95]

Integral to this ministry is its continuity. Using the example of a river in the Sacramento valley which suddenly disappears, Cheney continued:

> It would be yet more strange in the spiritual world, if Christ, whose love to man, unsealed in apostolic days the flowing stream of the gospel ministry, had in later times suffered it to perish from the earth. He promised that His presence with those whom He sent on this special work should continue 'unto the end of the world' . . . In monastery cells, in lonely Alpine valleys, in the courts of kings, and in the humble homes of the poor, Christ's Spirit prepared His ministers.[96]

On the other side of the Atlantic, a similar view was held. For the old Free Church of England, too, ordination is 'an institution observed in the Apostolic Church'.[97] The strong emphasis on ordination in the 1863 Constitution has been noted in Chapter 9.

Both traditions also accepted that while the hands of a bishop may give a man outward authority to minister the Word and Sacraments, only the Holy Spirit can make a man a minister of Christ. The two are not, of course, incompatible. Whitefield, for example, had been certain of the grace of the Holy Spirit. On the night before his ordination as priest he wrote, 'Oh, that I might be prepared for receiving the Holy Ghost tomorrow by the imposition of hands.'[98] A few weeks later, after a Sunday full of ministry, he could triumphantly assert: 'Now know I, that I did receive the Holy Ghost at the imposition of hands, for I feel it as much as Elisha did when Elijah dropped his mantle.'[99] As seen in Chapter 11, prayer at ordination for the Holy Spirit was adopted at an early stage.

As in the Church of England the diaconate is currently essentially a probationary ministry. Back in the 1940s Vaughan floated the possibility of a 'small staff of "Permanent Deacons"', but nothing has yet been developed along these lines.[100]

It should perhaps be noted that, unlike for example the Methodist Church,[101] there is no tradition of lay presidency at the Eucharist. When a congregation has no presbyter, deacons have from time to time been licensed by their bishop to preside at the Eucharist, but never when a presbyter is present. Congregations without a presbyter or deacon receive sacramental ministrations from visiting clergy. Lay presidency is not resorted to. Canon 44 explicitly states that a Lay Reader may not administer the Sacraments.

The pre-union Free Church of England inherited from its Connexional past the ministry of lay preachers. This coalesced with the ministry of Readers contributed from the Reformed Episcopal Church, and the lay preaching ministry is recognized in the denomination today.[102]

As in all other areas of its life, the situation regarding the Orders and Ministry of the Free Church of England falls well within the boundaries of Anglican norms – and hence of catholic norms. Despite the dire situation that the community has been in at times, the ministry in general and the episcopate in particular have been responsibly maintained. As in any Church there have been individuals who proved unworthy of their office, but the ministry itself has been faithfully exercised and handed on.

Notes

1. Published Malvern, 1881.
2. Kenneth E. Kirk, *The Apostolic Ministry: Essays on the History and the Doctrine of Episcopacy* (London, Hodder & Stoughton, 1946), p. 40.
3. Ibid.
4. Ibid., p. 36.
5. *Baptism, Eucharist and Ministry* (Faith and Order Paper no.111) (Geneva, WCC, 1982). There have been many reprints. The document is sometimes referred to as the Lima text or *BEM*.
6. This is discussed in Chapter 10. The text is repeated here for convenience.
7. *Called to Witness and Service: The Reuilly Common Statement* (London, Church House Publishing, 1999), p. 36.
8. *Declaration of Principles.*
9. GS Misc 432 (London, General Synod, 1994). For the debate on the Porvoo Documents with reference to *Apostolicity and Succession*, see *General Synod: Report of Proceedings*, 9 July 1995, pp. 185ff.
10. GS Misc 432, para. 26.
11. Ibid., para. 35 (quoting BEM, Ministry 34).
12. Merryweather, p. 11.
13. Ibid., p. 21.
14. F. H. Easton, *Know Your Church* (London, FCE, 1964), p. 8.
15. Quoted in *Apostolicity and Succession*, p. 26.
16. Seymour, *Life and Times*, vol. 2, pp. 445ff.
17. *Church History*, I, x–xi; quoted in Skevington Wood, *Thomas Haweis*, p. 223.
18. *The Circular of the Free Church of England*, no. 1, October 1863, p. 18.
19. *Porvoo Common Statement*, para 57, p. 29.
20. In this it differed from, for example, Presbyterians, Congregationalists or Methodists who would have to restructure their polities.
21. Quoted in Guelzo, *For the Union*, p. 201.
22. Quoted in Vaughan, *History*, (1st edn), p. 47 (italics not in original).
23. Quoted in Guelzo, *For the Union*, p. 143.
24. Ibid., p. 159.
25. Ibid., pp. 152, 199ff.
26. Quoted in ibid., p. 195.
27. Cheney, *What Reformed Episcopalians Believe* (1888 edn), p. 98. The final sentence has been omitted from the 1978 edition.
28. Vaughan, *History*, (1st edn), p. 72.
29. Cheney, *What Reformed Episcopalians Believe*, p. 64.
30. *Handbook for Ministers*, p. 23. The *Handbook* also uses the language of 'confer[ring] the episcopal character' in consecration, and notes that the per-

manent feature in the historic succession is 'that only a bishop validly consecrated, invested by the Church with authority, should pass on authority to another' (pp. 30f.).

31. See Chapter 7. As an interesting point of comparison, it should be noted that until well into the twentieth century consecrations of bishops in the Church of England were private affairs, often conducted in Lambeth Palace Chapel, with very few people in attendance.

32. An exception might be Gregg's consecration of Toke in 1878, which seems to have been a hasty affair in defiance of the General Council. Interestingly, it does not feature in the official list of consecrations.

33. Vaughan, *History*, (1st edn), p. 250.

34. Ibid. p. 120 in both the 1960 and 1964 editions.

35. *Porvoo Common Statement*, para. 51.

36. *Handbook for Ministers*, p. 24.

37. Kallistos Ware, 'Patterns of Episcopacy: an Orthodox view' in Peter Moore (ed.), *Bishops: But What Kind?* (London, SPCK, 1982), p. 13.

38. John Zizioulas, *Being as Communion* (New York, St Vladimir's Seminary Press, 1985), p. 197, n. 94.

39. Ibid., p. 198. The absence of stable, structured communities is a powerful argument against the 'validity' of the Orders of most *episcopi vagantes*.

40. See, for example, Irenaeus, *Adv. Haereses*, III.3,4, in J. Stevenson, *A New Eusebius* (London, SPCK, 1970), pp. 118f. Hegesippus, quoted in Eusebius, *The Ecclesiastical History* IV.22, (London, William Heinemann, 1975), p. 375.

41. Guelzo, *For the Union*, p. 158.

42. Thus, for example, on 11 September 1999 Arthur Bentley-Taylor was consecrated to the 'throne' of the Northern Diocese, left vacant by the death of Bishop Cyril Milner.

43. *Five Lambeth Conferences*, p. 98,

44. *Conference Report 1888*, pp. 359–63.

45. The statement noted that Cummins had performed a second consecration (assisted by Cheney) – that of William Nicholson on 24 February 1874. As this was well beyond the expiry of the six-month canonical period, it was discounted by the PECUSA bishops even more strongly.

46. *Five Lambeth Conferences*, p. 150.

47. *The Code of Canon Law of the Catholic Church* (London, Collins, 1983), Canon 1014.

48. 'De Duobus Episcopis' *Acta Pii Pp XII*, (30 November 1944) pp. 131ff.: 'It is lawful for the validity of episcopal consecration that only one bishop is required, when he performs the necessary rites ...'

49. See C. B. Moss, *The Old Catholic Movement* (London, SPCK, 2nd edn, 1964), *passim*.

50. See Lars Osterlin, *Churches of Northern Europe in Profile* (Norwich, The Canterbury Press, 1995), p. 82. The bishop in question, Paul Juusten, was simply one of those taking part in the laying on of hands on the new Archbishop of Uppsala, Laurentius Petri II (Gothus).

51. The consecration was that of Joseph Mar Koorilose IV of Thozhiyoor by Metropolitan Mathews Mar Athanasios in 1856. See J. R. K. Fenwick, *The Malabar Independent Syrian Church* (Nottingham, Grove Books, 1992), p. 29. In the West Syrian rite, even if other bishops are present, they do not take part in the laying on of hands.

52. Quoted in Bede, *A History of the English Church and People*, trans. Leo Shirley-Price, (London, Penguin Books, 1988), p. 75.

53. *Reformed Episcopal Orders Examined. Objections Answered* (Chicago, 1908); reprinted in Vaughan, *History*, (1st edn), pp. 158–74. The quotation is from p. 163. The author is identified as 'A Clergyman of the Anglican Church'.

54. *Conference Report 1888*, p. 362.

55. *Reformed Episcopal Orders Examined*, (Vaughan, p. 168; see n. 53 above).

56. For the text see Chapter 4, p. 93. That currently in use in the Free Church of England is 'Almighty God, grant unto thee the gift of the Holy Ghost, for the Office and Work of a Bishop in the Church of God, now committed unto thee by the imposition of our hands . . .' It is closer to an invocation of the Holy Spirit than that of 1662.

57. *Reformed Episcopal Orders Examined*, (Vaughan, p. 169; see n. 53 above).

58. Ibid.

59. Bower, *Orders*, p. 49.

60. Ibid.

61. *Reformed Episcopal Orders Examined*, (Vaughan, p. 170; see n. 53 above).

62. See the photograph in Lars Osterlin, *Churches of Northern Europe*, p. 303.

63. Perhaps the most famous is Lesslie Newbigin, who was consecrated bishop on 27 September 1947 having previously been ordained by the Presbytery of Edinburgh on 12 July 1936 (*idem., Unfinished Agenda* (London, SPCK, 1985), pp. 37, 94f. See also John Gibaut, 'Sequential or Direct Ordination?' in *Joint Liturgical Study* 55 (Alcuin/GROW. Cambridge, Grove Books, 2003).

64. FOAG Report on Episcopi Vagantes (1960), para. 24 (Lambeth Palace Archives).

65. Ibid., para. 26.

66. Ibid., para. 27. The phrase to which FOAG took exception in fact comes from p. 30 of F. H. Easton's booklet, *Know Your Church*, already referred to. Easton had arguably gone beyond the Declaration of Principles.

67. FOAG Report (1960) para. 28.

68. Ibid., para. 30.

69. Ibid., para. 31.

70. Hugh Montefiore in R. W. Franklin (ed.), *Anglican Orders: Essays on the*

Centenary of Apostolicae Curae 1896–1996 (London, Mowbray, 1996), p. 4. The essays show how the Roman judgment haunted Anglican thinking about Orders for most of the following century.

71. FOAG Report (1960), para. 31.
72. GS 694.
73. Brandreth, *Episcopi Vagantes*, p. 116.
74. Lambeth Palace Archives/CFR. Letter from Herbert Waddams to John Andrew, 28 November 1963.
75. Lambeth Palace Archives. Letter to the Revd John Lang, 3 December 1963.
76. Consecrated Bishop of Stafford in 1996.
77. 'A Note on CFR and Episcopi Vagantes' 11 September 1979 (BMU/FO/79/10).
78. Haweis, *Plea for Peace and Union*,(1796) p. 29.
79. Ibid.; quoted in Skevington Wood, *Thomas Haweis*, p. 205.
80. See official list of consecrations and *The Lambeth Conference 1888*, section XXXVI, p. 362. The invitation to Methodist bishops in the Arminian Wesleyan tradition is particularly noteworthy.
81. See the statement issued (as a Press Release) by Cardinal Basil Hume, 26 April 1994.
82. *Code of Canon Law of the Catholic Church*, Canon 1024.
83. Ibid., Canon 1012.
84. The patronage system in the Church of England presents some parallels.
85. Bye-law III.5. This procedure has at times been omitted by bishops, sometimes with unfortunate results.
86. Recent examples include presbyters from the Church of England and the Roman Catholic Church.
87. The denomination currently has one presbyter ordained in the Congregational Union.
88. In 1876 when the historic episcopate was received, there was no re-ordination of existing presbyters, just as there was not in Scotland in 1610 and 1661.
89. This requirement, too, has sometimes been neglected.
90. Bye-law III.11.2.
91. The following is a recent example of the latter: 'You have been shipwrecked and cast ashore on a remote island where the entire population is Roman Catholic. Fortunately, you have managed to save copies of the 39 Articles of Religion and the Epistle to the Galatians. Show how you would explain the Christian Gospel to the natives (20 marks).' Many will find the presuppositions breathtaking.
92. Canon 39.
93. Merryweather, p. 137.
94. The texts may be found among the canonical forms appended to the Constitution and Canons Ecclesiastical, pp. 90f.

95. Cheney, *What Reformed Episcopalians Believe*, p. 46.
96. Ibid.
97. Merryweather, p. 143.
98. *Journals*, p. 199 (Saturday 13 January 1739).
99. Ibid., p. 206 (Sunday 4 February 1739).
100. Vaughan, 'Memories', p. 25.
101. At the time of writing, the Diocese of Sydney in Australia is said to be contemplating lay presidency.
102. The office of Reader, known in the early Church, was revived in the Church of England in 1866 (after a brief experiment by Archbishop Parker in the 1560s) and spread rapidly throughout the Anglican Communion. Some were stipendiary – Frank Vaughan being an example of such.

CHAPTER 13

The Final Chapter?

In 1995, at the end of his detailed study of the denomination's history, Richard Fenwick concluded that if the discussions with the Church of England did not succeed the Free Church of England might 'still carry on for perhaps 20, 30 or even 40 years to come'.[1] Three years earlier, addressing Convocation, Bishop Arthur Ward had told the denomination, 'If we do not move forward with these Unity discussions, then ultimately, we will die.'[2] In 2002, following the collapse of the discussions with the Church of England, Bishop Shucksmith (who had helped bring about the collapse) stated that 'at the present rate of decline, the Free Church of England could disappear within two decades'[3] and gave the denomination no more that 10 years if it continued 'committed solely to traditional language' in its worship.[4]

Certainly, the denomination currently has fewer congregations than at any time since the 1860s.[5] The current (2003) number of congregations is 24. Several of those that remain are small and vulnerable. The high hopes of many (especially in the 1870s) have remained unfulfilled. The present chapter attempts a preliminary analysis of some of the factors that may have contributed to this. Particular attention is given to two similar analyses by Bishop Vaughan to which some reference has already been made. The first is his Centenary Charge, *Prospect and Retrospect*, published in 1944;[6] the second is his private compilation, 'Memories and Reflections', of 1949. Use of these should keep the analysis less personal (though present members of the Free Church of England will have no difficulty fitting modern names to ancient faults) and illustrate the deeply ingrained nature of some of the problems. At the time he produced the two documents Vaughan (who remains one of the most influential bishops the movement has produced) had over 40 years of experience in the Reformed Episcopal Church and in the united Church after 1927. A third point of reference is James Packer's recent lecture 'Anglicanism for Tomorrow'.[7] Packer has consistently stood for and defended a view of Anglicanism perhaps indistinguishable from that of the founding fathers of the Free Church of England and Reformed Episcopal Church. He speaks very much from inside the tradition the denomination exists to represent and therefore his comments (though not initially addressed to the Free Church of England) are of particular relevance.[8]

Reasons for failure

A negative ethos

As the present study has shown, there are three main strands in the tradition of the present-day denomination. The first strand might be characterized as the eighteenth-century Evangelical Revival with its roots in warm-hearted Christ-centred evangelism. The second strand was the opposition to Tractarianism from the 1840s onwards. The third strand was the commitment to ecumenism which prompted Cummins's moment of decision in the genesis of the Reformed Episcopal Church.

Undeniably, it is the second of these that has predominated in the Church's self-understanding. Much of the literature contains references to the darkness and corruption under Rome in the Middle Ages and the need to avoid falling under such domination once more. Though any non-Roman Catholic must presumably view the Reformation as necessary, there is a tendency to repeat crude accusations and caricatures, without showing any awareness of recent historical studies of the Reformation period or of developments since. The instinct to be condemnatory still remains. As recently as 2002, Shucksmith could seriously argue that 'We also believe it essential, in view of modern trends, to re-emphasize that our *church is not only singularly evangelical, but evidently anti-tractarian*',[9] a theme recently repeated, as noted in Chapter 8, by Bentley-Taylor. The tragedy of using such 'slogans' is perhaps twofold.

First, they have no meaning to the unchurched population (or, indeed, to many practising Christians), and when explained often serve merely to create or reinforce prejudices and stereotypes. Secondly, such labelling shows no awareness of changes that have taken place over the last 150 years, nor does it allow that there might be any good in the Tractarian tradition as it has developed. By contrast, Packer in 'Anglicanism for Tomorrow' can say

> Anglo-Catholicism, which incurred such hostility for its Romanising style . . . has at its heart love for Christ as Saviour and Lord, and a high view of the Bible, which sets it *with* Evangelicalism against relativism, pluralism and agnosticism regarding the fundamentals of faith. We are infinitely closer to Anglo-Catholics than we are to liberals, radicals, people who want to reconstruct and restate the faith in the way that so many do today. . . All who are concerned to [maintain biblical orthodoxy] must be regarded as our friends.

If the Free Church of England were able to follow Packer's lead, then much of the anxiety and fear that characterize some of its members would ease away.

It has also been the case that a Calvinistic theological position has often been associated with unattractive, judgmental attitudes and bigotry. This association (however unjust it may be) goes back into the Evangelical Revival itself. As long ago as 1741 Whitefield feared that John Wesley's aversion to predestination might be because he had been 'disputing with some warm narrow-spirited men that held election'.[10] Not all who held the doctrine were 'persecutors', pleaded Whitefield in response to Wesley's contention that marks of holiness, such as meekness and love, were lacking in its proponents. Whitefield is obviously correct, but it is interesting that the stereotype was already in existence. It can still be found in the Free Church of England.

One result of these attitudes has been the endowing of the denomination with a negative disposition. Free Church of England people, it has often seemed, are *against* something. Some of them have displayed what the *Church Times* in 1902 called 'the inherent cantankerousness of Protestant Dissent'.[11] This negativity has produced (like the Roundheads in Sellar and Yeatman's *1066 and All That*) a 'Right but Repulsive' image at times.[12] Doctrinal orthodoxy has not always been accompanied by a Christlike attractiveness.

Throughout the history of the movement some of its most passionate defenders have pleaded for a charitable tolerance. At the height of the nineteenth-century controversies, when painful separations were taking place and feelings running high, Merryweather could still ask

> that we should be prepared to recognize in the Christian Church the presence of much diversity of talent and the existence of many shades of thought . . . in a spirit of comprehensiveness, bounded by, and consistent with, the evangelical truth. A rigid formal and forced uniformity of thought upon non-essentials is not necessary or desirable.[13]

Vaughan was only too well aware of the consequences of 'forced uniformity' and was highly critical of the judgmental attitude found within the denomination: 'that condition which cannot tolerate any point of view but its own and which builds a judgement throne and sits upon it, assuming superiority in the name of Christ . . .'.[14] Contrasting the loving mercy of Christ in his earthly dealings with others, with the attitude of the Free Church of England, Vaughan did not hesitate to identify where the latter fell short: 'The earlier hopes that crowds of disturbed, concerned and sympathetic people would rally to *this* standard, was doomed to disappointment. When the air became charged with *accusation, persecution and denunciation*, the masses moved away.'[15] The sheer unloveliness of the Free Church of England in some of its manifestations has helped to keep it small. Some in the denomination need to hear Vaughan's warning: 'Truth . . . will do its work, more constructively and more gracefully than condemnation and denunciation can ever be expected to do.'[16]

A failure to face its Anglican identity

Legally and constitutionally the identity of the Free Church of England is resolved. It is a traditionally ordered episcopal community committed to following the laws, customs and liturgy of the Church of England. By virtually every conceivable test that can be applied, 'the Free Church of England, otherwise called the Reformed Episcopal Church' is an Anglican Church.[17] Its origins lie in Provinces of the Anglican Communion, its episcopate derives from the see of Canterbury, its Constitution, doctrinal basis, liturgy, concepts, visual appearance and terminology all bind it

irrevocably to historic Anglican norms. This has been the declared intention since the eighteenth century, as expressed by a sequence of representative authorities. Cummins, in particular, had

> no wish that it should be a Methodist or Presbyterian Church . . . Had he
> wished to unite with his Presbyterian, or Methodist, or Reformed brethren,
> he could easily have done so; and great suffering and sacrifice on his part
> would have been saved; But when asked, in Nov. 1873, whether he meant to
> unite with any of these sister Churches, he answered, '*No*; I wish a pure
> *Episcopal* Church . . .'[18]

A decade later Bishop Newman reminded members of the Free
Church of England (which at the time, it will be recalled, was *less* Anglican
than the Reformed Episcopal Church) that 'We are essentially of the
Church of England in the laws and regulations of our Deed Poll and
Canon Law.'[19] To this day, in areas not provided for in the Free Church of
England's own Constitution, the Church of England is the authority to be
followed. The Free Church of England is arguably more 'Anglican' than
some Provinces of the Anglican Communion.

Such a linkage was, as has been seen, meant to provide an entrée
into a rich heritage – both Catholic and Reformed – and to facilitate the
transfer of members of the Church of England and other parts of the
Anglican Communion to the Free Church of England and its sister
Churches. In practice, however, the Free Church of England has found
itself locked into a 'love–hate' relationship with the Church of England.
The Church of England is both the revered Mother to be emulated *and*
the grossly distorted monster to be feared and attacked whenever possible. At different times the leadership has oscillated between the two
poles. Inevitably there is a deep suspicion of the Church of England's
motives; many older members of the denomination were reared on
stories of legal action against their parents and grandparents by incumbents and bishops of the Established Church. The consequent emotional
estrangement contributes towards an inability to recognize and appreciate developments within the Church of England of which the founding
fathers of the Free Church of England and Reformed Episcopal Church
would most definitely have approved. For all his antagonistic stance
against the Church of England at the time of the Lambeth Appeal,
Vaughan testifies to relationships with Church of England clergy at the
local level that were 'often kindly and courteous . . . We often receive more

courtesy and consideration from the Ritualistic clergy than from the Evangelicals with whom we are, at least doctrinally, one.'[20] As in other dialogues, the Free Church of England and the Church of England need to move beyond stereotypes and seek what that Anglican–Methodist *Common Statement* calls a 'Healing of Memories', if further progress is to be possible.[21]

Arguably, however, once it ceases to navigate by its Anglican 'pole star', the Free Church of England is directionless. There is no obvious alternative direction. Conservative Evangelicals in the various small denominations with which the leadership has recently consorted are not remotely interested in the episcopal and liturgical aspects of the denomination. Claims to look to 'the Bible alone' all too often produce further fragmentation, as the story of Protestantism shows depressingly clearly. Packer, while utterly committed to the unique authority of Scripture as God's Word written, defends the Anglican theological method which, 'involves the use of reason and tradition for the better understanding and applying Scripture'. Moreover, Packer rejoices in the normative nature of Anglicanism: 'Ideal Anglicanism . . . is . . . mere Christianity, the Apostolic religion of the New Testament without addition, subtraction or distortion.' For him this is fully consistent with full-blooded Evangelicalism: 'The emphases of Evangelicalism are no more and no less than underlinings of aspects of Anglicanism . . .'[22] Frequently, by contrast, the theology of the denomination's leaders has not been integrated with the denomination's ecclesiology in the way that Packer shows it can be, with resultant tensions. The reality is, however, that the title deeds of the Free Church of England belong to the Anglican-minded among her members. There is nothing in the denomination's history or constitution to support an alternative identity.[23]

In view of the failure of recent leaders to face this fact it is not surprising that the Free Church of England in recent years has done no strategic thinking about how it might provide an alternative home for those leaving the Church of England or other Churches as a result of current controversies. Deliberately enticing away members of another Church may not be morally or theologically defensible, but the Free Church of England has made no attempt to offer a home to thousands of people who (if the statistics are to be believed) *had decided to leave the Church of England anyway*, whether through their inability to accept recent changes or for other reasons. Historically the denomination saw itself as existing to provide a home for Anglicans who can no longer pursue their discipleship in the Church of England. It is currently making no attempt to do so. Part of the reason must be that it does not portray itself as sufficiently Anglican for such transfer to be possible.

Unlike some of the recent leadership of the Free Church of England, the founding fathers of the movement in Britain and North America gloried in their Anglican heritage and commended it to others. Despite what Packer call the recent 'bad patch'[24] that Anglicanism is currently going through, it is still capable of proving attractive to Christians – including Evangelical Christians – of other traditions.[25] The Free Church of England needs to come to a more positive assessment of its own inherent Anglican identity – not as a 'believe what you like' portmanteau, but as the Catholic Church cleansed and revitalized by the word of God.

A failure to appreciate its Catholic and patristic heritage

The knowledge of Church Fathers displayed by figures such as Merryweather and Cummins is striking. Patristic precedent was important to them. For Merryweather, for example, the Fathers are not the *foundation* – that is Christ Himself (1 Corinthians 3.11) – nevertheless, 'it can be proved that in all essential points [the Free Church of England] is supported by the testimony of the earlier Fathers'.[26] Newman was critical of those who 'have fallen below the standard of the ancient Church'.[27] Time and time again the point is made by the denomination's apologists that this is not a community that began 'yesterday' or even in the sixteenth century, but which traces its continuity back through the Medieval, Saxon and Celtic Churches to the patristic and apostolic communities.

This is explicit in the Anglican foundations of the denomination. The historic creeds and the liturgical formularies are the products of ancient Christian communities. It has often been argued that 'being patristic' is an indispensable element in being Anglican.[28] In the Free Church of England today (as in much of the Church of England) this sense is latent rather than explicit.[29] Part of the cause of this lies in changed theological education. The eighteenth- and nineteenth-century presbyters were very often men with a classical Oxford, Cambridge or Dublin education. They knew Greek and Latin and were familiar with the ancient world. The vocabulary and thought-world of the Fathers was familiar to them.[30] This is no longer the case. There is no space to explore the reasons for this here, but the Free Church of England (and other Churches) needs to consider how it might compensate for this.

A further reason for the estrangement is the infiltration of a particular kind of Protestant culture which in practice thinks that a commitment to scriptural authority means that all other 'authorities' can be ignored or even ridiculed. Such an approach is usually selective and susceptible to manipulation, since a wider perspective is disallowed. The 1978 *Chicago Call*, an appeal to Evangelicals, recognized the failure of this approach:

> We confess that we have often lost the fullness of our Christian heritage, too readily assuming that the Scriptures and the Spirit make us independent of the past. In so doing, we have become theologically shallow, spiritually weak, blind to the work of God in others and married to our cultures.[31]

Packer, too, is able to affirm 'the use of reason and tradition for the better understanding and applying of Scripture'.[32] The Anglican Reformers and apologists – Hooker in particular – were conscious that they were part of, and indebted to, a catholic heritage in which the teaching of the Fathers occupies a prominent place. The Evangelical authors of the *Chicago Call* were conscious of the damage that loss of the wider heritage had caused: 'We decry the poverty of sacramental understanding among evangelicals. This is largely due to the loss of our continuity with the teaching of many of the Fathers and Reformers . . .'[33]

By contrast, too often members of the Free Church of England have shown a theological and historical 'isolationism', often linked with an implicit cultural superiority or imperialism. A particular form of nineteenth-century Protestant culture is seen as the 'norm' and as superior to other ecclesiastical cultures.

The Free Church of England has not yet caught up with the recent contacts between the Evangelical Alliance (of which it is a member) and the Orthodox Church.[34] Some of its current members would certainly disapprove of such contact. Yet, as an episcopal and liturgical Church, the denomination ought to be able to make a significant contribution to such a dialogue. It is noteworthy that recent studies are rediscovering the extent to which the sixteenth-century Reformers were themselves aware of their patristic heritage.[35] Protestantism is not the 'new beginning' that some of its defenders would like to believe. The Reformed Episcopal

Church in North America is currently rediscovering the patristic aspect of its identity, and from 2002 has included a list of the Seven Ecumenical Councils among its foundational documents. Interestingly, too, the recently formed 'Church of England (Continuing)', which shares a Reformed ethos, has at the same time shown a commitment to the patristic heritage:

> Underlying the founding principles of the Reformed English Church is the ethos that constantly appeals to the Holy Scriptures, Apostolic tradition, Patristic witness in the first five centuries, the Creeds of undivided Christendom and the Augustinian remnant in the Medieval period as marking the boundaries of Anglican doctrine, i.e. Catholic orthodoxy that upholds the Nicene Faith and preserves the Chalcedonian Definition in all its pristine purity and logical implications, as was rediscovered by the Reformers and passed down to successive divines . . .[36]

The official website of the Free Church of Scotland lists the Chalcedonian Definition and the Anathemas of the Second Council of Constantinople (553) along with other Confessions among the 'Historical Documents of the Reformed Faith'.[37] The Free Church of England has yet to rediscover the commitment to the Fathers intrinsic in its heritage.

A failure to fulfil its ecumenical commitment

For a denomination that professes to take its Declaration of Principles seriously, the neglect of the commitment required by this clause stands as a serious rebuke.

A Church formally committed to 'set forth . . . quietness, peace and love, among all Christian people' ought, one might suppose, to be at the forefront of the ecumenical endeavour. The reality, as has been shown, is the precise opposite. Not only has the denomination distanced itself from 'mainline' ecumenical activities such as the British Council of Churches (BCC) or Churches Together in England (CTE), it has also failed to integrate in any significant way into any alternative network or grouping. While it has been a member of the Free Church Federal Council (now the Free Churches Group in CTBI) since 1954, it can hardly be said to have been an enthusiastic member. As seen in Chapter 8, some of its present leadership are unhappy even with membership of that body.

In view of the vast discrepancy between the Free Church of England's stated intent and its actual performance in this area, it is worth looking further at some of the background.

As far back as the leadership of Thomas Haweis, warm and courteous fellowship with other Christians was encouraged. Haweis himself in 1793 entertained the (Roman Catholic) Archbishop of Aix and the Bishop of Comminges (both of them exiles from the French Revolution). He also assisted émigré Roman Catholic presbyters (some of whom even attended his services) to obtain teaching posts.[38] Some present-day members of the denomination would find such openness towards 'the traditional enemy' very difficult. Among non-Roman Catholics, Haweis was even more open. He declared that he would willingly join in Communion with a wide range of traditions: in Scotland with 'the High Church' as well as with the Seceders, Burghers or Anti-Burghers:

> if I were in Saxony, my Lutheran brethren would meet me at their table; at Nimes I would sit down with St Etienne under the rock; at Berne break bread with that gracious Swiss correspondent as cordially as with the prelate of Upsala, if I were in Sweden. I need not add that they would be equally welcome to the bread I break, for the same is my brother, my sister and mother.[39]

The inclusion of both German and Swedish (vestment-wearing) Lutherans is significant. Lutherans and Calvinists had become polarized in the sixteenth century and Haweis might have been expected to keep them at arm's length. On the contrary, his sympathies transcended even the great divide that had split the Evangelical Revival:

> Really spiritually minded men are all one in Christ Jesus, and however, when disputes arise, the difference between Calvinist and Arminian seems vast and irreconcilable, yet, when we converse in love and the spirit of weakness, rejoicing if Christ be preached by whomsoever, or whensoever, we can stretch out the right hand of fellowship and press the hand with true fraternal affection.[40]

Haweis's open and generous attitude towards other Christians, even those whose theology differed considerably from his own, seems to have been lost among his successors during the course of the nineteenth century. Price, despite his anti-Roman convictions, nevertheless came to see that 'the spirit of our movement . . . Evangelical in doctrine and

Catholic in principle' necessitated an openness to Christians of other traditions. In 1871 he even went so far as to advocate 'the free interchange of pulpits in this country among the various sections of the Christian Church, established and non-established'.[41] Such an interchange would 'be a second Pentecost . . . and would, more than any other event, hasten on that blessed day for which our Lord prayed, "that they all may be one"'.[42] But the openness of Price had been followed by the bigotry of Dicksee. Nor does Bishop Cummins's strong ecumenical concern seem to have crossed the Atlantic. Not only did he wish to draw into Reformed episcopalianism a wide range of Evangelicals but, as Guelzo points out, he 'went out of his way to establish parallels between his movement and the post-Vatican Council Old Catholics'.[43] In marked contrast, by the end of the nineteenth century the Free Church of England and Reformed Episcopal Church in the United Kingdom were settling down into a narrow sectarian mentality, quite alien to the spirit of their founders.

By the time of his Centenary Charge, Vaughan realized that a wrong direction had been taken. Virtually the entire Charge is composed of two 'responsibilities'. The first of these is 'Responsibility to maintain the fellowship of the Universal Church'.[44] It is in this context that he made his remarks about truth rather than denunciation as the right course to follow, already quoted above. He then went on to reflect on the way in which the concept of 'unity in diversity', seen in the material world, needs to be applied to the Church. This led Vaughan to conclude:

> Given agreement on fundamental facts – man's need of salvation, the sovereignty of Grace, the inspiration of the Word and the Divinity of the Man of Nazareth – there must be varying approaches to the treasure house of Truth, and each seeker must find his own portion of that Truth; no mind can contain it all; for the finite cannot comprehend the infinite.

Vaughan admitted that he found 'some modes of government and worship' abhorrent to him, and some doctrines repugnant, but would 'not deny [to those that held them] their claim to have discovered what, for them, is the Truth'. Vaughan reserved the right to test such beliefs by the Scriptures, but claimed from such Christians what he was also prepared to give to them:

> credit for devotion to our one common Lord and Saviour. For while I must make my witness in my own way, they are still my brethren and I am their

brother. Their Father is my Father. Their Saviour is my Saviour. Their hope for a place in the eternal rest is my hope too.[45]

The evidence suggests that the denomination did not respond to Vaughan's remarkable plea for a more open attitude. The logical step would have been for the Free Church of England to join the British Council of Churches which came into existence the very year of the Centenary Charge. It did not. A decade later, as noted, it joined the Free Church Federal Council, but against the wishes of some members. Thereafter, the denomination never really caught up with the changes of attitude and thought that were making honest ecumenical co-operation and dialogue possible. An example may be found in the paper presented by the Revd W. B. Makin of the Free Church of England at a 'Teach In' held at Liverpool University on 21 November 1967.[46] The religious leaders present included the Roman Catholic Archbishop of Liverpool (G. A. Beck) and the Bishop of Liverpool (Stuart Blanch). Makin prefaced his remarks by saying, 'we rejoice that the intolerance and even occasional rudeness, between Christians of different denominations is largely a thing of the past, and that whatever our differences may be, we can at least regard each other with Christian charity and courtesy'.[47] These encouraging words were followed by a listing of truths that must never be surrendered, a naming of Roman Catholic practices that 'we cannot accept', references to members of the Church of England having been 'betrayed by Romanists within their borders' and similar remarks. It must have been offensive to many present and is a far cry from Vaughan's plea that 'Affirmation, not denunciation, is the surest way to propagate truth.'[48] Makin has his successors in the Free Church of England today.

In its anti-ecumenical stance the denomination is not only out of step with its heritage, but with such Reformed Anglican Evangelicals as Packer. His words are worth quoting at length:

> Anglicanism is ecumenical. Always has been . . . Anglicanism pays attention to all Christian traditions, thus seeking both the fullness of the Catholic faith for itself and the fullest communion with the rest of the Christian world as well . . . I do think that the Anglican heritage is the richest heritage in Christendom . . . The ecumenical dimension, seeking all the riches of wisdom that God has given anywhere in Christendom is one of the qualities of Anglicanism that I most admire.[49]

There is (to the present writer at least) an illogicality in the position of those in the denomination who seek to distance themselves from ecumenical contact. Much is made of the sovereign protection of God, yet the actions taken suggest that those concerned do not actually believe in it. The implication is that God could not protect them from being 'sullied' by contact with other Christians, that His Word would not actually prevail if uttered in 'mixed company'. There is, almost certainly, a collective insecurity which prevents the Free Church of England fulfilling this aspect of its foundational charter and its founders' vision. It needs to experience Packer's discovery that a Church committed to biblical truth has nothing to fear from seeking the riches of God's wisdom outside its own confines.

An Adullam's cave

It was Bishop Newman of the pre-union Free Church of England who, in October 1883 warned the denomination that, 'our Church must not be turned into a sort of Cave of Adullam – a refuge for all sorts and conditions of men'.[50] This comparison of the denomination to the place where 'all those who were in distress or in debt or discontented gathered'[51] has been uncomfortably accurate at times – at least as far as the 'discontented' are concerned. By the very nature of events the first congregations (whether in the 1780s or the post-1844 phase) were composed of people who had the strength of character to leave – whether reluctantly or defiantly – the Church of England. For the clergy involved, the step was often only taken after years of protesting and agitation within the Established Church. Being a member of the Free Church of England was a deliberate choice, usually made in protest. This self-selecting nature was often a recipe for instability. As the decades passed, however, this became less true of the laity. Today many members of the denomination are three or four generations removed from their forefathers who originally joined. This makes for a sense of continuity, stability and harmony. There are many lifelong friendships within and between congregations. It is this 'core' that has over the years had to absorb a continual stream from other traditions.

On the other side of the Atlantic the Reformed Episcopal Church had encountered the same problems that Newman was addressing. As Benjamin Leacock observed, 'some of the men who joined us, and whom after a few days' contact [Cummins] described as "Splendid fellows",

"Valuable accessions", "Men of the first ability", have proven utter failures, and others have given us much trouble'.[52] There were also 'the
simple incompetents, who were unable to make a decent livelihood for
themselves in their own denominations and were fleeing to the Reformed
Episcopalians as a convenient port in a storm'.[53]

Vaughan had no illusions about some of those who had joined the
Free Church of England for unworthy motives:

> There are place-hunters; spiritual adventurers; unstable, restless souls . . .
> Perhaps the type of person who has caused us most real pain is the unctu-
> ous piety professor, who strives to convince all around him that they come
> sadly short of the spiritual experience and standing he enjoys . . . They
> think that God Almighty is concerned with every petty fogging event in
> their drab and wretched lives . . . and appear to have no sense of God's
> Majesty, or their own inconsiderable insignificance.[54]

A large denomination or congregation can safely 'absorb' a number
of unstable or 'damaged' people. In a small body like the Free Church of
England their influence is disproportionately great, particularly as they
may be forceful and verbose. No doubt this contributed to Headlam's
assessment of the denomination in 1920 as 'a body of malcontents'. A
former presbyter of the denomination has shared with the present writer
his view that the Free Church of England contains a disproportionate
number of people 'who don't fit in anywhere else'. Such an analysis has
implications for the future of the denomination. Among other possibilities, it suggests that the last thing the denomination needs is a sudden
influx of strong-minded people with their own 'agendas', fleeing the
Church of England or other parent denomination, and seeking to make
the Free Church of England their new 'platform'. There have been too
many of them in the past.

The quality of the clergy

It is perhaps true of any Church that its greatest strength and its greatest
weakness is its clergy. That polarization has been seen particularly clearly
in the Free Church of England.

For Price in 1871, what the movement needed was 'men with warm
hearts and strong faith, and filled with the Holy Ghost and with power'.[55]

Though spiritual qualities were paramount, Price realised the value of other qualities: 'We require men of culture and education . . . men of mental acquirements and intellectual power – men of refinement and gentlemanly bearing.'[56]

Newman, Price's co-worker in the episcopate, reinforced his Primus's call:

> For the work of the ministry amongst us, we require men called by God to the work . . . men of education and intellectual power, men of talent, Christian gentlemen, that we may be equal to the clergy of any denomination . . . We do not require the services of those who have been unsuccessful elsewhere, nor of those who imagine they can find an entrance into the Church on very easy terms.[57]

Sixty years later Vaughan's testimony shows that these high ideals about the quality of the clergy had not been achieved: 'I suggest that there should be a narrowing of the doorway of entrance to our ministry even now.'[58] Vaughan was concerned not just with the educational standards of the clergy but with the lack of real loyalty to the Free Church of England and its ethos. A whole section of his 'Memories' is entitled 'Ministerial Insubordination and Ambition'. He inveighed against those who, once they become ministers in the denomination,

> are apt to instruct your Bishops as to their duties, or their personal character . . . they can see the cloven hoof in ancient Protestant ceremonial, which is habitual in our Church . . . One cannot avoid the conclusion that such persons or their prototypes must have been in the mind of the prophet Isaiah, when he wrote or spoke his Chapter 65, and verse 5 ['an obstinate people . . . who say, "Keep away; don't come near me, for I am too sacred for you!"'].[59]

Clearly Vaughan had had his fill of such 'unstable men' who, after ordination, revealed an 'inability to sense and respond to our type of authority and tradition, habits and customs' and 'have demanded changes of traditional custom for their own personal interest'.[60] Many such ultimately 'have found us to be a Church in which they can no longer work happily. So they departed . . .'.[61] What particularly hurt Vaughan was that such people departed with Holy Orders which they could not have obtained elsewhere and which they seldom resigned on leaving the Free Church of England.

Interestingly, of those clergy who came already ordained from other denominations, Vaughan had found that the experience of receiving

Anglicans or Methodists had 'not been at all happy either for the ministers themselves or the congregations they have served'.[62] Congregationalists and Independent Evangelical pastors made, in Vaughan's experience,
better Free Church of England presbyters. A detailed analysis of the background of the ministry in recent decades would be instructive. Currently
it contains presbyters ordained in the Church of England, the Roman
Catholic Church and the Congregational Union, in addition to those
ordained by the denomination's bishops.

Both Newman and Vaughan (and many other bishops) believed
that good quality training (preferably residential) was the chief remedy
against the doctrinal and personal inadequacies of the clergy. A residential element, Vaughan believed, would enable candidates to acquire those
things that 'cannot be learned from books, but are absorbed in atmosphere; traditions, customs, implications, becoming part of the mind furniture for the sense of the "fitness of things"'.[63] Current clergy training
(which was briefly described in Chapter 12) does not go very far towards
addressing this issue, though the regular residential meetings are clearly
valuable.

Part of the problem is the relatively few candidates who come from
within the Free Church of England itself. The bishops in office in 2002
illustrate the situation. Only one of them (Powell) was a 'cradle Free
Church of England man'; Bishop McLean had been in the denomination
over half a century, having come from the Scottish Episcopal Church;
Bentley-Taylor (who had been a layman in an independent Presbyterian
Church and was ordained immediately on entering the denomination[64])
first appears in the clergy list in the 1994–95 Year Book, and Shucksmith
(who resigned from the Church of England in which he had been an
incumbent) the following year. The first two had over 120 years of experience in the Free Church of England; the latter two only 15.

The 'patchiness' of quality is a continuing problem. It is compounded by the lack of a central structure for examining and vetting candidates. The two dioceses currently operate separate systems. Some of
those admitted or ordained over the years have simply lacked the necessary skills for leadership and ministry. This has repercussions for the
Church's ability to engage with contemporary issues. A Christian community with clergy who are poorly equipped to deal with intellectual
matters is, in Packer's words, prone to resort to 'ignoring them or using
the big stick to silence those that voice them'.[65]

Against this must be set the conditions of sacrifice and poverty in which many of them have had to minister – and still minister. The stipend in 2004 is a mere £4,000 per annum. Quite a few of the ministers receive no payment at all. There is no doubt that some of the clergy experience a considerable degree of financial hardship.

Given the geographical isolation from each other of most of the clergy, the non-Anglican background of many of them, and the limited degree of training some have received, it is remarkable that the present-day denomination manages to maintain the sense of identity that it does. Clearly, however, there is considerable room for improvement.

A failure to address contemporary issues

The outgoing confidence of the eighteenth century had by the late nineteenth and early twentieth centuries given way to a drawbridge mentality.

As already noted, in large part this was a product of the educational and social standards of the clergy. Instead of the men of 'education and intellectual power' desired by Newman, there have been too many

> persons who need through personal insecurity to believe that the particular foundation on which they are resting their lives is beyond all question as firm and unshakeable as a rock, and will therefore commit intellectual suicide and repel all questions unanswered in order to sustain their otherwise untenable position.[66]

The situation is self-perpetuating. Men of greater ability who join the denomination often end up leaving it again, worn down by the mental restrictions of their peers.[67]

The isolation of the denomination has prevented it from co-operating with others in clergy and lay training schemes. This could have been one of the greatest benefits of continuing the Conversations with the Church of England.

The insularity of congregations and dioceses

The 1863 Constitution spoke of incorporating the 'Congregational' principle in its ordering of the Church. This has been a mixed blessing to the denomination. On the positive side, the strength and semi-independence of the local churches probably saved them at times when central leadership failed, as for example in the 1890s. Allied to this is the issue of Trusts. The piecemeal way in which the pre-union Free Church of England, Reformed Episcopal Church and Reformed Church of England came into existence led to a situation where many of the properties were controlled by local trustees. Like the patronage system in the Church of England this was capable of being hailed as a blessing (when it prevented, for example, a bishop overriding the wishes of a congregation) and a hindrance (when, for example, it allowed congregations to stand aloof from worthwhile denominational initiatives).[68]

This independence has, however, worked against denominational unity. As Fenwick described it:

> The negative side of an essentially *congregationalist* system meant that the independent-minded churches were very self-centred. To many of the clergy and laity involved, *only* their church with its trust was central to their vision. The problems of another trust on the other side of the country would have elicited little sympathy . . .[69]

This is seen most clearly in the area of finance. Time and again denominational treasurers have appealed to the congregations for funding for various aspects of the Church's life, usually with very little success. Yet the same congregations were often (particularly at the end of the nineteenth century) giving generously (by the standards of the day) to overseas missions. In more recent decades the situation has changed somewhat. Many congregations do not have the money to give *either* to overseas missions *or* denominational funds, though most do what they can, despite the costs of maintaining their own plant.

The legacy of independence, however, is not just seen in the realm of finance. It is very difficult to get the congregations to unite around a common vision, particularly when the distance between them makes interaction infrequent and limited. The situation has been compounded by internal divisions. It is significant that Vaughan devoted the second half of his Centenary Charge to 'The Responsibility to maintain the Unity of my own Church'.[70] Writing in 1944, Vaughan drew from international events an urgent lesson, and warned the denomination of 'the bitter harvest of arrogant dictatorship . . . a spirit no longer teachable'.[71] Five years later he complained about 'weak minds and weaker characters, often bawling about their complete trust in their Saviour, but never by any chance trusting the honour of their fellow-Christians; suspicious because themselves unworthy of confidence, ready to credit others with the social sins they habitually commit'.[72] Recurring episodes of internal conflict have no doubt been a contributing factor to the paralysis the Church has often suffered.

A particularly acute form of this paralysis has undoubtedly been the inability from time to time of bishops (and hence their dioceses) to co-operate. Where there are only two dioceses, the catholic heritage of a proper degree of episcopal and diocesan independence in fact produces polarization. It is remarkable how often the election system has produced pairs of bishops who are unable to work with each other.[73] The denomination has not addressed some of the issues discussed in, for example, *Bishops in Communion: Collegiality in the Service of the Koinonia of the Church*, issued by the House of Bishops of the Church of England in 2000.[74] As with congregational insularity, this has been a mixed blessing. It has allowed one diocese to provide the denomination with stability at a time when the other has, for one reason or another, been destabilized. Equally, it has allowed one diocese to veto another, as in the response to the 1920 Lambeth Conference Appeal. In the absence of leadership capable of gathering the whole Free Church of England around a common vision, such fragmentation is inevitable.

Financial problems

'The cause of God', Price told Convocation in 1871, 'can no more do without money than commerce can.'[75] The history of the Free Church of England bears this out very clearly. A repeated theme is of bishops and treasurers calling for increased giving. It is probably true that most congregations that failed did so ultimately for financial reasons. There has been immensely sacrificial giving (not least by some of the clergy) but there has also been totally inadequate financial support.[76] All too often, withholding finance has been a means of 'punishing' the minister. Changes in society have 'democratized' giving. There are now few individuals with the levels of disposable wealth enjoyed by the Duke of Somerset or the mill-owners who supported the new movement. This means that there is very little chance of any significant capital development, especially where elderly congregations are struggling to pay the weekly bills.

In part this is itself a product of poverty and isolation. The denomination has not had the means in recent decades to finance a Stewardship Officer, such as are now common in the Church of England. Isolationism has prevented it using the resources of such officers in other Churches.

A hugely important factor is loss of vision. In the nineteenth century substantial sums of money were raised to purchase land and build churches, halls and schoolrooms because people had a strong sense of purpose. Theirs was a cause in which they passionately believed. Their successors now struggle to maintain the buildings their grandparents erected, and have little energy for anything else.

Fear

There is much unspoken, underlying fear within the Free Church of England. Fear of absorption. Fear of the loss of all the movement has stood for. Fear of not being able to pay bills. Fear of doctrinal 'pollution'. Fear of compromise with a polluted world. Fear of change. Fear of loss of influence. Fear of moving out into new possibilities. Fear of extinction. The description of the early Reformed Episcopalians in America as people 'who fear that if wheat and tares grow together, the tares will assuredly root out the wheat', sums up well the mentality of some members of the British denomination.[77]

Some such fear is understandable at the human level. It sits uncomfortably, however, with the vision of the sovereignty of God so often proclaimed from the denomination's pulpits. The message is in fact the opposite of the words. Many clearly do *not* believe that God will protect them as His people if they allow themselves to come into contact with other people and situations. The community is reluctant to leave the foot of Mount Sinai. People who see themselves as timorously guarding a tiny, guttering flame in the midst of the impenetrable darkness of a 'Gothic night',[78] find it difficult to step out into the storm they believe is raging outside.[79]

Such fears existed among Evangelicals in the Church of England for most of the first half of the twentieth century. Buchanan wrote of Church of England Evangelicals in the late 1960s:

> With some caution, the Evangelical constituency at last was ready to move forward out of [the] last ditch, ready even to move without being absolutely sure what the point of arrival would be, but with a deep sense that, under God and with due regard for his word and for the realities of the Church and the nation, there were certain moves which were right in themselves to take, irrespective of narrow issues of advantage and disadvantage.[80]

While there are some in the Free Church of England who are clearly itching to climb out of the ditch, they have not yet persuaded the rest of the denomination to do so.

Many of the above points are aspects of a single phenomenon – the narrowing of the original vision. The denomination is not sufficiently conscious of the breadth of its tradition or of the links it already has, by its history and constitution, with the wider Christian community. The result is that it has no clear vision of what it, corporately, has to offer to the other Churches and to the unchurched of England. It is ironic that the Free Church of England is currently turning its back on the wider Christian community at the very time that it is being accorded greater recognition than ever before, and its position on a number of issues is being adopted by others.[81]

The foregoing list adds up to a depressing catalogue. However, to compress two centuries of failure into a few pages is to some extent misleading. As Vaughan acknowledged, 'I suppose if all the hidden history of other denominations were known, it would be similar.'[82] The failures are extremely serious, but they are not the whole picture. Some of the clergy, for example, have been men of education and stature, figures well known and respected in their local communities.[83] Many of the laity have been sincere, devout, courteous and hard-working people. In some places the Free Church of England presence eclipsed other denominations and even that of the Established Church. It is important, too, to distinguish the failures of the *membership* from the potential strengths of the *denomination as an institution*. This final section looks at some possible futures for the Free Church of England.

The Future?

Many different futures can be envisaged for the Free Church of England. Some of them are explored briefly below. None of them is here presented as the 'right' way forward. All of them, except the first three, presuppose the denomination's willingness to change to a greater or lesser extent and that the besetting issues of leadership quality can be overcome.

Further shrinkage

No recent commentator – from inside or outside the denomination – predicts growth for the Free Church of England if it continues with its current attitudes. The Church is simply too old-fashioned, too 'churchy' and too isolationist to attract independent Evangelicals, and the supply of members of the Church of England seeking a Church which uses 'the old services' is inevitably drying up. Humanly speaking, perhaps half its congregations are likely to fail in the next decade. Some congregations may choose to become independent[84] or seek alternative affiliations. Whether the surviving congregations could maintain any corporate identity is debatable. Beyond that lies the possibility of extinction as a denomination. The Free Church of England would not be the first Christian community, born in great hope, to suffer such a fate.[85]

Degeneration into episcopus vagans status

The story of Alfred Richardson in the late nineteenth century is a salutary warning of a possible fate for the denomination. Richardson had been involved in the Reformed Episcopal Church venture from the very beginning, yet ended up unwisely involved with small groups of dubious character and origin. To date, the denomination has been preserved from going down such a path by its (relative) breadth and constitutional behaviour. It is, however, not difficult to imagine a further reduced Free Church of England being seduced by a perhaps unstable or eccentric bishop into entering the 'twilight world' of episcopi vagantes bodies. An alternative scenario is of a frustrated presbyter seeking consecration from such a group in order to gain status in a struggle for control of the remains of the Free Church of England. It would be a sad end for the heritage of Whitefield and Cummins.

Unravelling of the strands

It would be possible to interpret recent tensions in the Free Church of England as stemming from the fact that the denomination, like the feet of the statue in Nebuchadnezzar's vision, is part iron and part clay.[86] It could be argued that, even after 1927, the old Free Church of England and Reformed Episcopal elements never really merged. Such an analysis would not in fact be true. What *is* true is that some who have joined the denomination over the years have been selective in their understanding of it. Nevertheless, as the present work has shown, although the Free Church of England element is the older, it is the 'pure' Anglicanism of the Reformed Episcopal Church that prevailed in the union. The Declaration of Principles, Constitution, Prayer Book and historic succession all derived predominantly from the Reformed Episcopal Church. Furthermore, many of those who would invoke the pre-union Free Church of England, are unaware of how strongly 'Churchy' it was, both in its founders' intention and in practice. Attempts to 'de-Anglicanize' the present-day denomination are not true to the history of any of its component parts.

It would, nevertheless, be possible to envisage the current Free Church of England splitting along Anglican/Non-Anglican lines as it did in 1877 and nearly did again the following year.[87] The 'Non-Anglican' section would be free to pursue its own vision of the Church. The 'Anglican' section would be able to explore unimpeded the breadth of its heritage and perhaps engage ecumenically. Whether either section would have the resources or energy to pursue these paths is an open question.

Modest growth

It is possible that, with a sensitive adoption of modern liturgical provision, and a modest openness towards the larger Christian community, the Free Church of England may indeed attract significant numbers of new members, perhaps disenchanted members of the Church of England. In such a development local factors are likely to play a part, as they often did in the nineteenth century. Members of a Church of England congregation, unable, for example to accept a woman priest or a woman bishop, or an incumbent advocating homosexual unions, may choose to affiliate to the Free Church of England. The denomination would need to be flexible enough to respond pastorally, sensitively and competently to any such requests. It would also have to face the fact that various expectations – for example, music and worship styles – may be different from the denomination's practice hitherto.

Non-Provincial Diocese

One model aired informally at the time of the Conversations with the Church of England was that of the Spanish Reformed Episcopal Church and the Lusitanian Church. These tiny episcopal Churches organize their own internal affairs and ecumenical relations, but since 1980 have been under the ultimate metropolitical jurisdiction of the Archbishop of Canterbury.[88] Despite their small size – each has substantially fewer clergy and congregations than the Free Church of England – the two Churches are members of the World Council of Churches and the Conference of European Churches.

It would obviously be harder to create such an arrangement in England, where jurisdictions would overlap. One possible structure might not be so very different from that of a network of proprietary chapels (church buildings, usually governed by specific trusts, that function as part of the Established Church, but have no geographical parish) or the family of churches 'owned' by a particular patronage body.

Nucleus of a Third Province

For the last few decades, as the likelihood of the ordination of women to the presbyterate in the Church of England drew closer and eventually became a reality, there have been calls for a Third Province to be created in England alongside those of Canterbury and York. This would be non-geographical, but would consist of those parishes that 'opted into' it. It would be a full part of the Church of England, but be served by a traditional male ministry. In a sense of course, the Free Church of England already forms such a body – an Anglican jurisdiction alongside the Provinces of Canterbury and York. The difference of course lies in its independence – it is not part of the structures of the Church of England, nor has it any access to its resources of buildings, money and manpower.

Faced with the likelihood of further disruption in the Established Church if women bishops are allowed, the Archbishop of Canterbury has expressed himself prepared to consider the Third Province option (among many others). It is unlikely that the Free Church of England would wish to join such a Province if the majority of its parishes were Anglo-Catholic in character.

Nucleus of a United Church of England

In 1970, following the collapse of the Anglican–Methodist Unity Scheme, four members of the Church of England, two Evangelical (Colin Buchanan and James Packer) and two Anglo-Catholic (Graham Leonard and Eric Mascall) produced an alternative which they published as *Growing Into Union*.[89] The proposal commenced with what the authors believed was a more coherent theological basis than the defeated Scheme, then went on to propose a unique mechanism for achieving a united Church. Instead of imposing a nationwide unity, irrespective of the willingness of local congregations, they proposed the creating of four embryonic dioceses to which parishes and congregations would transfer *when they were ready to do so.*

> The united Church would start as one or two isolated parish-type areas, grow into an archipelago, and eventually approach a solid shape in region after region, until the participating denominations finally disappeared and a new English Church had replaced them. In every case the transfer would occur only when the local Christians were agreed in desiring it.[90]

Looking at the *Growing Into Union* proposals, it is not impossible to see that the Free Church of England already bears some resemblance to the 'embryonic dioceses' envisaged by the authors. It is episcopal (which was an agreed feature of the united Church), but without the nuances of the Establishment or of unchurching exclusivity, and with a pattern of small dioceses.[91] It already has a Constitution and is used to operating as a body with widely scattered congregations.

Obviously, the situation has changed radically since 1970, not least because of the ordination of women. It is still possible, however, to posit a possible future for the Free Church of England as the nucleus of a future United Church of theologically conservative identity, formed by a process similar to that envisaged in *Growing Into Union*. Whether the denomination would be prepared to contemplate the changes necessary to facilitate such a development is another matter.

Inherent Potential?

Leaving aside the most negative scenarios, theoretically, the Free Church of England has a lot to commend it.

a) Its origins in the eighteenth-century Evangelical Revival give it an immediate point of contact and sympathy with other Churches that trace their origins to the Revival. Like them, it has a long experience of being a minority Church in England. It should be capable of being Anglican without being 'superior'.

b) The fact that it is not a recent breakaway in reaction to the ordination of women will commend it in some quarters. It is not, from this perspective, a 'one issue' body and should be able to operate in accordance with a wider vision

c) It is possible to be a member of the Free Church of England and enjoy a strong sense of continuity with the historic Church in the British Isles – with the Celtic and Saxon Churches, the builders of the medieval cathedrals, the events of the Reformation and the Evangelical Revival. Its bishops are in continuity with Augustine, Theodore, Anselm, Becket, Cranmer, Whitgift, Laud, Juxon, Wake and Moore. This sense of not being cut off from the nation's ecclesiastical history and culture is important to many.

d) The Free Church of England is non-Established Anglicanism. It shares this status within the British Isles with the Anglican Churches of Ireland, Scotland and Wales, but is unique in England. While this is attractive to some members of the Church of England, the story of the Free Church of England also contains warnings of some of the potential problems facing a Church stripped of any 'protection'. Nevertheless, it provides a context in which to explore the theological and practical consequences of an independent episcopal identity.

e) The Free Church of England operates in a narrower 'doctrinal spectrum' than the Church of England. This would be true even if it were to explore the full breadth of its heritage. This should be seen as a strength. The extremes of liberalism or Tractarianism could not flourish in its ambit. Nor, theoretically, could an indifference to doctrine. It has the potential to 'pick up the Anglican story' from the point it was at before the huge polarizing changes of the nineteenth and twentieth centuries. Its members could be described as 'Old Anglicans', by analogy with their counterparts in the Union of Utrecht.

f) It is perhaps unique among Churches in the United Kingdom in being the only Christian body to have adopted the sign of the historic episcopate. It provides a precedent for other Churches considering 'taking episcopacy into their system', and a potential source of the historic sign itself.

g) Compared with recently formed 'Continuing Churches' the Free Church of England, for all its troubles, is well established and comparatively stable. It operates on the basis of a substantial fully-working Constitution.[92] There is still a lot of uncertainty and suspicion about the 'Continuing Churches' and their fissiparous nature, making them unattractive. The Free Church of England can point to 76 years of relative institutional stability in its present form, and nearly a century and a half of independent existence before that.[93]

h) The structures of the Free Church of England approximate closely to the *desiderata* not only for a United Church in England, but to those of a restructured Church of England as posited more recently by Colin Buchanan.[94] Buchanan would like to see no more than 90 incumbencies in a diocese. The present Free Church of England diocesan bishops each have fewer than 20. Each Free Church of England parish has direct representation on the Diocesan Synod (unlike their Church of England opposite numbers) *and* on Convocation (totally unlike the situation with General Synod). Nor is the Free Church of England encumbered with cathedrals and the structures that accompany them. In Buchanan's phrase, it 'travels light'. While the Free Church of England clearly does have its own 'baggage', it is, by comparison with other bodies, an episcopal Church stripped down to its essentials, and therefore theoretically with the flexibility to adapt rapidly. The fact that, ironically, the opposite has been the case in the past, should not be allowed to obscure the potential that exists.

i) Having stood back from the various 'movements' of the twentieth century, the Free Church of England should be in a position to make a balanced assessment. It should, for example, be able to distinguish between the excesses of the Charismatic Movement and what has been of God and enduring in it. It should be able to pick the best fruits of liturgical reform without having to go through the unsettling decades of experimentation. It should be able to distinguish between the false hopes and wrong turns of the ecumenical movement, and the positive gains that have been made. Non-involvement has spared it the traumas which might have torn it apart. It should now be able to harvest the fruit of others' labours.

j) Far from having to be a narrow, monochrome, 'one-dimensional' body, the Free Church of England is the heir to a multifaceted heritage. Each of the three 'strands' identified in this study contributes to this richness. The eighteenth-century origins provide a passionate commitment to evangelism – to taking a life-changing experience of Jesus Christ to the people of Britain and beyond. The nineteenth-century vision was of a commitment to preserve the biblical and historic heritage of the Anglican tradition against those who would distort it by addition or subtraction. From North America comes the challenge to create a Gospel Catholicism that will provide a nucleus for reuniting separated traditions. An episcopal Church committed to evangelism, catholicity and ecumenism should have a major contribution to make to the spiritual life of the British Isles.

Even those most optimistic about the Free Church of England, however, acknowledge that its situation is precarious. Without change, its survival is very uncertain. Humanly speaking, the denomination has to make some painful decisions. Vaughan believed that it had been preserved 'for some yet unrevealed purpose'.[95] Can the Free Church of England turn its marginalization into a positive, deeply committed involvement in the corporate life of the Church in England? That would certainly be in line with the vision of the founding fathers. It *is* possible for tiny Anglican Churches to grow dramatically. The General Convention which met in the newly independent United States in 1789 was composed of only 2 bishops and 20 clergy, yet was to grow into the Protestant Episcopal

Church, spanning the entire continent. The Scottish Episcopal Church had dwindled to 4 bishops and an estimated 40 presbyters in total by the late eighteenth century.[96] Like the latter, the Free Church of England is reduced, in Sir Walter Scott's famous phrase, to 'a mere shadow of a shade'. Ironically, however, the very fact that the denomination still exists and functions robs it of a certain kind of nostalgic attractiveness. Bishops who live in semi-detached houses, have no cathedrals, and are consecrated in small, run-down, brick-built churches lack something of the romanticism of the Non-Jurors or of the Scottish 'bishops in the heather', worshipping with their persecuted flock, celebrating 'with mournful privacy the most august solemnity of the Catholic Church'.[97]

Yet there *is* something inspiring about the story and witness of the Free Church of England. The words of the Archbishop's Commission concerning the small Churches of the Iberian peninsula could equally well be applied to their British counterpart: 'Their struggle to foster and maintain a Church life of a recognisably Anglican type in circumstances of extreme difficulty must command our respectful admiration.'[98]

The question is whether the Free Church of England will, like the remnants of the Church of England in the American colonies or the Scottish Episcopal Church, draw back from the brink of extinction, or whether it will follow the Non-Jurors and have its candlestick removed.

Notes

1. Fenwick, *Thesis*, p. 507.
2. Quoted in, ibid.
3. Shucksmith, 'Agenda for Renewal 2002–2012', p. 1.
4. Ibid., p. 6.
5. It is possible that recent events will result in the loss of a few more congregations
6. *Prospect and Retrospect 1844–1944*, printed by the Wallasey and Wirral Newspaper Co., Wallasey, 1944.
7. Delivered on 11 October 2002. This has not yet been published. Copies of the talk on tape are available from Trinity College, Stoke Hill, Bristol, BS9 1JP.
8. On 20 January 2003 the conservative Evangelical Archbishop of Sydney, Australia, Dr Peter Jensen, urged Evangelicals 'to unite around, and promote, the central truths of Dr John Stott and Dr Jim Packer' (quoted in the *Church Times*, 24 January 2003, p. 3). Jensen described Packer as 'actually more famous than any other leader of the Anglican Communon' (ibid.).

Packer's statements are therefore extremely apposite to the Free Church of England, some of whose members have occasionally looked to the Diocese of Sydney as a possible ally. They have an authority that cannot easily be dismissed.

9. Shucksmith, 'Agenda for Renewal', p. 2 (underscoring in original).
10. *A Letter to the Reverend Mr John Wesley*, printed in Whitefield, *Journals*, p. 577. 'Warm' here has its eighteenth-century connotation of 'quickly or easily aroused'.
11. *Church Times*, 22 August 1902.
12. W. C. Sellar and R. J. Yeatman, *1066 And All That* (Harmondsworth, Penguin, 1967), p. 71. By contrast, the Cavaliers were 'Wrong but Wromantic'.
13. Merryweather, p. 97.
14. Vaughan, *Prospect*, p. 3.
15. Ibid., p. 6; italics in original.
16. Ibid., p. 4.
17. Put negatively, it clearly is not Roman Catholic, Orthodox, Methodist, Presbyterian, Congregationalist, Baptist, etc., etc. Perhaps the only test which the Free Church of England fails is that of not being formally in Communion with the Archbishop of Canterbury.
18. Letter from Alexandrine Cummins (the Bishop's wife) to Colonel Aycrigg; quoted in Guelzo, *For the Union*, p. 235.
19. *FCE Magazine*, October 1883, p. 216. Price's affirmation of the special relationship with the Church of England has already been noted. Other examples could be quoted.
20. Vaughan, 'Memories', p. 8.
21. Anglican–Methodist *Common Statement*, p. 14.
22. Packer, 'Anglicanism for Tomorrow'.
23. This finding was one that the present writer did not anticipate when commencing this study.
24. Packer, 'Anglicanism for Tomorrow'.
25. See, for example, the testimonies in Robert E. Webber, *Evangelicals on the Canterbury Trail* (Waco, Texas, World Books, 1985).
26. Merryweather, p. 92.
27. *FCE Magazine*, October 1883, p. 214.
28. For a recent exploration of some of the issues see Arthur Middleton, *Fathers and Anglicans*, (Leominster, Gracewing, 2001).
29. There are exceptions. Bishop Shucksmith quoted St John Chrysostom in his sermon at Covocation 2002 (*FCE Year Book 2002–2003*, p. 13).
30. It was said of Daniel Rowland, for example, that, 'His illustrations are profoundly biblical, but he freely uses Greek classical authors and the early Church Fathers as well.' Evans, *Daniel Rowland*, p. 370.

31. 'The Chicago Call: An Appeal to Evangelicals' in Robert Webber and Donald Bloesch (eds) *The Orthodox Evangelicals* (Nashville, Thomas Nelson, 1978), p. 12.
32. Packer, 'Anglicanism for Tomorrow'.
33. Webber and Bloesch, *Orthodox Evangelicals*, p. 14.
34. See Grass, *Evangelicalism and the Orthodox Church*.
35. See, for example, Anthony N. S. Lane, *John Calvin: Student of the Church Fathers* (Edinburgh, T&T Clark, 1999).
36. Letter from Jason Loh of Abersystwyth in the *English Churchman*, no. 7598, 15–22 November 2002.
37. The official website of the Presbyterian Church in Wales in December 2002 described as 'a good idea' another website where icons for incorporation into electronic messages could be obtained (*www.ebcpcw.org.uk/english/publications/treasury-02–12–website.htm*).
38. Skevington Wood, *Thomas Haweis*, p. 186.
39. *A Plea for Union*, pp. 29f.; quoted in ibid., p. 206.
40. *Diary*, p. 178. quoted in ibid., p. 253.
41. *FCE Magazine*, July 1871, p. 177.
42. Ibid. Merryweather pleaded for 'the closest bonds' to be created between the Church of Ireland, the Countess of Huntingdon's Connexion and Evangelicals in the Established Church (p. 188).
43. Guelzo, *For the Union*, p. 192.
44. Vaughan, *Prospect*, pp. 3ff.
45. Ibid., p. 5.
46. Published in 1967 by the FCE as a booklet entitled *Ecumenism and the Free Church of England*.
47. Ibid., p. 3.
48. Vaughan, *Prospect*, p. 5.
49. Packer, 'Anglicanism for Tomorrow'.
50. *FCE Magazine*, October 1883, p. 215.
51. 1 Samuel 22.2.
52. Quoted in Guelzo, *For the Union*, p. 236.
53. Ibid., p. 237.
54. Vaughan, 'Memories', p. 24.
55. *FCE Magazine*, July 1871, p. 175.
56. Ibid.
57. Ibid., October 1883, p. 215.
58. Vaughan, 'Memories', p. 25.
59. Ibid., p. 24.
60. Ibid., p. 16. Hints of the deep-rootedness of clerical disloyalty to the denomination's traditions can be seen in Newman's reminder that the clergy 'must

learn to feel that they are amenable to our Church law, and must act within its scope'; *FCE Magazine*, October 1883, p. 216.

61. Vaughan, 'Memories', p. 16. Some left after, in Vaughan's phrase, 'missing their way' financially or morally.

62. Ibid., p. 15.

63. Ibid., p. 24.

64. This practice, relatively common in the denomination, was identified by Vaughan as long ago as 1949 as contributing to some of the Church's problems ('Memories', pp. 24f.). Back in the 1560s Archbishop Parker and Bishop Grindal had also come to regret performing hasty ordinations. See, for example, W. H. Frere, *The English Church in the Reign of Elizabeth and James I* (London, MacMillan, 1924), p. 60.

65. Packer, 'Anglicanism for Tomorrow'.

66. Buchanan, *Is the Church of England Biblical?*, p. 260.

67. An example of a former Free Church of England presbyter of considerable intellectual stature who left the denomination is the Revd Dr Paul Avis, General Secretary of the Council for Christian Unity of the Church of England since 1998. Avis has written extensively on ecclesiological matters. Many of the points he makes in *The Anglican Understanding of the Church* (London, SPCK, 2000) are consonant with Free Church of England positions.

68. See Fenwick, *Thesis*, pp. 407ff. for a discussion of the Trust situation.

69. Ibid.

70. Vaughan, *Prospect*, pp. 5f.

71. Ibid., p. 7.

72. Vaughan, 'Memories', p. 26.

73. Gregg and Sugden; Richardson and Greenland; Dicksee and Meyers; Eldridge and Vaughan; Powell and Shucksmith; McLean and Bentley-Taylor.

74. London, Church House Publishing, (GS Misc 580).

75. *FCE Magazine*, October 1871, p. 175.

76. The present writer has seen IOUs for £2.50 on the collection plate.

77. The quotation is from Tiffany, *A History*, p. 563.

78. The phrase is Merryweather's.

79. A world-view can be self-created. One is reminded of the dwarves in C. S. Lewis's *The Last Battle*, who were surrounded by the wonders of Aslan's country, but preferred to believe they were in the filth of a stable: 'Their prison is in their own minds, yet they are in that prison . . .' (Harmondsworth, Penguin Books, 1964), pp. 131ff.).

80. Buchanan, *Is the Church?*, p. 11.

81. An illustration of the way in which the denomination has even gone *backwards* in terms of national profile is the fact that one of its bishops was invited

to attend Queen Victoria's Golden Jubilee service, but none was invited to that of Elizabeth II.

82. Vaughan, 'Memories', p. 24.

83. William Troughton's funeral in 1917, for example, was attended by the Mayor of Morecambe and the Vicar of Morecambe. Over a generation later he still merited a mention as 'a preacher of note' in the history of his native town (Henry F. Birkett, *The Story of Ulverston* (Kendal, Titus Wilson & Son, 1949), p. 136). There is still a Troughton Terrace in Ulverston.

84. In the first part of the twentieth century there was a network of 'Unattached Church of England Congregations'.

85. The fate of Benjamin Ingham's Connexion shows what can happen. In the 1750s Ingham had been 'General Overseer' of approximately 80 societies. In 1761, following an attempt to introduce practices advocated by John Glas in Scotland (such as foot-washing and the Kiss of Peace) Ingham's Connexion broke up, only 13 congregations remaining loyal to him. These were reinforced in 1813 by a merger with a similar group of Scottish origin, the Old Scots Independents, which had 15 societies. (Ingham himself had died in 1772, aged 60, a broken man.) By the 1960s the number of congregations had shrunk to 7. Today (2004) there are only two Inghamite chapels left, in Wheatley Lane and Salterforth. It is easy to imagine the Free Church of England following such a path. For further details on the history of the Inghamite chapels see Pickles, *Benjamin Ingham, passim*.

86. Daniel 2.33ff.

87. See Chapter 6.

88. Currently the Spanish Church has 1 bishop, 22 presbyters and 20 congregations. The Lusitanian Church has 1 bishop, 9 presbyters, 16 congregations, 1,500 communicants (see *www.episcopalchurch.org/europe/coacce*). Both Churches claim a membership of 5,000 (*Church of England Year Book 2002*, pp. 378f.).

89. Buchanan *et al.*, *Growing Into Union: Proposals for forming a United Church in England*, (London, SPCK, 1970).

90. Ibid., pp. 132f. The actual process would of course be extremely complex, involving Parliamentary legislation.

91. The proposals recommend that when a diocese reached about 75 congregations, it should divide. Buchanan *et al.* also suggest that the consecration of bishops for the United Church need not be exclusively by *Anglican* (by which they seem to mean *Church of England*) bishops. Presumably (all other conditions being right) the Free Church of England would be an acceptable source of the historic succession.

92. The published Constitution of the 'Church of England (Continuing)' occupies one side of A5. That of the Free Church of England runs to 7 pages, with a further 81 pages of Canons and canonical forms.

93. In one of its publicity pamphlets produced in the late 1980s entitled 'What is the Free Church of England?' the denomination actually describes itself as 'the oldest of the "Continuing Anglican Churches"'.

94. Buchanan, *Is the Church?*, pp. 354ff.

95. Vaughan, 'Memories', p. 29.

96. Goldie, *Short History*, p. 61.

97. I have not been able to trace the source of the quotation. It appears in Goldie, *Short History*, p. 38.

98. *The Faith and Order of the Lusitanian and Spanish Reformed Episcopal Churches*, The Report of a Commission appointed by the Archbishop of Canterbury (London, Church Information Office, 1963), p. 8.

The Declaration of Principles

The text set out here is as it is found in the first and second Articles of the Constitution.

Ordinary type indicates material from the 1873 Declaration of Principles drafted by Bishop Cummins and still one of the foundational documents of the Reformed Episcopal Church.[1] Words underlined are from William Muhlenberg's 1854 Exposition of the Memorial presented to the House of Bishops of the Protestant Episcopal Church.[2] Words in **bold type** are from the **1870 Preamble and Declaration of the Church of Ireland**.[3] Words in *italic* are unique to the Free Church of England text, or are derived from another source. The bold capital letters in square brackets ([A], [B], etc) are not part of the text but are added to make cross-referencing easier.

ARTICLE I

Declaration of Principles

[A] *The Free Church of England, otherwise called the Reformed Episcopal Church, which is a branch of the Holy Catholic Church of the Lord Jesus Christ, united by Faith to Him* **who is the Head over all things to the Church** *which is His body; and recognising the essential unity of all who, by* *a like Faith, are united to the one Divine and Common Head, doth make declaration of its Principles as follows:-*

1. [B] *The Free Church of England, otherwise called the Reformed Episcopal Church,* holding "the faith once delivered unto the saints," declares its belief in the Holy Scriptures of the Old and New Testaments as the Word of God, and the sole Rule of Faith and Practice; in the creed "commonly called the Apostles' Creed"; in the Divine Institution of the Sacraments of Baptism and the Lord's Supper; and in the Doctrines of grace substantially as they are set forth in the Thirty-nine Articles of Religion.

2. [C] This Church recognises and adheres to Episcopacy, not as of Divine right, but as a very ancient and desirable form of Church polity.

3. [D] This Church, retaining a Liturgy which shall not be repressive of freedom in prayer, accepts the Book of Common Prayer, as it was revised, prepared, and recommended for use by the General Convention of the Protestant Episcopal Church, A.D.1785, reserving full liberty to alter, abridge, enlarge, and amend the same, as may seem most conducive to the edification of the people, "providing that the substance of the faith be kept entire."

4. This Church condemns and rejects the following erroneous and strange doctrines as contrary to God's Word:-

[E] Firstly, That the Church of Christ exists only in one order or form of ecclesiastical polity;

[F] Second, That Christian ministers are "priests" in another sense than that in which all believers are "a royal priesthood";

[G] Third, That the Lord's Table is an altar on which the oblation of the Body and Blood of Christ is offered anew to the Father;

[H] Fourth, That the presence of Christ in the Lord's Supper is a presence in the elements of Bread and Wine;

[I] Fifth, that Regeneration is inseparably connected with Baptism.

[J] *In accordance with the liberty given in Article 3 of the above Declaration of Principles, this Church accepts the Book of Common Prayer of the Church of England, with such revisions as shall exclude sacerdotal doctrines and practices.*

[K] This Church, as a Reformed and Protestant Church, doth hereby re-affirm its constant witness against all those innovations in doctrine and worship, whereby the primitive Faith hath been from time to time defaced or overlaid, and which at the Reformation were disowned and rejected.

[L] This Church will maintain communion with all Christian Churches, and will set forth, so far as in it lieth, quietness, peace and love, among all Christian people.

ARTICLE II

[M] *The Free Church of England, otherwise called the Reformed Episcopal Church, in the United Kingdom of Great Britain and Northern Ireland,* deriving its authority from Christ, Who is the Head over all things to the Church, doth declare that *the Convocation of the said Church,* consisting of the *Bishop Primus,* Bishops, *Presbyters and Deacons, together with the* representatives of the Laity, shall in all matters therein, have chief legislative power *and jurisdiction.*

Notes

1. See, for example, Guelzo, *For the Union*, pp. 155f. or the Reformed Episcopal Church website.
2. Text in Guelzo, *For the Union*, pp. 63f.
3. Text in *The Constitution of the Church of Ireland: Being Statutes passed at the General Convention 1870* (Dublin, Hodges, Foster and Co., 1870), pp. 3ff. or the Church of Ireland website.

The List of Serving Bishops in the UK (as printed in the 2002–2003 Year Book)

THE FREE CHURCH OF ENGLAND
OTHERWISE CALLED THE
REFORMED EPISCOPAL CHURCH
List of
THE CONSECRATION OF BISHOPS
(ENGLAND)
EXTRACTED FROM OFFICIAL RECORDS

1. JOHN MOORE, D.D., Archbishop of Canterbury 1783–1805, Consecrated by the Archbishop of Canterbury (Frederick Cornwallis) and the Bishops of Ely (Edmund Keene), Oxford (Robert Lowth) and Rochester (John Thomas), 12 February, 1775 in Lambeth Palace Chapel, London.
2. WILLIAM WHITE, D.D., Bishop of Pennsylvania Presiding Bishop of the Protestant Episcopal Church in the USA, was consecrated by the Archbishop of Canterbury (John Moore), the Archbishop of York (William Markham) and the Bishops of Peterborough (John Hinchcliffe) and Bath and Wells (Charles Moss) 4 February, 1787 in Lambeth Palace Chapel, London.
3. JOHN HENRY HOPKINS, D.D., Bishop of Vermont, Presiding Bishop of the Protestant Episcopal Church in the USA, was consecrated by Bishops White, Griswold and Bowen, 31 October 1832, in St. Paul's Chapel, New York.

4. GEORGE DAVID CUMMINS, D.D., born 11 December, 1822. Consecrated by Bishops Hopkins, Smith, H. W. Lee, Talbot, Quintard, Clarkson and Kerfoot, of the Protestant Episcopal Church, Louisville, Kentucky, 15 November, 1866. Elected Presiding Bishop of the Reformed Episcopal Church, 2 December 1873.

5. CHARLES EDWARD CHENEY, D.D., S.T.D., was consecrated by Bishop Cummins and five Presbyters in Christ Church, Chicago, Illinois, 14 December 1873.

6. WILLIAM RUFUS NICHOLSON, D.D., was consecrated by Bishops Cummins, Cheney and Simpson and nine Presbyters in St. Paul's Reformed Episcopal Church, Philadelphia, Pennsylvania, 24 February 1876.

7. EDWARD CRIDGE, B.A. (Cantab.), was consecrated by Bishops Cheney, Nicholson and Carman and nine Presbyters, in Emmanuel Church, Ottowa, Ontario, 17 July 1876.

8. BENJAMIN PRICE was consecrated by Bishop Cridge, assisted by several Presbyters, in Christ Church, Teddington, 15 August 1876.

9. JOHN SUGDEN, B.A., D.D., was consecrated by Bishops Cridge and Price, assisted by several Presbyters, in Christ Church, Lambeth, England, 20 August 1876.

10. THOMAS HUBAND GREGG, M.A., M.D., was consecrated by Bishops Fallows, Cheney and Nicholson, and eight Presbyters, in the First Reformed Episcopal Church, New York City, 20 June 1877.

11. ALFRED SPENCER RICHARDSON, D.D., was consecrated by Bishops Nicholson and Fallows, assisted by several Presbyters, in St. Paul's Reformed Episcopal Church, Philadelphia, Pennsylvania, 22 June 1879.

12. FREDERICK NEWMAN was consecrated by Bishops Price and Sugden, assisted by several Presbyters in Christ Church, Teddington, 2 July 1879.

13. HUBERT BOWER was consecrated by Bishops Sugden and Richardson, assisted by several Presbyters, at St. Saviour's Church, Littlehampton, 19 August 1879.

14. HENRY ORION MEYERS was consecrated by Bishops Newman and Sugden, assisted by several Presbyters, in Emmanuel Church, Putney, 22 October 1883.

15. THOMAS GREENLAND, M.A., was consecrated by Bishops

Richardson, Sugden, Bower and Meyers, assisted by several Presbyters, in Christ Church, Carlton Hill, London, 11 June 1888.

16. SAMUEL, J. C. DICKSEE, D.D., was consecrated by Bishops Price and Meyers, assisted by several Presbyters, in Christ Church, Lambeth, London, 6 November 1889.

17. WILLIAM BAKER was consecrated by the same Bishops at the same time as Bishop Dicksee, 6 November 1889.

18. PHILIP X. ELDRIDGE, D.D., was consecrated by Bishops Sugden, Greenland and Baker, assisted by several Presbyters, in Emmanuel Church, Gunnersbury, London, 24 June 1892.

19. JAMES RENNY, D.D., was consecrated at the same time and place as Bishop Eldridge, and by the same Bishops, 24 June 1892.

20. WILLIAM TROUGHTON was consecrated by Bishop Meyers, assisted by several Presbyters, at Hounslow, Middlesex, 5 August 1901.

21. RICHARD BROOK LANDER, D.D., was consecrated by Bishop Troughton, assisted several Presbyters at Christ Church, Teddington, 18 October 1904.

22. FRANK VAUGHAN, D.D., was consecrated by Bishops Eldridge and Brook Lander, assisted by several Presbyters, in Christ Church, Harlesden, London, on 25 April 1913.

23. JOSEPH LOUIS FENN, D.D., LL.D., was consecrated by Bishops Vaughan, Brook Lander and H. Mumford (Presiding Bishop of the Moravian Church), assisted by several Presbyters, in Christ Church, Harlesden, London, on 21 September 1921.

24. WILLIAM EDWARD YOUNG, O.B.E., D.D., was consecrated by Bishop Brook Lander, assisted by several Presbyters, in Emmanuel Church, Putney, on 28 July 1925.

25. JOHN CHRISTIE MAGEE, D.D., was consecrated by Bishops Vaughan, Fenn and Young, assisted by several Presbyters, in Christ Church, Harlesden, London, on 7 July 1932.

26. GEORGE MARSHALL was consecrated by the same Bishops and Presbyters at the same time and in the same place as Bishop Magee, on 7 July 1932.

27. ALEXANDER M. HUBLY, D.D., was consecrated by Bishops Cloak and Marshall, assisted by several Presbyters, in Christ Church, Shaw Street, Toronto, Canada, on 11 May 1933.

28. GEORGE W. FORBES SMITH, M.A., was consecrated by Bishops

Vaughan, Magee and T. H. Shaw (Presiding Bishop of the Moravian Church), assisted by several Presbyters, in Christ Church, Harlesden, 29 September 1938.

29. DONALD A. THOMPSON was consecrated by the same Bishops and Presbyters at the same time and in the same place as Bishop Forbes Smith, on 29 September 1938.

30. THOMAS CAMERON was consecrated by Bishops Vaughan, Magee, Forbes Smith and W. G. MacLeavy, M.A., B.D. (Bishop of the Moravian Church) assisted by several Presbyters in St. John's Church, Tottington, Bury, Lancs., on 21 September 1950.

31. WILLIAM RODGERS was consecrated by Bishops Forbes Smith and Cameron assisted by the Rev. F. P. Copeland Simmons, M.A. (Moderator of the Free Church Federal Council 1955) and several Presbyters, at Christ Church, Liscard on 18 October 1957.

32. AMRBOSE MARTIN BODFISH was consecrated by Bishops Cameron, Forbes Smith and Ernest W. Porter (Bishop of the Moravian Church), assisted by several Presbyters, at St. John's Church, Tottington, Bury, Lancs., on 4 September 1963.

33. JAMES DUDLEY BURRELL was consecrated by the same Bishops and Presbyters, at the same time and in the same place as Bishop Bodfish, on 4 September 1963.

34. WILLIAM CHARLES WATKINS was consecrated by Bishop Cameron, Forbes Smith, Bodfish and Burrell, assisted by several Presbyters, at St. Jude's Church, Balham, London, on 8 October 1969.

35. CYRIL MILNER, F. Th., D.D., was consecrated by Bishops Cameron, Burrell and Watkins, assisted by several Presbyters, at St. Paul's Church, Fleetwood, Lancs., on 29 August 1973.

36. ARTHUR WARD, B.D. Th.B., D.D., was consecrated by Bishops Milner, Cameron, Theophilus J. Herter, Th.D., D.D., Presiding Bishop of the Reformed Episcopal Church of America, The Rt. Rev. Russell B. White, M.A. Bishop of the Church of England, and several Presbyters, at Christ Church Teddington, Middlesex, on 11 September 1976.

37. KENNETH JOHN WESLEY POWELL was consecrated by Bishops Milner and Ward, assisted by the Rev. Rowland Graves, President of the Wesleyan Reform Union, and several Presbyters, at Christ Church, Teddington, Middlesex on 1 October 1986.

38. JOHN BARRY SHUCKSMITH, B.D., M.A., Ph.D., was consecrated by Bishops Milner, Powell and the Rt. Rev. Leonard W.
Riches, D.D., Presiding Bishop of the Reformed Episcopal Church
of America, assisted by several Presbyters, at Christ Church,
Teddington, Middlesex, on 16 October 1996.

39. ARTHUR BENTLEY-TAYLOR, B.D., M.A., was consecrated by
Bishops Powell, the Rt. Rev'd Royal U. Grote, Jr., D.D., (Bishop of
the REC of America) and the Rt. Rev. Leonard W. Riches, D.D.,
Presiding Bishop of the Reformed Episcopal Church of America,
assited by the Rt. Rev'd J. B. Shucksmith and several Presbyters, at
Christ Church, Liscard, on 11 September 1999.

40. JOHN DALY MORTON McLEAN, B.A., A.C.I.S., D.M.A., was
consecrated by the same Bishops and Presbyters at the same time
and in the same place as Bishop Bentley-Taylor on 11 September
1999.

Notes

The following notes invariably accompany the List of Consecrations
As some who are unacquainted with Church history may object to a consecration by a single Bishop instead of the Nicene Canonical three, they
are referred to Bingham's Antiquities of the Church for Precedents of consecration by one Bishop only. 'Siderius of Palaebisca was ordained by one
Bishop. Paulinus, Bishop of Antioch, ordained Evangus without any
other Bishop to assist him.'

'The orders of the early Anglo-Saxon Church were derived from a
single Bishop. In A.D. 604, Augustine ordained as Bishops, Melletus and
Justus. Melletus was the first Bishop of London, and Justus the first
Bishop of Rochester; also Lawrence, Archbishop of Canterbury, was consecrated by one Bishop only.'

St. Gregory wrote to Augustine. 'In the English Church wherein
there is no other Bishop but thyself thou canst not ordain a Bishop otherwise than alone.' – Bede's Eccles History.

Canon Liddon in 1876 wrote: 'A consecration by one Bishop is valid,
but it is not canonical. The result, however, is that all orders conferred by
a Bishop are undoubtedly valid'. To this Archbishop Bramhall agreed.

Table of Consecrational Descent

The chart below indicates the tactile succession from Archbishop John Moore of Canterbury enjoyed by the bishops of the Free Church of England in office in November 2003. The sequence of consecrations is the 'shortest route'. Consecrations of bishops not in the direct line are not shown except where a bishop from another Church was involved. Presbyters 'assisted' in all consecrations after 1873.
(Information from PECUSA and FCE printed sources.)

APPENDIX 3

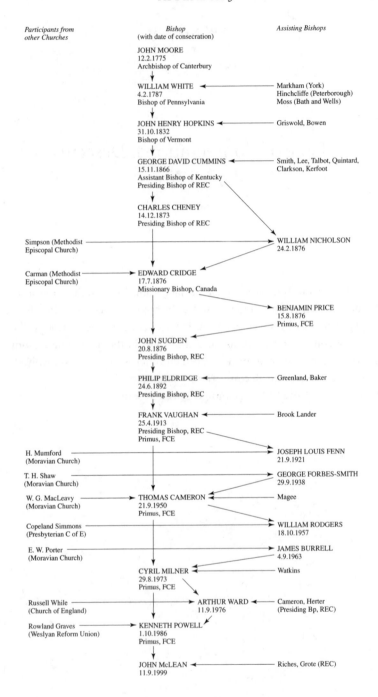

Participants from other Churches	Bishop (with date of consecration)	Assisting Bishops

JOHN MOORE
12.2.1775
Archbishop of Canterbury

WILLIAM WHITE ◄————— Markham (York)
4.2.1787   Hinchcliffe (Peterborough)
Bishop of Pennsylvania   Moss (Bath and Wells)

JOHN HENRY HOPKINS ◄————— Griswold, Bowen
31.10.1832
Bishop of Vermont

GEORGE DAVID CUMMINS ◄————— Smith, Lee, Talbot, Quintard,
15.11.1866   Clarkson, Kerfoot
Assistant Bishop of Kentucky
Presiding Bishop of REC

CHARLES CHENEY
14.12.1873
Presiding Bishop of REC

Simpson (Methodist ——————————————► WILLIAM NICHOLSON
Episcopal Church)   24.2.1876

Carman (Methodist ————► EDWARD CRIDGE
Episcopal Church)   17.7.1876
                             Missionary Bishop, Canada

                                              ► BENJAMIN PRICE
                                                15.8.1876
                                                Primus, FCE

JOHN SUGDEN
20.8.1876
Presiding Bishop, REC

PHILIP ELDRIDGE ◄————— Greenland, Baker
24.6.1892
Presiding Bishop, REC

FRANK VAUGHAN ◄————— Brook Lander
25.4.1913
Presiding Bishop, REC
Primus, FCE

H. Mumford ————————————————► JOSEPH LOUIS FENN
(Moravian Church)   21.9.1921

T. H. Shaw ————————————————► GEORGE FORBES-SMITH
(Moravian Church)   29.9.1938

W. G. MacLeavy ————► THOMAS CAMERON ◄————— Magee
(Moravian Church)   21.9.1950
                         Primus, FCE

Copeland Simmons ————————————► WILLIAM RODGERS
(Presbyterian C of E)   18.10.1957

E. W. Porter ————————————————► JAMES BURRELL
(Moravian Church)   4.9.1963

                                              ◄————— Watkins
CYRIL MILNER ◄
29.8.1973
Primus, FCE

Russell While ————————————► ARTHUR WARD ◄————— Cameron, Herter
(Church of England)   11.9.1976   (Presiding Bp, REC)

Rowland Graves ————► KENNETH POWELL
(Weslyan Reform Union) 1.10.1986
                        Primus, FCE

JOHN McLEAN ◄————— Riches, Grote (REC)
11.9.1999

APPENDIX 4

Presidents, Presiding Bishops and Bishops Primus

The accompanying table shows those who have exercised *episkope* over the whole of the community through which the present-day Free Church of England traces its continuity.

Thomas Haweis described the leadership of the Connexion following the Countess's death as 'essentially episcopal – with us a few preside'. In the event it was Haweis himself who exercised leadership/*episkope* over the whole movement (in collaboration with the other Trustees) until his death in 1820. He was in that sense the first *Episkopos* of the independent tradition (though it is possible to argue from a tradition of oversight going back to Whitefield himself).

Following Haweis's death the ministers of the chapels began to meet in annual Conference and to elect a President. In the earliest years, two of these were laymen (Arundel and Trueman, who were Trustees of the Connexion), but after 1829 the President was always an ordained man. Election was usually for one year, though individuals could be elected again at a later date. A few served for two or more years at a time. The names for three years have been lost. The pattern was very similar to that of contemporary Methodism where the annual Conference also elected a President.

The resolution of 1863 bringing the Free Church of England into legal existence spoke of the annual Connexional gathering as 'a general Conference of Presbyters, under the guidance of a President Bishop', thus affirming the episcopal nature of the role.

From its inauguration, the Free Church of England is described as having an episcopal element, expressed supremely in the person of the President of Convocation. Thus, for the years 1863–68, when Conference and Convocation were in effect the same body, the Presidents may fairly be described as the first 'bishops' of the newly constituted body. In this sense Benjamin Price is not the first bishop of the Free Church of England.

In 1876 this tradition of *episkope*, reaching back 85 years, received the sign of the historic succession and has maintained it to the present day.

The Reformed Episcopal Church and the Reformed Church of England have always had a Presiding Bishop in the historic succession.

PRESIDENTS, PRESIDING BISHOPS AND BISHOPS PRIMUS

Countess of Huntingdon's Connexion	Free Church of England	Reformed Episcopal Church		Reformed Church of England	
Principal Trustee	*(1863–1868 President of Conference)*	1877–1878	Thomas Gregg	1878–1891	Thomas Gregg
1791–1820 Thomas Haweis	1863–1865 George Jones	1878–1885	John Sugden		
	1865–1866 E. C. Lewis	1885–1892	Alfred Richardson		
President of Conference	1866–1868 Benjamin Price	1892–1893	John Sugden		
1823 James Arundel		1893–1921	Philip Eldridge		
1824 Joseph Trueman	*(From 1868 Presiding Bishop/Primus)*	1921–1927	Frank Vaughan		
1825–1827 James Arundel and J. Finley	1868–1896 Benjamin Price				
1827–1829 J. Trueman and J. Finley	1896–1901 Samuel Dicksee				
1829 A. Start	(June–Oct) 1901 Henry O. Meyers				
1830–1837 J. Meffen	1901–1917 William Troughton				
1837 J. Mather	1917–1927 Richard Brook Lander				
1838 J. Jones					
1839 J. Meffen					
1840 J. Williams					
1842 J. Jones					
1845–1847 T. Keyworth					
1847 J. Wood					
1848 J. Jones					
1850 J. Wood					
1851 J. Sherman					
1852–1853 J. Owen					
1854–1856 B. T. Hollis					
1856–1858 T. E. Thoresby					
1858 L. J. Wake					
1859 J. K. Foster					
1860 T. Dodd					
1861–1863 W. Woodhouse					

The Free Church of England otherwise called The Reformed Episcopal Church

1927–1930	Richard Brook Lander
1930–1962	Frank Vaughan
1962–1975	Thomas Cameron
1975–1998	Cyril Milner
1998–2000	Kenneth Powell
2000–2003	Arthur Bentley-Taylor
2003–	Kenneth Powell

APPENDIX 5
Diocesan Bishops

Free Church of England	Reformed Episcopal Church	The Free Church of England otherwise called The Reformed Episcopal Church
North	*North*	*North*
1889–1897 William Baker	1881–1892 Alfred Richardson	1927–1958 Frank Vaughan
(1897–1901 William Troughton *President of Northern Synod*)	(1892–1915 Philip Eldridge *had oversight of whole Church*)	1958–1967 Thomas Cameron
1901–1917 William Trougton	1915–1921 Philip Eldridge	1967–1973 James Burrell
(1917–1927 A. V. Bland *President of Northern Synod*)	1921–1927 Joseph Fenn	1973–1998 Cyril Milner
		1999–2003 Arthur Bentley-Taylor
		2003– John McLean
South	*South*	*South*
1889–1896 Benjamin Price and Samuel Dicksee	1881–1885 John Sugden	1927–1934 Joseph Fenn
1896–1901 Samuel Dicksee	(1885–1892 Alfred Richardson *had oversight of whole Church*)	1934–1955 John Magee
(1901–1904 William Troughton *had oversight of whole Church*)	(1892–1915 Philip Eldridge *had oversight of whole Church*)	1955–1968 George Forbes Smith
1904–1927 Richard Brook Lander	1915–1926 Frank Vaughan	1968–1971 Ambrose Bodfish
		1972–1976 William Watkins
		1977–1990 Arthur Ward
		1990– Kenneth Powell
		Central
		1927–1937 William Young
		1938–1942 George Forbes Smith

APPENDIX 6

The Current Congregations
(November 2003)

(The date in brackets is the year the congregation was founded or joined the FCE or REC.)

Northern Diocese

St George's, Mill Hill, Blackburn, Lancs. (1907)
St Paul's, Darbishire Road, Fleetwood, Lancs. (1907)
St James's, Byron Street, Hollinwood, Oldham (1866)
The John Knowles Memorial Church, High Street, Hoyland, Barnsley S. Yorks. (1912)
Christ Church, Manston Gardens, Crossgates, Leeds (1949)
Christ Church, Buckingham Road, Tuebrook, Liverpool (1881)
St Stephen's, Woodlands Road, Middlesbrough, Cleveland (1908)
Emmanuel, Marine Road East, Morecambe, Lancs. (1886)
Holy Trinity, New Lane, Oswaldtwistle, Lancs. (1870)
St David's, Eldon Street, Preston, Lancs. (1939)
St John's, Kirklees Street, Tottington, Bury, Lancs. (1853)
Christ Church, Martin's Lane, Liscard, Wallasey, Wirral (1880)
Emmanuel, Vulcan's Lane, Workington, Cumbria (1939)

Southern Diocese

Emmanuel, Alum Rock Road, Birmingham (1903)

Christ Church, Osborne Road, Broadstairs, Kent (1904)

Christ Church, Grosvenor Place, Blackboy Road, Exeter (1844)

Christ Church, North Street, Exmouth, Devon (1896)

Emmanuel, South Street, Farnham, Surrey (1889)

Christ Church, Pall Mall, Leigh-on-Sea, Essex (1889)

St Jude's, Heslop Road, Balham, London (1887)

Christ Church, St Alban's Road, Harlesden, London (1886)

Christ Church, Station Road, Teddington, Middlesex (1864)

St Andrew's, Wolverhampton Road West, Bentley, Walsall, W. Midlands (1943)

St Jude's, Eldon Street, Walsall, W. Midlands (1947)

Christ Church, Hythe Road, Willesborough, Kent (1874)

Bibliography

Addleshaw, G. W. O. *The High Church Tradition*, London, Faber & Faber, 1941

Anglican–Evangelical Church in Germany Conversations, *The Meissen Declaration*, London, Council for Christian Unity, 1991 (GS 951)

Anglican–French Lutheran and Reformed Conversations, *Called to Witness and Service: The Reuilly Common Statement*, London, Church House Publishing, 1999 (GS 1329)

Anglican–Methodist Conversations, *An Anglican–Methodist Covenant. Common Statement of the Formal Conversations between the Methodist Church of Great Britain and the Church of England*, Peterborough, Methodist Publishing House/London, Church House Publishing, 2001

Anglican–Moravian Conversations, *The Fetter Lane Common Statement with Essays in Moravian and Anglican History*, London, Council for Christian Unity of the General Synod, 1996 (GS 1202)

Anglican–Nordic/Baltic Lutheran Conversations, *Together in Mission and Ministry. The Porvoo Common Statement with Essays on Church and Ministry in Northern Europe*, London, Church House Publishing, 1993 (GS 1083)

Anglican–Reformed Conversations, *God's Reign and our Unity*, London, SPCK/Edinburgh, The St Andrew Press, 1984

Anglican–Roman Catholic International Commission (ARCIC), *The Final Report*, London, SPCK/Catholic Truth Society, 1982

Avis, Paul, *The Anglican Understanding of the Church*, London, SPCK, 2000

Aycrigg, Benjamin, *Memoirs of the Reformed Episcopal Church*, New York, 1878

Ayres, Anne (ed.), *Evangelical Catholic Papers: A Collection of Essays, Letters and Tractates from the Writings of Rev. William Augustus Muhlenberg*, New York, Thomas Whittaker, 1875

——, *The Life and Work of William Augustus Muhlenberg*, New York, Thomas Whittaker, (5th edn) 1894

Bain, Alan, *Bishops Irregular*, Bristol, published by author, 1985

Baker, Eric W., *A Herald of the Evangelical Revival: A critical inquiry into the relationship of William Law to John Wesley and the beginnings of Methodism*, London, Epworth Press, 1948

Balleine, G. R., *A History of the Evangelical Party in the Church of England*, London, Church Book Room Press, 1908

Baptism, Eucharist and Ministry (Faith and Order Paper no. 111), Geneva, WCC, 1982

Bede, *A History of the English Church and People* (trans. Leo Shirley-Price), London, Penguin Books, 1988

Bell, G. K. A., *Christian Unity: The Anglican Position*, London, Hodder and Stoughton, 1948

Birkett, Henry F., *The Story of Ulverston*, Kendal, Titus Wilson & Son, 1949

Bower, H., *The Orders of the Reformed Episcopal Church Examined*, Malvern, The Advertiser Office, 1881

Bradshaw, T., *The Olive Branch: An Evangelical Anglican Doctrine of the Church*, Carlisle, Paternoster Press, 1992

Brandreth, H. R. T., *Episcopi Vagantes and the Anglican Church*, London, SPCK (2nd edn) 1961

Bray, G., *The Anglican Canons 1517–1947*, London, Boydell Press/Church of England Records Society, 1998

Breward, Ian, *A History of the Church in Australasia*, Oxford, Clarendon Press, 2001

Brook, V. J. K., *A Life of Archbishop Parker*, Oxford, Clarendon Press, 1962

Brown, Stewart J., *The National Churches of England, Ireland and Scotland 1801–1846*, Oxford, OUP, 2001

Buchanan, C. O., *Is the Church of England Biblical?*, London, Darton, Longman & Todd, 1998

Buchanan, C. O., E. L. Mascall, J. I. Packer and the Bishop of Willesden

[Graham Leonard], *Growing Into Union: Proposals for forming a United Church in England*, London, SPCK, 1970

Bullard, J. V., *Constitutions and Canons Ecclesiastical 1604*, London, Faith Press, 1934

Carpenter, Edward, *Archbishop Fisher – His Life and Times*, Norwich, The Canterbury Press, 1991

Chadwick, Owen, *The Victorian Church*, London, A & C Black, (2nd edn) 1970

Cheney, Charles Edward, *What Reformed Episcopalians Believe*, Philadelphia, The Reformed Episcopal Publication Society, 1978 (1st edn 1888)

Code of Canon Law of the Catholic Church, London, Collins, 1983

Constitution and Canons of the Reformed Episcopal Church . . . otherwise called the Reformed Church of England, London, E. Marlborough & Co., 1883

The Constitution of the Church of Ireland: Being Statutes passed at the General Convention 1870, Dublin, Hodges, Foster & Co., 1870

Cook, Faith, *Selina, Countess of Huntingdon*, Edinburgh, Banner of Truth Trust, 2001

Cuming, G. J., *A History of Anglican Liturgy*, London, Macmillan, (2nd edn) 1982

Dallimore, Arnold, *George Whitefield: The Life and Times of the Greatest Evangelist of the Eighteenth-Century Revival*, London, Banner of Truth Trust, 1970

Davidson, Randall T. (ed.), *The Lambeth Conferences of 1867, 1878, and 1888, with the Official Reports and Resolutions, together with the Sermons Preached at the Conference*, London, SPCK, 1898

Dearing, Trevor, *Wesleyan and Tractarian Worship*, London, Epworth Press/SPCK, 1966

Digest of the Canons for the Government of the Protestant Episcopal Church in the United States of America . . . together with the Constitution (printed for the Convention) 1875

Doe, N., *The Legal Framework of the Church of England*, Oxford, Clarendon Press, 1996

—, *Canon Law in the Anglican Communion*, Oxford, Clarendon Press, 1998

Douglas, J. D. (ed.), *The New International Dictionary of the Christian Church*, Exeter, Paternoster Press, 1974.

Dyer, Mark, *et al.* (eds), *The Official Report of the Lambeth Conference 1998*, Harrisburg, PA, Morehouse Publishing, 1999

Easton, F. H., *Know Your Church*, London, FCE, 1964

Emerson, N. D., 'The Last Phase of the Establishment', in Phillips (ed.), *History of the Church of Ireland*, vol. III, pp. 325–59

Episcopal Ministry: The Report of the Archbishops' Group on The Episcopate, London, Church House Publishing, 1990 (GS 944)

Eusebius, *The Ecclesiastical History*, London, William Heinemann, 1975

Evans, Eifion, *Daniel Rowland and the Great Evangelical Awakening in Wales*, Edinburgh, Banner of Truth Trust, 1985

Evans, G. R. and J. R. Wright (eds), *The Anglican Tradition*, London, SPCK, 1991

The Faith and Order of the Lusitanian and Spanish Reformed Episcopal Churches, The Report of a Commission appointed by the Archbishop of Canterbury, London, Church Information Office, 1963

Fawcett, Timothy J., *The Liturgy of Comprehension 1689: An abortive attempt to revise the Book of Common Prayer* (Alcuin Club Collection 54), Southend-on-Sea, Mayhew–McCrimmon, 1973

Fenwick, J. R. K., *The Malabar Independent Syrian Church*, Nottingham, Grove Books, 1992

Fenwick, R. D., 'The Free Church of England otherwise called the Reformed Episcopal Church c.1845 to c.1927', Ph.D. Thesis, University of Wales, 1995

Figgis, J. B., *The Countess of Huntingdon and her Connexion*, London, Partridge & Co., 1891

The Five Lambeth Conferences, London, SPCK, 1920

Ford. A., J. McGuire and K. Milne (eds), *As By Law Established: The Church of Ireland since the Reformation*, Dublin, Lilliput Press, 1995

Forrester, Duncan and Douglas Murray (eds), *Studies in the History of Worship in Scotland*, Edinburgh, T & T Clark, 1986

Forsyth, P. T., *Church and Sacraments*, London, Independent Press, 1917

Franklin, R. W. (ed.), *Anglican Orders: Essays on the Centenary of Apostolicae Curae 1896–1996*, London, Mowbray, 1996

The Free Church of England otherwise called the Reformed Episcopal Church in the United Kingdom of Great Britain and Northern Ireland, Constitution and Canons Ecclesiastical, enrolled in the Chancery Division of the High Court 10th November 1927, published by Order of Convocation, 1983 edn.

Frere, W. H., *The English Church in the Reign of Elizabeth and James I*, London, Macmillan, 1924

Goldie, Frederick, *A Short History of the Episcopal Church in Scotland*, Edinburgh, St Andrew Press, 1976

Grass, T. (ed.), *Evangelicalism and the Orthodox Church*, London, The [Evangelical] Alliance Commission on Unity and Truth among Evangelicals (ACUTE), 2001

Guelzo, Allen C., *For the Union of Evangelical Christendom*, Pennsylvania, Pennsylvania State University Press, 1994

Hamilton, J. T. and K. G., *The History of the Moravian Church*, Bethlehem, PA, 1967

Hatchett, Marion J., *The Making of the First American Book of Common Prayer*, New York, Seabury Press, 1982

Hattersley, R., *A Brand from the Burning: The Life of John Wesley*, London, Little, Brown, 2002

Haweis, Thomas, *A Plea for Peace and Union among the Living Members of the Real Church of Christ*, London, 1796

Hooton, W. S. and J. Stafford Wright, *The First Twenty-five Years of the Bible Churchmen's Missionary Society 1922–1947*, London, BCMS, 1947

House of Bishops Occasional Paper *Apostolicity and Succession*, London, General Synod, 1994 (GS Misc 432)

Hylson-Smith, Kenneth, *Evangelicals in the Church of England 1734–1984*, Edinburgh, T&T Clark, 1998

Jasper, R. C. D., *Prayer Book Revision in England 1800–1900*, London, SPCK, 1954

—, *The Development of the Anglican Liturgy 1662–1980*, London, SPCK, 1989

Jones, R. Tudur, 'Charles, Thomas' in Douglas (ed.), *New International Dictionary of the Christian Church*

The Judgement of the Judicial Committee of the Privy Council, delivered March 8th 1850, London, Seeleys, 1850

Kirby, Gilbert W., *The Elect Lady*, Rushden, The Trustees of the Countess of Huntingdon's Connexion, (2nd edn) 1990

Kirk, Kenneth E. (ed.), *The Apostolic Ministry: Essays on the History and the Doctrine of Episcopacy*, London, Hodder & Stoughton, 1946

Lane, Anthony N. S., *John Calvin: Student of the Church Fathers*, Edinburgh, T & T Clark, 1999

Langton, Edward, *History of the Moravian Church*, London, George Allen & Unwin, 1956

Lewis, C. S., *The Last Battle*, Harmondsworth, Penguin Books, 1964

Lewis, James, *Frances Asbury: Bishop of the Methodist Episcopal Church*, London, Epworth Press, 1927

Lightfoot, J. B., *The Christian Ministry*, London, MacMillan & Co., 1901

Long, Charles (ed.), *Who are the Anglicans?*, Cincinnati, Forward Movement Publications, 1988

Makin, W. B. *Ecumenism and the Free Church of England*, (no place of publication given) FCE, 1967

McKim, Donald (ed.), *The Westminster Handbook to Reformed Theology*, Louisville, Westminster John Knox Press, 2001

Merryweather, F. S., *The Free Church of England: Its History, Doctrines and Ecclesiastical Polity*, London, Partridge & Co., 1873

Middleton, Arthur, *Fathers and Anglicans*, Leominster, Gracewing, 2001

Moore, Peter (ed.), *Bishops: But What Kind?*, London, SPCK, 1982

Moss, C. B., *The Old Catholic Movement*, London, SPCK (2nd edn) 1964

Munden, Alan, *The History of St John's College Nottingham. Part 1: Mr Peache's College at Kilburn*, Nottingham, St John's College, 1995

A New International Dictionary of the Christian Church, Grand Rapids, MT, Michigan Zondervan, 2001

New, Alfred H., *The Coronet and the Cross*, London, Partridge & Co, 1858

Newbigin, Lesslie, *Unfinished Agenda*, London, SPCK, 1985

Nias, J. C. S., *Gorham and the Bishop of Exeter*, London, SPCK, 1951

Noll, Mark A., *A History of Christianity in the United States and Canada*, London, SPCK, 1992

Norris, Richard A., 'Episcopacy', in Sykes and Booty (eds), *The Study of Anglicanism*, pp. 296–309

Osterlin, Lars, *Churches of Northern Europe in Profile*, Norwich, The Canterbury Press, 1995

Packer, J. I., *Evangelism and the Sovereignty of God*, London, IVP, 1961

Park, Trevor, *St Bees College 1816–1895*, Barrow-in-Furness, St Bega Publications, 1982

Peaston, A. E., *The Prayer Book Revision in the Free Churches*, London, James Clarke & Co., 1964

Penner, J. E., *Law Dictionary*, London, Butterworths, 2001

Perry, William Stephens, *Historical Notes and Documents illustrating the*

Organisation of the Protestant Episcopal Church in the United States of America, Claremont, NH, Claremont Manufacturing Co., 1874

Phillips, W. A. (ed.), *History of the Church of Ireland*, London, OUP, 1933 (3 vols)

Phillpotts, H., *The Case of the Rev. Mr. Shore: A Letter to His Grace the Archbishop of Canterbury*, London, 1849

Pickles, H. M., *Benjamin Ingham: Preacher amongst the Dales of Yorkshire, the Forests of Lancashire, and the Fells of Cumbria*, Coventry, published by author, 1995

Podmore, Colin, *The Moravian Church in England 1728–1760*, Oxford, Clarendon Press, 1998

Pollock, John, *George Whitefield and the Great Awakening*, London, Hodder & Stoughton, 1972

Potter, Alonzo (ed.), *Memorial Paper: The Memorial with Circular and Questions of the Episcopal Committee*, Philadelphia, E. Butler & Co., 1857

Prayer Book of the Church of England in South Africa, Gillitts, CESA, 1992

Price, Anne Elizabeth, *The Organisation of the Free Church of England, being Extracts from the Autobiography of the late Bishop Price . . .*, Ilfracombe, W.H. Smith & Son, 1908

Price, Charles P., 'Whence, Whither and What?' in Wright, *Quadrilateral at One Hundred*, pp. 79–97

Rack, Henry, *Reasonable Enthusiast: John Wesley and the Rise of Methodism*, London, Epworth Press (3rd edn) 2002

Riding, Christine and Jacqueline (eds), *The Houses of Parliament: History, Art, Architecture*, London, Merrell, 2000

Ryle, J. C., *Knots Untied*, London, James Clarke & Co, (32nd edn) 1959

Sellars, W. C. and R. J. Yeatman, *1066 And All That*, Harmondsworth, Penguin, 1967

Seymour, A. C. H., *The Life and Times of Selina, Countess of Huntingdon*, London, William Painter, 1840 (2 vols)

Shucksmith, J. B., *Honest for God*, J & B Books, Cosham, 1996

—, 'Agenda for Renewal 2002–2012' (paper circulated for 2002 Convocation)

Skevington Wood, A., *Thomas Haweis 1734–1820*, London, SPCK, 1957

Smith, J. D., *The Eucharist Doctrine of the Later Nonjurors*, (Alcuin/ GROW Joint Liturgical Study 46) Cambridge, Grove Books Ltd, 2000.

BIBLIOGRAPHY

Spinks, Bryan, *Sacraments, Ceremonies and the Stuart Divines*, Aldershot, Ashgate, 2002

Stevenson, J., *A New Eusebius*, London, SPCK, 1970

Stow, Walter Herbert (ed.), *The Life and Letters of Bishop William White*, New York, Morehouse Publishing Co., 1937

Sykes, Stephen and John Booty (eds), *The Study of Anglicanism*, London, SPCK, 1988

Thomas, W. H. Griffith, *Principles of Theology*, London, Church Book Room Press, 1945

Tiffany, Charles C., *A History of the Protestant Episcopal Church in the United States of America*, New York, Charles Scribner's Sons, (3rd edn) 1907

Tracts for the Times by Members of the University of Oxford, London, J. G. & F. Rivington, 1834

Vatican Council II: The Conciliar and Post-Conciliar Documents, (ed. Austin Flannery), Leominster, Fowler Wright Books, 1981

Vaughan, Frank, *A History of the Free Church of England otherwise called the Reformed Episcopal Church*, (published by authority of Convocation) 1st edn Bath, 1936; 2nd edn Bungay, 1960, 3rd edn Wallasey, 1994

—, *Prospect and Retrospect: The Centenary Charge*, printed by the Wallasey and Wirral Newspaper Co., Wallasey, Cheshire, 1944

—, 'Memories and Reflections of Forty-Five Years in the Ministry of the Free Church of England' (typescript circulated privately) 1949

Walker, William, *The Life and Times of John Skinner, Bishop of Aberdeen*, Aberdeen, Edmond & Spark, 1887

Wand, J. W. C., *The High Church Schism*, London, The Faith Press, 1951

Ware, Kallistos, 'Patterns of Episcopacy: An Orthodox view' in Moore (ed.), *Bishops: But What Kind?*, pp. 1–24

Webber, Robert E., *Evangelicals on the Canterbury Trail*, Waco, Texas, World Books, 1985

Webber, Robert and Donald Bloesch (eds) *The Orthodox Evangelicals*, Nashville, Thomas Nelson, 1978

Webster, C. A., 'The Reconstruction of the Church, 1869' in Phillips (ed.), *History of the Church of Ireland*, vol. III, pp. 360–86

Whitefield, George, *Journals*, Edinburgh, Banner of Truth Trust, 1960

Wigan, Bernard, *The Liturgy in English*, London, OUP, 1962

Willcocks, F. W., *An Old Attendant [F. W. Willcocks]. Spa Fields Chapel and its Associations 1779–1884*, London, *c.* 1888

Woodhouse-Hawkins, Michelle, 'Maurice, Huntington and the Quadrilateral', in Wright (ed.), *Quadrilateral at One Hundred*, pp. 61–78

Wright, Robert, J. (ed.), *Quadrilateral at One Hundred*, Cincinnati, Forward Movement Publications, 1988

—, 'Heritage and Vision: the Chicago–Lambeth Quadrilateral', in Wright (ed.), *Quadrilateral at One Hundred*, pp. 8–46

Zahl, Paul F. M., *The Protestant Face of Anglicanism*, Grand Rapids, MI, William Eerdmans, 1998

Zizioulas, John, *Being as Communion*, New York, St Vladimir's Seminary Press, 1985

Index

INDEX